THE
POLITICS
OF
LAW
A PROGRESSIVE CRITIQUE

THE POLITICS OF LAW

A PROGRESSIVE CRITIQUE

EDITED BY DAVID KAIRYS

PANTHEON BOOKS  NEW YORK

Grateful acknowledgment is made to the following for permission to reprint previously published material:

The National Law Journal: Excerpts from the article "Why Precedents Aren't Treated Equally" by David Kairys, from the June 9, 1980 issue of the *National Law Journal*. Copyright © 1980 by The National Law Journal. All rights reserved. Reprinted with permission of The National Law Journal.

Teachers College Press: Alan David Freeman's article "School Desegregation Law: Promise, Contradiction, Rationalization" in Derrick Bell, Editor, *Shades of Brown: New Perspectives on School Desegregation*, pp. 71–89. Copyright © 1980 by Teachers College, Columbia University. All rights reserved. Reprinted by permission of Teachers College Press.

University of Pennsylvania Law Review, and Fred B. Rothman & Co.: Excerpts from book review by David Kairys, 126 *University of Pennsylvania Law Review* 930 (1978). Copyright © 1978 by University of Pennsylvania Law Review. Reprinted by permission of University of Pennsylvania Law Review and Fred B. Rothman & Co.

Library of Congress Cataloging in Publication Data
Main entry under title:
The politics of law.
    Includes bibliographical references.
    1. Law—United States—Addresses, essays, lectures. I. Kairys, David.
KF380.P64   1982   349.73   82–47868
ISBN 0–394–51981–7   347.3   AACR2
ISBN 0–394–71110–6 (pbk.)

Manufactured in the United States of America

Text designed by Dana Kasarsky Design

987654

CONTENTS

II
SELECTED FIELDS OF LAW AND SUBSTANTIVE ISSUES

III
ALTERNATIVE PROGRESSIVE APPROACHES

ACKNOWLEDGMENTS

Many people made important contributions to this book. Among the authors, all of whom met relatively short deadlines, Duncan Kennedy, Karl Klare, and David Rudovsky regularly provided helpful comments and suggestions. Revisions of the initial drafts were made with input from many of the authors. And the book was greatly enhanced by the efforts of our editors at Pantheon, Philip Pochoda and Don Guttenplan; the copy editor, Donna Bass; and the entire Pantheon organization.

Homage should also be extended to the National Lawyers Guild, which has engaged for almost 50 years in a progressive struggle to understand, challenge and change the law, and to the Guild's Theoretical Studies Committee and the Conference on Critical Legal Studies, which have provided organizational bases for dialogue and support in the effort to develop a progressive critique of the law.

EDITOR'S DEDICATION
To my parents,
Bernard Kairys and Julia Lovett Kairys,
and to the memory of David Lovett.

INTRODUCTION

We Americans turn over more of our society's disputes, decisions, and concerns to courts and lawyers than does any other nation. Yet, in a society that places considerable value on democracy, courts would seem to have a peculiarly difficult problem justifying their power and maintaining their legitimacy. The judiciary is a nonmajoritarian institution, whose guiding lights are neither popularly chosen nor even expected to express or implement the will of the people. Rather, its legitimacy rests on notions of honesty and fairness and, most importantly, on popular perceptions of the judicial decision-making process.

Basic to the popular perception of the judicial process is the notion of government by law, not people. Law is depicted as separate from—and "above"—politics, economics, culture, or the values or preferences of judges. This separation is supposedly accomplished and ensured by a number of perceived attributes of the decision-making process, including judicial subservience to a Constitution, statutes, and precedent; the quasi-scientific, objective nature of legal analysis; and the technical expertise of judges and lawyers.

Together, these attributes constitute a decision-making process in which (1) the law on a particular issue is preexisting, clear, predictable, and available to anyone with reasonable legal skill; (2) the facts relevant to disposition of a case are ascertained by objective hearing and evidentiary rules that reasonably ensure that the truth will

1

emerge; (3) the result in a particular case is determined by a rather routine application of the law to the facts; and (4) except for the occasional bad judge, any reasonably competent and fair judge will reach the "correct" decision.

Of course, there are significant segments of the bar and trends in legal scholarship that repudiate this idealized model. The school of jurisprudence known as legal realism long ago exposed its falsity; and later jurisprudential developments, such as theories resting the legitimacy of law on the existence of widely shared values, at least implicitly recognize the social and political content of law. Moreover, concepts like public policy and social utility, while limited to certain notions of the public good, are generally acknowledged as appropriate considerations for judges, and it is commonly known that the particular judge assigned to a case has a significant bearing on the outcome.

But most of this thinking is either limited to law journals or compartmentalized, existing alongside and often presented as part of the idealized process. For example, balancing tests, where judges decide which of two or more conflicting policies or interests will predominate, are presented and applied as if there were objective and neutral answers, as if it were possible to perform such a balance independent of political, social, and personal values that vary among our people and (to a lesser extent) among our judges.

Despite the various scholarly trends and the open consideration of social policy and utility, legal decisions are expressed and justified, and the courts as well as their decisions are depicted and discussed throughout society, in terms of the idealized process. The public perception—the crucial perception from the standpoint of legitimacy—is generally limited to the idealized model. One will often hear cynical views about the law, such as "the system is fixed," but even such observations are usually meant to describe departures from, rather than characteristics of, the legal process. While this perception is not monolithic or static (at various times substantial segments of society have come to question the idealized model), it has fairly consistently had more currency in the United States than in any other country.

Indeed, public debate over judicial decisions usually focuses on whether courts have deviated from the idealized model rather than on the substance of decisions or the nature and social significance of judicial power. Perceived deviations undermine the legitimacy and power of the courts, and are usually greeted with a variety of institutional and public challenges, including attacks by politicians and the press, proposals for statutory or constitutional change, and, occasionally, threats or attempts to impeach judges.

While there is presently considerable dissatisfaction with the courts and their decisions from a variety of political perspectives, it is usually expressed in terms of this notion of deviation from the idealized model. Thus, the conservative criticism that the courts have overstepped their bounds—going beyond or outside legal reasoning and the idealized process—is now commonplace, as is the accompanying plea for judicial restraint to allow our "democratic processes" to function.

The authors of this book are also dissatisfied, but the content and implications of our critique are very different. At this early stage there appear to be four basic elements of our evolving legal theory.

First, we reject the idealized model and the notion that a distinctly legal mode of reasoning or analysis characterizes the legal process or even exists. The problem is not that courts deviate from legal reasoning. There is no legal reasoning in the sense of a legal methodology or process for reaching particular, correct results. There is a distinctly legal and quite elaborate system of discourse and body of knowledge, replete with its own language and conventions of argumentation, logic, and even manners. In some ways these aspects of the law are so distinct and all-embracing as to amount to a separate culture; and for many lawyers the courthouse, the law firm, the language, the style, become a way of life. But in terms of a method or process for decision making—for determining correct rules, facts, or results—the law provides only a wide and conflicting variety of stylized rationalizations from which courts pick and choose. Social and political judgments about the substance, parties, and context of a case guide such choices, even when they are not the explicit or conscious basis of decision.

Judges are the often unknowing objects, as well as among the staunchest supporters, of the myth of legal reasoning. Decisions are predicated upon a complex mixture of social, political, institutional, experiential, and personal factors; however, they are expressed and justified, and largely perceived by judges themselves, in terms of "facts" that have been objectively determined and "law" that has been objectively and rationally "found" and "applied." One result is a judicial schizophrenia that permeates decisions, arguments, and banter among lawyers.

Second, we place fundamental importance on democracy, by which we mean popular participation in the decisions that shape our society and affect our lives. While there is a very real sense of powerlessness that pervades contemporary society, to blame this solely or even principally on the courts misses the point.

Those democratic processes that the courts are supposedly invading in the conservative view consist essentially of the right to vote and freedom of speech and association. Our society allows no democracy outside this "public" sphere of our lives. For example, the economic decisions that most crucially shape our society and affect our lives, on basic social issues like the use of our resources, investment, the energy problem, and the work of our people, are regarded as "private" and are not made democratically or even by the government officials elected in the public sphere. The public/private split ideologically legitimizes private—mainly corporate—dominance, masks the lack of real participation or democracy, and personalizes the powerlessness it breeds.

The law plays a crucial role in this: the idealized model, the notion of technical expertise, and the notion of the law as neutral, objective, and quasi-scientific lend legitimacy to the judicial process, which in turn lends a broader legitimacy to the social and power relations and ideology that are reflected, articulated, and enforced by the courts. However, existing democratic processes do not provide meaningful choices or constitute meaningful mechanisms for popular control or input, which is, perhaps, why half our people do not vote. These processes—and the law—provide a false legitimacy to existing social and power relations.

The current and seemingly endless debate over judicial restraint or activism also misses the point. There is no coherent framework or principled resolution of this debate within the legal system, just as and because there is no legal reasoning. Rather, with very few exceptions, the pleas for judicial restraint and activism, sometimes unintentionally or unconsciously, mask a political direction and are wholly dependent on the historical and social contexts. If one favored Social Security and restriction of child labor over maximization of profits during the New Deal, one was for judicial restraint; if one favored racial equality and justice over maintenance of white privilege and the historical oppression of black people in the 1960s, one was for judicial activism; if one favors prohibition of abortions by choice in the 1980s, one is for judicial restraint. There is afoot these days a conservative brand of "democracy," using, in part, the fashionable label of judicial restraint, that allows little or no room for popular participation or scrutiny. In this view, powerful, largely corporate, interests; the patriarchal, authoritarian family; and, in selected areas, government officials are not to be interfered with, by the courts or by the people.

Third, we reject the common characterization of the law and the state as neutral, value-free arbiters, independent of and unaffected by social and economic relations, political forces, and cultural phenomena. Traditional jurisprudence largely ignores social and historical reality, and masks the existence of social conflict and oppression with ideological myths about objectivity and neutrality. The dominant system of values has been declared value free; it then follows that all others suffer from bias and can be thoughtlessly dismissed.

Left thinking about the law and the state has long recognized this political content and lack of neutrality. However, there has been a tendency to oversimplify with analyses that often seem to seek an almost mystical, linear, causal chain that translates economics into law. For example, a common orthodox Marxist explanation is that law is a "superstructural" phenomena that is mysteriously governed and determined by an underlying "base" of economic relations and/or instrumentally controlled by the ruling elite or class. But the law is not simply an armed receptacle for values and priorities determined elsewhere; it is part of a complex social totality in which it constitutes as well as is constituted, shapes as well as is shaped. Moreover, such analyses lose sight of the fact that the law consists of people-made decisions and doctrines, and the thought processes and modes of reconciling conflicting considerations of these people (judges) are not mystical, inevitable, or very different from the rest of ours. It is often difficult to resist dehumanization of one's opponents and a blanket rejection of all institutions and people that constitute and symbolize a system one deeply wishes to completely transform, and such analyses have characterized left thinking for some time.

However, judges are not robots that are—or need to be—mysteriously or conspiratorily controlled. Rather, they, like the rest of us, form values and prioritize conflicting considerations based on their experience, socialization, political perspectives, self-perceptions, hopes, fears, and a variety of other factors. The results are not, however, random; their particular backgrounds, socialization, and experiences— in which law schools and the practice of largely commercial forms of law play an important role—result in a patterning, a consistency, in the ways they categorize, approach, and resolve social and political conflicts. This is the great source of the law's power: it enforces, reflects, constitutes, and legitimizes dominant social and power relations without a need for or the appearance of control from outside and by means of social actors who largely believe in their own neutrality and the myth of legal reasoning.

Fourth, while the law has many important functions, the legitimation function is crucial to an understanding of its doctrines, rationalizations, results, and social role. The law's ultimate mechanism for control and enforcement is institutional violence, but it protects the dominant system of social and power relations against political and ideological as well as physical challenges. The law is a major vehicle for the maintenance of existing social and power relations by the consent or acquiescence of the lower and middle classes. The law's perceived legitimacy confers a broader legitimacy on a social system and ideology that, despite their claims to kinship with nature, science, or God, are most fairly characterized by domination by a very small, mainly corporatized elite. This perceived legitimacy of the law is primarily based on notions of technical expertise and objectivity and the

idealized model of the legal process—in short, as described above, on
the distorted notion of government by law, not people. But it is also
greatly enhanced by the reality, often ignored in orthodox left thinking, that the law is, on some occasions, just and sometimes serves to
restrain the exercise of power.

A realistic, understandable approach to the law that explains its
operation and social role must acknowledge the fundamental conflicts
in society; the class, race, and sex basis of these conflicts; and the
dominance of an ideology that is not natural, scientifically determined,
or objective. The discretionary nature of court decisions, the importance of social and political judgments, and the dominance of the
ideology of advanced capitalism characterize our judicial process far
better than any notions of objectivity, expertise, or science.

This book is an attempt to present a progressive, critical analysis
of the operation and social role of the law in contemporary American
society. Our approach is interdisciplinary, including authors and
methods based in sociology, economics, history, and political science as
well as law, and draws upon the experience of law practitioners as well
as teachers. We seek a theoretical and practical understanding of the
law that places its institutions and individual actors in their social and
historical contexts, and views the law as part of and intimately connected to a social totality.

This is not a new task. In a broad sense, this effort is a continuation of the realists' project (see chapter 2). However, it is also a
beginning, because left legal (and social) theory has been for several
decades caught in a crippling choice between liberal theory and
mechanical, determinist forms of Marxism-Leninism.*

It is our hope that this book will provide insight, understanding,
and an impetus and basis for further development to a wide variety of
readers. These include, in addition to legal theorists, law teachers, and
members of the legal profession generally, law students seeking an
understanding of the bewildering world of law school and the discipline that is largely being mystified rather than revealed in their classes
(see chapter 3); law practitioners and legal workers seeking an understanding of the meaning of their work; students and teachers concerned with the social role and operation of the law and the state in
legal studies, sociology, political science, economics, history, and other
disciplines; Marxists, neo-Marxists, and other progressives interested in
the nature and role of the law and the state in contemporary society;
and progressive people and groups seeking a better understanding of

---

* While portions of this book are critical of some Marxist thinking, many of us
place ourselves in or draw heavily on the Marxist tradition and current trends in
Marxist thought.

their law-related goals and strategies. We have assumed the reader has only a general grasp of the legal process and little or no legal training, although due to space limitations it has not been possible to explain every legal term or concept used.

The book is divided into three parts. Part 1 considers the idealized model and the notion of legal reasoning (chapter 1), traditional jurisprudence (chapter 2), and legal education (chapter 3). Part 2 consists of ten chapters that discuss and analyze the social role and operation of the law, focusing on selected substantive issues and fields of law. The first four of these chapters concern four major social and legal issues (the conflict between labor and capital, race and sex discrimination, freedom of speech). The remaining chapters in part 2 concentrate on several selected fields of law and law-school courses (contracts, torts, criminal law) and some selected issues (causation, corporations and free speech, welfare entitlements). This focus on substantive issues is intended to result in a more accessible and significant analysis than would attempts to discuss the law abstractly. Part 3 presents four short essays that introduce and discuss a variety of progressive approaches to the law.

This book originated in 1979 as a project of the Theoretical Studies Committee of the National Lawyers Guild and proceeded, at first informally and later formally, as a joint project of the Theoretical Studies Committee and the Conference on Critical Legal Studies. The Guild, founded in 1937, is a national organization of progressive lawyers, law students, and legal workers with over seven thousand members and offices in most major cities. The Conference, founded in 1977, is primarily composed of law teachers and holds a yearly weekend conference open to all interested persons.*

The reader will see reflected in this book a variety of political perspectives and methodologies, and some variance in the audiences to which the selections are addressed. While the book is intended to be more coherent as a whole than collections usually are, we have not attempted to harmonize the contributions or to present a single, fully developed approach. Each author is responsible for the content of his or her selection.

> *David Kairys*
> *Philadelphia*
> *September 1981*

---

* The Conference on Critical Legal Studies can be contacted c/o Mark Tushnet, Secretary, 1416 Holly St., N.W., Washington, D.C. 20012; the Guild's national office is at 853 Broadway, NY, NY 10003; the Guild's Theoretical Studies Committee can be contacted at 1425 Walnut Street, Philadelphia, PA 19102.

A Note on the Notes

The bibliographic style of the notes generally follows that speci-
fied for footnotes in *A Manual of Style*, by the University of Chicago
Press. However, legal citations generally follow *A Uniform System of
Citations* (12th ed., 1976), published by the Harvard Law Review
Association, except that many words usually abbreviated have been
written out to aid the non-law-trained reader. The content of the notes
has generally been limited to citations to authority.

I

LEGAL REASONING, TRADITIONAL JURISPRUDENCE, AND LEGAL EDUCATION

1 LEGAL REASONING
David Kairys

The idealized model of the legal process discussed in the introduction is based on the notion that there is a distinctly legal mode of reasoning and analysis that leads to and determines "correct" rules, facts, and results in particular cases. The concept of legal reasoning is essential to the fundamental legitimizing claim of government by law, not people; it purports to distinguish legal analysis and expertise from the variety of social, political, and economic considerations and modes of analysis that, in a democratic society, would be more appropriately debated and determined by the people, not judges.

This chapter focuses on one of the basic elements or mechanisms of legal reasoning, *stare decisis*, which embodies the notion of judicial subservience to prior decisions or precedents. The notion is that judges are bound by and defer to precedents, thereby restricting their domain to law rather than politics.

If legal reasoning has any real meaning, *stare decisis*, applied by a skilled and fair legal mind, should lead to and require particular results in specific cases. But anyone familiar with the legal system knows that some precedents are followed and some are not; thus, not all precedents are treated similarly or equally. Moreover, the meaning of a precedent and its significance to a new case are frequently unclear. The important questions, largely ignored by judges, law teachers, and commentators, are: How do courts decide which precedents to follow? How do they determine the significance of ambiguous precedents? Do precedents really matter at all? Why do lawyers spend so much time talking about them?

The Supreme Court's recent decisions concerning exercise of free-speech rights in privately owned shopping centers provide a good illustration (illustrations in private law areas are contained in other portions of this book). In *Amalgamated Food Employees Union Local 590* v. *Logan Valley Plaza* (1968),[1] the Court upheld the constitutional right of union members to picket a store involved in a labor dispute in the shopping center where it was located. The Court recognized that shopping centers have to a large extent replaced inner-city business districts. The best, and perhaps only, place to communicate with sub-urbanites is in shopping centers. Citing *Marsh* v. *Alabama* (1946),[2] in which First Amendment freedoms were held applicable to a "company town," the Court ruled that the interest in free speech outweighed the private-property interests of shopping-center owners.

However, only four years later, in *Lloyd* v. *Tanner* (1972),[3] the Court held that an antiwar activist had no right to distribute leaflets in a shopping center, even though this center regularly attracted political candidates by avowing that it provided the largest audience in the state. The majority opinion justified the decision by claiming to differentiate the facts involved from those in *Logan Valley* primarily on the ground that speech concerning a labor dispute relates more closely to the activities of a shopping center than does antiwar speech. (In legal parlance, this is called distinguishing a precedent.)

Then, in *Hudgens* v. *NLRB* (1976),[4] the Court announced that, contrary to explicit language in *Lloyd*, the Court had actually over-ruled *Logan Valley* in the *Lloyd* case. The Court said that to treat labor speech differently from antiwar speech would violate the norm that First Amendment freedoms do not depend on the content of the speech, a result that surely was not intended in *Lloyd*. Having rewritten *Lloyd*, the *Hudgens* court went on to say that it was bound by *Lloyd* (as rewritten) and to hold that union members involved in a labor dispute with a store located in a shopping center do not have a constitutional right to picket in that shopping center. The stated rationale for this complete turnabout, within only eight years, was *stare decisis*: "Our institutional duty is to follow until changed the law as it now is, not as some members of the Court might wish it to be."[5]

The Court offered no explanation of what happened to this "institutional duty" in *Lloyd*, since the *Lloyd* court would seem to have been bound by *Logan Valley* (which the *Hudgens* court held had decided the same issue decided in *Lloyd*). Nor did the Court explain how its duty to "follow until changed the law as it now is" binds it in any real sense, since even within the system of *stare decisis* it is understood that the Court can change the law or overrule, ignore, or rewrite prior decisions. The Supreme Court is never really *bound* by a precedent. Finally, the majority opinion in *Hudgens* castigated the dissenting justices for deciding cases on the basis of what they "might wish [the law] to be," but there is no indication of how the majority's decision-making process is different. The majority simply outnumbered the minority.

There were ample precedents supporting each of the conflicting policies in *Hudgens*. Freedom of speech was favored over private property in *Marsh* (from an earlier period when First Amendment rights were being expanded) and in *Logan Valley* itself. Private property and the interests of suburbanites in isolation were favored in earlier cases and recently in *Lloyd*. This policy conflict clearly was not—and could not be—resolved by some objective or required application of *stare decisis* or any other legal principle.

Unstated and lost in the mire of contradictory precedents and justifications was the central point that none of these cases was or could be decided without ultimate reference to values and choices of a *political* nature. The various justifications and precedents emphasized in the opinions serve to mask these little-discussed but unavoidable social and political judgments. In 1968, a majority of the members of the Court resolved the conflict in favor of freedom of speech; in 1972, a majority retreated from that judgment; in 1976, a majority decided that property interests would prevail.

In short, these cases demonstrate a central deception of traditional jurisprudence: the majority claims for its social and political judgment not only the status of law (in the sense of binding authority), which it surely has, but also that its judgment is the product of distinctly legal reasoning, of a neutral, objective application of legal expertise. This latter claim, essential to the legitimacy and mystique of the courts, is false.

Stare decisis is so integral to legal thinking and education that it becomes internalized by people trained in the law, and its social role and ideological content become blurred and invisible. To see these aspects of and to understand *stare decisis*, it is helpful to separate the social role from the functional impact on the decision-making process.

Our legal norms are broadly and vaguely stated. They do not logically lead to particular results or rationales concerning most important or difficult issues.[6] A wide variety of interpretations, distinctions, and justifications are available; and judges have the authority and power to choose the issues they will address and to ignore constitutional provisions, statutes, precedents, evidence, and the best legal arguments.

Moreover, there are prior decisions similar or related by analogy to both sides of almost any difficult or important issue. This should not be surprising, since issues are difficult or important largely because there are significant policies, rooted in social reality and/or legal doctrine, supporting both sides. Each such policy, or a closely related policy, will have been favored or given high priority in some context and/or during some period. Usually the various relevant precedents will provide some support for both sides rather than lead to a particular rule or result.

Indeed, often the same precedent will provide support for both sides. For example, suppose after *Hudgens* an antinuclear activist claimed the right to distribute leaflets and picket in a privately owned railroad terminal. The terminal's counsel would argue that *Hudgens* should be broadly construed as definitively resolving the issue of speech on private property that is open to the public. He or she would emphasize the physical and functional similarities of shopping centers and train terminals. On the other hand, the activist's counsel would urge that *Hudgens* be narrowly construed as applicable only to the particular problem of labor picketing and only to the shopping center involved in that case or, at most, to shopping centers generally. He or she would emphasize the differences between train terminals and shopping centers. Much of legal education consists of training students to make arguments and distinctions of this kind. Both sides would argue that *Hudgens*, properly construed (a phrase likely to be found in both briefs), supports each of them. The judge would then decide the case, citing *Hudgens* as support for his or her decision regardless of which side won. There is no *legal* explanation in any of this; the law has provided a falsely legitimizing justification for a decision that is ultimately social and political.

Thus, *stare decisis* neither leads to nor requires any particular results or rationales in specific cases. A wide variety of precedents and a still wider variety of interpretations and distinctions are available from which to pick and choose. Social and political judgments about the substance, parties, and context of the case guide such choices, even when they are not the explicit or conscious basis of decision. In the shopping-center cases, justices who placed a preeminent value on freedom of speech found *Marsh* and *Logan Valley* precedents that should be followed, while justices who viewed property rights as more important placed considerable precedential weight on *Lloyd*.

Judicial decisions ultimately depend on judgments based on values and priorities that vary with particular judges (and even with the same judge, depending on the context) and are the result of a composite of social, political, institutional, experiential, and personal factors. The socially and legally important focus of judicial decision making—hidden by *stare decisis* and the notion of legal reasoning, and largely ignored in law schools, opinions, and law review articles—should be on the content, origins, and development of these values and priorities.

This does not mean that judicial values and priorities, or the results in particular cases, are random or wholly unpredictable. The shared backgrounds, socialization, and experience of our judges, which include law school and usually law practice, yield definite patterns in the ways they categorize, approach, and resolve social and political conflicts. Moreover, some rules and results are relatively uncontroversial and predictable in a particular historical context, not based on *stare decisis* or any other legal principle but because of widely shared social and political assumptions characteristic of that context.

While seeming to limit discretion and to require objective and rational analysis, *stare decisis* in fact provides and serves to disguise enormous discretion. This discretion is somewhat broader in the higher courts, but it exists at all levels. Lower courts have an added institutional concern, since their decisions can be reviewed, but they also have added discretion stemming from their relatively larger control over the facts and the credibility of witnesses.

Functionally, *stare decisis* is not a process of decision making or a mechanism that ensures continuity, predictability, rationality, or objectivity. Precedents are largely reduced to rationalizations, not factors meaningfully contributing to the result; they support rather than determine the principles and outcomes adopted by judges.

There are, however, difficult and important cases where *stare decisis* or continuity seems to have considerable significance. For example, it is widely believed (and I will here assume) that a majority of the Supreme Court would decide *Miranda* v. *Arizona*[7] differently now than it did in 1966, and yet the Court has not overruled *Miranda*. There are two major, alternative explanations.

First, if one regards *stare decisis* as a decision-making process and accepts traditional jurisprudence, the Court is bound by *Miranda*. I obviously reject this: the *Hudgens* court also should have been bound by *Logan Valley*, and there is no objective explanation for the difference based in legal reasoning.

Second, although a present majority may substantively favor overruling *Miranda*, based on a different social and political judgment concerning police conduct and the rights of criminal defendants, there is not a majority willing to do so for institutional and political reasons unrelated to the substance of the issue, to any "duty" to follow precedent, or to any legal decision-making process. Rather, their decision not to overrule is based on the likely public perception of and reaction to such a decision and the effect on the Court's power and legitimacy. Thus, hypothetically (and without consulting any law clerks), there may be six justices whose substantive judgment is to overrule *Miranda*, but perhaps two or more of these six will not so vote. The "constrained" justices are not and do not view themselves as substantively, analytically, or institutionally "bound"; their judgment is to overrule. However, if the Court overrules *Miranda*, a well-known symbol, the decision would be widely perceived as political—and therefore raise the spector of government by people, not law. In fact, such a decision would not be any more political than was *Miranda* itself (just a different politics and a different context). But the popular perception could create a serious crisis of legitimacy and undermine the Court's power.[8]

Stare decisis is integral to the popular conception of the judicial process and an important component of the ideology with which judicial power is justified and legitimized. This ideological role is perhaps easiest to see if one looks at the historical development of *stare decisis*. Viewing *stare decisis* as a component of a neutral, objective, or quasi-scientific discipline, one would expect a progressive development and a general tendency toward reliance on precedent, or at least toward concrete, rational standards for determining when precedent will not be followed. However, it is clear that *stare decisis* has not developed this way. The meaning and importance of *stare decisis* are not fixed or independent of social and historical circumstances, and there has been no long-term tendency toward refinement. Rather, *stare decisis* has conveniently fallen by the wayside in periods when the legitimacy and power of the courts stood to be enhanced by openly rejecting continuity in favor of politically popular change.

For example, in the early 1800s, long-established legal principles of property, exchange, and relations among people clashed with an evolving social commitment to economic development. Widespread construction of mills and dams, for instance, was inconsistent with established rights of downstream and upstream landowners (based on the earlier conception of land as a source of enjoyment in its natural state rather than as a productive asset). In this context, *stare decisis* was explicitly rejected by the courts; rather, the law was seen as an active promoter of socially desirable goals and conduct (*i.e.*, capitalist economic growth). After a basic substantive transformation was accomplished (circa 1850), the new legal values were consolidated and entrenched by limiting the effect of social concerns on the law and by the reemergence of legal formalism and *stare decisis*. However, the renewed deference to precedent, though often expressed in terms of principles derived from time immemorial, looked back only as far as the early 1800s to the recently transformed legal norms.[9]

In sum, *stare decisis*, while integral to the language of legal discourse and the mystique of legal reasoning, serves a primarily ideological rather than functional role. Nor is there any more validity to the notion of legal reasoning when the source of law is a statutory or constitutional provision or the language of an agreement. Courts determine the meaning and applicability of the pertinent language; similar arguments and distinctions are available; and the ultimate basis is a social and political judgment. Indeed, even the facts relevant to a particular controversy (largely reduced to uncontroversial givens in law schools) are not capable of determination by any distinctly legal or nonpolitical methodology. Law is simply politics by other means.

In a broader sense, the ideological role of concepts like legal reasoning is but one aspect of a larger social phenomenon. In many areas of our lives, essentially social and political judgments gain legitimacy from notions of expertise and analysis that falsely purport to be objective, neutral, and quasi-scientific. For example, cost-benefit analyses have been used to lend a false scientific gloss to people-made judgments about workplace safety standards that place profits above human life. If religion is the opiate of the masses, it seems that objectivity, expertise, and science have become the tranquilizers.

NOTES

1. 391 U.S. 308 (1968).
2. 326 U.S. 501 (1946).
3. 407 U.S. 551 (1972).
4. 424 U.S. 507 (1976). On remand, a statutory right to picket in the shopping center concerning the labor dispute was recognized. 230 NLRB 414 (1977).
5. 424 U.S. at 518.
6. There are, of course, cases and areas of the law where there is considerable clarity and predictability. For example, some aspects of the law of commercial transactions are quite detailed, thorough, and currently uncontroversial, and continuity has more meaning there.
7. 384 U.S. 436 (1966).
8. There is possibly a third major alternative: although *stare decisis* is not a determinate decision-making process in the sense that it requires or explains the unwillingness to overrule *Miranda*, justices may earnestly believe in it apart from the political calculation that characterizes the second alternative. However, unless a justice always follows precedent (which none do) or has objective standards for determining when he or she will do otherwise (which is impossible), his or her honest belief in *stare decisis* is but an unconscious variant of the second alternative. For example, former Justice Potter Stewart is widely thought to have an unusually deep belief in the importance of continuity, but he wrote the majority opinion in *Hudgens*. Various judges place different emphases on various values and factors, and although Justice Stewart has a strong commitment to continuity, institutional and political factors—not technical expertise or objective analysis—determine when and where he deviates from that commitment.
9. *See* M. Horwitz, *The Transformation of American Law, 1780–1860* (Harvard University Press: Cambridge, Mass., 1977).

2 THE HISTORY OF MAINSTREAM LEGAL THOUGHT
Elizabeth Mensch

The most corrosive message of legal history is the message of contingency.[1] Routinely, the justificatory language of law parades as the unquestionable embodiment of Reason and Universal Truth; yet even a brief romp through the history of American legal thought reveals how quickly the Obvious Logic of one period can become the silly formalism of another, or how easily Enlightened Modern Policy can, from another perspective, be perceived as irresponsible judicial meddling. The account that follows is a short, and necessarily superficial, summary of the major changes that have taken place in American legal thought since the onset of the nineteenth century. There will be no attempt to examine the complex causes of those changes, nor their relation to the social and economic contexts within which they have, of course, occurred. The goal is more limited: to describe the legal consciousness of distinct (although overlapping) periods of American legal thought. Since the effort is to reconstruct the world-view of those who have been most directly concerned with making, explaining, and applying legal doctrine, many theorists who have written on the fundamental questions of jurisprudence are not included.* This is an

---

* The key modern omissions are Rawls and Dworkin. While they are presently the most widely read liberal legal theorists, the significance of their contribution to jurisprudential thought has been vastly overrated. Rawls, somewhat whimsically,

account of conventional, and therefore often wholly unreflecting and unselfconscious, legal consciousness.[2]

PRE-CLASSICAL CONSCIOUSNESS (1776–1885)

During the disruptive and potentially radical period that immediately followed the Revolution, elite American jurists devoted themselves to reestablishing legal authority. As the embodiment of reason and continuity, law seemed to offer the only source of stability in a nation that otherwise threatened to dissolve into the chaotic, leveling passions of a people now so dangerously declared to be sovereign.

In a flowery vocabulary drawn largely from the natural-law tradition, late-eighteenth- and early-nineteenth-century legal speakers made extravagant claims about the role of law and lawyers. Law was routinely described as reflecting here on earth the universal principles of divine justice, which, in their purest form, reigned in the Celestial City. For example, the single most popular legal quotation, for rhetorical purposes, was taken from the Anglican theologian Hooker: "Of law no less can be acknowledged, than that her seat is the bosom of God; her voice harmony of the world."[3]

Similarly, lawyers portrayed their own professional character as the embodiment of republican virtue; ideally, within each well-educated lawyer reason had subdued the unruly passions, and that triumph rendered the lawyer fit to consecrate himself to the service of law, as a "priest at the temple of justice." In this role the lawyer/priest was to act, not as an instrument of his client's unbridled will, but as a "trustee" for the interests of the whole community. As advisor and guardian, he would attempt to elicit elevated rather than base motives

---

has simply resurrected seventeenth-century social contract theory in an effort to universalize liberal thought. He postulates a hypothetical initial position of "rational" people who are essentially atomized monads with an interest in attaining their own private stock of social goods, but who demonstrate no interest in promoting the welfare of others or in building a society of true participation, equality, or shared values. This Rawlsian conception of reason as the amoral, instrumental selection of means to achieve private, subjective ends is of course deeply rooted in liberal market ideology and is a key premise in the current law and economics literature (see infra, pp. 36–37); but it can hardly lay claim to providing an ahistorical Archimedian point from which to transcend the problem of contingency. See Roberto Unger, Knowledge and Politics (New York: The Free Press, 1975). Dworkin, on the other hand, simply vascillates between an implicit reliance on natural law theory and reliance on the inherent legitimacy of the judicial tradition. The first is obviously bankrupt absent a real theory of substantive value, which is impossible within liberalism's own most basic assumptions. The second renders Dworkin's theory of rights as self-referencing as classical rights theory (see infra, pp. 23–26) and is premised on the same legitimacy that it sets out to demonstrate.

in his clients, guiding them to promote a social order consistent with those universal principles that were ordained by God and most clearly understood by lawyers.

This special trusteeship meant that lawyers played a crucial political role in the new democracy, where principle and legal right constantly faced the threat of mass assault. Leaders of the bar often described lawyers as sentinels, placed on the dangerous outposts of defense, preserving the virtue of the republic from the specifically democratic threats of irrational legislation and mob rule. Not surprisingly, many nineteenth-century jurists cited with satisfaction de Tocqueville's observation that the legal profession constituted a distinctively American aristocracy, providing order in an otherwise unstable democracy.

The universal principle that seemed to require the most zealous protection was the sanctity of private property. With something approaching paranoia, leading American jurists explained that the redistributive passions of the majority, if ever allowed to overrun the barrier of legal principle, would sweep away the nation's whole social and economic foundation. Thus Joseph Story, upon his inauguration as professor of law at Harvard, announced that the lawyer's most "glorious and not infrequently perilous" duty was to guard the "sacred rights of property" from the "rapacity" of the majority. Only the "solitary citadel" of justice stood between property and redistribution; it was the lawyer's noble task to man that citadel, whatever the personal cost. "What sacrifice could be more pure than in such a cause? What martyrdom more worthy to be canonized in our hearts?"[4]

The ornate legal rhetoric of the period obscured a number of dilemmas deep at the core of early American legal theory. First, despite the rhetorical appeal to natural law as a source of legitimacy, most jurists readily conceded that natural law alone was too indeterminate to guide judicial decision making in specific cases. Natural law provided divine sanction but yielded few concrete rules or results. Moreover, pure natural-law theory could lead in unwanted directions. The notion of natural reason upon which it rested, for example, could be translated to mean the natural reason of the sovereign people— Thomas Paine's common sense—rather than the reason of trained lawyers. That suggested precisely the unlimited popular will, which most jurists feared. Furthermore, the moral content of natural-law theory often led in contradictory directions. One key example was the right to property; while a Lockean natural-law tradition asserted the sanctity of private property, an even older (and alarmingly popular) natural-law tradition questioned the morality of all social and economic inequality.[5]

Most early-nineteenth-century lawyers were thus ready to concede that the most immediate, practical source and definition of law was to be found in positive law[6]—not statutes, which were feared because of their origin in unpredictable representative assemblies[7]—but the complex, ancient forms of the English common law. The legitimacy of those forms was said to derive not from universal moral principle but from custom and long usage. It was the extraordinary technicality of the common law that provided lawyers with their claim to expertise and served, by its very artificiality, to distinguish legal reasoning from the "common-sense" reason of the general populace.[8] Moreover, common-law rules, however quirky, seemed able to supply the certainty and formal realizability impossible to find in the vague morality of natural law.

The precise relation between natural-law and common-law forms was inevitably problematic. Occasionally, it was announced that the common law and natural law were simply identical, but that claim was inherently implausible. Many technical rules of the common law seemed purely whimsical, obviously rooted exclusively in the English legal tradition, and often derived from the history of feudal property relations, which Americans had explicitly repudiated. Some rules had already been declared wholly inapplicable to the New World, where they had been modified, in quite various ways, in each of the colonies; even in England there had been obvious changes within the supposed changelessness of the common law. Thus, it was hard to argue that each common-law rule was an expression of immutable, universal truth.

The potential conflict between natural-law conceptions and the common-law tradition, as well as between contradictory assertions within natural law, was obscured in the early-nineteenth century by a surprisingly self-confident belief that one would always reach a just conclusion by employing two techniques of legal reasoning: liberality of interpretation and implication. By the first, judges and treatise writers meant a willingness to interpret technical common-law rules—which were still unquestioningly assumed to form the bulk of the law—with a flexible, progressive American spirit and, in particular, with concern for commerical utility. Lord Mansfield in England, who had often drawn on civil law to modify rigid common-law rules in the name of commercial good sense, was often cited as an example to be followed by enlightened American decision makers.

This notion of utility became a key mediating concept in liberal interpretation. It suggested that one did not have to choose *between* a strict, rigid adherence to common-law technicalities and the less certain demands of substantive justice, nor *between* commercial utility and the moralistic claims of traditional natural law. Instead, it was common to cite utility as a justification for departing from common-law rules, often on the claim that the common law itself, properly understood by liberal judges like Mansfield, had always allowed for utilitarian change; and then to further explain that in the form of commercial "reasonableness," utility was implicit in natural reason and therefore in the whole natural-law and civil-law tradition. Thus, modern departures from common-law rules could be seen as both consistent with the long "changing changelessness" of the common-law tradition[9] and also as evidence of the common law's link to natural reason and universal principle.

The technique of implied intent, also basic to early-nineteenth-century legal thought, performed a similar function. Routinely, judges appealed to the intent of the parties as a basis for decision making, which coincided with the increased use of contract imagery in judicial opinions. The emphasis on implied intent did not, however, necessarily evidence concern with the actual, subjective intent of individual parties; instead, it represented a fusion of subjective intent with socially imposed duty. Legal thinkers self-confidently assumed that they could find the "law" within the obligations inherent in particular social and commercial relations, obligations which, it could be claimed, parties intended to assume when they entered the relationship.

For example, in his important treatise on contract law,[10] Parsons devoted over 90 percent of the pages to a description of various types of parties (e.g., agents, guardians, servants) and relational contexts (e.g., marriage, bailment, service contracts, sale of goods). Each category represented a social entity with its own implicit duties and reasonable expectations. A party entering into a particular relationship would be said to have intended to conform to the standards of reasonable behavior that inhered in such a relationship. Specific rules could then be defended or modified depending upon whether they promoted the principles and policies basic to that relationship (encouraged transactions in goods, promoted honorable dealing between merchants, etc.). Subjectivity and free will were thus combined with the potentially conflicting imposition of objective, judicially created obligations; and both notions were integrated into the amorphous blend of natural law, positive law, morality, and utility, which made up the justificatory language of early-nineteenth-century law.

Despite the confidence with which early-nineteenth-century judges invoked liberality and implied intent, the conceptual mush they made of legal theory posed serious problems for the emerging liberal conception, in constitutional law, of a sovereignty limited by private legal rights. Public law thinking was dominated by the Lockean model of the individual rightholder confronting a potentially oppressive sovereign power. Within that world-view, there ideally existed a realm of pure private autonomy, free from state intrusion. It was a realm in which individuals owned property protected from the encroachment of others and made self-willed, freely bargained for choices. Of course there was also a legitimate public realm, comprised of state and federal institutions entrusted with maintaining public order and serving clearly delineated public functions. Nevertheless, the public realm and the private were vacuum-bounded: in other words, they were conceived as wholly separate, in-or-out categories that could allow for no blurring or intermeshing.[11] It was, in effect, the vacuum boundary between public and private that jurists of the early-nineteenth century promised to guard with such everlasting zeal.

Yet, in order to justify protecting private rights from public power, it was necessary to conceive of the private as purely private. This demanded, in turn, a fully rationalized structure of private law, which, in theory, did no more than protect and facilitate the exercise of private will and which could also give concrete, objective content to the private rights supposedly protected by the Constitution. The loose hodge-podge of conflicting premises that made up early-nineteenth-century private law was insufficient for that purpose, and the great thrust of nineteenth-century legal thought was toward higher and higher levels of rationalization and generalization. Eventually, that process produced a grandly integrated conceptual scheme that seemed, for a fleeting moment in history, to bring coherence to the whole structure of American law, and to liberal political theory in general.

CLASSICAL LEGAL CONSCIOUSNESS (1885–1935)

The nineteenth century's process of legal rationalization resulted in the abstraction of law from both particularized social relations and substantive moral standards. By the "rule of law" classical jurists meant quite specifically a structure of positivised, objective, formally defined rights. They viewed the legal world not as a multitude of discrete, traditional relations but as a structure of protected spheres of rights and powers. Logically derivable vacuum boundaries defined for each individual her own sphere of pure private autonomy while simultaneously defining those spheres within which public power could be exercised freely and absolutely.

This conception of social action as the exercise of absolute rights and powers within bounded spheres extended to all possible relations: in a way inconceivable to the early-nineteenth century, the relation of private parties to each other was seen as deeply analogous to the relation of private parties to states, of states to each other and to federal powers, etc. In every instance of dispute, the key legal question was whether the relevant actors had stayed within their own protected sphere of activity or had crossed over the boundary and invaded the sphere of another. To the classics, freedom *meant* the legal guarantee that rights and powers would be protected as absolute within their own sphere, but that no rightholder/powerholder would be allowed to invade the sphere of another.

In that classical scheme, the utterly crucial task of boundary definition was assigned to the judiciary. Necessarily, this task required objectivity and impartiality. Other actors were free, within their own spheres, to exercise unbridled will in pursuit of their particular (subjective) moral, political, or economic goals. In contrast, the judicial role of boundary finding required the exercise of reason—a reason now conceived, however, not as embodying universal moral principles and knowledge of the public good but strictly as the application of objective methodology to the task of defining the scope of legal rights. Upon the supposed objectivity of that method hinged the liberal faith that the rule of law resolved the conflict between freedom as private, civil right and freedom as public participation in a democracy.

The supposed judicial objectivity upon which the classical structure depended was based in turn upon the intersection of constitutional language and an increasingly generalized, rationalized conception of private law. First, jurists pointed out that by enacting the Constitution, the sovereign American people had unequivocally (and wisely) adopted a government premised on private rights and strictly limited public powers. Thus, while it was certainly the exalted function of the judiciary to protect private rights from uncontrolled public passion, this function required merely the application of positive constitutional law—there was no painful choice to be made between positive law and natural rights.

Second, and of prime importance, the objective definition given to rights protected by the Constitution could be found within the common-law tradition, which had been wonderfully cleansed of both messy social particularity and natural-law morality. Classical jurists claimed that as a result of an enlightened, scientific process of rationalization, the common law could now properly be understood as based upon a few general and powerful—but clearly positivised—conceptual categories (like property and free contract), which had also been incorporated into the Constitution as protected rights. All of the specific rules of the common law (at least the "correct" rules) were said to be deduced from those general categories. For example, Williston's monumental treatise on contracts[12] assumed that from the general principle of free contract one could derive the few central doctrines around which the treatise was organized—offer and acceptance, consideration, excuse, etc.—and from the logic of those central doctrines one could derive all of the specific rules that made up the law of contracts. Those rules could then be applied, rigidly and formally, to *any* particular social context; in fact, failure to do so would be evidence of judicial irrationality and/or irresponsibility. More-over, because every rule was based upon the principle of free contract, the logical coherence of a contract doctrine, correctly applied, ensured that private contracting was always an expression of pure autonomy. With no small amount of self-congratulation, classical jurists con-trasted their conceptualization of private autonomy to Parson's de-scription of contract law as something to be found *within* numberless particular social relations. In retrospect, Parsons could be viewed as naïve and unscientific.

The new rationalization of common law meant that the old con-flict between formally realizable "rules" and substantive "justice" seemed resolved. Common-law rules were no longer a quirky relic from the English feudal past. Instead, they were both an expression and a definition of rights, and of course the protection of rights constituted the highest form of justice. Furthermore, as integrated into the con-stitutional law structure, the rationalization of private law meant that the boundary between the realm of private autonomy and the realm of public power could be objectively determined by reference to specific common-law doctrine.

The notorious case of *Coppage* v. *Kansas*[13] provides a clear example of the classical approach. In that case the Kansas state legisla-ture had passed a statute outlawing yellow-dog contracts (*i.e.*, con-tracts in which workers agreed not to engage in union activities). The question was whether this was a reasonable exercise of police power (*i.e.*, fell within the bounded sphere of public power) or whether it constituted an invasion of private contract right, a right considered implicit in the even more general category of liberty protected by the Fourteenth Amendment.

An earlier case, *Adair* v. *United States*,[14] had declared that a similar federal regulation was invalid; and through the Fourteenth Amendment, the constitutional protection of liberty as against the fed-eral government was made applicable to the states—evidence of the deep analogy now perceived in what were once conceived as quite different relationships. In response to the argument that *Adair* con-trolled, however, Kansas argued that its statute was designed specifi-cally to outlaw contracts formed under coercion. Since workers had no realistic choice but to accept the terms obviously imposed by em-ployers, the agreement to sign yellow-dog contracts was not an ex-pression of freedom, and it was no violation of liberty to regulate a "choice" that was never freely made. The Court refused to accept that argument, *not* because it denied the obvious inequality between work-ers and employers, but because freedom of contract as a legal category had to be defined objectively, which meant according to common-law doctrine. Since the common law had excluded economic pressure from its definition of duress as a legal excuse for nonperformance of contracts, then *by definition* yellow-dog contracts were not formed under duress and were therefore freely entered. It then followed logically that the statute constituted an invasion of liberty protected by the Constitution.

Cases like *Coppage* are now commonly cited as representing a judiciary determined to impose its own econonmic biases on the country. This both trivializes the underlying power of the classical conceptual scheme and, more significantly, trivializes the importance of the realist assault that revealed its incoherence. In fact, courts during the classical period described a police power as absolute in its sphere as were private rights in theirs, and they by no means overruled all legislation designed to regulate corporate power. Their key claim was that they could objectively "find" the boundary that separated private from public, and it was that supposed objectivity that gave the appearance of coherence and reality to the legal (and social/political) model of bounded rights and powers. That basic model, although in bankrupt form, is with us still, despite the realist challenge that demolished all of its premises. The message the model conveys is that actual power relations in the real world are by definition legitimate and most go unchallenged.

THE REALIST CHALLENGE (1920–1939)

The realist movement was a part of the general twentieth-century revolt against formalism and conceptualism. As applied to law, that revolt was directed against the whole highly conceptualized classical legal structure. More specifically and politically, realism was also a reaction against Supreme Court decisions like *Coppage*, which had invalidated progressive regulatory legislation favored even by many business leaders.

Some of the realists confined their attack to the relatively mild suggestion that legal thought should be more in accord with changing times and public sentiment. That meant recognizing the growing importance of government—especially administrative agencies—in an advanced industrial economy. Thus judges should defer to legislators on economic issues, and law students should prepare themselves to be policy makers in the new regulatory state. Meanwhile, in private law, enlightened, progressive judges should be willing to sacrifice rigid adherence to the logic of doctrine for the sake of doing a more commonsense and overtly policy-oriented "justice" within the particular context of each case.[15]

The best of the realist critique, however, cut so deeply into the premises of American legal thought that no amount of enlightened policy making and informed situation sense could ever really put Humpty Dumpty together again. Chiefly, the realists undermined all faith in the objective existence of "rights" by challenging the coherence of the key legal categories that gave content to the notion of bounded public and private spheres. Traditionally, legal discourse had justified decisions by making reference to rights; an opinion, for example, would set out as a reason for finding the defendant liable that she had invaded the property rights of the plaintiff—or, similarly, would justify declaring a statute unconstitutional by saying that it violated the right of property. Yet, as the realists pointed out, such justifications are inevitably circular. There will be a right if, and *only* if, the court finds for the plaintiff or declares the statute unconstitutional. What the court cites as the *reason* for the decision—the existence of a right—is, in fact, only the *result*.

Moreover, in every dispute, both sides' interests or goals can be asserted and formulated in terms of rights. In a nuisance case, for example, one party's "right" to complete security from the other's invasion (as in the form of industrial pollutants, noise from animals, or whatever) can be countered by an equally coherent "right" to complete freedom to use property as one chooses. Thus, instead of a preexisting right that compels a particular result, there are, in fact, conflicting (and contradictory) rights between which the court must always choose. It is that legal *choice* which then determines the result and forms the so-called right.

This attack upon the logic of rights theory was closely linked to an attack upon the logic of precedent. The realists pointed out that no two cases are ever exactly alike; there will always be some difference in the multitude of facts surrounding them. Thus, the "rule" of a former case can never simply be applied to a new case; rather, the judge must *choose* whether or not the ruling in the former case should be extended to include the new case. That choice is essentially a choice about the relevancy of facts, and those choices can never be logically compelled. Given shared social assumptions, some facts might seem obviously irrelevant (e.g., the color of socks worn by the offeree should not influence the enforceability of a contract), but decisions about the relevance of other distinguishing facts are more obviously value-laden and dependent on the historical context (e.g., the relative wealth of the parties).

That dilemma does not vanish when the "law" to be applied comes not from cases but from the language of statutory or constitutional provisions, or the language of a private contract. There was a time when words were thought to have a fixed, determinate content, a meaning partaking of objective Platonic forms. In the absence of a belief in Platonic intelligible essences, however, no interpretation or application of language can be logically required by the language itself. Words are created by people in history, and their definition inevitably varies with particular context and with the meaning brought to them by the judges who are asked to interpret them. That act of interpretation is, in every instance, an act of social choice.

Thus, the realists claimed that the effort of the nineteenth century to cleanse law of messy social particularity and moral choice was inevitably a failure. There was *no such thing* as an objective legal methodology behind which judges could hide in order to evade responsibility for the social consequences of legal decision making. Every decision they made was a moral and political choice.[16]

Furthermore, the realists understood, as had the classics, that the whole structure of the classical scheme depended upon the coherence of private law and the public/private distinction. Thus, the realists spent little time attacking the methodology of constitutional law and concentrated instead upon undermining the coherence of the key private-law categories that purported to define a sphere of pure autonomy. For example, Morris Cohen's essay "Property and Sovereignty"[17] pointed out that property is necessarily public, not private. Property *means* the legally granted power to withhold from others; as such, it is created by the state and given its only content by legal decisions that limit or extend the property owner's power over others. Thus, property is really an (always conditional) delegation of sovereignty, and property law is simply a form of public law. Whereas the classics (and liberal theorists generally) had drawn a bright line separating (private) property from (public) sovereignty, Cohen simply collapsed the two categories.

Hale made a similar point about the supposed private right of free contract: state enforcement of a contract right represents, like property, a delegation of sovereign power.[18] Moreover, he also pointed out, coercion, including legal coercion, lies at the heart of every "freely" chosen exchange. Coercion is inherent in each party's legally protected threat to withhold what is owned; that right to withhold creates the right to force submission to one's own terms. Since ownership is a function of legal entitlement, every bargain is a function of the legal order. Thus, there is no "inner" core of free, autonomous bargaining to be protected from "outside" state action; the inner and outer dissolve into each other.

Potentially, that collapse of spheres carried with it the collapse of the whole structure of American legal thought. Realism had effectively undermined the fundamental premises of liberal legalism, particularly the crucial distinction between legislation (subjective exercise of will) and adjudication (objective exercise of reason). Inescapably, it had also suggested that the whole liberal world-view of (private) rights and (public) sovereignty mediated by the rule of law was only a mirage, a pretty fantasy that masked the reality of economic and political power.

Since the realists, American jurists have dedicated themselves to the task of reconstruction; indeed, the realist message was so corrosive that many of the most influential realists evaded the full implications of their own criticism and quickly sought instead to articulate a new justification for legal reasoning's old claim to objectivity and legitimacy. That effort seemed especially crucial after the rise of fascism in Europe: If the liberal model of legally protected private rights was mere illusion, then where could one look for protection against totalitarian statism?[19] Nevertheless, the modern search for a new legitimacy, however earnest, was destined always to have a slightly defensive tone; after realism, American legal theorists had, as it were, eaten of the tree of knowledge, and there could be no return to the naïve confidence of the past.

ATTEMPTS AT MODERN RECONSTRUCTION (1940–PRESENT)

During the 1940s, Laswell and McDougal at Yale[20] followed out the implications of realism by announcing that since law students were destined to be the policy makers of the future, Yale should simply abandon the traditional law school curriculum and teach students how to make and implement policy decisions. Their simultaneously antidemocratic and antilegalist message was a bit jarring; most of the major post-realist reconstructors of American legal thought have been somewhat more restrained. Indeed, much of the reconstruction has consisted of simply conceding a number of key realist insights and then attempting to incorporate those insights into an otherwise intact doctrinal structure. What were once perceived as deep and unsettling logical flaws have been translated into the strengths of a progressive legal system. For example, the indeterminancy of rules has become the *flexibility* required for sensible, policy-oriented decision making; and the collapse of rights into contradiction has been recast as "competing interests," which are inevitable in a complex, tragic world and which obviously require an enlightened judicial *balancing*. In other words, we justify as legal sophistication what the classics would have viewed as the obvious abandonment of legality.

The most elaborate attempt to resurrect the legitimacy of the whole American lawmaking structure can be found in the extraor-

dinarily influential Hart and Sacks legal process materials of the
1950s.[21] Those materials were premised on a vision of American society which, it seemed for a time, offered a viable alternative to the
whole classical world-view. Hart and Sacks started by explaining that
the critical view of law as a "mask for force, providing a cover of
legitimacy" for the exercise of political and economic power, was
based on "the fallacy of the static pie." According to Hart and Sacks,
the "pie" of both tangible and intangible goods was in fact ever-
expanding, and a primary, shared purpose of social life was to keep the
pie growing.

Within the Hart and Sacks description of American society, the
essentially private actors who shared the goal of expansion also shared a
belief in the stability afforded by the institutional settlement (by law)
of the few disputes that were likely to arise, and more specifically in
the particular distribution of functions that was set out in the American Constitution; that distribution was itself designed to ensure both
the maximization of valid human wants and a "fair" (although not
necessarily equal) distribution of tangible and intangible goods.

The effect was to postulate not particular substantive rights but
rather a shared social value in the *process* by which rights were defined
—a shared value in distinct institutional competencies. That implied, in
turn, a differentiation of the processes by which judges, in contrast to
legislators and administrators, reached decisions. According to Hart
and Sacks, judges had the competence to settle questions that lent
themselves to a process of "reasoned elaboration"—that could, in other
words, be justified by reference to general, articulated standards which
could be applied in all like cases: that process was to be contrasted
with the "unbuttoned discretion" enjoyed by legislators. Presumably,
it was the judiciary who decided which questions lent themselves to
this process of reasoned elaboration.

The shift from an emphasis on substance to an emphasis on process seemed for a time to satisfy the realist critique of substantive
rights; but of course it still rested on the distinction between reasoned
elaboration and discretion, which in turn rested on the availability of
principled, objective, substantive categories to which judges could
make reference. More generally, it also rested on the complacent, simplistic assumption that American society consisted of happy, private
actors maximizing their valid human wants while sharing their profound belief in institutional competencies. That may have reflected the
mind-set of many in the 1950s, but by the end of the 1960s it seemed
oddly out of touch with reality.

Another response to the collapse of clear conceptual categories has
been less self-consciously articulated than Hart and Sacks', but pervades modern case law. The prevailing pattern is to accept as inevitable

and "in the nature of things" the absence of vacuum-bounded categories. Instead, the boundaries between categories are portrayed as fluid, or "live," meaning that many particular examples will occupy a mushy middle position, which includes attributes of two nonetheless distinct categories. Thus, the collapse of spheres is not total, and the goal is to deal comfortably with a world made up largely of middle positions.[22]

This livening up of boundaries cuts across all doctrinal lines. For example, the traditional rule of jurisdiction was that a state court could exercise jurisdiction only over a defendant who was within the borders of the state; the line was as clear as the state's boundary marker. That straightforward "in or out" conception has now given way to a conception that recognizes "presence" as often a middle ground, sort-of-in sort-of-out notion, to be determined by standards of "fair play and substantial justice" and by a "balance" of the interests of the relevant parties and forums.[23] Similarly, whereas classical doctrine had drawn a clear line, at the moment of formation, between contract and no contract, modern reference to reliance breaks down that clarity by recognizing a sort-of contract prior to formation, based on one party's reasonable reliance on the other's precontract negotiating promises.[24] The same notion also breaks down the once sharp contract/tort distinction (i.e., obligations agreed to by the parties as distinct from obligations imposed by law), since reliance is the basis of neither a recognized tort nor a fully contractual cause of action.

At this point in time it would be hard to state any pair of categories still legally conceived as vacuum-bounded. Even life/death and male/female have been treated by courts as live-bounded, as in the Karen Quinlan case[25] and cases involving parties who have undergone sex transformations.[26] Similarly, in the landmark abortion case, Roe v. Wade,[27] the Supreme Court recognized a woman's abortion decision as protected by the right to privacy during the first trimester, as legitimately subject to public power during the last trimester, and during the middle trimester as partly private but also subject to some limited public control. Notably, however, courts have still refused to recognize a live boundary between capital and labor.[28]

Closely paralleling the emergence of live rather than vacuum boundaries has been the breakdown of the deep sense of analogy and uniformity that once characterized classical thought. Private-law categories such as property or contract were then thought to have fixed meanings that did not vary with differences in context; that uniformity was conceived to be crucial to the ideal of rationality and formal equality. Now, however, it is common to concede that rights may vary depending upon status and relationship. As Justice Robert Jackson explained in United States v. Willow River Power Company,[29] simply because a particular water-flow level might constitute property as between two private parties, that did not necessarily mean that the same flow constituted property as between a private party and the federal government.

Despite the breakdown of vacuum boundaries and uniform, generally applicable categories, modern American legal thought continues to be premised on the distinction between private law and public law. Private law is still assumed to be *about* private actors with private rights, making private choices, even though sophisticated judges tend quite frankly to refer to public policy when justifying private-law decision making. Similarly, the major post-realist reconstructors of private-law theory, like Edward Levi and Karl Llewellyn, acknowledged the necessary role of policy choice in legal decision making but described judicial choices as still specifically "legal" because judges worked within a long-established judicial tradition, which exerted a steadying (if not precisely "logical") constraint. By training, judges acquire a "craft-consciousness," which leads them to respond to new situations through a "reworking of the heritage" rather than through unguided impulse. The result is neither unbridled choice nor inflexible formalism but "continuity with growth" and "vision with tradition."[30] The new private-law heroes were therefore not the rigorous Willistonians, who refused to acknowledge the role of social change in shaping law, but (once again) Mansfield in England, America's own preclassical nineteenth-century judges, and, in more recent times, Benjamin Cardozo.

As an example of enlightened decision making, Levi[31] described with admiration Cardozo's opinion in *McPherson* v. *Buick Motors Company*.[32] There, Cardozo had modified the classical privity of contract rule (according to which a manufacturer's liability for personal injuries due to a defective product extended only to those with whom he had directly entered a contract) in order to hold Buick liable for a "foreseeable" injury to a party not in privity. As justification, Cardozo had specifically referred to changes in automobile retailing practices, because of which only retailer middlemen, and rarely consumers, directly contracted with manufacturers. Under the privity rule, consumers would almost always be left unprotected when defective cars caused injuries, an "anomalous" result, Cardozo's said, which he did not want to reach.

Cardozo also justified his decision by referring to the category of "abnormally dangerous" products, which had evolved as an exception to the privity rule and to the standard of "foreseeability" upon which Cardozo claimed the exception was based. Using the notion of foreseeability, Cardozo masterfully suggested that his decision was a reasoned application of past doctrine, not simply a result-oriented exercise of judicial policy choice. Nevertheless, the skilled craft of the opinion obscured rather than solved the key realist point: for every rule there is bound to be a counterrule, *because* the choice to be made is always between the contradictory claims of freedom and security. In their extreme form here, that would mean freedom as complete absence of manufacturer liability versus consumer security as manufacturer liability for all injuries caused by use of his product. Within legal logic there is no reason for drawing the line at any particular point, and recasting the problem as one of a supposedly neutral public policy does not resolve the dilemma. Trite, conventional policy arguments can always be made for *either* freedom or security.

As with policy, modern private-law thinking has both conceded and evaded the inevitability of value choice in legal decision making. The great post-realist treatise writers, Corbin on contracts and Prosser on torts, appeal at least as often to presumably neutral, shared standards of substantive "justice" and "reasonableness" as they do to fixed rules; but the vocabulary of modern treatises is still the vocabulary of classical doctrine—questions of justice emerge *within* discussions of offer and acceptance, the elements of a cause of action in negligence, etc. The message is that we can advance beyond the silly stage of formalism while still retaining the basic structure and premises of classical thought. Both Prosser and Corbin, however, leave unresolved the old conflict between formal realizability and general standards of substantive justice; and neither explains where, within liberalism's supposed subjectivity of values, one is to find a source for objective standards of justice.

The most sophisticated version of private-law reconstruction can be found in the Sales Article of the Uniform Commercial Code—essentially Llewellyn's revamping of traditional contract law. Like Corbin and Prosser, Llewellyn relied on standard doctrine for most of his vocabulary, but he also sought to replace a formalistic application of rules with standards of good faith and reasonableness. Those standards were to be known not as the abstract universals of natural law but through a judicial understanding of actual intent and reasonable expectations within each specific fact situation and within the customs and usages of specific trades. This was Llewellyn's famous "situation-sense," which, he insisted, was distinctly "legal" because it drew on the legal tradition of craft, reason, and principle, and at the same time saw (universal) reason as embodied *within* the particularity of specific commercial practice.

Llewellyn's "singing reason," as he perhaps unfortunately termed it,[33] has already raised methodological problems. The facts of particular customs or situations tend to elude objective judicial determination; some courts have simply refused to hear all of the conflicting testimony with which they are confronted. The choice as to relevency, of course, remains a *choice*; and even if objectively "known," the precise role of custom and usage in relation to traditional rules is still problematic. It is commonly said, for example, that custom and usage can be used to interpret contracts but not to create them; yet it is unclear why the line should be drawn at that point, or whether the distinction is even an intelligible one. Equally problematic is the precise relation between reason and custom[34]—a problem as old as the coexistence of a natural-law and a (supposedly customary) common-law tradition. Without standards of reasonableness *outside* existing practice, singing reason is simply ratification of the status quo—the "is" automatically becomes the "ought." Yet absent a fully developed natural-law theory, the source of any such normative standard remains unavailable. Moreover, taking custom and usage as a source of legal standards does not really avoid the problem of self-referencing, which was inevitable in rights theory, since social practice and reasonable expectations are, like "free" bargains, in large measure a *function* of the legal order. The wholly spontaneous custom and usage is rare, if it exists at all; thus, by reflecting "custom," the law in large measure reflects only itself, and the nagging problem of legitimacy reemerges.

The hodge-podge of policy, situation-sense, and leftover doctrine that now makes up the indeterminate body of private law provides scant basis for a rationalization of constitutional rights; and the search for some coherent foundation for rights analysis, particularly for judicial review, has been the preoccupation of modern constitutional law theorists. That search has led to two distinct branches in constitutional law thought. The first is based on a model of deference to legislative bodies, while the second is based on various attempts to formulate affirmative, substantive bases for constitutional rights.

During the New Deal, the Supreme Court virtually abandoned to the legislature the field of economic regulation, once subject to invalidation under the categories of property and free contract. Deference in that area, however, left unresolved the fate of other supposed constitutional rights. For some theorists, deference simply became the preferred model for all cases. Alexander Bickel,[35] for example, created a new category, somewhere between general principle and mere expediency, which he called prudence. A prudent Supreme Court would avoid judicial review by using procedural grounds (e.g., problems of ripeness or standing) to justify a refusal to reach the merits. The Court could thereby avoid both the criticism that it stood in the way of the democratic majority (the basic argument against judicial review) and the criticism that it legitimated, by finding constitutional, action that seemed to violate fundamental rights. One of Bickel's examples was the notorious *Korematsu* case,[36] where the Supreme Court upheld the detention of all Japanese Americans living on the West Coast in holding camps during World War II. Bickel argued that the Court should have dodged the question rather than label the detention and its underlying statute constitutional. The exercise of such prudence would have gained the trust of the country and placed the Court in the position of "teacher" in the public discussion of values. Then, when a time of *real* crisis to the Constitution arose, the court would have been in a position to act on principle, with the backing of the people.

Bickel's "passive virtues" inevitably represent something of a retreat from the juristic model of rights and sovereignty. The person in a concentration camp is presumably not comforted with the knowledge that her case has been prudently decided on procedural rather than constitutional grounds; and a Court unprepared to make hard decisions in such a case is in a weak position to then hold out legal rights as the ultimate protection against totalitarianism. Bickel maintained that the prudent Court could still act when the dictator's troops came marching down Massachussetts Avenue, but his claim rang a bit hollow.

Moreover, the Bickel approach of deference to the legislative process, while on the surface the most obvious answer to the claim that judicial review is undemocratic, evades questions about the nature of our particular form of representation. The American legislative model is not, under our constitutional structure, itself a model of pure, participatory consensualism; its particular form is not more unquestionably democratic or legitimate than is judicial review. *Both* are part of a total constitutional structure, as interpreted by past legal decision making. In fact, an attack on any single part of that structure inevitably calls into question the legitimacy of the whole structure. Also, Hale's critique of free choice in the market can be applied to the political process (the marketplace of ideas) as well. So-called free political choice takes place within a system of legally protected economic power, which is a function of past legal decision making and which profoundly affects outcomes in the political decision-making process. The Court, by suddenly avoiding judicial review, cannot escape responsibility for the social decisions that are made.

Alternatively, other theorists have sought a more affirmative defense of constitutional rights. Herbert Wechsler,[37] for example, advocated a return to "general" and "neutral" principles as the only sound basis for judicial review. He complained, for example, that in the *Brown* case[38] the Court rested its decision on sociological fact rather than on constitutional principle. Yet he also acknowledged that the only available, general principle that seemed to cover the case was "freedom of association," which quickly confronts an equally neutral and general but contradictory principle barring forced association. As he conceded, at the level of pure, ahistorical· generality there was no

logical resolution; yet the necessary move to greater particularity raises
the dilemma of necessarily illogical choice somewhere *between* abstract, transcendental generality and ad hoc, "unprincipled" case-by-
case decision making. The choice is bound to appear arbitrary.

The most recent attempts to derive a substantive basis for fundamental constitutional rights have vascillated between a more or less
veiled reliance on natural-law theory (David Richards, Kenneth Karst,
Lawrence Tribe), and recourse to a model, only somewhat more
sophisticated than Hart and Sacks', of shared American values (Harry
Wellington, Michael Perry).[39] John Ely,[40] criticizing both approaches, has attempted to take a stand somewhere between the assertion of affirmative substantive rights and complete deference. He has
postulated instead a supposedly value-neutral "participation-oriented,
representation-reinforcing" standard for judicial review. Drawing on
Justice Harlan Fiske Stone's suggestion,[41] Ely argues that the judiciary
should actively scrutinize only that legislation (1) "which restricts
those political processes which can ordinarily be expected to bring
about repeal of undesirable legislation," or (2) which is based on
"prejudice against discrete and insular minorities." Yet this approach
too rests on a conception of substantive values—the value of participation within this particular form of representative structure and the
"badness" of prejudice as opposed to all those other values which the
legislature would be left free to implement.[42] As in the Hart and Sacks
materials, the nagging problem of asserting objective, substantive values within a system premised on a pluralistic subjectivity of values
inevitably reemerges.

Currently, perhaps the most influential attempt to provide a general, legitimating rationale for American legal decision making has
been through a blending of legal theory and free-market economic
theory. Scholars within the law and economics movement have happily
embraced the realist view that legal language, which purports to be
about preexisting rights, simply obscures what courts do. Their claim
is that, in fact, American judges have succeeded, with surprising consistency, in mimicking those solutions that would be reached through
unimpeded market exchange, solutions that can therefore be described
as most efficient (least costly). Furthermore, shifting from the de-
scriptive to a normative claim, they argue that efficiency provides a
neutral, objective standard for judicial decision making, unlike obviously value-laden rights analysis.[43]

The most frequently cited "rule" that emerges from the law and
economics literature—the Coase theorem[44]—is that courts should simply assign any "right" in question to the party who would find it
worthwhile to purchase that right if it were assigned to the other party

and if transaction costs were zero. By definition, any other result would be costly in that it would either give the right to the party for whom it had less value—a failure of exchange equilibrium—or else lend to unnecessary exchange transaction costs in order to achieve equilibrium. While law and economic theorists concede that in some cases the application of the Coase theorem might lead to unwanted distributional consequences, those should be ignored by judges. Distribution is essentially a political question that should be left to legislation, and judges should confine themselves to applying the objective, neutral exchange calculus.

Most of those who are used to assuming that law is really "about" rights find the instrumental tone of the law and economics literature startling;[45] indeed, the assertion that the common law has traditionally served to mimic the market under the guise of protecting rights sounds starkly Marxist. On another level, however, most current law and economics theory represents neoconceptualism strikingly similar to the classical conceptualism successfully undermined by the realists. The law and economics model is the model of free, value-enhancing exchange, yet as Hale pointed out with reference to free contract theory, market exchanges are in fact a function of the legal order; the terms of so-called free bargains (and, taken collectively, the supposedly objective market price) are determined by the legally protected right to withhold what is owned. Exchange "value" (and "costs") is a function of that right, so that the rationale of exchange is ultimately as circular and self-referencing as the rationale for legal rights. The legitimacy of every exchange calculus depends upon the legitimacy of prior legal decisions: it neither establishes that legitimacy nor evades the problem of legitimacy by a purported ahistorical objectivity. Similarly, judges cannot escape responsibility for the distributional consequences of legal decisions. The exchange calculus cannot be divorced from the question of distribution, since exchange is a function of the existing distribution of legal entitlement, and every new legal decision (including those that rigorously apply the law and economics approach) will inevitably affect subsequent distribution and, in turn, affect subsequent exchanges, costs, values, etc. Like the older spheres of private and public, questions of market exchange and of distribution simply collapse into each other.[46]

Nevertheless, despite all of their fairly obvious intellectual incoherences, the various efforts to reconstruct American legal thought continue daily, filling numberless volumes of case reports and law reviews. Presumably, they still play the role Rousseau identified: "The strong is never strong enough to be always the strongest, unless he transforms strength into right, and obedience into duty."[47]

NOTES

1. *See*, especially, Robert Gordon, "Historicism in Legal Scholarship," 90 *Yale Law Journal* 1017 (1981), and Comment, "The Historical Contingency of the Role of History," 90 *Yale Law Journal* 1057 (1981).

2. By far, the best and most thorough account of these changes is to be found in Duncan Kennedy, "The Rise and Fall of Classical Legal Thought" (Unpublished manuscript, 1975). This essay is in part based upon that manuscript.

3. This assertion and some of the others that follow are based upon a reading of collected but unpublished nineteenth-century addresses, speeches, and other miscellaneous examples of legal discourse. The collection is to be found, uncatalogued under a single title, in the Cornell Law School Library. Hooker's quotation is still inscribed, in large letters, on the wall of the Harvard Law School Library.

4. Joseph Story, Discourse upon the Inaguration of the Author as Dane Professor of Law, 1829 (Cornell Law School Collection).

5. For the early background to that tradition, *see*, *e.g.*, Norman Cohn, *The Pursuit of the Millennium* (New York: Harper Brothers, 1961).

6. *See*, *e.g.*, Ogden v. Saunders, 25 U.S. (12 Wheat.) 213 (1827).

7. *See* Morton Horwitz, *The Transformation of American Law, 1780–1860* (Cambridge, Mass.: Harvard University Press, 1977), p. 257.

8. The claim was as old as the confrontation between Sir Edward Coke and King James I, in which Coke explained that whereas others besides judges (including, especially, the king) had excellent natural reason, they did not have the "artificial reason" of the law, which "is an art which requires long study and experience, before that a man can attain to the cognizance of it." 12 Coke's Reports 63, 65, 77 English Reports 1342, 1343 (King's Bench, 1608).

9. Again, nineteenth-century jurists were able to draw on a long English tradition for such notions. *See* Matthew Hale, "Considerations Touching the Amendment and Alteration of Laws," *A Collection of Tracts Relative to the Law of England*, ed. Francis Hargrave (Dublin: W. Colles, 1787), 1:249.

10. Theophilus Parsons, *Law of Contracts* (Boston: Little Brown, 1855).

11. *See* Al Katz, "Studies in Boundary Theory" (Unpublished manuscript, 1980).

12. Samuel Williston, *The Law of Contracts*, 1st ed. (New York: Baker, Voorhis, 1920).

13. Coppage v. Kansas, 236 U.S. 1 (1915).

14. Adair v. United States, 208 U.S. 161 (1908).

15. As an early example of that approach, *see* Roscoe Pound, "Mechanical Jurisprudence," 8 *Columbia Law Review* 605 (1908).

16. For one of the best single examples of the realist assault upon the objectivity of rights theory and legal analysis in general, *see* Felix Cohen, "Transcendental Nonsense and the Functional Approach," 35 *Columbia Law Review* 809 (1935).

17. Morris Cohen, "Property and Sovereignty," 13 *Cornell Law Quarterly* 8 (1927).

18. Robert Hale, "Bargaining, Duress and Economic Liberty," 43 *Columbia Law Review* 603 (1943); Robert Hale, "Coercion and Distribution in a Supposedly Non-Coercive State," 38 *Political Science Quarterly* 470 (1923).

19. For a discussion of this dilemma, and of American realism in general, *see* Edward Purcell, *The Crisis of Democratic Theory: Scientific Naturalism and the Problem of Value* (Lexington: University of Kentucky Press, 1973).

20. Howard Laswell and Myres McDougal, "Legal Education and Public Policy: Professional Training in the Public Interest," 52 *Yale Law Journal* 203 (1943).

21. Henry Hart and Albert Sacks, *The Legal Process: Basic Problems in the Making and Application of Law* (tent. ed. 1958).

22. *See* Katz, *supra* note 11.
23. International Shoe Co. v. State of Washington, 326 U.S. 310 (1945), the landmark modern case on personal jurisdiction.
24. Hoffman v. Red Owl Stores, Inc., 26 Wis. 2d 683 (1965).
25. *In re* Quinlan, 70 N.J. 10 (1976).
26. *See, e.g.*, Chicago v. Wilson, 75 Ill. 2d 525 (1978).
27. Roe v. Wade, 410 U.S. 113 (1973).
28. *See* Lee Smith, "The Opinions of Justice Lewis Powell: A Study of Balancing" (Unpublished manuscript, 1979).
29. United States v. Willow River Power Co., 324 U.S. 499 (1945).
30. Karl Llewellyn, *The Common Law Tradition, Deciding Appeals* (Boston: Little, Brown, 1960).
31. Edward Levi, *An Introduction to Legal Reasoning* (Chicago: University of Chicago Press, 1948).
32. McPherson v. Buick Motors Co. 217 N.Y. 382 (1916).
33. Llewellyn, *supra* note 30.
34. *See, e.g.*, Franklin Schultz, "The Firm Offer Puzzle: A Study of Business Practice in the Construction Industry," 19 *Chicago Law Review* 237 (1952).
35. Alexander Bickel, "The Passive Virtues," 75 *Harvard Law Review* 40 (1961).
36. Korematsu v. United States, 323 U.S. 214 (1944).
37. Herbert Wechsler, "Toward Neutral Principles of Constitutional Law," 73 *Harvard Law Review* 1 (1959).
38. Brown v. Board of Education, 347 U.S. 483 (1954).
39. *See* Paul Brest, "The Fundamental Rights Controversy: The Essential Contradictions of Normative Constitutional Scholarship," 90 *Yale Law Journal* 1063, 1067–80 (1981).
40. John Ely, *Democracy and Distrust: A Theory of Judicial Review* (Cambridge, Mass.: Harvard University Press, 1980).
41. United States v. Carolene Products Company, 304 U.S. 144, 152, n. 4 (1938).
42. *See* Paul Brest, "The Substance of Process," 42 *Ohio State Law Journal* 131 (1981).
43. Richard Posner, *Economic Analysis of Law*, 2d ed. (Boston: Little, Brown, 1977).
44. Ronald Coase, "The Problem of Social Cost," 3 *Journal of Law and Economics* 1 (1960).
45. *See, e.g.*, Frank Michelman, "Norms and Normativity in the Economic Theory of Law," 62 *Minnesota Law Review* 1015 (1978).
46. For radical critiques of the law and economics literature, *see* Mark Kelman, "Consumption Theory, Production Theory, and Ideology in the Coase Theorem," 52 *Southern California Law Review* 669 (1979); Duncan Kennedy, "Cost-Benefit Analysis of Entitlement Problems: A Critique," 33 *Stanford Law Review* 387 (1981). For a liberal critique that stresses, with explicit normative overtones, alternative efficiency arguments (cost spreading, cost avoiding) *see* Guido Calabresi, *The Costs of Accidents* (New Haven, Conn.: Yale University Press, 1970).
47. As described by Duncan Kennedy, "The Structure of Blackstore's *Commentaries*," 28 *Buffalo Law Review* 209 (1979).

3

LEGAL EDUCATION AS TRAINING FOR HIERARCHY

Duncan Kennedy

Law schools are intensely political places despite the fact that the modern law school seems intellectually unpretentious, barren of theoretical ambition or practical vision of what social life might be. The trade-school mentality, the endless attention to trees at the expense of forests, the alternating grimness and chumminess of focus on the limited task at hand, all these are only a part of what is going on. The other part is ideological training for willing service in the hierarchies of the corporate welfare state.

To say that law school is ideological is to say that what teachers teach along with basic skills is wrong, is nonsense about what law is and how it works; that the message about the nature of legal competence, and its distribution among students, is wrong, is nonsense; that the ideas about the possibilities of life as a lawyer that students pick up from legal education are wrong, are nonsense. But all this is nonsense with a tilt; it is biased and motivated rather than random error. What it says is that it is natural, efficient, and fair for law firms, the bar as a whole, and the society the bar services to be organized in their actual patterns of hierarchy and domination.

Because students believe what they are told, explicitly and implicitly, about the world they are entering, they behave in ways that fulfill the prophecies the system makes about them and about that world. This is the link-back that completes the system: students do more than accept the way things are, and ideology does more than damp opposition. Students act affirmatively within the channels cut for them, cutting them deeper, giving the whole a patina of consent, and weaving complicity into everyone's life story.

In this chapter, I take up in turn the initial first-year experience, the ideological content of the law school curriculum, and the noncurricular practices of law schools that train students to accept and participate in the hierarchical structure of life in the law.

THE FIRST-YEAR EXPERIENCE

A surprisingly large number of law students go to law school with the notion that being a lawyer means something more, something more socially constructive than just doing a highly respectable job. There is the idea of playing the role an earlier generation associated with Brandeis: the role of service through law, carried out with superb technical competence and also with a deep belief that in its essence law is a progressive force, however much it may be distorted by the actual arrangements of capitalism. There is a contrasting, more radical notion that law is a tool of established interests, that it is in essence superstructural, but that it is a tool that a coldly effective professional can sometimes turn against the dominators. Whereas in the first notion the student aspires to help the oppressed and transform society by bringing out the latent content of a valid ideal, in the second the student sees herself as part technician, part judo expert, able to turn the tables exactly because she never lets herself be mystified by the rhetoric that is so important to other students.

Then there are the conflicting motives, which are equally real for both types. People think of law school as extremely competitive, as a place where a tough, hard-working, smart style is cultivated and rewarded. Students enter law school with a sense that they will develop that side of themselves. Even if they disapprove, on principle, of that side of themselves, they have had other experiences in which it turned out that they wanted and liked aspects of themselves that on principle they disapproved of. How is one to know that one is not "really" looking to develop oneself in this way as much as one is motivated by the vocation of social transformation?

There is also the issue of social mobility. Almost everyone whose parents were not members of the professional/technical intelligentsia seems to feel that going to law school is an advance in terms of the family history. This is true even for children of high-level business managers, so long as their parents' positions were due to hard work and struggle rather than to birth into the upper echelons. It is rare for parents to actively *disapprove* of their children going to law school, whatever their origins. So taking this particular step has a social meaning, however much the student may reject it, and that social meaning is success. The success is bittersweet if one feels one should have gotten into a better school, but both the bitter and the sweet suggest that one's motives are impure.

The initial classroom experience sustains rather than dissipates ambivalence. The teachers are overwhelmingly white, male, and deadeningly straight and middle class in manner. The classroom is hierarchical with a vengeance, the teacher receiving a degree of deference and arousing fears that remind one of high school rather than college. The sense of autonomy one has in a lecture, with the rule that you must let teacher drone on without interruption balanced by the rule that teacher can't *do* anything to you, is gone. In its place is a demand for a pseudo-participation in which one struggles desperately, in front of a large audience, to read a mind determined to elude you. It is almost never anything as bad as *The Paper Chase* or *One-L*, but it is still humiliating to be frightened and unsure of oneself, especially when what renders one unsure is a classroom arrangement that suggests at once the patriarchal family and a Kafka-like riddle-state. The law school classroom at the beginning of the first year is culturally reactionary.

But it is also engaging. You are learning a new language, and it *is* possible to learn it. Pseudo-participation makes one intensely aware of how everyone else is doing, providing endless bases for comparison. Information is coming in on all sides, and things that you knew were out there but you didn't understand are becoming intelligible. The teacher offers subtle encouragements as well as not-so-subtle reasons for alarm. Performance is on one's mind, adrenaline flows, success has a nightly and daily meaning in terms of the material assigned. After all, this is the next segment: one is moving from the vaguely sentimental world of college, or the frustrating world of office work or housework, into something that promises a dose of "reality," even if it's cold and scary reality.

It quickly emerges that neither the students nor the faculty are as homogeneous as they at first appeared. Some teachers are more authoritarian than others; some students other than oneself reacted with horror to the infantilization of the first days or weeks. There even seems to be a connection between classroom manner and substantive views, with the "softer" teachers also seeming to be more "liberal," perhaps more sympathetic to plaintiffs in the torts course, more willing to hear what are called policy arguments, as well as less intimidating in class discussion. But there is a disturbing aspect to this process of differentiation: in most law schools, it turns out that the tougher, less policy-oriented teachers are the more popular. The softies seem to get less matter across, they let things wander, and one begins to worry that their niceness is at the expense of a metaphysical quality called rigor, thought to be essential to success on bar exams and in the grownup world of practice. Ambivalence reasserts itself. As between the conservatives and the mushy centrists, enemies who scare you but subtly reassure you may seem more attractive than allies no better anchored than yourself.

There is an intellectual experience that somewhat corresponds to the emotional one: the gradual revelation that there is no purchase for left or even for committed liberal thinking on any part of the smooth surface of legal education. The issue in the classroom is not left against right, but pedagogical conservatism against moderate, disintegrated liberalism. No teacher is likely to present a model of either left pedagogy or vital left theoretical enterprise, though some *are* likely to be vaguely sympathetic to progressive causes, and some may even be moonlighting as left lawyers. Students are struggling for cognitive mastery and against the sneaking depression of the pre-professional. The actual intellectual content of the law seems to consist of learning rules—what they are and why they have to be the way they are— while rooting for the occasional judge who seems willing to make them marginally more humane. The basic experience is of double surrender: to a passivizing classroom experience and to a passive attitude toward the content of the legal system.

The first step toward this sense of the irrelevance of liberal or left thinking is the opposition in the first-year curriculum between the technical, boring, difficult, obscure legal case and the occasional case with outrageous facts and a piggish judicial opinion endorsing or tolerating the outrage. The first kind of case—call it a cold case—is a challenge to interest, understanding, even to wakefulness. It can be on any subject, so long as it is of no political or moral or emotional significance. Just to understand what happened and what's being said about it, you have to learn a lot of new terms, a little potted legal history, and lots of rules, none of which is carefully explained by the casebook or the teacher. It is difficult to figure out why the case is there in the first place, difficult to figure out whether you have grasped it, and difficult to anticipate what the teacher will ask and what one should respond.

The other kind of case—call it a hot case—usually involves a sympathetic plaintiff—say, an Appalachian farm family—and an unsympathetic defendant—say, a coal company. On first reading, it appears that the coal company has screwed the farm family by renting their land for strip mining, with a promise to restore it to its original condition once the coal has been extracted, and then reneging on the promise. And the case should include a judicial opinion that does something like award a meaningless couple of hundred dollars to the farm family rather than making the coal company perform the restoration work. The point of the class discussion will be that your initial reaction of outrage is naïve, nonlegal, irrelevant to what you're supposed to be learning, and maybe substantively wrong into the bargain. There are "good reasons" for the awful result, when you take a legal and logical "large" view, as opposed to the knee-jerk passionate view; and if you can't muster those reasons, maybe you aren't cut out to be a lawyer.

Most students can't fight this combination of a cold case and a hot case. The cold case is boring, but you have to do it if you want to become a lawyer. The hot case cries out for response, seems to say that if you can't respond you've already sold out; but the system tells you to put away childish things, and your reaction to the hot case is one of them. Without any intellectual resources, in the way of knowledge of the legal system and of the character of legal reasoning, it will appear that emoting will only isolate and incapacitate you. The choice is to develop some calluses and hit the books, or admit failure almost before you've begun.

THE IDEOLOGICAL CONTENT OF LEGAL EDUCATION

One can distinguish in a rough way between two aspects of legal education as a reproducer of hierarchy. A lot of what happens is the inculcation through a formal curriculum and the classroom experience of a set of political attitudes toward the economy and society in general, toward law, and toward the possibilities of life in the profession. These have a general ideological significance, and they have an impact on the lives even of law students who never practice law. Then there is a complicated set of institutional practices that orient students to willing participation in the specialized hierarchical roles of lawyers. Students begin to absorb the more general ideological message before they have much in the way of a conception of life after law school, so I will describe this formal aspect of the educational process before describing the ways in which the institutional practice of law schools bear on those realities.

Law students sometimes speak as though they learned *nothing* in school. In fact, they learn skills to do a list of simple but important things. They learn to retain large numbers of rules organized into categorical systems (requisites for a contract, rules about breach, etc.). They learn "issue spotting," which means identifying the ways in which the rules are ambiguous, in conflict, or have a gap when applied to particular fact situations. They learn elementary case analysis, meaning the art of generating broad holdings for cases so they will apply beyond their intuitive scope, and narrow holdings for cases so that they won't apply where it at first seemed they would. And they learn a list of balanced, formulaic, pro/con policy arguments that lawyers use in arguing that a given rule should apply to a situation despite a gap, conflict, or ambiguity, or that a given case should be extended or narrowed. These are arguments like "the need for certainty" and "the need for flexibility," "the need to promote competition" and the "need to encourage production by letting producers keep the rewards of their labor."

One should neither exalt these skills nor denigrate them. By comparison with the first-year students' tendency to flip-flop between formalism and mere equitable intuition, they represent a real intellectual advance. Lawyers actually do use them in practice; and when properly, consciously mastered, they have "critical" bite. They are a help in thinking about politics, public policy, ethical discourse in general, because they show the indeterminacy and manipulability of ideas and institutions that are central to liberalism.

On the other hand, law schools teach these rather rudimentary, essentially instrumental skills in a way that almost completely mystifies them for almost all law students. The mystification has three parts. First, the schools teach skills through class discussions of cases in which it is asserted that law emerges from a rigorous analytical procedure called legal reasoning, which is unintelligible to the layperson but somehow both explains and validates the great majority of the rules in force in our system. At the same time, the class context and the materials present every legal issue as distinct from every other—as a tub on its own bottom, so to speak—with no hope or even any reason to hope that from law study one might derive an integrating vision of what law is, how it works, or how it might be changed (other than in any incremental, case-by-case, reformist way).

Second, the teaching of skills in the mystified context of legal reasoning about utterly unconnected legal problems means that skills are taught badly, unselfconsciously, to be absorbed by osmosis as one picks up the knack of "thinking like a lawyer." Bad or only randomly good teaching generates and then accentuates real differences and imagined differences in student capabilities. But it does so in such a way that students don't know when they are learning and when they aren't, and have no way of improving or even understanding their own learning processes. They experience skills training as the gradual emergence of differences among themselves, as a process of ranking that reflects something that is just "there" inside them.

Third, the schools teach skills in isolation from actual lawyering experience. "Legal reasoning" is sharply distinguished from law practice, and one learns nothing about practice. This procedure disables students from any future role but that of apprentice in a law firm organized in the same manner as a law school, with older lawyers controlling the content and pace of depoliticized craft training in a setting of intense competition and no feedback.

The Formal Curriculum: Legal Rules and Legal Reasoning

The intellectual core of the ideology is the distinction between law and policy. Teachers convince students that legal reasoning exists, and is different from policy analysis, by bullying them into accepting as valid in particular cases arguments about legal correctness that are circular, question-begging, incoherent, or so vague as to be meaningless. Sometimes these are just arguments from authority, with the validity of the authoritative premise put outside discussion by professorial fiat. Sometimes they are policy arguments (e.g., security of transaction, business certainty) that are treated in a particular situation as though they were rules that everyone accepts but that will be ignored in the next case when they would suggest that the decision was wrong. Sometimes they are exercises in formal logic that wouldn't stand up for a minute in a discussion between equals (e.g., the small print in a form contract represents the "will of the parties").

Within a given subfield, the teacher is likely to treat cases in three different ways. There are the cases that present and justify the basic rules and basic ideas of the field. These are treated as cursory exercises in legal logic. Then there are cases that are anomalous—"outdated" or "wrongly decided" because they don't follow the supposed inner logic of the area. There won't be many of these, but they are important because their treatment persuades students that the technique of legal reasoning is at least minimally independent of the results reached by particular judges and is therefore capable of criticizing as well as legitimating. Finally, there will be an equally small number of peripheral or "cutting-edge" cases the teacher sees as raising policy issues about growth or change in the law. Whereas in discussing the first two kinds of cases the teacher behaves in an authoritarian way supposedly based on his objective knowledge of the technique of legal reasoning, here everything is different. Because we are dealing with "value judgments" that have "political" overtones, the discussion will be much more freewheeling. Rather than every student comment being right or wrong, all student comments get pluralist acceptance, and the teacher will reveal himself to be either a liberal or a conservative rather than merely a legal technician.

The curriculum as a whole has a rather similar structure. It is not really a random assortment of tubs on their own bottoms, a forest of tubs. First, there are contracts, torts, property, criminal law, and civil procedure. The rules in these courses are the ground rules of late-nineteenth-century laissez-faire capitalism. Teachers teach them as though they had an inner logic, as an exercise in legal reasoning, with policy (e.g., commercial certainty in the contracts course) playing a relatively minor role. Then there are second- and third-year courses that expound the moderate reformist program of the New Deal and the administrative structure of the modern regulatory state (with passing reference to the racial egalitarianism of the Warren Court). These courses are more policy oriented than first-year courses, and also much more ad hoc. Teachers teach students that limited interference with the market makes sense and is as authoritatively grounded in statutes as the ground rules of laissez-faire are grounded in natural law. But each problem is discrete, enormously complicated, and understood in a way that guarantees the practical impotence of the reform program. Finally, there are peripheral subjects, like legal philosophy or legal history, legal process, clinical legal education. These are presented as not truly relevant to the "hard" objective, serious, rigorous analytic core of law; they are a kind of playground or finishing school for learning the social art of self-presentation as a lawyer.

This whole body of implicit messages is nonsense. Teachers teach nonsense when they persuade students that legal reasoning is distinct, *as a method for reaching correct results*, from ethical and political discourse in general (*i.e.*, from policy analysis). It is true that there is a distinctive lawyers' body of knowledge of the rules in force. It is true that there are distinctive lawyers' argumentative techniques for spotting gaps, conflicts, and ambiguities in the rules, for arguing broad and narrow holdings of cases, and for generating pro and con policy arguments. But these are *only* argumentative techniques. There is never a "correct legal solution" that is other than the correct ethical and political solution to that legal problem. Put another way, everything taught, except the formal rules themselves and the argumentative techniques for manipulating them, is policy and nothing more. It follows that the classroom distinction between the unproblematic, legal case and the policy-oriented case is a mere artifact: each could as well be taught in the opposite way. And the curricular distinction between the "nature" of contract law as highly legal and technical by contrast, say, with environmental law is equally a mystification.

These errors have a bias in favor of the center liberal program of limited reform of the market economy and pro forma gestures toward racial and sexual equality. The bias arises because law school teaching makes the choice of hierarchy and domination, which is implicit in the adoption of the rules of property, contract, and tort, look as though it flows from and is required by legal reasoning rather than being a matter of politics and economics. The bias is reinforced when the center liberal reformist program of regulation is presented as equally authoritative but somehow more policy oriented, and therefore less fundamental. The message is that the system is basically OK, since we have patched up the few areas open to abuse, and that it has a limited but important place for value-oriented debate about further change and improvement. If there is to be more fundamental questioning, it is relegated to the periphery of history or philosophy. The real world is kept at bay by treating clinical legal education, which might bring in a lot of information threatening to the cozy liberal consensus, as free legal drudge work for the local bar or as mere skills training.

It would be an extraordinary first-year student who could, on his own, develop a theoretically critical attitude toward this system. Entering students just don't know enough to figure out where the teacher is fudging, misrepresenting, or otherwise distorting legal thinking and legal reality. To make matters worse, the two most common kinds of left thinking the student is likely to bring with her are likely to hinder rather than assist in the struggle to maintain some intellectual autonomy from the experience. Most liberal students believe that the left program can be reduced to guaranteeing people their rights and to bringing about the triumph of human rights over mere property rights. In this picture, the trouble with the legal system is that it fails to put the state behind the rights of the oppressed, or that the system fails to enforce the rights formally recognized. If one thinks about law this way, one is inescapably dependent on the very techniques of legal reasoning that are being marshalled in defense of the status quo.

This wouldn't be so bad if the problem with legal education were that the teachers *misused* rights reasoning to restrict the range of the rights of the oppressed. But the problem is much deeper than that. Rights discourse is internally inconsistent, vacuous, or circular. Legal thought can generate equally plausible rights justifications for almost any result. Moreover, the discourse of rights imposes constraints on those who use it that make it almost impossible for it to function effectively as a tool of radical transformation. Rights are by their nature "formal," meaning that they secure to individuals legal protection for as well as from arbitrariness—to speak of rights is precisely *not* to speak of justice between social classes, races, or sexes. Rights discourse, moreover, simply presupposes or takes for granted that the world is and should be divided between a state sector that enforces rights and a private world of "civil society" in which atomized individuals pursue their diverse goals. This framework is, *in itself*, a part of the problem rather than of the solution. It makes it difficult even to conceptualize radical proposals such as, for example, decentralized democratic worker control of factories.

Because it is logically incoherent and manipulable, traditionally individualist, and willfully blind to the realities of *substantive* inequality, rights discourse is a trap. As long as one stays within it, one can produce good pieces of argument about the occasional case on the periphery where everyone recognizes value judgments have to be made. But one is without guidance in deciding what to do about fundamental questions and fated to the gradual loss of confidence in the convincingness of what one has to say in favor of the very results one believes in most passionately.

The alternative left stance is to undertake the Procrustean task of reinterpreting every judicial action as the expression of class interest. One may adopt a conspiracy theory in which judges deliberately subordinate "justice" (usually just a left liberal rights theory) to the short-run financial interests of the ruling class, or a much more subtle thesis about the "logic" or "needs" or "structural prerequisites" of a particular "stage of monopoly capitalism." But however one sets out to do it, there are two difficulties. The first is that there is just too much drek, too much raw matter of the legal system, and too little time to give everything you have to study a sinister significance. It would be a full-time job just to give instrumental Marxist accounts of the cases on consideration doctrine in first-year contracts. Just exactly why was it that late-nineteenth-century capitalism needed to render an uncle's promise to pay his nephew a handsome sum if he didn't smoke till age twenty-one, a legal nullity? Or was it the other way around: that capitalism *needed* such promises to be enforceable?

The second difficulty is that there is no "logic" to monopoly capitalism, and law cannot be usefully understood, by someone who has to deal with it in all its complexity, as "superstructural." Legal rules the state enforces and legal concepts that permeate all aspects of social thought constitute capitalism as well as responding to the interests that operate within it. Law is an aspect of the social totality, not just the tail of the dog. The rules in force are a factor in the power or impotence of all social actors (though they certainly do not determine outcomes in the way liberal legalists sometimes suggest they do). Because it is part of the equation of power rather than simply a function of it, people struggle for power through law, constrained by their limited understanding and limited ability to predict the consequences of their maneuvers. To understand law is to understand this struggle as an aspect of class struggle *and* as an aspect of the human struggle to grasp the conditions of social justice. The outcomes of struggle are not preordained by any aspect of the social totality, and the outcomes within law have no "inherent logic" that would allow one to predict outcomes "scientifically" or to reject in advance specific attempts by judges and lawyers to work limited transformations of the system.

Left liberal rights analysis submerges the student in legal rhetoric but, because of its inherent vacuousness, can provide no more than an emotional stance against the legal order. The instrumental Marxist approach is highly critical of law but also dismissive. It is no help in coming to grips with the particularity of rules and rhetoric because it treats them, a priori, as mere window dressing. These theories fail left students because they offer no base for the mastery of ambivalence. What is needed is to think about law in a way that will allow one to enter into it, to criticize it without utterly rejecting it, and to manipulate it without self-abandonment to *their* system of thinking and doing.

Student Evaluation

Law schools teach a small number of useful skills. But they teach them only obliquely. It would threaten the professional ideology and the academic pretensions of teachers to make their students as good as they can be at the relatively simple tasks that they will have to perform in practice. But it would also upset the process by which a hierarchical arrangement analogous to that of law school applicants, law schools, and law firms is established within a given student body.

To teach the repetitive skills of legal analysis effectively, one would have to isolate the general procedures that make them up, and then devise large numbers of factual and doctrinal hypotheticals where students could practice those skills, knowing what they were doing and learning in every single case whether their performance was good or bad. As legal education now works, on the other hand, students do exercises designed to discover what the "correct solution" to a legal problem might be, those exercises are treated as unrelated to one another, and students receive no feedback at all except a grade on a single examination at the end of the course. Students generally experience these grades as almost totally arbitrary—unrelated to how much you worked, how much you liked the subject, how much you thought you understood going into the exam, and what you thought about the class and the teacher.

This is silly, looked at as pedagogy. But it is more than silly when looked at as ideology. The system generates a rank ordering of students based on grades, and students learn that there is little or nothing they can do to change their place in that ordering, or to change the way the school generates it. Grading as practiced teaches the inevitability and also the justice of hierarchy, a hierarchy that is at once false and unnecessary.

It is unnecessary because it is largely irrelevant to what students will do as lawyers. Most of the process of differentiating students into bad, better, and good could simply be dispensed with without the slightest detriment to the quality of legal services. It is false, first, because in so much as it does involve the measuring of the real and useful skills of potential lawyers, the differences between students could be "leveled up" at minimal cost, whereas the actual practice of legal education systematically accentuates differences in real capacities. If law schools invested some of the time and money they now put into Socratic classes in developing systematic skills training, and committed themselves to giving constant, detailed feedback on student progress in learning those skills, they could graduate the vast majority of all the law students in the country at the level of technical proficiency now achieved by a small minority in each institution.

Law schools convey their factual message to each student about his or her place in the ranking of students along with the implicit corollary that place is individually earned, and therefore deserved. The system tells you that you learned as much as you were capable of learning, and that if you feel incompetent or that you could have become better at what you do, it is your own fault. Opposition is sour grapes. Students internalize this message about themselves and about the world, and so prepare themselves for all the hierarchies to follow.

Incapacitation for Alternative Practice

Law schools channel their students into jobs in the hierarchy of the bar according to their own standing in the hierarchy of schools. Students confronted with the choice of what to do after they graduate experience themselves as largely helpless: they have no "real" alternative to taking a job in one of the conventional firms that hires from their school. Partly, faculties generate this sense of student helplessness by propagating myths about the character of the different kinds of practice. They extol the forms that are accessible to their students; they subtly denigrate or express envy about the jobs that will be beyond their students' reach; they dismiss as ethically and socially suspect the jobs their students won't have to take.

As for any form of work outside the established system—for example, legal services for the poor and neighborhood law practice—they convey to students that, although morally exalted, the work is hopelessly dull and unchallenging, and that the possibilities of reaching a standard of living appropriate to a lawyer are slim or nonexistent. These messages are just nonsense—the rationalizations of law teachers who long upward, fear status degradation, and above all hate the idea of risk. Legal services practice, for example, is far more intellectually stimulating and demanding, even with a high case load, than most of what corporate lawyers do. It is also more fun.

Beyond this dimension of professional mythology, law schools act in more concrete ways to guarantee that their students will fit themselves into their appropriate niches in the existing system of practice. First, the actual content of what is taught in a given school will incapacitate students from any other form of practice than that allotted graduates of that institution. This looks superficially like a rational adaptation to the needs of the market, but it is in fact almost entirely unnecessary. Law schools teach so little, and that so incompetently, that they cannot, as now constituted, prepare students for more than one career at the bar. But the reason for this is that they embed skills training in mystificatory nonsense and devote most of their teaching time to transmitting masses of ill-digested rules. A more rational system would emphasize the way to learn law rather than rules, and skills rather than answers. Student capacities would be more equal as a result, but students would also be radically more flexible in what they could do in practice.

A second incapacitating device is the teaching of doctrine in isolation from practice skills. Students who have no practice skills tend to exaggerate how difficult it is to acquire them. There is a distinct lawyers' mystique of the irrelevance of the "theoretical" material learned in school, and of the crucial importance of abilities that cannot be known or developed until one is out in the "real world" and "in the trenches." Students have little alternative to getting training in this dimension of things after law school. It therefore seems hopelessly impractical to think about setting up your own law firm, and only a little less impractical to go to a small or political or unconventional firm rather than to one of those that offer the standard package of postgraduate education. Law schools are wholly responsible for this situation. They could quite easily revamp their curricula so that any student who wanted it would have a meaningful choice between independence and servility.

A third form of incapacitation is more subtle. Law school, as an extension of the educational system as a whole, teaches students that they are weak, lazy, incompetent, and insecure. And it also teaches them that if they are willing to accept dependency, large institutions will take care of them almost no matter what. The terms of the bargain are relatively clear. The institution will set limited, clearly defined tasks and specify minimum requirements in their performance. The student/associate has no other responsibilities than performance of those tasks. The institution takes care of all the contingencies of life, both within the law (supervision and backup from other firm members; firm resources and prestige to bail you out if you make a mistake) and in private life (firms offer money but also long-term job security and delicious benefits packages aimed to reduce risks of disaster). In exchange, you renounce any claim to control your work setting or the actual content of what you do, and agree to show the appropriate form of deference to those above and condescension to those below.

By comparison, the alternatives are risky. Law school does not train you to run a small law business, to realistically assess the outcome of a complex process involving many different actors, or to enjoy the feeling of independence and moral integrity that comes of creating your own job to serve your own goals. It tries to persuade you that you are barely competent to perform the much more limited roles it allows you, and strongly suggests that it is more prudent to kiss the lash than to strike out on your own.

THE MODELING OF HIERARCHICAL RELATIONSHIPS

Law teachers model for students how they are supposed to think, feel, and act in their future professional roles. Some of this is a matter of teaching by example, some of it a matter of more active learning from interactions that are a kind of clinical education for lawyerlike behavior. This training is a major factor in the hierarchical life of the bar. It encodes the message of the legitimacy of the whole system into the smallest details of personal style, daily routine, gesture, tone of voice, facial expression—a plethora of little p's and q's for everyone to mind. Partly, these will serve as a language—a way for the young lawyer to convey that she knows what the rules of the game are and intends to play by them. What's going on is partly a matter of ritual oaths and affirmations—by adopting the mannerisms, one pledges one's troth to inequality. And partly it is a substantive matter of value. Hierarchical behavior will come to express and realize the hierarchical selves of people who were initially only wearers of masks.

Law teachers enlist on the side of hierarchy all the vulnerabilities students feel as they begin to understand what lies ahead of them. In law school, students have to come to grips with implications of their social class and sex and race in a way that is different from (but not necessarily less important than) the experience of college. People discover that preserving their class status is extremely important to them, so important that no alternative to the best law job they can get seems possible to them. Or they discover that they want to rise, or that they are trapped in a way they hadn't anticipated. People change the way they dress and talk; they change their opinions and even their emotions. None of this is easy for anyone, but progressive and left students have the special set of humiliations involved in discovering the limits of their commitment and often the instability of attitudes they thought were basic to themselves.

Another kind of vulnerability has to do with one's own competence. Law school wields frightening instruments of judgment, including not only the grading system but also the more subtle systems of teacher approval in class, reputation among fellow students, and out-of-class faculty contact and respect. Left students sometimes begin law school with an apparently unshakable confidence in their own competence and with a related confidence in their own left analysis. But even these apparently self-assured students quickly find that adverse judgments—even judgments that are only imagined or projected onto others—count and hurt. They have to decide whether this responsiveness in themselves is something to accept, whether the judgments in question have validity and refer to things they care about, or whether they should reject them. They have to wonder whether they have embarked on a subtle course of accommodating themselves intellectually in order to be in the ball park where people win and lose teacher and peer approval. And they have, in most or at least many cases, to deal with actual failure to live up to their highest hopes of accomplishment within the conventional system of rewards.

A first lesson is that professors are intensely preoccupied with the status rankings of their schools, and show themselves willing to sacrifice to improve their status in the rankings and to prevent downward drift. They approach the appointment of colleagues in the spirit of trying to get people who are as high up as possible in a conventionally defined hierarchy of teaching applicants, and they are notoriously hostile to affirmative action in faculty hiring, even when they are quite willing to practice it for student admissions and in filling administrative posts. Assistant professors begin their careers as the little darlings of their older colleagues. They end up in tense competition for the prize of tenure, trying to accommodate themselves to standards and expectations that are, typically, too vague to master except by a commitment to please at any cost. In these respects, law schools are a good preview of what law firms will be like.

Law professors, like lawyers, have secretaries. Students deal with them off and on through law school, watch how their bosses treat them, how they treat their bosses, and how "a secretary" relates to "a professor" even when one does not work for the other. Students learn that it is acceptable, even if it's not always and everywhere the norm, for faculty to treat their secretaries petulantly, condescendingly, with a perfectionism that is a matter of the bosses' face rather than of the demands of the job itself, as though they were personal body servants, utterly impersonally, or as objects of sexual harassment. They learn that "a secretary" treats "a professor" with elaborate deference, as though her time and her dignity meant nothing and his everything, even when he is not her boss. In general, they learn that humane relations in the workplace are a matter of the superior's grace rather than of human need and social justice.

These lessons are repeated in the relationships of professors and secretaries with administrators and with maintenance and support staff. Teachers convey a sense of their own superiority and practice a social segregation sufficiently extreme so that there are no occasions on which the reality of that superiority might be tested. As a group, they accept and willingly support the division of labor that consigns everyone in the institution but them to boredom and stagnation. Friendly but deferential social relations reinforce everyone's sense that all's for the best, making hierarchy seem to disappear in the midst of cordiality when in fact any serious challenge to the regime would be met with outrage and retaliation.

All of this is teaching by example. In their relations with students, and in the student culture they foster, teachers get the message across more directly and more powerfully. The teacher/student relationship is the model for relations between junior associates and senior partners, and also for the relationship between lawyers and judges. The student/ student relationship is the model for relations among lawyers as peers, for the age cohort within a law firm, and for the "fraternity" of the courthouse crowd.

In the classroom and out of it, students learn a particular style of deference. They learn to suffer with positive cheerfulness interruption in mid-sentence, mockery, *ad hominem* assault, inconsequent asides, questions that are so vague as to be unanswerable but can somehow be answered wrong all the same, abrupt dismissal, and stinginess of praise (even if these things are not always and everywhere the norm). They learn, if they have talent, that submission is most effective flavored with a pinch of rebellion, to bridle a little before they bend. They learn to savor crumbs, while picking from the air the indications of the master's mood that can mean the difference between a good day and misery. They learn to take it all in good sort, that there is often shyness, good intentions, some real commitment to your learning something behind the authoritarian façade. So it will be with many a robed curmudgeon in years to come.

Then there is affiliation. From among many possibilities, each student gets to choose a mentor, or several, to admire and depend on, to become sort of friends with if the mentor is a liberal, to sit at the feet of if the mentor is more "traditional." You learn how he or she is different from other teachers, and to be supportive of those differences, as the mentor learns something of your particular strengths and weaknesses, both of you trying to prevent the inevitability of letters of recommendation from corrupting the whole experience. This can be fruitful and satisfying, or degrading, or both at once. So it will be a few years later with your "father in the law."

There is a third, more subtle, and less conscious message conveyed in student/teacher relations. Teachers are overwhelmingly white, male, and middle class; and most (by no means all) black and women law teachers give the impression of thorough assimilation to that style, or of insecurity and unhappiness. Students who are women or black or working class find out something important about the professional universe from the first day of class: that it is not even nominally pluralist in cultural terms. The teacher sets the tone—a white, male, middle-class tone. Students adapt. They do so partly out of fear, partly out of hope of gain, partly out of genuine admiration for their role models. But the line between adaptation to the intellectual and skills content of legal education and adaptation to the white, male, middle-class cultural style is a fine one, easily lost sight of.

While students quickly understand that there is diversity among their fellow students and that the faculty is not really homogeneous in terms of character, background, or opinions, the classroom itself becomes more rather than less uniform as legal education progresses. You'll find Fred Astaire and Howard Cosell over and over again, but never Richard Pryor or Betty Friedan. It's not that the teacher punishes you if you use slang or wear clothes or give examples or voice opinions that identify you as different, though that *might* happen. You are likely to be sanctioned, mildly or severely, only if you refuse to adopt the highly cognitive, dominating mode of discourse that everyone identifies as lawyerlike. Nonetheless, the indirect pressure for conformity is intense.

If you, alone in your seat, feel alienated in this atmosphere, it is unlikely that you will do anything about it in the classroom setting itself, however much you gripe about it with friends. It is more than likely that you'll find a way, in class, to respond as the teacher seems to want you to respond—to be a lot like him, as far as one could tell if one knew you only in class, even though your imitation is flawed by the need to suppress anger. And when some teacher, at least once in some class, makes a remark that seems sexist or racist, or seems unwilling to treat black or women students in quite as "challenging" a way as white students, or treats them in a more challenging way, or cuts off discussion when a woman student gets mad at a male student's joke about the tort of "offensive touching," it is unlikely that you'll do anything then either.

It is easy enough to see this situation of enforced cultural uniformity as oppressive, but somewhat more difficult to see it as training, especially if you are aware of it and hate it. But it is training nonetheless. You will pick up mannerisms, ways of speaking, gestures, that would be "neutral" if they were not emblematic of membership in the universe of the bar. You will come to expect that as a lawyer you will live in a world in which essential parts of you are not represented, or are misrepresented, and in which things you don't like will be accepted to the point that it doesn't occur to people that they are even controversial. And you will come to expect that there is nothing you can do about it. One develops ways of coping with these expectations—turning off attention or involvement when the conversation strays in certain directions, participating actively while ignoring the offensive elements of the interchange, even reinterpreting as inoffensive things that would otherwise make you boil. These are skills that incapacitate rather than empower, skills that will help you imprison yourself in practice.

Relations among students get a lot of their color from relations with the faculty. There is the sense of blood brotherhood, with or without sisters, in endless speculation about the Olympians. The speculation is colored with rage, expressed sometimes in student theatricals or the "humor" column of the school paper. ("Put Professor X's talents to the best possible use: Turn him into hamburger." Ha, ha.) There is likely to be a surface norm of noncompetitiveness and co-operation. ("Gee, I thought this would be like *The Paper Chase*, but it isn't at all.") But a basic thing to learn is the limits of that cooperativeness. Very few people can combine rivalry for grades, law review, clerkships, good summer jobs, with helping another member of their study group so effectively that he might actually pose a danger to them. You learn camaraderie and distrust at the same time. So it will be in the law-firm age cohort.

And there is more to it than that. Through the reactions of fellow students—diffuse, disembodied events that just "happen," in class or out of class—women learn how important it is not to appear to be "hysterical females," and that when your moot court partner gets a crush on you, and doesn't know it, and is married, there is a danger he will hate you when he discovers what he has been feeling. Lower-middle-class students learn not to wear an undershirt that shows, and that certain patterns and fabrics in clothes will stigmatize them no matter what their grades. Black students learn without surprise that the bar will have its own peculiar forms of racism, and that their very presence means affirmative action, unless it means "he would have made it even without affirmative action." They worry about forms of bias so diabolical even they can't see them, and wonder whether legal reasoning is intrinsically white. Meanwhile, dozens of small changes through which they become more and more like other middle- or upper-middle-class Americans engender rhetoric about how the black community is not divided along class lines. On one level, all of this is just high school replayed; on another, it's about how to make partner.

The final touch that completes the picture of law school as training for professional hierarchy is the placement process. As each firm, with the tacit or enthusiastically overt participation of the schools, puts on a conspicuous display of its relative status within the bar, the bar as a whole affirms and celebrates its hierarchical values and the rewards they bring. This process is most powerful for students who go through the elaborate procedures of firms in about the top half of the profession. These include, nowadays, first-year summer jobs, dozens of interviews, fly-outs, second-year summer jobs, more interviews, and more fly-outs.

This system allows law firms to get a *social* sense of applicants, a sense of how they will contribute to the nonlegal image of the firm and to the internal system of deference and affiliation. It allows firms to convey to students the extraordinary opulence of the life they offer, adding the allure of free travel, expense-account meals, fancy hotel suites, and parties at country clubs to the simple message of big bucks in a paycheck. And it teaches students at fancy law schools, students who have had continuous experience of academic and careerist success, that they are not as "safe" as they thought they were.

When students at Columbia or Yale paper dorm corridors with rejection letters, or award prizes for the most rejection letters and for the most unpleasant single letter, they show their sense of the meaning of the ritual. There are many ways in which the boss can persuade you to brush his teeth and comb his hair. One of them is to arrange things so that almost all students get good jobs, but most students get their good jobs through twenty interviews yielding only two offers.

By dangling the bait, making clear the rules of the game, and then subjecting almost everyone to intense anxiety about their acceptability, firms structure entry into the profession so as to maximize acceptance of hierarchy. If you feel you've succeeded, you're forever grateful, and you have a vested interest. If you feel you've failed, you blame yourself, when you aren't busy feeling envy. When you get to be the hiring partner, you'll have a visceral understanding of what's at stake, but by then it will be hard even to imagine why someone might want to change it.

Inasmuch as these hierarchies are generational, they are easier to take than those baldly reflective of race, sex, or class. You, too, will one day be a senior partner and, who knows, maybe even a judge; you will have mentees and be the object of the rage and longing of those coming up behind you. Training for subservience is training for domination as well. Nothing could be more natural and, if you've served your time, more fair than that you as a group should do as you have been done to, for better and for worse. But it doesn't *have* to be that way, and remember, you saw it first in law school.

I have been arguing that legal education is one of the causes of legal hierarchy. Legal education supports it by analogy, provides it a general legitimating ideology by justifying the rules that underlie it, and provides it a particular ideology by mystifying legal reasoning. Legal education structures the pool of prospective lawyers so that their hierarchical organization seems inevitable, and trains them in detail to look and think and act just like all the other lawyers in the system. Up to this point I have presented this causal analysis as though legal education were a machine feeding particular inputs into another machine. But machines have no consciousness of one another; inasmuch as they are coordinated, it is by some external intelligence. Law teachers, on the other hand, have a vivid sense of what the profession looks like and of what it expects them to do. Since actors in the two systems consciously adjust to one another and also consciously attempt to influence one another, legal education is as much a product of legal hierarchy as a cause of it. To my mind, this means that law teachers must take personal responsibility for legal hierarchy in general, including hierarchy within legal education. If it is there, it is there because they put it there and reproduce it generation after generation, just as lawyers do.

THE STUDENT RESPONSE TO HIERARCHY

Students respond in different ways to their slowly emerging consciousness of the hierarchical realities of life in the law. Looking around me, I see students who enter wholeheartedly into the system—for whom the training "takes" in a quite straightforward way. Others appear, at least, to manage something more complex. They accept the system's presentation of itself as largely neutral, as apolitical, meritocratic, instrumental, a matter of craft. And they also accept the system's promise that if they do their work, "serve their time," and "put in their hours," they are free to think and do and feel anything they want in their "private lives."

This mode of response is complex because the messages, though sincerely proffered, are not truly meant. People who accept the messages at face value often seem to sense that what has actually transpired is different. And since the law is neither apolitical nor meritocratic nor instrumental nor a matter of craft (at least not exclusively these things), and since training for hierarchy cannot be a matter merely of public as opposed to private life, it is inveitable that they do in fact give and take something different than what is suggested by the overt terms of the bargain. Sometimes people enact a kind of parody: they behave in a particularly tough, cognitive, lawyerlike mode in their professional selves, and construct a private self that seems on the surface to deliberately exaggerate opposing qualities of warmth, sensitivity, easygoingness, or cultural radicalism.

Sometimes one senses an opposite version: the person never fully enters into "legal reasoning," remaining always a slightly disoriented, not-quite-in-good-faith role player in professional life, and feels a parallel inability ever to fully "be" their private self. For example, they may talk "shop" and obsess about the day at work, while hating themselves for being unable to "relax," but then find that at work they are unable to make the tasks assigned them fully their own, and that each new task seems at first an unpleasant threat to their fragile feelings of confidence.

For progressive and left students, there is another possibility, which might be called the denunciatory mode. One can take law school work seriously as time serving and do it coldly in that spirit, hate one's fellow students for their surrenders, and focus one's hopes on "not being a lawyer" or on a fantasy of an unproblematically leftist legal job on graduation. This response is hard from the very beginning. If you reject what teachers and the student culture tell you about what the first-year curriculum means and how to enter into learning it, you are adrift as to how to go about becoming minimally competent. You have to develop a theory on your own of what is valid skills training and what is merely indoctrination, and your ambivalent desire to be successful in spite of all is likely to sabotage your independence. As graduation approaches, it becomes clearer that there are precious few unambiguously virtuous law jobs even to apply for, and your situation begins to look more like everyone else's, though perhaps more extreme. Most (by no means all) students who begin with denunciation end by settling for some version of the bargain of public against private life.

I am a good deal more confident about the patterns that I have just described than about the attitudes toward hierarchy that go along with them. My own position in the system of class, sex, and race (as an upper-middle-class white male) and my rank in the professional hierarchy (as a Harvard professor) give me an interest in the perception that hierarchy is both omnipresent and enormously important, even

while I am busy condemning it. And there is a problem of imagination
that goes beyond that of interest. It is hard for me to know whether I
even understand the attitudes toward hierarchy of women and blacks,
for example, or of children of working-class parents, or of solo practitioners eking out a living from residential real-estate closings. Members
of those groups sometimes suggest that the particularity of their experience of oppression cannot be grasped by outsiders, but sometimes
that the failure to grasp it is personal rather than inevitable. Often it
seems to me that all people have at least analogous experiences of the
oppressive reality of hierarchy, even those who seem most favored
by the system—that the collar feels the same when you get to the end
of the rope, whether the rope is ten feet long or fifty. On the other
hand, it seems clear that hierarchy creates distances that are never
bridged.

It is not uncommon for a person to answer a description of the
hierarchy of law firms with a flat denial that the bar is really ranked.
Lawyers of lower-middle-class background tend to have far more direct political power in the state governments than "elite" lawyers, even
under Republican administrations. Furthermore, every lawyer knows
of instances of real friendship, seemingly outside and beyond the distinctions that are supposed to be so important, and can cite examples of
lower-middle-class lawyers in upper-middle-class law firms, and vice
versa. There are many lawyers who seem to defy hierarchical classification, and law firms and law schools that do likewise, so that one can
argue that the hierarchy claim that everyone and everything is ranked
breaks down the minute you try to give concrete examples. I have
been told often enough that I *may* be right about the pervasiveness of
ranking, but that the speaker has never noticed it himself, himself
treats all lawyers in the same way, regardless of their class or professional standing, and has never, except in an occasional very bizarre
case, found lawyers violating the egalitarian norm.

When the person making these claims is a rich corporate lawyer
who was my prep school classmate, I tend to interpret them as a willful
denial of the way he is treated and treats others. When the person
speaking is someone I perceive as less favored by the system (say, a
woman of lower-middle-class origin who went to Brooklyn Law
School and now works for a small, struggling downtown law firm), it
is harder to know how to react. Maybe I'm just wrong about what it's
like out there. Maybe my preoccupation with the horrors of hierarchy
is just a way to wring the last ironic drop of pleasure from my own
hierarchical superiority. But I don't interpret it that way. The denial
of hierarchy is false consciousness. The problem is not whether hierarchy is there, but how to understand it, and what its implications are
for political action.

II

SELECTED
FIELDS
OF
LAW
AND
SUBSTANTIVE
ISSUES

4 CRITICAL THEORY AND LABOR RELATIONS LAW
Karl E. Klare

LABOR LAW AND RADICAL CRITIQUE

Labor law is often regarded as unusually accessible to radical analysis and criticism. While the political implications of the rise of promissory estoppel doctrine or comparative negligence may seem opaque, labor cases frequently evidence quite transparent struggles over power in the workplace. Particularly since passage of the National Labor Relations Act (NLRA) in 1935, working people have indelibly imprinted the law of labor relations with their aspirations, values, and struggles, both in victory and in anguishing defeat. Accordingly, labor law lends itself naturally to discussion in terms of whether this doctrine or that case expands or diminishes worker power.

But the fact that political issues are so close to the surface in labor law can also be a liability for radical legal theory. The relative ease of focusing on workers' intrasystemic interests may discourage us from seeking answers to broader questions, such as: Why did the doctrines and institutions of collective bargaining develop as they have? What are the meanings and social functions of the collective bargaining system and of the distinctive mode of intellectual practice we call labor law? What is the developmental path of collective bargaining, its future prospects, its inner tensions? To what extent does the collective bargaining system contribute to and/or detract from the ideal of industrial democracy?

Until recently most discussions of labor law from a radical perspective have emphasized the overt, short-run impact of decisional law on workers' interests. Explanation usually then proceeded by way of a leap from the immediate to the global: whether employees had won or lost a case, doctrinal developments were viewed as "expressions" or "emanations" of a unified, pre-given historical subject (e.g., "monopoly capitalism"). We have lacked a theoretical paradigm capable of transcending the constricted and deformed definitions of "workers' interests" available to us within liberal collective bargaining law. But we have also lacked an explanatory model that goes significantly beyond referring the results in all instances to the omnipresent "needs of capital"; that is, we have been slow to develop a theory of capitalist society as a "constructed totality" of the diverse dimensions of social and political life, of the multifarious relations of power, forms of organization, and institutional and communication patterns that together constitute our social world.[1] In particular, we should not rest with a theory that simply ascribes all labor-law doctrine to the "needs of capital," precisely because the development and elaboration of collective bargaining law contributes to making American capitalism what it *is*.

The most sophisticated mainstream liberal students of labor relations law have fashioned an elaborate theory of the social function of collective bargaining. These writers have understood the need for theory to go beyond the horizon of the intrasystemic "interests" of the parties. While liberal collective bargaining law justifies itself by reference to a conception of "industrial democracy" that ultimately rests on management decision making and command in the workplace, a hallmark of liberal labor law is its active promotion of workers' rights in certain well-defined and circumscribed contexts. The complexity and nuance of liberal collective bargaining doctrine have made it a remarkable contribution to post–World War II American political thought.

Radical theorists must develop a model for comprehending the "deep structure" of labor law, both in terms of its internal doctrinal coherence and in terms of its social import. We need a theory that accounts for the contribution of collective bargaining, as a functioning institution and as a set of political symbols, to fashioning and shaping the character of contemporary American life. Without such a theory we will not be able to understand either the developmental path of labor law or its hegemonic function in reinforcing and legitimating workplace hierarchy. Absent such a theory, we are unable to distill from labor law the enduring and emancipatory values with which it has been imbued by popular struggle. Above all, we are hindered from developing a radical, nonliberal conception of workplace democracy in concrete terms that are related (even if only by way of contrast) to the actual problems, institutions, and emerging contradictions of industrial life.

In recent years there has been an effort to develop a radical or "critical" theory of labor law. This project draws inspiration from the movements toward worker and community control of enterprises; toward combatting racism and sexism in the workplace and the unions; toward organizing new sectors of the work force, expanding the scope of employee participation in workplace governance, and democratizing the labor movement itself. Inspiration is also forthcoming from the struggles of workers in other countries to redefine and to build industrial democracy. With particular reference to the analysis of collective bargaining law, growing numbers of writers have committed their energies to the task of constructing a critical labor jurisprudence.[2]

My purposes in this article are: (1) to point to some of the complexities of approaching collective bargaining law from a radical perspective; (2) to share in outline form some of the preliminary conclusions of the new critical labor law theory; and (3) to suggest some of the problems that the radical critique of collective bargaining law poses for the attempt to fashion a left politics. I will begin with a discussion of a highly significant Supreme Court labor law case, *Boys Markets, Inc.* v. *Retail Clerks Local 770*.[3] This case capsulizes the current crisis of labor and the law, the predicaments of labor law theory, and the possibilities for constructing a radical labor jurisprudence.

THE *BOYS MARKETS* CASE: WORKER SELF-ACTIVITY AND THE LAW

The Boys Markets, Inc., operates a chain of retail supermarkets. On February 18, 1969, a dispute developed at one of their stores in Cudahy, California, when unionized clerks observed a supervisor and other nonunion personnel rearranging merchandise in the frozen-food cases. The employees believed that their collective bargaining contract required such work to be performed by nonsupervisory, union-represented personnel. The union demanded that the counters be stripped of all merchandise and restocked by unionized employees.

Many Americans do not understand the vital job-preservation function of this type of demand. The management-dominated media call them, pejoratively, restrictive practices and point to such demands in portraying the labor movement as "anti-consumer," "anti-progress," and "anti-public interest." It is symptomatic of its most fundamental

problems that for all its bargaining leverage and much-vaunted political clout, the American labor movement has so little input into national
economic planning and development that it operates in an economic
environment premised on the inevitability of job scarcity, one in
which there is no fundamental public policy or plan for guaranteeing
employment. Accordingly, labor fights to protect jobs on an ad hoc,
industry-by-industry basis, through work-preservation rules, open alliance with management to obtain favorable tariff and regulatory treatment from government, and, most recently, through concessions
("give-backs") at the collective bargaining table.

Management declined the union's demand that the shelves be restocked. In the ordinary and approved course of events, the union
was entitled at this point to file a grievance. The grievance would lead
to conferences and, if the parties could not reach agreement, to a
ruling by an arbitrator on whether management had violated any work-
preservation provisions of the contract. Having filed a grievance the
employees must return to work. The law is clear that management's interpretation of disputed workplace rules prevails and must be obeyed,
no matter how patently erroneous, while the grievance is being pro-
cessed.

These particular supermarket clerks decided not to go the grievance route; instead, they went on strike. Perhaps they had found the
grievance procedure frustrating or interminable in the past. It is unlikely that any of them expected to go down in history. Apparently
they simply did what workers often do when they feel deeply aggrieved: they exercised the elemental tool of worker protest, the concerted withholding of labor power. Their action led to one of the most
important labor cases since the New Deal.

As is typically the case, the clerks' grievance strike was in violation of the "no-strike" clause contained in the collective bargaining
contract, *i.e.*, the union's promise that no work stoppage would occur
during the term of the contract. A strike during the term of a contract
is called a wildcat strike. Employees do not ordinarily have the protection of law when they strike in the face of a no-strike clause; therefore, they can be disciplined or fired. Likewise, direct or indirect
approval of a wildcat strike subjects the union to liability for monetary
damages. But the delay and transaction costs of replacing employees or
of suing the union for money damages may make these remedies unat-
tractive to employers. What management really wants is to force the
employees back on the job. This requires an injunction, a court order
compelling the employees to go back to work. Failure to obey such an
order is punishable by fines and prison as "contempt of court." In *Boys
Markets* the company played for these higher stakes by seeking an
injunction against the clerks' strike. The question that eventually

reached the Supreme Court was whether the courts are permitted to enjoin and thereby to break grievance strikes.

The "labor injunction" casts a long shadow over the history of the American worker. In the period from the end of the nineteenth century through the 1930s, employers, assisted by the courts, used the injunction in thousands of cases to combat union organization and strikes. The injunction became employers' favorite legal weapon for a variety of technical and procedural reasons. Chief among these is the speed with which an injunction can be obtained. "Psychological factors"—spontaneity, solidarity, the acuteness of the sense of grievance, and courage—are all critical to union success in labor disputes. Since the spirit underlying a strike or organizational campaign can dissipate, timing is obviously a crucial factor in labor disputes. The injunction provided employers a mechanism for nearly instantaneous legal intervention against strikes. Likewise, the preliminary phases of injunction proceedings could occur *ex parte* (*i.e.*, with only one party —the employer—appearing before the judge) or upon affidavits (*i.e.*, without witnesses being subject to cross examination). Nor was there a right to a jury at the preliminary (or for that matter any) injunction proceedings. The truth had a way of getting lost in these shabby preliminary proceedings. But given that an initial, temporary injunction could often break a strike, the union's theoretical right to a subsequent trial with full procedural guarantees was often meaningless. As Felix Frankfurter and Nathan Greene wrote, "the tentative truth results in making ultimate truth irrelevant." Labor injunctions swept very broadly; they could, as in a famous case involving Eugene V. Debs, forbid "all persons whomsoever" from engaging in any conduct "whatsoever" in furtherance of a strike.[4]

For these and other reasons the injunction became "[t]he prime instrument used by the courts to limit union action. . . ."[5] The labor injunction was a much-despised symbol of a largely pro-employer judiciary. Use of the labor injunction

became so extensive and conspicuous that the protests against the particular remedy merged with and poisoned the debate over the substantive rights of the parties. The term "labor injunction" became an epithet for anti-union court decisions, a fighting word for unions and their supporters, and a flaming political issue. The Democratic platform in [1896] condemned "government by injunction as a new and highly dangerous form of oppression by which federal judges . . . become at once legislators, judges and executioners."[6]

Generations of anti-injunction agitation finally culminated in the Norris-LaGuardia Act (1932). Section 4(a) of that law expressly forbids the federal courts from issuing injunctions against concerted refusals to perform work, that is, against peaceful strikes.[7] Many of the states subsequently passed "little Norris-LaGuardia acts" curtailing the injunction powers of their own courts in labor cases.

If the Norris-LaGuardia Act essentially forbids injunctions against peaceful strikes, on what basis could the company ask for an injunction in the *Boys Markets* case? Following the lead of prominent commentators the company argued that the general commands of Norris-LaGuardia must be "accommodated" to the policies underlying another, subsequent congressional enactment, namely Section 301(a) of the Taft-Hartley Act of 1947. On its face Section 301(a) seems to deal only with jurisdiction in the federal courts to enforce collective bargaining contracts. But by 1970 it had long been interpreted as embodying a mandate to the federal judiciary to promote the national labor policy of ensuring industrial peace by enforcing contractual no-strike clauses and by underwriting grievance-arbitration procedures.[8]

The Supreme Court accepted the company's argument that the policy of industrial peace embodied in Section 301(a) overrides Norris-LaGuardia and authorizes injunctions against grievance strikes. In the face of an act of Congress and generations of popular struggle against the hated labor injunction, the Court held, and the law remains today, that a strike over an arbitrable grievance may be enjoined. Put another way, employees may not ordinarily use collective action to prosecute their grievances no matter how deeply they have been injured by management's actions. The Court has taken the *Boys Markets* doctrine so far as to allow the courts to issue injunctions against strikes provoked by potentially life-threatening coal mine safety hazards.[9]

It is symbolic that *Boys Markets* is the enthusiastic product of the liberal Justice William J. Brennan, who in turn relies heavily upon the great labor opinions of another distinguished liberal jurist, William O. Douglas. The case epitomizes the triumph of two paramount themes in *liberal* thinking about collective bargaining law.

The first theme symbolized by *Boys Markets* is the law's hostility to employee self-help in industrial dispute-resolution. The law manifestly prejudices employee collective self-activity and equally plainly favors "peaceful" resolution of industrial disputes within formalized, bureaucratic channels, notably grievance arbitration. Justice Brennan is brutally frank on this point:

As labor organizations grew in strength and developed toward maturity, congressional emphasis shifted from protection of the nascent labor movement to the encouragement of collective bargaining and to *administrative techniques* for the peaceful resolution of industrial disputes.[10]

Public policy does *not* generally favor the use of "administrative techniques" to establish fair rates of pay or decent working conditions.

This is largely left to the "free play" of so-called market forces, *i.e.*, to the relative bargaining power of management and labor. Accordingly, labor's use of concerted activity is accorded a narrow, legitimate role, notably in the private-sector primary economic strike, as Brennen elsewhere acknowledges.[11] But most other forms of employee self-help—e.g., grievance strikes, minority protest, secondary pressure, recognitional and work-assignment activity, and, of course, public employee strikes—are either outlawed entirely or heavily regulated.

"Contractualism" is the second key theme. The primary source of rights and of law in the private-sector organized workplace is the collective bargaining contract. Since World War II the courts have placed great emphasis on enhancing the enforceability of the collective contract. A fundamental premise of this approach is that collective bargaining can be functional for management. In the words of a famous Senate committee report on Taft-Hartley:

The chief advantage which an employer can reasonably expect from a collective labor agreement is assurance of uninterrupted operation during the term of the agreement.[12]

The prospect of this and similar advantages was deftly utilized by liberal labor theorists to encourage employer reconciliation to collective bargaining. *Boys Markets* culminates a generation of efforts to make good on the promise by rendering the collective contract judicially enforceable. The *Boys Markets* injunction enforces the union's contractual no-strike pledge with a vengeance. It in effect immunizes employers from concerted worker protest against management's front-line administration of shop rules.[13]

The collective bargaining contract, in conjunction with the legal gloss provided by the courts, is functional for management in other ways as well. Contracts foster long-range economic planning. Contractual grievance procedures provide a device by which higher-level management controls and polices its own line supervisors. Contractual grievance procedures provide a mechanism for generating operating rules for the enterprise and for obtaining a modicum of employee consent and reconciliation to the hierarchical command of the workplace. Indeed, the law of the collective contract co-opts unions into the uncomfortable position of performing certain managerial functions.[14]

The collective bargaining contract is the institutional device by which employees surrender, for a price, their statutory rights. The union's contractual waiver of the right of employees to make their concerns heeded by concertedly withholding their labor power is the keystone of "mature" collective bargaining. Moreover, the law allows employers to use their bargaining leverage to obtain a "management rights" clause. Under these clauses, the contract carves out a sheltered area of unreviewable employer prerogative beyond the reach of employee input during the contract term. Thus, the typical collective bargaining contract is a legal mechanism by which employees waive their statutory rights, such as they are, to "co-participation" in establishing working conditions.[15] It is often said that the *quid pro quo* for labor's waiver of statutory rights, particularly the right to strike, is management's acquiescence to review of its actions in arbitration. Staughton Lynd has exposed the mythical character of the "*quid pro quo* doctrine." While the union's no-strike pledge is ordinarily absolute and unlimited, arbitral oversight of management conduct does not extend to "non-arbitrable" issues, that is, to issues within the employer's reserved managerial prerogatives.[16] In sum, the collective bargaining agreement is the legal form by which organized employees consent to their own domination in the workplace.

Finally, under the contractualist regime the quality of working life and remuneration of labor turn, beyond minimal standards, on the vagaries of relative bargaining power, not upon considerations of substantive justice. The terms and conditions of employment are just, we are taught, if they result from a "fair" bargaining process. Contractualism makes justice a function of the relative, that is *disparate*, bargaining power of the parties. Yet curiously, the moral rhetoric of contractualism is compelling only if the parties are assumed to stand in a rough relationship of *equality*. Though it may seem a contradiction, contractualist labor cases are at some pains to reassure that labor and capital ordinarily bargain from an initial position of parity.[17] The upshot of all this is that the appearance of "due process" in the bargaining that determines conditions of employment endows such conditions with an imprimatur of legitimacy, no matter how onerous or unfavorable they are. The separation of procedure and substance is one of the most conspicuous features of labor law as ideology.

THE APPROACH OF CRITICAL LEGAL THEORY

How can we explain *Boys Markets?* Was it simply a bad decision by an antilabor Court? How then do we account for the prominent role of the liberal justices in bringing it about?[18] Indeed, the crucial intellectual groundwork for the Court's partial repeal of the Norris-LaGuardia Act was a set of precedents from cases brought to and won in the Supreme Court by *unions*, not by employers, cases that significantly *enlarged* unions' rights.[19] Likewise, it is inadequate simply to ascribe *Boys Markets* to a repressive, anti-working-class "essence" of labor law or attitude of the judiciary. It will not do to say that "capitalist law" cannot tolerate the grievance strike. As it happens, a case presenting virtually the same issues as *Boys Markets* came before the Supreme Court in 1962, and at that time the Court held that the Norris-LaGuardia Act *forbids* injunctions against grievance strikes.[20] Thus, the task of critical theory is to make sense of the case situated as it is in the context of a developing labor law system. This system was originally brought into being in large measure because of working-class struggle,[21] and it has always espoused a substantial solicitude for workers' needs. *Boys Markets* must therefore be understood as the product of an ideological and institutional structure that has enormously expanded workers' rights.

Critical labor law approaches problems like this by attempting to reconstruct the inner logic of collective bargaining law as a whole rather than by focusing on the strategic impact of particular cases. The endeavor is to uncover the moral and political vision embedded in the doctrines, the values and images of justice and workplace rights that the cases evince. We need to do this not only to better understand the cases. An effort of this kind reveals that labor law is animated by a powerfully integrated set of beliefs, values, and political assumptions, liberal political assumptions. The labor movement, or at least much of its leadership, has to a large extent internalized this vision. Labor-law values form an aspect of the collective unconscious of the American labor movement. Many labor leaders accept a set of definitions of what is possible and desirable in the workplace that stands as a barrier to industrial freedom.

The latent value system of labor law is, in short, a legitimating ideology that reinforces the dominant institutions and hegemonic culture of our society. Totalistic criticism of labor law is therefore an indispensable prerequisite to progress toward freedom in the workplace. Considerable work has been done toward the goal of critically reconstructing collective bargaining law as a whole.[22] The space limitations and context of this article permit here only a truncated summary of that on-going project.[23]

THE LOGIC OF LIBERAL COLLECTIVE BARGAINING LAW

The repressive political content of some strands woven into the ideological tapestry of labor law is easily identified. These include the following basic ideas:

(a) Facile disinvestment and mobility of capital are of preeminent importance.[24]

(b) Employees make no "investment" and therefore acquire neither a stake in the direction of their company nor any legal interest in the fruits of their labor.[25] Neither may a community surrounding an enterprise, even one totally dominated by it, pretend to any legal interest in crucial decisions the company makes affecting that community.[26]

(c) Employees must obey the commands, discipline, resource-allocation choices, and operational decisions of the employer. This is deemed a natural and eternal feature of the employment relationship.[27] As already noted, it is settled law that employees must obey even *un*authorized employer commands pending completion of the grievance process.[28] Employees are said to owe an inviolable "duty of loyalty" to the employer,[29] although the employer owes no correlative duty to its employees. For example, in many instances the employer is privileged to inflict the devastating penalty of job loss upon its employees,[30] even sometimes without a business justification[31] and even sometimes with a motive to retaliate for the exercise of the statutory right to unionize.[32]

(d) Although the workplace is acknowledged to be uniquely suited for communication and social intercourse among employees,[33] the workplace is not treated by law as a place for employees to congregate, express themselves, grow as individuals and collectively, or to experience their creative potential and capacity for self-governance. The workplace is deemed a place solely to carry out production under employer command.[34] Though employees may spend the bulk of their waking lives in the plant or office, they acquire no entitlement to regard their workplace as in any sense their own. The workplace—both the physical premises and the existential space—"belongs" to the employer.[35]

In these areas the law generally dispenses with hidden messages. But matters are not so simple in other aspects of the field. Modern collective bargaining law not only advances the rhetoric of employee rights but has in a very real sense engendered the democratic participation of workers in enterprise governance. Labor unions provide an institutional context within which workers formulate and articulate their needs and aspirations, aggregate their voices, and combat the arbitrary and unilateral dictates of management. Since the New Deal period the national political climate has virtually required that the law authorize class conflict in the collective bargaining setting, and our political elites have acknowledged that organized workers do and should have some power.

At the same time the ultimate mission of collective bargaining law is to promote an ideology and evolve a set of institutions that legitimate and reinforce socially unnecessary hierarchy in the workplace. The political thrust of collective bargaining law is to institutionalize and thereby dampen industrial conflict. As an aspect of managerial practice, the interpretation of the collective bargaining laws aims to strengthen employer control over enterprise goals and the direction of the labor process.

Labor law has developed in light of these contrapuntal themes. Its doctrine is a product of an internal "double movement"[36] between repressive and democratic impulses. Accommodation of these discordant emphases in the interests of system maintenance requires imaginative elaboration of value systems and legal structures that will institutionalize and co-opt the authentic, emancipatory aspirations of collective bargaining while not succumbing inordinately to the repressive impulses constantly urged upon the courts by business interests. The development of this delicately balanced vision is one of the signal achievements of liberal thought since World War II. Summarized here and then discussed in the following sections are the three most important components of liberal collective bargaining theory:

First, conceiving "legitimate" collective action in such a way that the law simultaneously *encourages* and *confines* worker self-expression through industrial conflict. Labor law invites and authorizes workers to articulate and advance their interests through self-organization, yet carefully regulates and blunts workers' collective action. This is achieved by impeding solidarity and mutual aid, and by channeling collective action into narrow, institutionalized forms. The law limits worker self-expression through industrial conflict by establishing a highly formalized, atomizing, struggle-dissipating framework in which "legitimate" economic conflict is permitted.

Second, conceiving "industrial democracy" in such a way that the law simultaneously *values* and *limits* employee participation in workplace governance. The justice of worker participation is acknowledged, yet that participation is carefully controlled and restricted. This is achieved by sharply deflecting the exercise of worker power away from such concerns as the organization of the work process and long-range enterprise goals and planning. Rather, the "legitimate" exercise of worker participation and power tends to be confined to "market" (as opposed to "production") concerns, *i.e.*, to the terms of sale of labor power.

Third, conceiving the union's role in such a way that it is set off at a distance from rank-and-file employees and acquires institutional interests of its own. This is achieved by formulating the labor-management relationship as an institutional "partnership" in which "mature" unions do not serve as the uninhibited advocates of rank-and-file need but assume responsibility (without correlative power) for efficient operation of the business. The law works hard, often at the expense of individual employees, to enhance the institutional interests of unions in established collective bargaining relationships. In return unions assume the mantle of fiduciaries of a putative public interest in industrial peace, and perform managerial and disciplinary functions in the workplace.

Among the primary achievements of critical labor theory is its demonstration that most significant doctrines in contemporary collective bargaining law have developed in relationship to this three-pronged intellectual strategy for expanding workers' rights in a manner that ultimately diminishes and demeans them. Let me elaborate briefly on these points.

Confining Concerted Activity

Post–World War II liberalism accepts that conflict is a fact of industrial life. The liberal objective is to institutionalize and confine rather than repress class conflict. To meet that goal liberal theory must (1) redefine the causes and purposes of industrial conflict; (2) establish boundaries for the permissible use of economic weapons; and (3) develop alternative methods and institutions for dispute-resolution in situations in which overt struggle cannot be permitted, methods and institutions which can present a plausible claim to neutrality as between capital and labor.

In liberal management theory and political science, industrial conflict is stripped of any class-based or political character, and is said to be caused by the transnational and transhistorical logic of the modernization process. The purpose of industrial conflict is said to be intra-systemic advancement of group or sectoral interests. The precise structure of economic distribution is open to periodic renegotiation and revision, and groups may use self-help weapons in the process. But the fundamental organization of social life is not deemed at stake in industrial conflict. Everyone shares a common interest in maximizing output (so that the pie from which all groups get their slice is as large as possible). The basic ground rule is therefore that the strike weapon is not to be used to protest midcontract grievances; much less is it to be used as a mode of political expression. Grievance prosecution is confined to formalized legalistic channels.[37]

Collective bargaining law falls into line with this philosophy. The NLRA guarantees employees the right to engage in concerted activity for the purposes of collective bargaining or other mutual aid or protection and the right to strike.[38] Liberal theory not only contemplates that workers may exercise these rights but strives to protect them in doing so. Justice Brennan once emphasized:

[C]ollective bargaining . . . cannot be equated with an academic collective search for truth. . . . The parties—even granting the modification of views that may come from a realization of economic interdependence—still proceed from contrary and to an extent antagonistic viewpoints and concepts of self-interest. The system has not reached the ideal of the philosophic notion that perfect understanding among people would lead to perfect agreement among them on values. The presence of economic weapons in reserve, and their actual exercise on occasion by the parties, is part and parcel of the system that the Wagner and Taft-Hartley Acts have recognized.[39]

But the legitimate use of economic force is largely restricted to the biennial or triennial ritual of contract negotiation in the private sector, or, in rare cases, to protesting when an employer flagrantly abuses the basic rules of the game.[40] A great deal of labor doctrine concerns the suppression of other unacceptably disruptive forms of concerted activity. Included in that category are: any forms of worker protest smacking of class-conscious solidarity, notably the so-called secondary boycott;[41] concerted activity through which employees attempt to reorganize the labor process;[42] worker action of a "political nature" transcending the concerns of employees as employees;[43] minority-group dissenting protests;[44] recognitional activity (i.e., picketing or strikes designed to cut through the time-consuming legal procedures by which unions obtain representational rights);[45] sit-ins and other trespassory strikes;[46] routine economic strikes that occur in vital industries;[47] and almost all public employee strikes.

Additionally, one of the most profoundly important developments in modern labor law is the treatment accorded to the midcontract strike. The wildcat strike offends the basic rule that "thou shalt not interrupt operations." In the liberal vision of collective bargaining, the wildcat strike is the most basic form of social deviancy; it is the fundamental industrial crime.[48] It therefore comes in for brutal legal treatment (second in harshness only to secondary boycotts and public employee strikes).

To remain consistent with their overall "institutionalizing" project, the liberal theorists could not advocate mere repression of the wildcat strike without providing another means for employees to air their grievances and have them resolved. To telescope a very long story, under the urgings of liberal theorists and litigators the Supreme Court appropriated the institution of grievance arbitration to that end. Enforced adherence to grievance arbitration agreements, justified on the basis of the *quid pro quo* myth,[49] has become, in Justice Brennan's words, a "dominant motif," indeed, a "kingpin of federal labor policy."[50] It is fundamental that where the employer has agreed to submit disputes to the arbitral process, employees may not strike. By 1962 the Supreme Court had decided, in a rather significant departure from its contractualist refrain, that the employer's agreement to arbitrate gives rise to an "implied" contractual no-strike clause.[51] *Boys Markets*, authorizing injunctions against strikes over arbitrable grievances, brought the logic of liberal labor jurisprudence full circle.

Narrowing Employee Participation

The liberal vision of industrial democracy narrowly restricts workers' decision-making contributions. Partly this is a function of the systemic preference for highly stratified, representative organizational structures as opposed to more participatory models, a point connected to the bureaucratization of unions. The law goes beyond form, however, and immunizes employers from any collective bargaining duties respecting the substance of managerial decisions "fundamental to the basic direction of a corporate enterprise."[52] While NLRA-style "industrial democracy" reaches a wide variety of employee concerns related to compensation and working conditions, it stops short of mandating participation rights regarding "decisions . . . which lie at the core of entrepreneurial control."[53] The entrepreneurial core, of course, includes all major capital investment and disinvestment decisions. As a general rule, the more important a management decision is, the less likely is it that unions will have bargaining rights regarding it.[54]

The consequences of deflecting "industrial democracy" away from basic issues are particularly poignant with respect to the question of plant closing and relocation. In an incalculably destructive decision the Supreme Court recently applied the Reaganomic "cost-benefit" fetish to scope-of-bargaining doctrine. Justice Harry A. Blackmun first provides a remarkably candid description of what he calls the "neutral purposes"[55] of the NLRA:

A fundamental aim of the National Labor Relations Act is the establishment and maintenance of industrial peace. . . . Central to the achievement of this purpose is the promotion of collective bargaining as a method of defusing and channeling conflict between labor and management.[56]

He continues, in ruling that an employer's decision to close part of its business is outside the mandatory scope of employee participation:

[I]n establishing what issues must be submitted to the process of bargaining, Congress had no expectation that the elected union representative would become an equal partner in the running of the business enterprise in which the union's members are employed. . . . [I]n view of an employer's need for unencumbered decision making, bargaining over management decisions that have a substantial impact on the continued availability of employment should be required only if the benefit, for labor-management relations and the collective bargaining process, outweighs the burden placed on the conduct of the business.[57]

Worker participation is also constricted by the contractualist emphasis in collective bargaining law. As previously noted, contractualism makes labor's waiver of the rights to participate with and to pressure management during the life of the contract the centerpiece of "mature" collective bargaining. At a deeper level, the restriction of employee participation is reinforced by the contractualist separation of form and substance.[58] By emphasizing process at the expense of substance, indeed, by fostering the belief that "justice" is conceivable without regard to substance, collective bargaining law nurtures the idea that industrial democracy resides in the bargaining process itself, even if the "core" issues have been removed from the table before the bargaining gets started. Conceiving justice in procedural terms diverts attention from the top-heavy asymmetry of power in the employer-employee relationship. The forms of industrial due process become a substitute for democratic self-governance.

While this article focuses primarily on the law of collective bargaining proper, the procedure/substance dichotomy has a close parallel in the vast area of labor law governing the process by which unions organize employees and obtain the legal right to represent them, the "law of the organizational campaign." Liberal labor law obviously recognizes that unions must have a genuine opportunity to organize employees. By the same token, the law makes the organizational campaign an extremely difficult and treacherous undertaking.[59] The art of union busting relies heavily on delays obtainable through the technicalities of campaign law.[60] The underlying message here is that if a union loses an organizing drive it is because the union *deserves* to lose, because it has been rejected by its intended constituency. This blame-the-victim psychology derives from the proceduralist assumption that all anti-union tactics deployed by management may claim legitimacy from the very same laws that give the union a "fair" opportunity to acquire employee allegiance. The procedure/substance dichotomy is incarnated here in the false premise that democratic "free" choice is *possible* in an environment of crushing economic oppression.

Institutionalizing Workers' Organizations

Like the law of the campaign, the law governing the relationship of unions and individual employees is beyond the scope of this essay. This section concludes with a brief comment elaborating on the third theme, the institutionalization of the unions and the enforced distance the law places between unions and rank-and-file employees.

The Supreme Court has worked assiduously to expand and protect important institutional interests of unions vis-à-vis the rank and file. For example, the Court's cases upholding compulsory union-shop agreements in both the private[61] and public sectors,[62] as against very substantial constitutional attack, represent an extraordinary commitment of the American judicial elite to collective bargaining. Likewise, a nearly unanimous Supreme Court recently sought to protect the principle of majority rule from challenges posed by dissident minority groups.[63] But this solicitude for union institutional interests does not come without its price tag. In recent years unions have again and again been put in the position of performing disciplinary and managerial functions with respect to the employees they supposedly represent. Three examples illustrate this trend: the threat of vicarious union liability for even unsanctioned wildcat strikes;[64] decisions permitting discriminatory discipline of union stewards in wildcat-strike situations on the theory that union representatives have a special responsibility to ensure enforcement of the no-strike clause;[65] and recent fair-representation decisions obliging unions to share responsibility with management for making promotions under a so-called modified seniority clause.[66] The *Boys Markets* case fits this pattern. By exposing unions to injunctions in wildcat-strike situations, *Boys Markets* encourages unions to proceed "through channels" and to oppose "unruly" and "disruptive" worker protest. It induces unions to accept the role of guarantors of industrial peace carved out for them in liberal collective bargaining theory.

GOVERNANCE OF THE WORKPLACE AND THE RADICAL VISION OF DEMOCRACY

Liberal theorists found in collective bargaining law a superb terrain to develop approaches (e.g., the strategy of institutionalizing conflict, the theory of the "common interest" in uninterrupted production, technological determinist explanations of "modernization") to general problems in cold-war political theory. A generation later, critical theorists have an analogous opportunity to derive from the experience of collective bargaining law general approaches to forging a radical politics. We must rise to this challenge.

The argument of this paper is that the richly textured doctrine of labor law that envelops and pervades the daily lives of all union officials and activists induces us to think about workplace problems in ways that defeat the effort to create industrial freedom. Although labor law reform is a truly urgent priority, ultimately the problem cannot be solved by pouring better content into the supposedly shapeless vessel of labor legislation and adjudication. Radical labor activists must help to forge and disseminate an entirely new political vision. We must go beyond the liberal legalist vision of collective bargaining in which form and substance are separated and in which entitlements turn on bargaining power rather than human need; in which the prerogatives of capital are preferred to the democratic concerns of employees; in which unions go about arranging the sale of labor power but must leave to management the all-important decisions regarding the use of society's resources. Our political vision must encompass new notions of the meaning of work, indeed, the idea that work should *have* meaning, that it should be a mode of self-expression and development, that its content and purposes *matter*; new conceptions of how to reconcile the industrial production process with personal life and physical environment; a new set of values about the uses and allocation of social resources; and an end to racism, sexism, and all forms of illegitimate hierarchy in the workplace and in the labor movement.

In order even to begin to construct this new political vision, radical labor activists must rethink our relationship to and our dependency upon law. We must rethink the relationship the labor movement should have toward government. Put in general theoretical terms, the question we face is, what relationship between civil society and state does a radically democratic, socialist politics envision?

Its emphasis on worker self-activity and the antibureaucratic tone of this paper might suggest that its thrust is "anti-statist" or, in current parlance, "deregulatory." This is not my intent. In the prevailing political context, "deregulation" of the workplace means ratification of existing structures of economic inequality and hierarchy (themselves underwritten and maintained by political institutions and rules of law that by any definition surely constitute a regulatory system). A perspective placing great hope on heightened worker self-reliance and resort to concerted activity does not necessarily entail the conclusion that politics (*i.e.*, the collective, institutionalized self-regulation of society) should be disregarded. Radical critique of the co-optative and institutionalizing character of collective bargaining law should not culminate in a return to the Lockean position that political institutions are morally secondary to the social and economic arrangements of civil society.[67]

The National Labor Relations Act and similar workplace reforms resulted from the intersection of working-class aspirations and elite efforts to rationalize capitalist economic activity.[68] Although they were indelibly marked by workers' struggles, these reforms were in practice shaped by those for whom collective bargaining and labor law are modes of reconstituting the liberal capitalist social order.[69] Nonetheless, that the directive institutions of society ("state power") were deployed against workplace inequality and authoritarianism should be seen as a major advance in the moral development of the American people.[70] The NLRA made a public political issue of the structure of power and decision making on the shop floor: this was an exceptional historic achievement.

The problem with the attempt to achieve workplace reform through law is that law is itself subject to the same process of alienation as is work in capitalist society.[71] "Industrial democracy" in liberal collective bargaining law is a system for strengthening unnecessary hierarchy in work, and for confiscating and denying the expressive, developmental potentialities of work. Rather than enhancing workers' capacity for democratic self-government, collective bargaining law seeks to reconcile workers to their own domination and to unfettered management prerogative respecting the purposes, organization, and products of labor. Collective bargaining is therefore a classic instance of what Alan Wolfe calls "alienated politics"—the process by which peoples' communal, self-governing capacities are absorbed and returned to them in a form that, while falsely pretending to serve universal needs, in fact atomizes their sociality and collective sense, induces their consent to illegitimate hierarchy, and substitutes heteronomous control by the powerful for autonomous self-direction by the people.[72]

All of this suggests that it is misguided, if not nonsensical, to formulate issues, in labor relations or in any other aspect of the politics of social welfare, in terms of the regulation/deregulation dichotomy. The problem of social policy is not *whether* the organized self-regulatory power of society should be deployed to enhance participation and equality, and to serve our material and spiritual needs. The problem is, both in terms of critique and normative ideal, what are and should be the *forms* and *content* of such intervention.

In respect to critique, we must develop an understanding of precisely how and why the exercise of governmental power in the liberal democracies, even in periods of progressive reform, deflects and eviscerates popular participation, disserves human need, and reinforces the institutional infrastructure of capitalism. We must develop methodologies for understanding the complex of relational, organizational, and communicative patterns embedded in public policy and through which public policy plays its part in constituting capitalist social life as a totality. It is hoped that the analytical and interpretive techniques of critical labor jurisprudence have something to contribute to that methodological task.

What is true for our criticisms of contemporary institutions is also true for our efforts to fashion a normative political theory consonant with radical images of emancipation. If any conclusion is warranted from the historical trajectory of labor and the law it is that we need a considerably more complex and nuanced theory of the relationship between organized, institutionalized political power and the quest for human freedom than any currently available.

Two equally unsatisfactory approaches to normative political theory descend from the socialist tradition. The "statist" impulse, deriving from Marx's scientistic inclinations, tends to view state power and law as capable of being harnessed instrumentally to the goal of restructuring civil society. The statist approach has a variety of manifestations: welfare-state social democracy, the Leninist conception of proletarian dictatorship, and, in hideously perverted extreme, the experience of Stalinism. Statist versions of socialism are mirrored by a variety of statist expressions in the liberal tradition: the theories of Thomas Hobbes, the experience of the French Revolutionary terror, New Deal social engineering, and so on. The difficulty with even the most attractive versions of statist political theory is that they ultimately break faith with the most fundamental premise of the radical ideal: namely, that the highest aspiration of democratic culture should be to generate and nurture in all people the capacity for individual and collective *self*-governance and *self*-realization of their potentials.

My views on worker self-activity perhaps evoke the contrary political tradition, the "anti-statist" resonances associated with the workers' councils movements, syndicalism, the "proletarian positivity" of the early Antonio Gramsci and Georg Lukács, and the "prefigurative," cultural revolution tendency within the 1960s New Left. This perspective links up with the strand in Marx that teaches that freedom consists in the complete subordination of the state to civil society, in "immediate" popular self-management without need for institutional arrangements for organized decision making to ensure popular participation, to resolve disputes, and to secure political and economic guarantees. The anti-statist conception of freedom is not the instrumental use of law but its withering away. The socialist anti-statist impulse is reflected within the liberal tradition in the theories of John Locke, the laissez-faire faith in self-regulating markets, and radical civil libertarianism.

A weakness of the anti-statist perspective is its overly sanguine faith in the capacity of unalloyed popular action to restructure and democratize the whole of social life. An even more fundamental problem is the failure to appreciate that politics—the evolving of institutions for organizing peoples' collective, self-directive capacities and for nurturing each person's opportunity for and experience of their potentials and of the promise of social living—is an essential component of human freedom. If politics is conceived as the process and the institutions by which communities collectively guide their destinies, allocate their resources, resolve their disputes, and protect their members' experience of personhood, then politics should flourish, not disappear in the radical ideal.

The conceptions of the relationship between institutionalized power and social life that we inherit from the Marxist and other socialist traditions are inadequate both to comprehending our present experience and to projecting images of a free society. Obviously the task of theoretical reconstruction will draw upon the experience of all forms of oppositional political practice and upon learning derived from many disciplines. Critical labor law reveals that the problem of democratic governance in the workplace is in some respects paradigmatic of the problems of politics and law generally, and that work and law share aspects of the alienation characteristic of capitalist social life. The effort to conceptualize work as an experience of free, creative expression and the workplace as a locus of democratic self-governance may suggest general terms in which to conceive lawmaking and institution building as experiences of human self-development and self-realization. For these reasons, critical labor jurisprudence is inspired by the hope that systematic comparative reflection upon the ebb and flow of struggle and alienation at the intersection of the workplace and the legal process will yield fruitful contributions to the shared theoretical project radicals confront.

NOTES

1. On the concept of the "constructed totality" as a model for social and political analysis, *see* David Plotke, "The United States in Transition: Toward a New Order?" *Socialist Review*, no. 54 (November-December 1980): 87–90, 109.

2. Some of the most important contributions are: James Atleson, *Values and*

Assumptions in Labor Law (forthcoming); Kenneth Cloke, "Political Loyalty, Labor Democracy and the Constitution," 5 *San Fernando Valley Law Review* 159 (1976); Staughton Lynd, "Investment Decisions and the Quid Pro Quo Myth," 29 *Case Western Reserve Law Review* 396 (1979); "Employee Speech in the Private and Public Workplace: Two Doctrines or One?" 1 *Industrial Relations Law Journal* 711 (1977); "Workers' Control in a Time of Diminished Workers' Rights," *Radical America* (September-October 1976); "The Right To Engage in Concerted Activity After Union Recognition: A Study of Legislative History," 50 *Indiana Law Journal* 720 (1975); and Katherine Stone, "The Post-War Paradigm in American Labor Law," 90 *Yale Law Journal* 1509 (1981).

My work on labor law is contained in "The Quest for Industrial Democracy and the Struggle Against Racism: Perspectives from Labor Law and Civil Rights Law," *Oregon Law Review* (forthcoming, 1982): "The Bitter and the Sweet: Reflections on the Supreme Court's *Yeshiva* Decision," *Socialist Review* (forthcoming, 1982); "Labor Law as Ideology," 4 *Industrial Relations Law Journal* 450 (1981); and "Judicial Deradicalization of the Wagner Act and the Origins of Modern Legal Consciousness, 1937–1941," 62 *Minnesota Law Review* 265 (1978), reprinted as abridged in Piers Beirne and Richard Quinney, *Marxism and Law* (New York: John Wiley & Sons, 1981), pp. 138–68.

3. 398 U.S. 235 (1970).
4. The story of the labor injunction has been told many times, but it is less well known today than it should be. The classic work is Felix Frankfurter and Nathan Greene's *The Labor Injunction* (New York: Macmillan, 1930). Good summaries will be found in Irving Bernstein, *The Lean Years: A History of the American Worker, 1920–1933* (Boston: Houghton Mifflin Co., 1972), chapter 4; and Clyde Summers and Harry Wellington, *Cases & Materials on Labor Law* (Mineola, N.Y.: Foundation Press, 1968), pp. 163–206.
5. Summers and Wellington, *supra* note 4, at 163.
6. *Id.*
7. The *Boys Markets* case began in state court but was removed by the union to federal court.
8. *See* Local 174, Teamsters v. Lucas Flour Co., 369 U.S. 95 (1962); United Steelworkers of America v. Enterprise Wheel & Car Corp., 363 U.S. 593 (1960); United Steelworkers of America v. Warrior & Gulf Navigation Co., 363 U.S. 574 (1960); United Steelworkers of America v. American Mfg. Co., 363 U.S. 564 (1960); Textile Workers Union v. Lincoln Mills of Alabama, 353 U.S. 448 (1957).
9. Gateway Coal Co. v. United Mine Workers, 414 U.S. 368 (1974).
10. Boys Markets, Inc. v. Retail Clerks Local 770, 398 U.S. 235, 251 (1970) (emphasis added).
11. *See* text at and note 39 *infra*.
12. S. Rep. No. 105, 80th Cong., 1st Sess. 16 (1947).
13. *See generally* David Feller, "A General Theory of the Collective Bargaining Agreement," 61 *California Law Review* 663, 769–71 (1973).
14. *See generally id.* at 760–71.
15. This is the effect of the Court's decision in NLRB v. American National Insurance Co., 343 U.S. 395 (1952).
16. *See* Lynd, "Investment Decisions," *supra* note 2.
17. *See, e.g.,* American Ship Building Co. v. NLRB, 380 U.S. 300, 317 (1965): The National Labor Relations Act "protect[s] employee organization in countervailance to the employers' bargaining power, and . . . establishe[s] a system of collective bargaining whereby the newly coequal adversaries might resolve their disputes."
18. The theory underlying the *Boys Markets* injunction was supplied by Justice Brennan's dissenting opinion in the *Sinclair* case, *see* text at and note 20 *infra*, which was joined by Justice Douglas. Douglas voted with Brennan in

Boys Markets. Justice Marshall did not participate in *Boys Markets,* but later joined the Court's decision permitting a *Boys Markets* injunction against a coal mine safety strike, *see* note 9 *supra.* Justice Brennan joined the safety case as well. Much to his credit Justice Douglas dissented.

19. The most important precedents underlying the reasoning of *Boys Markets* are *Lucas Flour,* a series of three cases known as the *Steelworkers Trilogy,* and *Lincoln Mills.* These cases are all cited in note 8 *supra. Lucas Flour* was a fairly clear defeat for unions, but the others were all union victories. David Feller, one of the giants of the union bar, has written: "The result in *Boys Market [sic]* was in a very real sense a consequence of *Lincoln Mills* and the trilogy." Feller, *supra* note 13, at 714, n. 252.

20. *See* Sinclair Refining Co. v. Atkinson, 370 U.S. 195 (1962).

21. *See generally* Klare, "Judicial Deradicalization," *supra* note 2.

22. *See* note 2 *supra.*

23. I am very much indebted to the authors cited in note 2 *supra.* This article reflects my own slant on the issues discussed, and I am solely responsible for the formulations contained herein.

24. *See* First National Maintenance Corp. v. NLRB, 101 S. Ct. 2573 (1981); Textile Workers Union v. Darlington Mfg. Co., 380 U.S. 263 (1965).

25. *See generally* Steelworkers, Local 1330 v. United States Steel Corp., 492 F. Supp. 1 (N.D. Ohio 1980), *aff'd. in part & vacated and remanded in part* 631 F.2d 1264 (6th Cir. 1980).

26. *Id. See generally* Staughton Lynd, "Corporate Ruthlessness and Community Despair," *Labor Update,* February 1981, at 3; "Reindustrialization: Brownfield or Greenfeld?" *Democracy* (July 1981): 22–36.

27. *See* Elk Lumber Co., 91 N.L.R.B. 333 (1950).

28. *See* Ford Motor Co., 3 L.A. 779 (1944).

29. *See* NLRB v. Local 1229, IBEW (Jefferson Standard Broadcasting Co.), 346 U.S. 464 (1953).

30. *See* First National Maintenance Corp. v. NLRB, 101 S. Ct. 2573 (1981); Fibreboard Paper Products Corp. v. NLRB, 379 U.S. 203 (1964) (Stewart, J., concurring).

31. *See* NLRB v. Mackay Radio & Telegraph Co., 304 U.S. 333 (1938).

32. *See* Textile Workers Union v. Darlington Mfg. Co., 380 U.S. 263 (1965).

33. *See* NLRB v. Magnavox Co., 415 U.S. 322 (1974).

34. *See* Ford Motor Co., 3 L.A. 779 (1944); Peyton Packing Co., 49 N.L.R.B. 828 (1943), *enf'd.* 142 F.2d 1009 (5th Cir.), *cert. den.* 323 U.S. 730 (1944).

35. *See, e.g.,* Marshall v. Barlow's, Inc., 98 S. Ct. 1816 (1978); Hudgens v. NLRB, 424 U.S. 507 (1976); Central Hardware Co. v. NLRB, 407 U.S. 539 (1972); NLRB v. Babcock & Wilcox Co., 351 U.S. 105 (1956).

36. *Cf.* Karl Polanyi, *The Great Transformation* (Boston: Beacon Press, 1957) developing concept of "double movement" between "protective" and "deregulatory" aspects of public policy.

37. This portrait of liberal collective bargaining theory draws on Walter Korpi's summary in "Industrial Relations and Industrial Conflict: The Case of Sweden," *Labor Relations in Advanced Industrial Societies,* ed. Benjamin Martin and Everett Kassalow (Washington, D.C.: Carnegie Endowment for International Peace, 1980), pp. 90–93. I have elaborated on these arguments in my "Labor Law as Ideology," note 2 *supra.*

38. National Labor Relations Act, as amended, §§7 and 13, 29 U.S.C. §§157 and 163 (1976).

39. NLRB v. Insurance Agents' International Union, 361 U.S. 477, 488–89 (1960). *See also* American Ship Building Co. v. NLRB, 380 U.S. 300, 317 (1965): "the Act . . . contemplated resort to economic weapons should more peaceful measures not avail."

40. *See* Mastro Plastics Corp. v. NLRB, 350 U.S. 270 (1956).

41. *See* National Labor Relations Act, as amended, §§8(b) (4) and 10 (1), 29 U.S.C. §§158 (b) (4) and 160(1); and Labor Management Relations Act, 1947, §303, 29 U.S.C. §187 (1976).

42. *See* Elk Lumber Co., 91 N.L.R.B. 333 (1950).
43. *See* Eastex, Inc. v. NLRB, 437 U.S. 556, 567–70 (1978) (by implication). *Cf.* Cloke, *supra* note 2, at 160 (political neutrality for labor leadership a major principle of national labor policy).
44. *See* Emporium Capwell Co. v. Western Addition Community Organization, 420 U.S. 50 (1975).
45. *See, e.g.,* National Labor Relations Act, as amended, §§8(b) (4) and (7), 29 U.S.C. §§158 (b) (4) and (7) (1976); Linden Lumber Div., Summer & Co. v. NLRB, 419 U.S. 301 (1974).
46. *See* NLRB v. Fansteel Metallurgical Corp., 306 U.S. 240 (1939).
47. *See* the "national emergency" provisions of Title II of the Taft-Hartley Act, 29 U.S.C. §§176–180 (1976).
48. *Cf.* Clark Kerr and Abraham Siegel, "The Structuring of the Labor Force in Industrial Society: New Dimensions and New Questions," *Industrial and Labor Relations Review* (January 1955): 151, 162–63.
49. *See* text at note 16 *supra.*
50. Sinclair Refining Co. v. Atkinson, 370 U.S. 195, 225, 226 (1962) (Brennan, J., dissenting).
51. *See* note 19 *supra.*
52. Fibreboard Paper Products Corp. v. NLRB, 379 U.S. 203, 233 (1964) (Stewart, J., concurring).
53. *Id.*
54. *See* Lynd, "Investment Decisions," *supra* note 2, at 398–403.
55. First National Maintenance Corp. v. NLRB, 101 S. Ct. 2573, 2581 (1981).
56. *Id.* at 2578 (citation and footnote omitted).
57. *Id.* at 2579–81. It is extraordinary that seven justices of the Supreme Court could agree to this interpretation of a statute whose precise purpose is to "encumber" industrial decisions with employee participation out of a concern that workplace democracy, as well as managerial prerogative, is an important value.
58. *See* text at note 17 *supra.*
59. *See generally* Al Bilik, "Corrupt, Crusty, or Neither? The Poll-ish View of American Unions," 30 *Labor Law Journal* 323, 329:

   "Encouraged by self-serving 'consultants' who infest the labor relations field, employers are emboldened by the realization that . . . there is just no bite left in the teeth of the labor law. . . . Companies small and large, north and south, are now convinced that it pays to violate, even if found guilty by the NLRB. They measure the cost of violating against the cost of collective bargaining and coldly opt for the former. Given the weapons available to employers and their growing willingness to use them, it is surprising that so many workers today actually do vote for union representation."

60. On the new breed of union busters *see* Center to Protect Workers' Rights, *From Brass Knuckles to Briefcases: The Changing Art of Union-Busting in America* (pamphlet, Washington, D.C., 1979).
61. *See, e.g.,* International Association of Machinists v. Street, 367 U.S. 740 (1961); Railway Employes' Department v. Hanson, 351 U.S. 225 (1956).
62. *See* Abood v. Detroit Board of Education, 431 U.S. 209 (1977).
63. *See* Emporium Capwell Co. v. Western Addition Community Organization, 420 U.S. 50 (1975).
64. *See, e.g.,* Eazor Express, Inc. v. International Brotherhood of Teamsters, 520 F.2d 951 (3d Cir. 1975), *cert. den.* 424 U.S. 935 (1976); *but cf.* Carbon Fuel Co. v. United Mine Workers, 100 S. Ct. 410 (1979).
65. *See, e.g.,* Gould, Inc. v. NLRB, 612 F.2d 728 (3d Cir. 1979); Indiana & Michigan Electric Co. v. NLRB, 599 F.2d 227 (7th Cir. 1979).
66. *See* Smith v. Hussmann Refrigerator Co., 619 F.2d 1229 (8th Cir. 1980), *cert den. sub nom.* Local 13889, United Steelworkers v. Smith, 101 S. Ct. 116 (1980).
67. *See* C.B. Macpherson, *The Political Theory of Possessive Individualism:*

Hobbes to Locke (London/Oxford: Oxford University Press, 1962), pp. 194–251.

68. *See generally* Fred Block, "The Ruling Class Does Not Rule: Notes on the Marxist Theory of the State," *Socialist Review*, no. 33 (May-June 1977), pp. 6–28.

69. *See* Karl Klare, "Law-Making as Praxis," *Telos*, no. 40 (Summer 1979), pp. 123–35; Klare, "Judicial Deradicalization," *supra* note 2, at 336–39.

70. The Fourteenth Amendment "state action" requirement means that, at least as a matter of Constitutional theory, we still have not progressed so far in the areas of race and sex discrimination. *See generally* Ira Nerken, "A New Deal for the Protection of Fourteenth Amendment Rights: Challenging the Doctrinal Bases of the *Civil Rights Cases* and State Action Theory," 12 *Harvard Civil Rights—Civil Liberties Law Review* 297 (1977).

71. *See* Klare, "Judicial Deradicalization," *supra* note 2, at 338–39.

72. *See* Alan Wolfe, "New Directions in the Marxist Theory of Politics," *Politics & Society* (Winter 1974): 131, 144–49.

5 RACE DISCRIMINATION

LAW AND RACE IN AMERICA
W. Haywood Burns

The first essay in this chapter briefly traces the history of the law's role in reflecting and perpetuating racism starting with the colonial period, and the second critically analyzes contemporary antidiscrimination law. —Ed.

In 1855 white men sitting in the Kansas legislature, duly elected by other white men, passed a law that sentenced white men convicted of rape of a white woman to up to five years in prison, while the penalty for a black man convicted of the same offense was castration, the costs of the procedure to be rendered by the desexed.

The penalty of sexual mutilation appears at many points in the annals of American jurisprudence, Kansas in 1855 being but one of the more recent examples. What is special about the sentence of castration is that where it was in force, it was almost universally reserved for blacks (and, in some cases, Indians).

Apart from what this example reveals about the sexual psychopathology of white America, or at least of those in power, it graphically demonstrates the working of law in a racist society. The nexus between law and racism cannot be much more direct than this. Indeed, the histories of the African, Asian, Latin, and Native American peoples in the United States are replete with examples of the law and the legal process as the means by which the generalized racism in the society was made particular and converted into standards and policies of social control.* Going beyond the Kansas example cited, a systematic analysis of racism and law provides keen insight into the operations of both.[1]

In early-seventeenth-century colonial America, blacks and whites often existed and toiled side by side in various degrees of bondage. Though there were gradations of unfreedom, there was, at first, no clearly defined status of "slave." As the century drew to a close, however, the social reality and objective conditions changed sufficiently for the members of the colonial legislatures to recognize officially that the situations of the black person in bondage and the white person in bondage were diverging, with that of the black person becoming more debased. "Free choice" was hardly an issue for either whites or blacks who came in bondage to the New World. Still, there was a considerable difference in being, for example, an Irish indentured servant and a kidnapped African arriving in chains after the unspeakable horrors of the Middle Passage. There are vast differences between a societally enforced discrimination and an entire legal order founded explicitly on racism—a world of difference between "Irish need not apply," as reprehensible as that was, and statutory denial of legal personality, of humanity.

Black people were severed from much of their culture, language, kindred, religion, and all communication with the Old World of their fathers and mothers, from which they had been torn. The ugly sentiments of white racial superiority were beginning to sprout and rear their heads above the native soil. These facts, coupled with a growing understanding of the tremendous economic advantage to be gained from the long-term exploitation of black labor, brought about a social consensus (among whites) that sought to permanently relegate black people to the lowest stratum in a vertical relationship of white over black. This consensus found expression and implementation in the form of laws passed in colonial legislatures that made slavery for black people both a lifetime condition and a hereditary condition. Thus, through the operation of law, in this case legislated societal racism, the institution of American chattel slavery was created and perpetuated.

With the advent of the detailed and oppressive colonial slave codes of the early eighteenth century, law played a consistent role throughout the period, up to and including the American Revolution. The Revolution, of course, produced a golden opportunity to do business other than as usual. It was, after all, a revolution fought in the

---

* Although this short essay focuses mainly on the history of black people and American law, a similar analysis would apply to the historical experiences of other persons of color in the United States.

name of liberty and egalitarian principles. It was an opportunity that was nonetheless missed or, perhaps better said, rejected. The revolution of Jefferson, Washington, and Madison was never intended to embrace the ebony throngs of captured and enslaved people in their white midsts. It was too much for the eighteenth-century white American mind to view these captured and enslaved people fully as people. It was too much for the Founding Fathers and the economic interests they represented to tamper with that amount of property—even for those who on moral, philosophical, or religious grounds opposed slavery.

Thus, the birth of the new order in the establishment of the Republic brought with it no new day for the African on American soil. In erecting the new state, black people were still consigned to be the hewers of wood, the drawers of water, for there enshrined in the fundamental law of the land, the new Constitution itself was the guaranteed continuation of the slave trade; the guaranteed return of fugitive slaves; and the counting of black persons as three fifths human beings for purposes of taxation and political representation.

The pre-Revolutionary slave codes were more than ample models for the post–Revolutionary slave codes, which continued their detailed, oppressive harshness into the nineteenth century and into the new and expanding nation. The nineteenth-century slave codes provide an excellent example of law and state operating to impose a given social order. The slave codes legislated and regulated in minute detail every aspect of the life of a slave and of black/white interaction; assured white-over-black dominance; and made black people into virtual nonpersons, refusing to recognize any right of family, free movement, choice, and legal capacity to bring a suit or to testify where the interest of a white person was involved. This legal structure defining a black person's place in society was reinforced by statutes requiring cruel and brutal sanctions for any black man or woman who forgot his or her place and stepped, or even tried to step, out of it.

Even in the so-called Free States there was ample borrowing from the statutory schemes of the slavocracy to enforce a societal (white) view of the black person's rightful station in life. Thus, northern states systematically resorted to legislative devices to impose their collective view on the lives of "free" blacks, restricting them in employment, education, the franchise, legal personality, and public accommodation.

Logically, the Civil War should have made a decided difference in this racial legal dynamic. It did not, for though slavery itself was destroyed by this cataclysmic confrontation, the racism and economic exploitation undergirding slavery remained very much intact. Thus, even after the Emancipation Proclamation, after the war and the Thirteenth Amendment, the South set out to win the peace, despite having lost the war. The states of the South, where well over 90 percent of the nation's black people then lived, countered the emancipation by putting in place a series of laws known as the Black Codes, designed to approximate as closely as possible, in view of the legal abolition of slavery, a white-over-black, master/servant society. This legal order governed movement, marriage, work relations, and most major aspects of the freedperson's life.

In fact, there are many ways in which the Black Codes very much resembled the pre–Civil War slave codes. Laws were instituted against vagabonds to curtail black men from moving away from the land. Sharecropping and the convict-lease laws were designed to keep the former slaves on the land. Unlike other statutes, the vagabond- and convict-leasing statutes were not racial in their terms; however, their purpose and effect were entirely clear. The southern economy was predicated upon a large, exploited black labor force; and except for the brief and bright interregnum of Reconstruction, the law and the state throughout the last years of the nineteenth century and the early years of the twentieth operated to preserve the old order and to wring maximum advantage from white hegemony over an oppressed and economically ravaged black populace.

It was the law as well that played a crucial role in "the strange career of Jim Crow." In an uneven and nonsystematic way, culture and mores had provided for a separation of the races in many aspects of American life. For most of the nation's history, that was not even much of an issue because the presence of slavery took care of any need for social definition. However, during the late 1800s, states began to systematically codify separation of the races, *requiring* segregation literally from the hospital where one was born to the cemetery where one was laid to rest. Segregation no longer was open to local option, custom, and usage but was the state's legal order of the day. These developments occurred at the same point in time that an increasingly conservative Supreme Court was narrowing its interpretation of the Thirteenth, Fourteenth, and Fifteenth Amendments—the Civil War amendments. These trends culminated in the *Plessy* v. *Ferguson*[2] decision of the Supreme Court in 1896, in which "separate but equal" was approved as the law of the land, and the seal of approval of the nation's highest court was placed upon our own American brand of apartheid.

The use of the legal system to create and protect a racially segregated society was coincident with government's manipulation of the law to disenfranchise black citizens. Beginning with the Mississippi constitutional convention of 1890, revising that state's constitution through a series of legal stratagems and artifices—and greatly aided by the extra-legal depredations of lynch law—black people were stripped of the ballot and any real semblance of black political power. The poll tax, the literacy test, and the Grandfather Clause were legal devices employed in the service of this racist cause to desired effect.

As a result of state uses of the law in this fashion, black Americans entered the twentieth century segregated, sundered from full and free participation in American life, and politically powerless to do much about it. This situation largely obtained through this century, with minor indications of change and advancement from time to time but with no real major breakthrough in the wall of apartheid and power-lessness until the Supreme Court decision in *Brown* v. *Board of Education*.[3]

Brown and the struggle that followed in its wake—much of which involved use of the law to support and effect positive social change—obviously represent a highly significant advance in black Americans' quest for liberation. It would be an analytical mistake of considerable proportion, however, to view *Brown* as the end of explicitly racist legislation and court decisions, and the advent of civil rights laws as indicative of the end of the relationship among racism and the law and the state. For all our gains, America remains a country deeply infected by racism. Though this racism may not be as explicit or as obvious as it was in earlier times, it is present and no less real. The manifestations may not be as immediately apparent in the language of a statute or a judicial opinion, but there still is a close, intimate relationship between the operation of law and American (white) attitudes toward race.

Some modern manifestations of racism in the law are direct, obvi-ous, and overt. They are individual and often intentional, as with a racist remark by a judge, prosecutor, or clerk, or the refusal to use a courtesy title in addressing a person of color. These do not implicate the state in any systematic way, except to the extent that the individual perpetrators are state officials. Individual affronts of this nature can be directly engaged and combatted. Of greater moment are the institu-tional arrangements that are responsible, intentionally or unintention-ally, for racially disparate and racially discriminatory treatment. These are the arrangements, procedural rules, and substantive doctrines that cause the law in a racist society to reflect rather than transcend that society. Black people are no longer denied a legal personality and can testify in court, but their testimony is often devalued if not counted for naught by the trier of the facts, based on their blackness. Black people are no longer explicitly excluded from jury service by law, but the laws responsible for the formation of jury rolls and for the use of peremptory challenges make systematic jury exclusion on the basis of race a common courtroom occurrence. Black people and white people no longer receive different penalties for the same statutory infraction, but overall sentencing patterns often reveal sentencing differentials along racial lines. Nowhere is this more apparent than in the area of capital punishment, and nowhere within capital punishment is it more obvious than with capital punishment for rape. Sentencing is but one example of many areas where discretion is involved; and, thus, the opportunity for bias—conscious or unconscious—creeps in. The modern legal system is full of points of discretion—from the arresting officer on the beat through the prosecutor to the trial judge. The points of discretion are the portals through which much of the racism in the system enters.

Racially disparate treatment through the operation of law is also clearly a function as well of the ways in which procedural rules and substantive doctrines discriminate against the poor. The racial dimension to what amounts to a confluence of race and class bias is clear, since such a highly disproportionate number of poor people are Third World people. Thus, the operation of the money bail system is responsible for the incarceration of tens of thousands of black, Hispanic, Native American, and poor persons by reason of their poverty. These same persons are disadvantaged by the operation of a system for the provision of legal services that denies them an adequately financed right to counsel in criminal cases and entitles them to no assistance of counsel whatsoever in noncriminal cases.

Not only does racism show itself in the ways law is brought to bear upon persons of color, but also in the failure of law to work *for* black people when they have been victimized. This kind of nonaction is often the functional equivalent of action—negative action. It may take the form of a failure or a refusal to apprehend and charge those who physically and materially damage black people and their wherewithal, or the failure of juries to convict when black people have borne the brunt of some act of racial violence, whether from a police officer in blue or a Klansman in white.

The absence of statutes and judicial decisions that are literally racist on the surface does not mean that we are now free of racist legislation or judicial decision. There is a significant body of current law, legislation, and judicial decision that is racially biased in its operation, whether intentionally so or otherwise. Since other than a racial rationale is advanced for these actions, it is not always possible to evaluate them in the light of their true intent; but there can be little or no argument as to the racial dimension to their impact. Congressional legislation designed to limit the Voting Rights Act or to restrict the use of school busing is justified by the sponsors on a variety of grounds, which may or may not be creditible. A racist motivation usually cannot be proved in instances of this type, except by inference. Similarly, a growing body of Supreme Court doctrine makes access to the federal courts for redress of civil rights grievances increasingly difficult and proof of discrimination once before the courts subject to a more and more unreasonably stringent standard. One need not necessarily posit a racial motivation for these results to point out the racial effect of a judicial system that erects such barriers to racial justice. Conversely, neither is the absence of racial motivation demonstrated by advancing nonracial explanation for the judicial action taken. The point is that whatever the intent, and the complexity here is such that there is probably no single intent, the law is still operating to defeat progress, and black people are still experiencing the law as a facilitator of racism in the society.

NOTES

1. For good general treatment and historical overview, see Derrick Bell, Jr., *Race, Racism, and American Law* (Boston, Little, Brown & Co., 1980); Albert P. Blaustein, and Robert I. Zangrando, eds., *Civil Rights and the American Negro* (New York: Trident Press, 1968); Thomas F. Race Gossett, *The History of an Idea in America* (Dallas, Texas: Southern Methodist University Press, 1963); Oscar Handlin, *Race and Nationality in American Life* (Boston: Little, Brown & Co., 1957); A. L. Higginbotham, *In the Matter of Color*, vol. 1 (New York: Oxford University Press, 1980); Winthrop Jordan, *White Over Black* (Chapel Hill: University of North Carolina Press, 1968).
2. 163 U.S. 537 (1896).
3. 347 U.S. 483 (1954).

ANTIDISCRIMINATION LAW: A CRITICAL REVIEW
Alan D. Freeman

Few areas of law have seemed so significant over most of the past thirty years as that purporting to deal with racial discrimination. Beginning with the historic *Brown* v. *Board of Education* decision[1] in 1954, cases and statutes seemed to promise a real solution to the American practice of white supremacy. Yet, judged by the only sure criterion for assessing the success or failure of civil rights law—results —the effort has largely failed. Formal changes have occurred, to be sure, but substantive changes have been minimal.[2] Since 1974, Supreme Court decisions, with few exceptions,[3] have become increasingly oblivious to the history and contemporary reality of racial oppression; and despite the lack of results, there seems today to be a dominant mood of complacency, a sentiment, however inaccurate, that blacks and other minorities have gotten enough and should now make it on their own.

It is tempting to regard the adverse decisions as aberrations, as cases that just as easily could have "gone the other way" with better legal argument or incremental changes in judicial personnel. A more realistic explanation is that we have just gone through a "Second Reconstruction," perhaps less successful than the first one.[4] This Second Reconstruction has happened both in the world of outcomes and in the world of consciousness, for civil rights law serves as much more than "just law." It serves also as the evolving statement of dominant moral consciousnesss (supposedly of "our society") about civil rights. Consider, for example, the furor over the *Bakke* case,[5] and the massive and ritualistic "looking to the Supreme Court" for the latest moral pronouncement on the subject of race.

This paper will suggest that antidiscrimination law as it has evolved from 1954 to the present has served more to rationalize the continued presence of racial discrimination in our society than it has to solve the problem. The legal doctrine can be described more convincingly in this fashion than in the more conventional positivist, progressive, or reformist sense. To describe the evolution of civil rights law in such a critical way is to reject the liberal myth that sees the civil rights crusade as "a long, slow, but always upward pull that must, given the precepts of the country and the commitment of its people to equality and liberty, result eventually in the full enjoyment by blacks of all rights and privileges of citizenship enjoyed by whites."[6]

The last part of this paper will try to deal more explicitly with the tension between the experiential uniqueness of racial discrimination and its remedial intractability as a separate phenomenon. There is no doubt that racial discrimination in American life and history has been a distinct form of oppression, something different from other relations of exploitation. Nevertheless, the history of antidiscrimination law suggests that no genuine liberation or change in the conditions associated with the historical practice of racial discrimination can be accomplished without confronting class structure, for no matter how hard one tries to deal with the unique problem of race, deep structural obstacles make it difficult to proceed very much further than we have already.

VICTIM AND PERPETRATOR

The starting place for a discussion of racial discrimination would seem to be the concrete experience of a person who belongs to the group that has been discriminated against. What does it mean to such a person to be told that racial discrimination has now become illegal? The *Brown* case surely had to do with more than education; it was the official American statement that racial discrimination had become illegal (and immoral). The meaning of such a statement to a black American in the 1950s (or even now) must include an expectation that there will be, when the task is completed, some significant change in the conditions of life that one associates with the past practices of discrimination—segregated schools, lack of jobs, the least desirable jobs, lack of political power.

If making racial discrimination illegal is to make any sense, it must include some significant change in those conditions. If, after a supposed "elimination" of racial discrimination, substantially disproportionate numbers of black people still have the least desirable jobs, my reaction is that change has not occurred, discrimination has not been eliminated.

An alternative response that one hears with increasing frequency today is that jobs are not maldistributed because we have not eliminated racial discrimination but because blacks have insufficient merit and ambition or lack the necessary qualifications. In this view, the fact that such conditions persist well after the change in legality is explicable not as the product of a society that has practiced racial oppression, but as consistent with the way the good society should work. This quickly becomes what others have appropriately called the blaming-the-victim approach.[7] The idea is that if there is fault, it is the fault of the black people who have not made the best of the new era of lack of discrimination. But to make such a wild assertion seems to presuppose that the world that has transcended racial discrimination is already functioning—that, for example, the ideal of equality of opportunity is, in fact, a reality. My preference, faced with such a question, is to ask whether the ideal is not working, whether equality of opportunity is a myth. We should presume the opposite: when the very conditions that one used to associate with the most blatant forms of discrimination have not gone away, perhaps our "other institutions" are not yet the ones appropriate to future society. Perhaps there is still something very wrong.

Thus, results are crucial, but today we have a body of antidiscrimination law (discussed in the next section) that makes results largely irrelevant. The moral consciousness reflected in that law has become indifferent, for example, to whether a "desegregated" school becomes one that is integrated. By making results irrelevant, the law ultimately fails to speak to the concrete perception with which I began. I have called that concrete perception the victim perspective on racial discrimination. The core idea of the victim perspective is that doing something about the problem of racial discrimination necessarily means results.

Instead, modern American law has adopted what I have called the perpetrator perspective. It purports to be a stance of society as a whole, or of a disinterested third-party gaze looking down on the problem of discrimination, and it simply does not care about results. Discrimination becomes the actions of individuals, the atomistic behavior of persons and institutions who have been abstracted out of actual society as part of a quest for villains. It is a notion of racial discrimination as something that is caused by individuals, or individual institutions, producing discrete results that can be identified as discrimination and thereafter neutralized. The emphasis is negative—on the behavior of the perpetrator and not the life situation of the victim. It seeks to identify and catalogue perpetrators, to make sure that one has ascribed the correct evils to the correct perpetrator.

The perpetrator perspective, which is the principal model of contemporary antidiscrimination law, assumes that apart from the misguided conduct of particular actors the rest of our society is working, that future society is otherwise here. All we need do is root out the villains. Having done so, we can say with confidence that it was all their *fault*. A corollary of this fault notion is that those who, under current versions of the doctrine, are not labeled perpetrators have every reason to believe in their own innocence and their separation from the problem. If one is not a perpetrator, one must just be an innocent societal bystander. And why, then, should one be called to account or implicated at all in the business of eradicating the past? This pernicious aspect of the perpetrator perspective has a great deal to do with the psychic structure of the *Bakke* dispute.

While the perpetrator perspective captures the content of contemporary antidiscrimination law, it has not evolved neatly. The doctrinal evolution can best be described as having toyed with the victim perspective while retaining the form of the perpetrator perspective. That story begins with the *Brown* case.

THE DOCTRINAL EVOLUTION

Antidiscrimination law has passed through three eras of decision making since the *Brown* case. After a brief outline, each will be discussed in greater detail.

The first era I call the Era of Uncertainty. It covers the period from 1954 to 1965, when the law was preoccupied with identifying violators and violations, with extending the scope of antidiscrimination law rather than remedying what had been deemed violations. While it is true that lower courts during that era began to struggle with questions of remedy, at the level of Supreme Court doctrine answers remained uncertain.

The period from 1965 to 1974 I call the Era of Contradiction. The Supreme Court adhered ostensibly to the perpetrator form, concerning itself with questions of fault and causation at a formal level, but regularly deviated from the substantive requirements of the form—in fact, often it contradicted itself. The Court seemed to be incorporating the victim perspective in its decision making while steadfastly insisting that it was doing nothing of the kind.

The third period, the Era of Rationalization, began for school desegregation law with the 1974 decision in *Milliken* v. *Bradley* (*Milliken I*).[8] The Court reasserted the substantive primacy of the perpetrator perspective by pretending never to have strayed, by pretending away several earlier cases.

I do not suggest a cyclical view. The Court did not start with one view, adopt a new one for a while, and then simply return to the earlier one. It is crucial to this evolution that the return to strict perpetrator form occurred after having passed through the interim period, for that interim enables the Court to say today that there has been a cure. Because of what happened in the interim, the Court can posit, for example, that Detroit's schools are desegregated. But that is the end of the story.

The Era of Uncertainty (1954 to 1965)

As of the *Brown* case, there was no particular reason, as a matter of legal doctrine, to think about the victim/perpetrator dichotomy. At the same time, the victim perspective was crucial to the concrete expectations reasonably arising in the people whose liberation was announced by the decision.

Even as a matter of legal doctrine, there has been great debate about what the *Brown* decision "meant." In one sense, there is no issue: the *Brown* case was "about" white oppression of blacks, and segregation was illegal because of its role as part of that system of oppression.[9] But that accurate statement does not resolve the victim/perpetrator issue, yield an appropriate abstract principle, or resolve the ambiguities of the opinion.

For present purposes, it is most important to recognize that the *Brown* case produced a variety of doctrinal abstractions that responded to problems and needs other than the one to which they were ostensibly directed. The first of these was the view that the issue was one of freedom of association. That view cannot be said to capture the "meaning" of *Brown*, at least by way of hindsight; but it was in many ways an accurate statement of what *Brown* meant for the moral consciousness of the 1950s, for a world where, by and large, private discrimination (at least at the national level) was still regarded as ethically legitimate. Freedom of association is thus a way of rationalizing *Brown* for a world that had not yet, even as a matter of fashion, ruled out discrimination but was beginning to do so. The principle may be regarded as an interim ideology, pending the change in public fashion that now includes such powerful superficial symbols as black faces on television ads.

The second doctrinal abstraction, also far removed from the actuality of white oppression of blacks, was the theory of color-blindness, which has remained an important component of the legal ideology of antidiscrimination. The color-blind view seems to presuppose an abstract, ahistorical future world. The rules of color-blindness are the ones that would be appropriate, and would hence be superfluous, in a society that had never known racial discrimination.

The color-blind theory arose in a concrete setting, in a famous Harlan dissent,[10] as an objection to segregation. The curious ideological phenomenon is that color-blindness has become an abstraction that has taken on a life of its own, one that can turn around to disappoint the hopes of the very people on whose behalf it arose initially. Why should color-blindness be an end in itself, a reference point against which to test questions of racial discrimination? It has become a way of abstracting the American black experience out of its own historical setting to the point where all ethnics become fungible. The ideology of fungibility is part of the process of refusing to deal with the concreteness of black experience.

The color-blind approach maintains an insistent pressure on antidiscrimination law because it is supposedly one of those "cherished" and "shared" values. One had thought that color-blindness in its pure form had left antidiscrimination law, had been replaced by the sophistication of the perpetrator perspective. It has had a resurgence, however, with the fragile "majority" in the *Bakke* case. Justice Lewis F. Powell, in his crucial opinion, seemingly relies on the most rigid rhetoric of color-blindness, although in many ways undercutting himself with what must be interpreted as an implicit invitation to hypocritical practice.[11]

A third doctrine is based on the idea of equality of educational opportunity. The notion of equality of opportunity is an accurate way, as Judge Robert Carter suggested,[12] of describing what the litigants in *Brown* had in mind. That view is somewhat ironic, since the opinion has come to stand for both more and less than equality of educational opportunity—more to the extent it reached out to strike down other discriminatory practices, but much less to the extent there is no recognized right, no ethical claim for equality of resources or a substantively effective education as such. But equality of educational opportunity was never an end in itself. It was and is a means toward dealing with the greater problem of liberation, toward reversing the conditions associated with the history of oppression. And equality of educational opportunity is a functional goal only if one supposes a working system of equality of opportunity *in general*, operating in harmony with the educational system.

For the most utopian interpretators of *Brown*, it was the beginning of the end of racial discrimination, which would be achieved when, by the year 2200, everyone had become a creamy shade of beige and race had simply ceased to exist under the guiding hand of genetic entropy. Integration need not be an end in itself, however much it remained a powerful symbol of liberation. From the victim perspective, a choice of means other than integration may be no more than a choice of means, a strategic decision to seek the single end of liberation by another path; but an *apparent* choice (e.g., for racial separation) could too easily mask imposition or rationalization, especially where the resultant conditions seem so identical to those which have for years been a symbolic measure of oppression. And the problem is underscored by the fact that the perpetrator ideology employed as part of the rationalization process seems to presume the achievement of an integrated society. Conversely, integration remedies forced upon unwilling minorities may have nothing to do with liberation.

The *Brown* case simply set loose these various ideas and expectations, raising ambiguities to be resolved at a later time. On one occasion toward the end of the first era, however, the Court did have to confront the perpetrator/victim dichotomy. In a jury discrimination case, *Swain* v. *Alabama*,[13] the Court had to choose, and it chose the perpetrator perspective, making it irrelevant whether any black person served on the juries at issue. To support its position, the Court invoked the language of color-blindness, combining ethnic fungibility with the impropriety of claims to proportional representation.

The Era of Contradiction (1965 to 1974)

During the second era, the Court had to contend with the perpetrator/victim issue. In each of the major cases,[14] the Court adhered to the perpetrator form while incorporating the victim perspective, creating expectations that changes in conditions had become a matter of entitlement in antidiscrimination law.

Three recurring types of cases led the Court almost by necessity, if it was to preserve any integrity in its doctrine, to incorporate the victim perspective. The first was the "infinite-series" problem. Suppose a municipality has gerrymandered its districts so that the entire black population is in one district while every other district is white, and there is evidence of purposeful discrimination. Suppose further that the Court simply issues an order to the municipality that says "stop doing that," and a redistricting follows with a handful of people shifted but most of the black population still in the one district. Assuming there is no further evidence of "purposeful" discrimination, how can it be determined whether the new scheme is a violation? If the degree of change from the initial scheme is slight, further change would seem necessary, but how much? The problem is that remedying such a violation does not make much sense unless some notion of racial proportionality is incorporated; and rather than going through a process of repetitive litigation that approaches a limit of proportionality, it would obviously be easier and more convenient to impose such a remedy at the outset. But this is a victim perspective.

The Voting Rights Act (1965) exemplifies this problem and its solution, with the actual infinite-series litigations taking place in the South over voter-eligibility issues for years prior to the enactment of the statute. Once the notion of proportionality crept in, there was created an expectation that if a violation were proved, proportional representation would result. But, simultaneously, it is difficult to relate the remedy of proportionality to the violation, since all the violation demanded was a negation. In fact, what does proof of the violation really have to do with the legitimacy of the claim of proportionality— unless, of course, one is already in future society? Thus, what was clearly a perpetrator-perspective occasion for intervention led almost unwittingly to the creation of a victim-perspective expectation. And if there is a right to proportionality here, why not elsewhere?

The second typical case presents the "no-result" problem. For example, *Brown* declared school segregation illegal; but by relegating all remedial issues to the lower courts, it did nothing about the problem. The Court then waited, and the world changed. Neighborhood patterns shifted, with residential segregation increasing. By the time the Court returned to the original problem in *Swann v. Charlotte-Mecklenburg Board of Education*,[15] to do nothing but again outlaw segregation would be embarrassing and would undermine the court's credibility. Even Justice Felix Frankfurter had worried publicly during the oral argument in *Brown* that "nothing would be worse" than for the Court "to make an abstract declaration that segregation is bad and then have it evaded by tricks."[16]

But the Court could not go back in time. Thus, it had to order school districts to produce the result—racial balance—that would have followed from immediate and massive enforcement in 1955. By waiting fifteen years, however, the Court knew and simultaneously denied that something had happened in the interim to frustrate all possibility of success in the original expected terms. By proceeding that way, the Court created an expectation and an assumption that if the real relationship between the original violation and the current condition were really that tenuous, it must be the current condition that was significant regardless of the original violation. From the victim perspective,

the expectation became a change in conditions. The concrete expectation concerned results, while the Court indulged itself with verbal
gimmickry to "show," through the use of self-contradictory presumptions, as in *Swann*, how the current conditions related to the original
violation. The court used similar gimmicks in other cases.[17]

The net effect was the creation of a perception, consistent with
the victim perspective, that the problem was not just the old practice
of segregation but the current pattern of racially concentrated schools.
That perception gave rise to an expectation of entitlement, an affirmative right, to integrated schools (schools that are, in fact, integrated)
for some period of time sufficient to make credible to the black people
involved the claim that segregation had been outlawed.

The third type of case presents the problem of the ostensibly
neutral practice. The best illustration is an employment case, *Griggs* v.
Duke Power Co.,[18] which is the central case of the Era of Contradiction. *Griggs* was the only Supreme Court case that just about incorporated the victim perspective; and, not surprisingly, it is one of the
most currently repudiated cases.[19]

Griggs involved an ostensibly neutral practice—testing—that was
probably being employed for the purpose of racially discriminating.
However, there was no provable causal link between the substantive
invalidity of the test itself and the employer's prior practice of blatant
discrimination. The Court, dealing with a basically perpetrator-
perspective problem, embraced the victim perspective by focusing on
the test itself rather than on the prior practice of discrimination. The
test was viewed as a neutral practice that happened to fall with disproportionate severity on blacks. Under the perpetrator perspective,
the mere fact of a racially disproportionate result normally raises no
issue, since there is no guilty perpetrator from that fact alone. *Griggs*
set loose a different idea: ostensibly neutral practices had to be justified
if they produced disproportionate results. *Griggs* suggested that within
the perpetrator-perspective framework, the concept of intent in antidiscrimination law had been changed. Intentional continuation of a
course of conduct producing disproportionate results was actionable,
regardless of why one engaged in or continued the course of conduct.
This amounts to incorporation of the victim perspective.

There was no reason to suppose at the time of *Griggs* that it
would not be extended to all other areas of civil rights law, especially
school-desegregation law. One could read the school-desegregation
cases immediately following *Griggs* and assume application of the
Griggs idea to neutral school practices, particularly the practice of
neighborhood school assignment. Yet, all the while the Court steadfastly adhered to the perpetrator-perspective form. The Court reminded
us of the need to prove intentional discrimination but affirmed lower

court decisions that essentially found actionable segregation on the basis of disproportionate results. One is left puzzled: the victim perspective, though unacknowledged, had crept into the law.

The Era of Rationalization (1974 to the Present)

In *Milliken I* and the subsequent cases, the Court has rigidly insisted on strict compliance with the perpetrator form.[20] The neutral practice at issue in *Milliken* was jurisdictional districting, and the Court adopted a version of local autonomy that elevated the particular locally drawn districts at issue to the status of a cherished, constitutional value.

This is inconsistent with, for example, the Court's treatment of neighborhood school districts in the *Swann* case but characteristic of the Era of Rationalization. The Court demands proof of purpose, causation, and a neat correspondence between an identified violation and a permissible remedial obligation. Except in the narrowest and most limited sense, there is no concern for results. In effect, the Supreme Court seems to be saying, as singer Phil Ochs tried to do with the Vietnam War, that "the war is over" because we declare it's over, and for no other reason.

The basic task of the Era of Rationalization has been to restrict the concept of violation in civil rights law to a narrow, strictly interpreted perpetrator perspective.[21] However, some new ideas have emerged. Having narrowed the concept of violation, the Court is willing to tolerate at least, and perhaps to insist upon, intensive remedial efforts beyond what previously had been imposed.[22] It may be possible to seize upon the need to maintain the image of great remedial vigilance in the ever narrower areas of violation.

Another new notion, which has possibly been eroded by *Bakke*, is voluntarism. The idea is that conditions that will not be deemed violations of law may nevertheless be remediable through voluntary action. If you the school board can be convinced, then go ahead. The Court had said as much in *Swann*, as part of its insistence on perpetrator form, when it reminded us that the Constitution did not require racial balance but noted that a school board could try to achieve that goal if it wished to as a matter of educational policy. A number of recent opinions seems to underscore the voluntarism principle.[23] To relegate the problem to the tentative world of voluntarism, of course, reinforces the dissonance between the experience of burden imposed on those whites who are called upon to participate in such programs and the felt innocence of such persons created by the perpetrator perspective. And *Bakke* shows how voluntarism can be manipulated, can be made tantalizingly elusive by increasing its attendant costs.[24]

The major accomplishment of the Era of Rationalization has been to eradicate the victim perspective from the expectations created by antidiscrimination law. Its most significant case is not *Bakke*, which at most involved the permissible limits of voluntarism, but *Washington* v. *Davis*,[25] which illustrated how conditions associated with discrimination from the victim perspective could be rationalized into future society by presuming their validity rather than demanding their justification. In *Davis*, the failure rate on a verbal-ability test given to applicants for a police officer training school was four times greater for blacks than for whites. Even though there was no showing that the test had been validated to predict performance as a police officer, the court denied relief. That case and others[26] reaffirm the view that results are ultimately irrelevant.

RACE, CLASS, AND EQUALITY OF OPPORTUNITY

If I were content to stay within the structure of legal ideology and argument, I would write a brief in favor of the victim perspective as the appropriate form of judicial decision making in racial-discrimination cases. But surely the law's refusal to incorporate the victim perspective has had little to do with either the logic or effectiveness of legal argument or the subjective wishes of the participants in the legal process.

Suppose one drops the simplistic model of "white" society and "black" society and the pluralist, interest-group model, assumed in most discussion about antidiscrimination law, and replaces them with a social structure characterized more by conflict than by consensus, more by class structure than by community of interest, more by relations of domination and exploitation than by relations of cooperation or mutual benefit. In such a social structure, which I believe corresponds more closely with the real one, the basic contours of the rejection of the victim perspective, including both the fact and the manner of its rejection, can be understood as corresponding to the interests of a ruling class in a class society, as an instance of law as legitimation of the existing class structure. Of course, the doctrinal developments occurred largely through the internal tensions and dynamics of legal thought, without the guiding hand of either history or a conspiratorial elite, and with setbacks, interruptions, and mistakes. In addition, both the forms adopted by law as legitimation and that which is legitimated by the process are complex and contradictory, and cannot be squeezed into linear progressions. But with these qualifications as a backdrop, I offer an explanation of antidiscrimination law that emphasizes the fundamental social role of law as legitimation of existing social and power relations. The perpetrator perspective, even with its inherent illogic and disregard of the history and contemporary reality of racial oppression, has effectively served to legitimize, legally and morally, major institutions and a social structure that maintain a disproportionate number of black and other minority people as an underclass. This explanation is developed in the following two sections, which consider traditional Marxist approaches and an approach that focuses on the legitimation function of the law.

Traditional Marxist Approaches

Conventional Marxist treatments of racism leave one with a sense of dissatisfaction or, at least, incompleteness. They seem often to make the mistake of *either* collapsing racism into a problem of class domination generally, as if it were nothing more than a consequential incident of evolving capitalism, thereby denying its experiential reality, *or* treating racism as a mode of oppression so autonomous from capitalist social and economic relationships that it can be blamed on oppressors who appear as (classless?) "white society" and remedied without fundamental social change.

No one can deny that racism is a distinct and historically separate form of oppression. The statement is almost superfluous given the actual life experience of people who have been or who are being so oppressed. But that fact does not suggest that it is a problem that can be dealt with in isolation. However separate its origins and historical practices may be, racism must be confronted today within the context of contemporary American capitalist society. The problem is how to connect a unique history with a complex present.

One traditional Marxist view[27] sees racism as providing an underclass of wage laborers willling to work for wages far below workers now victimized by racism—the "reserve army of labor." Under this view, racism serves to hold down wages generally by offering the capitalists a ready market of cheap, unskilled labor. The net result is additional extraction of surplus value and greater capital accumulation. This is one of the views that seems to deny the historical reality of racism by almost collapsing it into an economically motivated capitalist plot.[28] In a less simplistic version, it cannot be denied that there is some truth to this explanation. Nevertheless, what was functional for a period of time in the service of capital accumulation (and the reserve army may well have been) need not have been invented by the capitalists or by the logic of capitalism. And it is questionable whether the reserve-army theory is functional at all in the service of capitalism any longer, or even consistent with the needs of the modern corporate liberal state. That racism persists (perhaps as a virulent ideological plague from the past) does not make it per se economically functional.

The question of function is difficult to resolve; one is quickly mired in debates about statistics, job categories, and correlations that may or may not amount to causations. It does seem questionable whether racism of the kind traditionally experienced by black Americans remains necessary to support capitalist exploitation or is even useful for that enterprise. Factors must be taken into account, such as the growth of technology, with its consequent and continuing displacement of unskilled workers; the growth of welfare systems that make membership in the reserve army less functional than it might be otherwise (for capital accumulation, that is);[29] the presence of continued high levels of unemployment, which provides a reserve army to some extent (one that is disproportionately populated, it is true, by black and other minority people, but that fact alone does not explain racism as functional to capitalism); and the presence of a genuine reserve army, in the classic sense, of "illegal" aliens (that many such persons are members of the same minority groups which have suffered under traditional American racism may make it ideologically easier for their exploitation to be tolerated, but does not transform the issue into one of racism per se).

The other traditional Marxist view, which is basically an economic explanation presented at the level of ideology, or consciousness, is that racism serves to divide the working class, to create internal conflicts and antagonisms that frustrate the creation or awareness of the genuine class consciousness essential to radical change.[30] While this view holds some truth, it too seems incomplete. First, as noted earlier with respect to the reserve-army theory, it does not explain the historical development of racism as a unique form of oppression but merely asserts its utility for the perpetuation of capitalist class structure. In addition, given the presence of other powerful ideologies that serve to arrest the development of class consciousness, racism seems only marginally necessary, and perhaps superfluous, if regarded from a functional point of view. Such ideologies include the "liberal" tradition, media-induced consumerism, equality of opportunity, as well as occasional bouts of hysterical nationalism.

Second, it fails to explain how the abolition of racism, at least at the formal level and in the realm of public moral consciousness, has become a project of America's dominant classes, at least in the period since the original *Brown* decision. This pattern of change, however limited to the formal and substantively inadequate, does at least suggest the presence of contradictory forces with respect to the perpetuation of racist practices in the United States.

Third, this variant of the traditional theory fails to acknowledge that too much racism may be just as destabilizing to the class structure as too little. Given our knowledge of twentieth-century world history, a critical level of racial division (a growing version of which may have been occurring with the Wallace movement in the late 1960s) may well create such white working-class hysteria, seizing on latent but powerful hostilities to bourgeois society as to set loose the uncontrollable and disordering forces of demagogic fascism.

The other traditional Marxist ways of looking at racism belong more in the realm of political strategy than of theory, but their theory is at least implicit in their practice. One is the perhaps opportunistic approach of targeting members of racial minorities as people already sufficiently aware of their own oppression within capitalist society as to be receptive to radical political ideas. The theory is that one has got to start somewhere if one is committed to radical political change (unless one believes entirely in the inevitable role of impersonal historical forces) and that people already aware of their oppressed status are most likely to form the core of an emerging radical political consciousness. This theory may even be progressive for those to whom it is addressed to the extent that it creates awareness of and effects some change with respect to racist practices in an era otherwise dominated by complacent racism. But this theory raises a real problem of who is using whom for whose self-conceived ends, and is ultimately counterproductive to the extent that it plays on the historical uniqueness of racism for its appeal but denies that uniqueness in its actual programmatic goals. For if the real goals deny that race and class are separate issues at all, this approach may alienate blacks, who will come to feel used, and create rather than alleviate racial tension.[31]

The final traditional Marxist approach is a version of the immediately preceding one as applied to legal struggles—which is to argue that the legal struggles, backed by mass political movements and demonstrations that have accomplished what progress there has been in civil rights have, in fact, constituted a substantive gain in the class struggle. The problem with this view is that the civil rights program would be achieved if blacks and other minorities were distributed in the American class structure similarly to whites. However elusive this goal has been and is, it does not necessarily threaten class structure generally. Thus, while I do not deny the actual achievements of the legal struggle for civil rights, I do suggest that this view overrates what has been accomplished, again forgets the historical uniqueness of racism by substituting for limited gains in the struggle against racism even limited gains against capitalist class structure generally, and, finally, ignores the possibility that some measure of racial change may well be in the self-interest of the contemporary dominant classes.

Antidiscrimination Law as Legitimation of the Reality and Ideology of Class Society

An adequate contemporary theory of racism must explain both the progressive efforts that have been accepted and the tenacity with which the conditions associated with racism remain in place. Contrary to some of the traditional Marxist views of racism, at least since the 1950s it has been in the interest of America's ruling classes to accept and partially implement a commitment to end racism in this country. The major goals associated with that project have been to hold the United States out as a genuinely equalitarian society that does not condone the racist practices of the past, to avoid embarrassment, and to stabilize the position of the United States in the world. These goals can be regarded as either traditionally economic or as bound up with the role of a state relatively autonomous from the capitalist class in its dealings with both its own oppressed classes and other states in the world arena.[32] Despite the massive struggles underlying the demand for civil rights reform, acceptance of that reform and the shape that it has ultimately taken must be understood in this context.

From this perspective, the goal of civil rights law is to offer a credible measure of tangible progress without in any way disturbing the basic class structure. The more specific version of what would be in the interest of the ruling classes would be to "bourgeoisify" a sufficient number of minority people in order to transform them into active, visible legitimators of the underlying and basically unchanged social structure.

This perspective has important implications for the development of particular strategies for fighting racism, which will only be suggested here. For example, affirmative action runs the risk of being caught up in the process of improving the lot of a small number of middle-class minority people while simultaneously consigning vast numbers of lower-class minority people (who disproportionately populate lower classes already) to a long-term underclass. The underlying theoretical question is not whether racism in all of its continuing manifestations is or is not different from class relationships generally— because it surely is different—but the extent to which anything significant can be done about the concededly unique problem of racism without paying attention to class structure and the forces that maintain it.

Ambiguous in application though consistent in form, the perpetrator perspective, through manipulation of remedy, offered substantial promises of liberation during the Era of Contradiction. As I suggested earlier, a combination of impatience, fear of embarrassment, and the need for some results (rather than none) gave rise to a judicially prompted expectation that incorporated the victim perspective. Is one to regard the subsequent rejection of the victim perspective (which had never been accepted formally) as a mere accident resulting from the fortuitous appointment of the Burger Court, or as symptomatic of a deeper structural problem? While the timing of individual decisions may be regarded as fortuitous, there seems a deep structural explanation for the jurisprudence of rationalization—one that forces a convergence of race and class.

In at least three ways, needs basic to the preservation of the class structure (not "American society" but the particular class relationships characteristic of contemporary American society) compel rejection of the victim perspective. The first is the problem of formal equality, which leads easily to evasion of remedial burdens by the rich, since American law sees no formal differences based on wealth, compounded by the legacy of blatant racism. A remedy that requires change in practical conditions will have some dislocative impact, since wealth or power must be redistributed from someone to someone else. And a regime of formal equality will ensure that the dislocative impact is disproportionately borne by lower-class whites (not to mention blacks, who are burdened either way). The best metaphor and concrete expression of this problem is the rich senators who favor bussing while sending their own kids to fancy private schools. Contemplate a legal response that would require participation of those children in a bussing plan. Measure the gap between that sort of legal response and that which is contained by the limits of legal ideology (think of the abstract universals to be hauled out in opposition—privacy, freedom of association, family autonomy, etc.). To argue that the remedial structure must necessarily overburden the ruling class is to meet the rigor of formal equality, which knows no such concept, and, in the end, necessarily burdens lower classes. This problem leads to hostility and instability, which alone might have been contained with coercive force.

The second way is a basic presupposition of legal ideology and of the existing class structure—the legitimacy of vested rights. The idea that vested rights might be treated as undeserved and therefore taken back directly (rather than through taxation, which is sufficiently manipulable to be nonthreatening) was probably too dangerous to be let out of confinement for very long.

The perpetrator perspective does not threaten vested rights, since it presupposes the innocence of those not directly implicated and the legitimacy of positions of advantage previously obtained. The victim perspective, by focusing on conditions rather than conduct, and on society rather than individuals, threatens the legitimacy of vested rights while tarnishing the "innocence" of their holders.

The principle of "no retroactivity" or "protection of expectations" is central to protecting and insulating vested rights, with exceptions requiring the most extraordinary justification (as, for example, where the principle could be violated to serve capitalism).[33] The Era of Contradiction exerted great pressure on the ideology of vestedness, though it pretended to be dealing with perpetrators. But a full-fledged adoption of the victim perspective destroys the presupposition of legitimacy of vested rights. All positions of advantage became potentially illegitimate. Formal equality ensures that the positions of advantage belonging to lower classes will be sacrificed first (and the process will likely go no further) but at risk to the legitimacy of the social structure. By reasserting its requirements of causation and individual responsibility, the perpetrator perspective reestablished the presupposition of legitimacy with respect to vested rights.

The third structural feature protected by the perpetrator perspective is the myth of equality of opportunity. Equality of opportunity is presented as both a description and a transcendent ideal. It incorporates the twin universals of personal desert (self-fulfillment) and societal advantage (maximize the product). In either form, with its two universals, it presupposes a world of atomistic individuals, without a class structure, and an objective, transcendent notion of merit or qualification. However much one debunks the lived reality of this myth (and great supportive forces operate to make up for its weaknesses—e.g., concepts of luck or fate), I suggest that equality of opportunity is neither a description nor an ideal but an institutional ideology—an ideology that is the major rationalization of class domination in this country. Central to its effectiveness is the lived, internalized experience of lower class status as personal failure, as lack of ability.[34] For this ideology to remain effective, there must be a credible, objective, positivist notion of "qualification."

But how can an ideology that serves to rationalize a system of class domination be expected to function as if it were an ideal? One discovers a gap so wide between the idea of equality of opportunity and its practical realization as to debunk it as a practice, unless the idea of "merit" works to legitimize class relationships. The *Griggs* case was the most radical case of the Era of Contradiction insofar as it dropped the presupposition that equality of opportunity was, in fact, working in the case of tests (which are both a concrete expression and the most powerful metaphor of meritocracy). *Griggs* demanded no more than that equality of opportunity be demonstrated as working in its own terms—that people who could do things best were actually being chosen to do them.

The scrutiny of testing opened up by this radical doctrine leads one to discover that tests are either irrational or meaningless (in that they correlate best with other tests but rarely with the underlying task for which the prediction is being made, assuming the remote possibility that the underlying task can be satisfactorily "measured" or "quantified"); or to discover that tests can be regarded as rational if perceived as an intergenerational device for class cloning. To discover the latter is to perceive equality of opportunity as ideology, and to perceive once again a purportedly objective social structure as reflecting the narrower interest of dominant classes. All of this is reinforced if one pursues the history and origins of testing in the United States and the continuing politics of "intelligence."[35]

The more that civil rights law threatened the "system" of equality or opportunity, which threat was essential to the production of victim-perspective results, the more it threatened to expose and delegitimize the relative situation of lower-class whites. The response of the Era of Rationalization was to restore, with *Washington* v. *Davis*, the protective insulation of presupposition around testing, to facilitate a return to the basic outlook of equality of opportunity—"blaming the victim." The spirit of the current period is to maintain the appearance of remedial effort while securing the hegemony of crucial presuppositions. In this context, the movement for "effective education," however pragmatic the impulse behind it, operates to place responsibility on "victims" while presupposing a structure of equality of opportunity ready to receive them. Similarly, I perceive academic efforts to denounce the worth of bussing, extol segregated schools as representative of "American pluralism," and recast the issue of *Brown* as never having had to do with anything but the measurable "effectiveness" of education, as, however sincerely offered, a structural part of the same process of rationalization represented by the recent Supreme Court cases.

To achieve the kind of massive results demanded by the victim perspective requires suspension of the equality-of-opportunity ideology for a time sufficient to bourgeoisify vast numbers of black people while maintaining that ideology simultaneously for everyone else lest the legitimacy of the entire class structure be threatened. To avoid the potential for instability in continuing such a course of action, legal ideology had to reject the victim perspective. The present goal would seem to be to legitimize the accomplishments of civil rights law by emphasizing and displaying a small but successful black middle class, and by seeking to gain its allegiance while ignoring the victim-perspective claims of the vast and disproportionate numbers of poor and unemployed black people.

Thus, despite the uniqueness of race as a historical problem of oppression, it cannot be remedied alone unless one is willing to accept nothing more than token bourgeoisification within the structure of a presupposed system of equality of opportunity—in short, one must become part of the legitimation process. To challenge that limited view is to tackle the pretense of equality of opportunity directly, to see it for what it is in relation to class structure.

NOTES

1. Brown v. Board of Education, 347 U.S. 483 (1954).
2. *See, e.g.,* Derrick A. Bell, Jr., *Race, Racism and American Law,* 2d ed. (Boston: Little, Brown, 1980).
3. Milliken v. Bradley, 418 U.S. 717 (1974); Pasadena City Board of Education v. Spangler, 427 U.S. 424 (1976); Beer v. United States, 425 U.S. 130 (1976); International Brotherhood of Teamsters v. United States, 431 U.S. 324 (1977); Washington v. Davis, 426 U.S. 229 (1976); Warth v. Seldin, 422 U.S. 490 (1975); Village of Arlington Heights v. Metropolitan Housing Development Corporation, 429 U.S. 252 (1977).
4. *See* Bell, *supra* note 2, at 37, 38.
5. Regents of the University of California v. Bakke, 438 U.S. 265 (1978).
6. *See* Bell, *supra* note 2, at 7, 8.
7. *See generally* William Ryan, *Blaming the Victim* (New York: Pantheon Books, 1976). *See also* Herbert G. Gutman, *The Black Family in Slavery and Freedom, 1750–1925* (New York: Pantheon Books, 1976), pp. xvii–xxii.
8. 418 U.S. 717 (1974).
9. Charles L. Black, Jr., "The Lawfulness of the Segregation Decisions," 69 *Yale Law Journal* 421 (1960); *accord,* Edmond Cahn, "Jurisprudence," 30 *New York University Law Review* 150, 159, 160 (1955).
10. Plessy v. Ferguson, 163 U.S. 537, 559 (Harlan, J., dissenting).
11. The public image of *Bakke* is one of a case that merely outlawed "bad" quotas while leaving intact the idea of voluntary affirmative-action programs that take race into account in admissions decision making. *See, e.g.,* Jerrold K. Footlick and Diane Camper, "New Issues for the Court," *Newsweek,* October 9, 1978, p. 54. The formal theory of Justice Powell's opinion is much more hostile to affirmative-action programs, invoking the most rigid rhetoric of color-blindness and explicitly rejecting the idea that race may be employed in admissions decisions for reasons having anything to do with securing racial justice or remedying racial discrimination (unless, of course, one has identified the increasingly elusive "violation"). *See* 438 U.S. at 288–315.

     The practical impact of the decision may, however, permit voluntary action to achieve results not unlike those struck down in *Bakke* while ensuring that strife and cost will precede the achievement of even minimal results. The decision does permit schools to make admissions decisions that take race into account so long as those decisions are part of a "diversity" program that is not designed (at least in theory) to promote racial justice and that treats race as equivalent to attributes like being a "farm boy for

Idaho." *See* 438 U.S. 323 (appendix). Such a program can benefit minority students if a faculty possesses sufficient will and concern to renew formally its commitment to such results through adoption of an "acceptable" program, to tolerate a more complex general admissions process, and to risk litigation.

12. *See* Robert Carter, "A Reassessment of *Brown v. Board*," *Shades of Brown*, ed. Derrick Bell (New York: Teachers College Press, Columbia University, 1980).

13. 380 U.S. 202 (1965).

14. Green v. County School Board, 319 U.S. 430 (1968); Monroe v. Board of Commissioners, 391 U.S. 450 (1968); Swann v. Charlotte-Mecklenburg Board of Education, 402 U.S. 1 (1971); Wright v. Council of Emporia, 407 U.S. 451 (1972); Keyes v. School District No. 1, 413 U.S. 189 (1973). For a discussion of the school cases, *see* Owen M. Fiss, "School Desegregation: The Uncertain Path of the Law," 4 *Philosophy & Public Affairs* 3, 15–35 (1974). I am indebted to the analysis in this discussion.

15. 402 U.S. 1 (1971).

16. Quoted in Richard Kluger, *Simple Justice* (New York: Alfred A. Knopf, 1976), p. 572.

17. *See, e.g.*, Swann v. Charlotte-Mecklenburg Board of Education, 402 U.S. 1 (1970); Keyes v. School District No. 1, 413 U.S. 189 (1973).

18. 401 U.S. 424 (1971).

19. *See, e.g.*, International Brotherhood of Teamsters v. United States, 431 U.S. 324, 348–55 (1977); General Electric Company v. Gilbert, 429 U.S. 125, 137–46 (1976); Washington v. Davis, 426 U.S. 229, 238–39, 248–52 (1976).

20. An exception has been made in the area of jury discrimination on the ground that unrepresentative juries compromise the legitimacy of the judicial process. *See* Duren v. Missouri, 439 U.S. 357 (1979); Taylor v. Louisiana, 419 U.S. 522 (1975).

21. The principal case is Washington v. Davis, 426 U.S. 229 (1976). Its counterpart in legal scholarship is Paul Brest, "The Supreme Court, 1975 Term—Foreword: In Defense of the Antidiscrimination Principle," 90 *Harvard Law Review* 1 (1976).

22. *See* Milliken v. Bradley, 433 U.S. 267 (1977) (Milliken II).

23. *See* United Jewish Organizations v. Carey, 430 U.S. 144 (1977); Weber v. Kaiser Aluminum and Chemical Corporation, 433 U.S. 193 (1979); Fullilove v. Klutznick, 448 U.S. 448 (1980).

24. *See* note 11, *supra*.

25. 426 U.S. 229 (1976).

26. *See, e.g.*, Pasadena City Board of Education v. Spangler, 427 U.S. 424 (1976); City of Mobile v. Bolden, 64 L. Ed. 2d 47 (1980); International Brotherhood of Teamsters v. United States, 431 U.S. 324 (1977).

27. For a general discussion, *see* Richard C. Edwards, Michael Reich, and Thomas E. Weisskopf, *The Capitalist System* (Englewood Cliffs, N.J.: Prentice Hall, 1972), pp. 287–321. *See also* David M. Gordon, *Problems in Political Economy: An Urban Perspective* (Lexington, Mass.: D.C. Heath, 1977), pp. 143–205.

28. For a sensitive critique of theories that merely collapse race into class, *see* Eugene D. Genovese, "Class and Nationality in Black America," *In Red and Black* (New York: Pantheon Books, 1971), pp. 55–72.

29. For a general discussion of the tensions between accumulation and legitimation, *see* James R. O'Connor, *The Fiscal Crisis of the State* (New York: St. Martin's Press, 1973).

30. For a discussion that relies on a number of explanatory factors, including this one, *see* Paul A. Baran and Paul M. Sweezy, *Monopoly Capital* (New York: Monthly Review Press, 1966), pp. 249–80.

31. For some critical views, *see* Harold Cruse, "Behind the Black Power Slogan," *Rebellion or Revolution?* (New York: William Morrow, 1968), pp. 193–258.

32. *Cf.* Fred Block, "The Ruling Class Does Not Rule: Notes on the Marxist

Theory of the State," *Socialist Revolution* (now *Socialist Review*), no. 33 (May/June 1977): 6–28. *See also* Theda Skocpol, *States and Social Revolutions* (New York: Cambridge University Press, 1979), pp. 14–33.

33.   *See, e.g.,* Home Building & Loan Company v. Blaisdell, 290 U.S. 398 (1934) (upholding moratorium on mortgage foreclosure during the Depression).

34.   For an exceptional treatment of this subject, *see* Richard Sennett and Jonathan Cobb, *The Hidden Injuries of Class* (New York: Alfred A. Knopf, 1973).

35.   *See, e.g.,* Stephen Jay Gould, *Ever Since Darwin* (New York: W. W. Norton, 1977), pp. 243–7; David B. Tyack, *The One Best System* (Cambridge, Mass.: Harvard University Press, 1974); Samuel Bowles and Herbert Gintis, "I.Q. in the U.S. Class Structure," *Social Policy*, nos. 4 and 5 (November/December 1972 and January/February 1973): 65–96.

6 PERSPECTIVES ON WOMEN'S SUBORDINATION AND THE ROLE OF LAW

Nadine Taub and Elizabeth M. Schneider

The Anglo-American legal tradition purports to value equality, by which it means, at a minimum, equal application of the law to all persons. Nevertheless, throughout this country's history, women have been denied the most basic rights of citizenship, allowed only limited participation in the marketplace, and otherwise denied access to power, dignity, and respect. Women have instead been largely occupied with providing the personal and household services necessary to sustain family life.

The work women perform in the domestic sphere is barely acknowledged, let alone valued. Institutional arrangements that preclude women's economic and sexual autonomy ensure that this work will be done primarily by women. Often, though not always, these institutions are expressed in legal form.

This chapter explores two aspects of the law's role in maintaining women in an inferior status. It first considers the way the law has furthered male dominance by explicitly excluding women from the public sphere and by refusing to regulate the domestic sphere to which they are thus confined. It then examines the way the law has legitimized sex discrimination through the articulation of an ideology that

The authors gratefully acknowledge the assistance of Ann Freedman, Associate Professor of Law, Rutgers Law School, Camden, New Jersey, in the development of this article.

117

justifies differential treatment on the basis of perceived differences
between men and women.

THE LEGAL ORDER AND THE
PUBLIC/PRIVATE SPLIT

Excluded in the past from the public sphere of marketplace and government, women have been consigned to a private realm to carry on
their primary responsibilities, *i.e.*, bearing and rearing children, and
providing men with a refuge from the pressures of the capitalist world.
This separation of society into the male public sphere and the female
private sphere was most pronounced during the nineteenth century,
when production moved out of the home.[1] But even today, women's
opportunities in the public sphere are limited by their obligations in
the private domestic sphere.

　　Men dominate both the public sphere and the private sphere. Male
control in the public sphere has often been consolidated explicitly by
legal means. The law, however, is in large part absent from the private
sphere, and that absence[2] itself has contributed to male dominance and
female subservience. In discussing the role of law in relation to this
public/private split, this section first reviews the legal means by which
women have been excluded from the public sphere, and then considers
the law's absence from the private sphere and how that absence fur-
thers male dominance.[3]

Legal Exclusion from the Public Sphere

The most obvious exclusion of women from public life was the denial
of the franchise. Although in colonial times unmarried, propertied
women were technically entitled to vote on local issues, all state constitutions that were adopted after the War of Independence, with the
temporary exception of New Jersey's, barred women from voting.
This initial exclusion gained even greater significance in the 1820s and
1830s, when the franchise was extended to virtually every white male
regardless of property holdings. Even after the Civil War, when black
men gained the right to vote, women of all races continued to be
denied the ballot. The Nineteenth Amendment, giving women the
vote, finally became law in 1920 after what has been described as "a
century of struggle."[4]

　　The amendment's passage, however, did not mean that women
were automatically accorded the rights and duties that generally ac-

companied elector status. For example, the exclusion of women from jury duty was upheld as late as 1961, when the Supreme Court explicitly rejected the equal-protection claim of a woman accused of murdering her husband. The Court found Florida's exclusion of women who did not voluntarily register for jury service "reasonable," since:

Despite the enlightened emancipation of women from the restrictions and protections of bygone years, and their entry into many parts of community life formerly considered to be reserved to men, woman is still regarded as the center of home and family life.[5]

Even today, women are excluded from what is viewed as a crucial test of citizenship—armed combat duty.[6] As a result, women who wish to participate on an equal basis in the military cannot do so. Moreover, because combat exclusion is used to justify an all-male draft registration system,[7] women are also exempted from the fundamental responsibility of deciding whether to join or resist their country's military efforts.

Women have likewise been excluded from full participation in the economy. Under English common law, not only were they barred from certain professions (such as law), but, once married, they were reduced to legal nonentities unable to sell, sue, or contract without the approval of their husbands or other male relatives.[8] Although these disabilities were initially rigidified by codification of laws, which began in the 1820s, they were gradually lifted in the middle and latter part of the nineteenth century. Starting in the 1840s, various states passed laws that gave women the right to hold certain property in their own name. Subsequent legislation, enacted over the following half-century, afforded them the right to conduct business and retain their own earnings. The enactments were, however, repeatedly subjected to restrictive judicial interpretations that continued to confirm male dominance in business matters.

Even as women moved into the paid labor force,[9] they were limited in their work opportunities and earning power by the ideological glorification of their domestic role reflected in the law. Women have been consistently excluded from certain occupational choices and denied equal earning power by statute and other governmental action.[10] Such explicit exclusions persist today despite the promise of equal treatment contained in the Fourteenth Amendment and affirmative antidiscrimination legislation enacted in the 1960s and 1970s.[11] For example, in 1977 the Supreme Court found it legal to deny women jobs as guards in maximum-security prisons on the ground that the very presence of women would prompt sexual assaults.[12] In so holding, the

Court simply ignored the fact that all guards are subject to assault by virtue of being guards and that a prison relies on the threat of future sanctions to maintain order. Women have also been and continue to be excluded from educational opportunities requisite to participation on an equal basis with men in the economy. As late as 1977, the Supreme Court upheld without opinion an appellate court decision finding that Philadelphia's two sex-segregated elite high schools were separate but essentially equal and that Philadelphia did not deny females equal protection by maintaining the dual schools.[13] Post–New Deal social-welfare legislation has likewise imposed barriers to women's participation in the public sphere. Reflecting and reinforcing the assumption that men are breadwinners and women are homemakers, Social Security legislation has denied female workers fringe benefits available to male workers.[14] Based on the same assumption, welfare and job programs have given men priorities in job placement and job training, with the result that women seeking work have been forced to stand by and watch the most desirable positions go to men.[15]

Legislation denying women the right to determine whether and when they will bear children has also served to exclude women from the public sphere. Beginning in the 1870s, legislative restrictions began to reinforce and supplement existing religious and cultural constraints on birth control. The Comstock Law forbidding obscene material (expressly including contraceptive devices) in the United States mail was invalidated in 1938,[16] while the Supreme Court did not invalidate state restrictions on the marital use of contraceptives until 1965[17] and their distribution to single persons until 1972.[18] Similarly, in the middle and late nineteenth century, most states enacted criminal statutes against abortion, although the procedure, at least in the pre-"quickening" stage, had not been a crime at the common law.[19] While a number of these statutes were liberalized in the 1960s, criminal sanctions remained in force until they were invalidated by the 1973 Supreme Court decisions.[20] Since then, provisions have been upheld that exclude abortion from Medicaid coverage and require the parents of many minors to be notified.[21]

Many nongovernmental practices also help to exclude women from the public sphere. Commercial concerns have refused women credit and work; trade unions and professional associations have excluded women from skilled employment; public accommodations and business clubs have denied women entrance. Only very recently and very incompletely have governments acted to remedy this discrimination.[22] As the introduction to this book points out, in distinguishing only between governmental and nongovermental agencies, and ignoring distinctions based on power, the law has tolerated and tacitly approved discriminatory conduct by a variety of powerful institutions.

The Absence of Law in the Private Sphere

While sex-based exclusionary laws have joined with other institutional and ideological constraints to directly limit women's participation in the public sphere, the legal order has operated more subtly in relation to the private sphere to which women have been relegated. On the one hand, the legal constraints against women retaining their earnings and conveying property—whose remnants endured well into the twentieth century—meant that married women could have legal relations with the outside world only through their husbands. In this sense, the law may be viewed as directing male domination in the private sphere. On the other hand, the law has been conspicuously absent from the private sphere itself. Despite the fundamental similarity of conflicts in the private sphere to legally cognizable disputes in the public sphere, the law generally refuses to interfere in ongoing family relationships. For example, the essence of the marital relation as a legal matter is the exchange of the man's obligation to support the women for her household and sexual services. Yet contract law, which purports to enforce promissory obligations between individuals, is not available during the marriage to enforce either the underlying support obligation or other agreements by the parties to a marriage to matters not involving property. A woman whose husband squanders or gives away assets during the marriage cannot even get an accounting. And while premarital property agreements will be enforced on divorce, courts' enormous discretion in awarding support and distributing property makes it highly unlikely that these decisions will reflect the parties' conduct during the marriage in regard to either the underlying support obligation or other agreements. It is as if in regulating the beginning and the end of a business partnership the law disregarded the events that transpired during the partnership and refused to enforce any agreements between the partners as to how they would behave.[23]

Similarly, tort law, which is generally concerned with injuries inflicted on individuals, has traditionally been held inapplicable to injuries inflicted by one family member on another. Under the doctrines of interspousal and parent-child immunity, courts have consistently refused to allow recoveries for injuries that would be compensable but for the fact that they occurred in the private realm.[24] In the same way, criminal law fails to punish intentional injuries to family members. Common law and statutory definitions of rape in most states continue to carve out a special exception for a husband's forced intercourse with his wife. Wife beating was initially omitted from the definition of criminal assault on the ground that a husband had the right to chastise his wife. Even today, after courts have explicitly rejected the definitional exception and its rationale, judges, prose-

cutors, and police officers decline to enforce assault laws in the family
context.[25]

The state's failure to regulate the domestic sphere is now often
justified on the ground that the law should not interfere with emotional relationships involved in the family realm because it is too heavy-
handed. Indeed, the recognition of a familial privacy right in the early
twentieth century[26] has given this rationale a constitutional dimension.
The importance of this concern, however, is undercut by the fact that
the same result was previously justified by legal fictions, such as the
woman's civil death on marriage. More importantly, the argument
misconstrues the point at which the law is invoked. Legal relief is
sought when family harmony has already been disrupted. Family
members, like business associates, can be expected to forego legal
claims until they are convinced that harmonious relations are no longer
possible. Equally important, the argument reflects and reinforces powerful myths about the nature of family relations. It is not true that
women perform personal and household services purely for love. The
family is the locus of fundamental economic exchanges, as well as
important emotional ties.

Isolating women in a sphere divorced from the legal order contributes directly to their inferior status by denying them the legal
relief that they seek to improve their situations and by sanctioning
conduct of the men who control their lives. For example, when the
police do not respond to a battered woman's call for assistance or when
a civil court refuses to evict her husband, the woman is relegated to
self-help, while the man who beats her receives the law's tacit encouragement. When the law does not allow for wage attachments or other
standard collection devices to be used to enforce orders for child
support, it leaves women in desperate financial straits.

But beyond its direct, instrumental impact, the insulation of
women's world from the legal order also conveys an important ideological message to the rest of society. Although this need not be the case
in all societies, in our society the law's absence devalues women and
their functions: women simply are not sufficiently important to merit
legal regulation. This message is clearly communicated when particular
relief is withheld. By declining to punish a man for inflicting injuries
on his wife, for example, the law implies she is his property and he is
free to control her as he sees fit. Women's work is discredited when
the law refuses to enforce the man's obligation to support his wife,
since it implies she makes no contribution worthy of support. Similarly, when courts decline to enforce contacts that seek to limit or
specify the extent of the wife's services, the law implies that household
work is not real work in the way that the type of work subject to

contract in the public sphere is real work. These are important messages, for denying woman's humanity and the value of her traditional work are key ideological components in maintaining woman's subordinate status. The message of women's inferiority is compounded by the totality of the law's absence from the private realm. In our society, law is for business and other important things. The fact that the law in general has so little bearing on women's day-to-day concerns reflects and underscores their insignificance. Thus, the legal order's overall contribution to the devaluation of women is greater than the sum of the negative messages conveyed by individual legal doctrines.

Finally, isolating women in a world where the law refuses to intrude further obscures the discrepancy between women's actual situation and our nominal commitment to equality. Like other collective ideals, the equality norm is expressed predominantly in legal form. Because the law as a whole is removed from women's world, the equality norm is perceived as having very limited application to women. In this way, people are encouraged to favor equality in the public sphere of government and business (e.g., "equal pay for equal work") while denigrating the need for any real change in social roles ("I'm not a woman's libber"). The law can thus purport to guarantee equality while simultaneously denying it.

In short, the law plays a powerful role, though certainly not an exclusive role, in shaping and maintaining women's subordination. The law has operated directly and explicitly to prevent women from attaining self-support and influence in the public sphere, thereby reinforcing their dependence on men. At the same time, its continued absence from the private sphere to which women are relegated not only leaves individual women without formal remedies but also devalues and discredits them as a group.

Acknowledging that the public/private split currently promotes male dominance is very different from suggesting that no division between the public and private is ever acceptable. While the concern that a rigid system of legal rights and wrongs will stifle feelings is a real one, a key aspect of women's present subordinate status is the failure to recognize work now performed in the domestic sphere as a real economic contribution rather than a spontaneous and gratuitous product of emotion. Our limited understanding of patriarchal relations makes it difficult to foresee the precise institutional arrangements, and thus the legal formulations, that will mark the end of male dominance; but it is apparent that the value of "women's work" will have to be acknowledged in a fundamental sense. Much of this work will most likely move out of the home. Consequently, a large portion of the activity that now takes place in the private sphere should come to be governed by law to the same extent as activities already located in the public sphere.

Delineating the extent of human relationships and activities that should ultimately escape collective judgments and prescribing the degree to which the "personal" and the "human" should be reserved to a special private realm is even more difficult. In other areas of the law, it has been argued that there is a continued role for organized institutional political power in the quest for human freedom and that law may enhance, rather than stifle, self-realization.[27] The recognition that immunizing the family realm has thus far reinforced women's identity as man's property and obscured her subordination should spur our efforts to explore this possibility.

THE LEGAL IDEOLOGY OF SEXUAL INEQUALITY

As we have seen, the law has enforced male dominance through its direct impact on the lives of individual women and men, and its symbolic devaluation of women and their functions. The law has also perpetuated inequality through the articulation of an ideology that camouflages the fundamental injustice of existing sexual relations. Because the law purports to be the embodiment of justice, morality, and fairness, it is particularly effective in performing this ideological function.

Historically, women's subservient status has been associated with a view of differences between the sexes and differential legal treatment. A succession of Supreme Court decisions[28] has legitimized that subservient status by upholding laws which, on their face, mandate that the sexes be treated differently. This section examines the principal doctrinal bases used by the Court by focusing on three illustrative Supreme Court decisions.[29] In an 1873 decision, differences between men and women were expressed in terms of gross overgeneralizations reflecting moral or religious views of women's nature and proper role. The ideology masked women's inferior treatment by glorifying women's separate role. In 1908, the differences focused to a much greater extent on the "facts" of women's physical limitations necessitated by their reproductive functions and their consequent dependence on men. These deficiencies called for special treatment for women to be on an equal footing with men. Present-day ideology is even more subtle. The Supreme Court espouses a concern for sexual equality and purports to reject stereotypical overgeneralizations about the sexes; yet it refuses to recognize classifications based on reproductive capacity as sex-based, and it regards legal and social disabilities that have been imposed on women as realistic differences sufficient to justify differential treatment. By continuing to make differential treatment appear fair, the current Court provides a rationale for present inequalities.

Women's "Separate Sphere": Bradwell v. Illinois

In *Bradwell* v. *Illinois*,[30] the Supreme Court upheld the Illinois Supreme Court's decision to refuse Myra Bradwell admission to the Illinois bar because she was a woman.[31] She studied law under her husband's tutelage; raised four children; ran a private school; was involved in civic work; and founded a weekly newspaper, the *Chicago Legal News*, which became an important legal publication. A feminist active in women's suffrage organizations, Myra Bradwell played an important role in obtaining Illinois legislation that removed women's legal disabilities. She took her case to the Supreme Court, arguing that admission to practice law was guaranteed by the privileges and immunities clause of the recently adopted Fourteenth Amendment.

The *Bradwell* litigation took place within the context of a particular conception of sex roles. Although women were in no way the equals of men during the colonial and Revolutionary periods, the nature of their subordination, particularly in the middle classes, changed dramatically between the end of the eighteenth century and the middle of the nineteenth century.[32] The early stages of industrial capitalism involved increasing specialization and the movement of production out of the home, which resulted in heightened sex segregation. Men went out of the house to work; and women's work, influence, and consciousness remained focused at home. Although women continued to be dependent on and subservient to men, women were no longer placed at the bottom of a hierarchy dominated by men. Rather, they came to occupy women's "separate sphere," a qualitatively different world centered on home and family. Women's role was by definition incompatible with full participation in society.

"Separate-sphere" ideology clearly delineated the activities open to women. Women's role within the home was glorified, and women's limited participation in paid labor outside the home[33] was most often in work that could be considered an extension of their work within the home. For example, native-born mill girls in the 1820s and 1830s, and immigrant women in the 1840s and 1850s, worked in largely sex-segregated factories manufacturing textiles, clothing, and shoes. Likewise, after a period of time, teaching became a woman's occupation. Unpaid charitable and welfare activities, however, were encouraged as consistent with women's domestic responsibilities.

Although ultimately quite constraining, the development of

women's separate sphere had some important benefits. While the
emphasis on women's moral purity and the cult of domesticity tended
to mask women's inferior position, it also allowed women a certain
degree of autonomy. It gave them the opportunity to organize exten-
sively into religious and secular welfare associations, afforded access to
education, and provided them with a basis for uniting with other
women. Evaluations of the cult of domesticity and women's separate
sphere by feminist historians have consequently ranged from the view
that women were victims of this ideology to the recognition that
women found a source of strength and identity in their separate
world.[34]

The development of separate-sphere ideology appears in large
measure to have been a consequence of changes in the conditions of
production. Behavior was then further channeled by a vast cultural
transformation promoted through books and magazines. The law does
not seem to have played an overt role in the initial articulation of the
separate-sphere ideology; but to the extent that the ideological transformation that occurred in the early part of the nineteenth century
was a reaction to a strict hierarchy imposed by the previous legal
order, the legal system may well have played an important part at the
outset.

In any event, the law appears to have contributed significantly
to the perpetuation of this ideology. Immediately following the Civil
War, feminists attempted to have women expressly included in the
protections of the Fourteenth and Fifteenth Amendments. The failure
of the Fourteenth and Fifteenth Amendments to address the needs
of women, and indeed for the first time to write the word "men"
into the Constitution, resulted in a long-lasting division in the women's
movement, which reflected differences regarding both ends and means,
and which lasted at least until the 1890s. Feminists aligned with the
Republican Party stressed black suffrage and saw women suffrage as
coming through a constitutional amendment at some future time. The
more militant and effective National Woman Suffrage Association
favored legal and political efforts to obtain a judicial or congressional
declaration that the Wartime Amendments also secured rights for
women.[35] Although Myra Bradwell's legal challenge was not known
to be part of an organized strategy, her attempt to use the Fourteenth
Amendment to challenge state prohibitions on occupational choices
legally reflected this tack. By invoking the cult of domesticity as a
legal rationale for rejecting this demand, the courts enshrined and
reinforced separate-sphere ideology while deferring women's rights.

In rejecting Myra Bradwell's challenge to Illinois's prohibition on
occupational choice, the Supreme Court had two options: to construe
the new constitutional guarantees narrowly so as to defeat all comers,

or to find special reasons for treating women differently. The majority adopted the first approach. It held that the decision was controlled by the Court's decision (the day before) in the *Slaughter-House Cases*,[36] which held that, even after the adoption of the Fourteenth Amendment, states retained the unmediated right to regulate occupations.

However, Justice Joseph Bradley, who dissented in *Slaughter-House*, opted for the second approach. His concurring opinion is the embodiment of the separate-sphere ideology:

[T]he civil law as well as nature itself, has always recognized a wide difference in the respective spheres and destinies of man and woman. Man is, or should be woman's protector and defender. The natural and proper timidity and delicacy which belongs to the female sex evidently unfits it for many of the occupations of civil life. . . . The constitution of the family organization, which is founded in the divine ordinance, as well as in the nature of things, indicates the domestic sphere as that which properly belongs to the domain and functions of womanhood. The harmony, not to say identity, of interests and views which belong, or should belong, to the family institution is repugnant to the idea of a woman adopting a distinct and independent career from that of her husband. . . .

It is true that many women are unmarried and not affected by any of the duties, complications, and incapacities arising out of the married state, but these are exceptions to the general rule. The paramount destiny and mission of woman are to fulfill the noble and benign offices of wife and mother. This is the law of the Creator. And the rules of civil society must be adapted to the general constitution of things, and cannot be based upon exceptional cases.[37]

Glorification of women's destiny serves to soften any sense of unfairness in excluding women from the legal profession. Since this "paramount destiny and mission" of women is mandated by "nature," "divine ordinance," and "the law of the Creator," the civil law need not recognize the claims of women who deviate from their proper role. By conceiving of the law as the means of enforcing reality as it "is or should be," Bradley can concede that some women do live apart from men—or even that some women who live with men are capable of functioning in the public domain—without exposing the law as unreasonable.

Women's Physical Differences: *Muller v. Oregon*

In the nineteenth century, the persisting separate-sphere ideology legitimized and reinforced women's marginal and secondary status in the work force. Working women were suspicious, inferior, and immoral. Those women who joined the work force were predominantly single or widowed, and confined to "women's jobs," serving as a reserve supply of cheap labor. The primary identification of women with the home also provided an ideological basis for keeping women out of unions.

With industrialization and urbanization in the late nineteenth century came deplorable work conditions for all workers, which prompted unions and social reformers to press for legislation regulating conditions of work, hours, and wages. By the turn of the century, both sex-neutral and sex-based protective laws had been passed and sustained against legal challenge. Women-only protective laws were enacted with the express support of such reform groups as the National Women's Trade Union League, the General Federation of Women's Clubs, and the National Consumers' League, which merged the energies of wealthy and working women. Although sex-based legislation might have conflicted with suffragists' initial argument that women were entitled to the role because they were fundamentally equal to men, it was entirely consistent with the more expedient position they had adopted in the 1890s, to the effect that women should be given the vote because their special perspective would benefit society.

Protective-labor legislation was countered legally by conservatives who, led by the American Bar Association, revived the natural-law notion of freedom of contract and located it in the due process clause of the Fourteenth Amendment. The effort culminated in *Lochner* v. *New York*,[38] a decision that, in striking down maximum-hour legislation for bakers by relying on the "common understanding" that baking and most other occupations did not endanger health, cast doubt on the validity of all protective legislation.

Advocates of state "protective" legislation for women could take two routes after *Lochner*: one, to displace the "common understanding" in *Lochner* with scientific evidence that all industrial jobs, when performed more than ten hours a day, were dangerous to a worker's health; or two, by arguing that women's need for special protection justified an exception to *Lochner*.[39] In *Muller* v. *Oregon*,[40] the Supreme Court was faced with a challenge to an Oregon statute that prohibited women from working more than ten hours a day in a laundry. The National Consumers' League, which played the major role in the middle- and upper-class reform movement, filed an *amicus* brief, written by Louis Brandeis, Josephine Goldmark, and Florence Kelly,[41] which attempted to combine both approaches. The brief portrayed as common knowledge pseudo-scientific data regarding physical differences between men and women, emphasizing the "bad effects" of long hours on women workers' health, "female functions," childbearing capacity, and job safety, and on the health and welfare of future generations. Adopting the view urged by the *amici*, the Court upheld the challenged legislation:

that woman's physical structure and the performance of maternal functions place her at a disadvantage in the struggle for subsistence is obvious. This is especially true when the burdens of motherhood are upon her. Even when they are not, by abundant testimony of the medical fraternity continuance for a long time on her feet at work, repeating this from day to day, tends to injurious effects upon the body, and as healthy mothers are essential to vigorous offspring, the physical well-being of woman becomes an object of public interest and care in order to preserve the strength and vigor of the race....

Still again history discloses the fact that woman has always been dependent upon man.... As minors, though not to the same extent, she has been looked upon in the courts as needing special care that her rights may be preserved.... Though limitations upon personal and contractual rights may be removed by legislation, there is that in her disposition and habits of life which will generate against a full assertion of these rights. She will still be where some legislation to protect her seems necessary to secure a real equality of right.... Differentiated by these matters from the other sex, she is properly placed in a class by herself, and legislation designed for her protection may be sustained, even when the legislation is not necessary for men and could not be sustained.[42]

Muller expresses a view of women as different from and more limited than men because of their "physical structure" and "natural functions." Although this view of women is every bit as fixed as that expressed in *Bradwell*, it purports to be grounded in physical fact. Legal reforms, such as the removal of "limitations upon personal and contractual rights," would be ineffective in changing women's rights because of women's "disposition and habits of life." These differences in physical structure and childbearing capacity are thus sufficient for women to be "properly placed in a class by themselves." Women's primary function as mother is now seen as physically incompatible with the demands of equal participation in the work force. Special work conditions for women are therefore justified.

Both social reformers and legal realists regarded the statute's survival and the Supreme Court's recognition of economic and social facts as important victories. However, as organized labor lost interest in protective legislation for men, the primary legal legacy of *Muller* was a view of women that justified excluding women from job opportunities and earning levels available to men.[43] The Court's focus on the apparently immutable facts of women's physique obscured the exploitation of workers generally and the social discrimination that assigned full-time responsibility for the household to women. As an ideological matter, the notion that women's different physiology requires special protection continues to legitimize a division of labor in which men are primary wage earners entitled to draw on the personal services of their wives, and women remain marginal workers available to replace more expensive male workers.[44]

Unequal Equal Protection: *Michael M.* v. *Sonoma County*

Although Supreme Court opinions of the 1960s began to acknowledge some changes in woman's position,[45] it took the rebirth of an active women's movement in the 1960s and the development of a legal arm to obtain a definitive legal determination that sex-based discrimination violated the equal-protection clause of the Fourteenth Amendment. In 1971, the Supreme Court, in *Reed* v. *Reed*,[46] for the first time invalidated a statute on the ground that it denied women equal protection. The Court unanimously struck down an Idaho statute preferring males to females in the performance of estate administration, refusing to find generalizations about women's business experience adequate to sustain the preference. Although the actual dispute involved a relatively trivial duty, a statute that already had been repealed, and facts that presented no major threat to the established social order, the opinion appeared to voice a view of women that seemed radically different from previous judicial expressions.

Equal protection rests on the legal principle that people who are similarly situated in fact must be similarly treated by the law.[47] In *Reed* the Court for the first time held that women and men are similarly situated. The Court recognized the social reality, through "judicial notice," that "in this country, presumably due to the greater longevity of women, a large proportion of estates . . . are administered by women."[48] By recognizing a departure from traditional social roles as so obvious as to be able to rely on judicial notice, the Court appeared to presage the erosion of the "differences" ideology.

Over the last ten years, in upholding equal-protection challenges to sex-based legislation, the Supreme Court has repeatedly rejected overgeneralizations based on sex.[49] For example, in *Frontiero* v. *Richardson*,[50] the Court upheld an equal-protection challenge to the military's policy of denying dependency benefits to male dependents of female servicewomen. The plurality opinion criticized *Bradwell* as reflective of an attitude of "romantic paternalism" that "in practical effect, put women not on a pedestal but in a cage."[51] Similarly, in *Stanton* v. *Stanton*,[52] the Court upheld an equal-protection challenge to a state statute specifying a greater age of majority for males than females with respect to parental obligation for support. In so doing, the Court appeared to understand the effect of stereotypes in perpetuating discrimination and the detrimental impact that differential treatment has on women's situation.[53]

However, the Supreme Court's developing application of equal protection has not lived up to its initial promise. The Court has adopted a lower standard of review for sex-based classifications[54] than for race-based classifications, reflecting its view that race discrimination is a more serious social problem than sex discrimination. The Court has rejected only those stereotypes that it perceives as grossly inaccurate. Indeed, the Court has developed a new and more subtle view of "realistically based differences," which encompasses underlying physical distinctions between the sexes, distinctions created by law, and socially imposed differences in situation, and frequently confuses the three. In these cases, the Court simply reasons that equal protection is not violated because men and women are not "similarly situated."

The paradigmatic physical distinction between the sexes, women's reproductive capacity, has been consistently viewed by courts as a proper basis for differential treatment. The present Court does so by refusing to recognize that classifications based on pregnancy involve sex discrimination and by ignoring the similarities between pregnancy and other temporary disabilities. In *Geduldig* v. *Aiello*,[55] the Supreme Court rejected an equal-protection challenge to California's disability insurance system, which paid benefits to persons in private employment who were unable to work but excluded from coverage disabilities resulting from pregnancy. The Court noted that

[w]hile it is true that only women become pregnant, it does not follow that every legislative classification concerning pregnancy is a sex-based classification like those considered in *Reed*, *supra* and *Frontiero*, *supra*. Normal pregnancy is an objectively identifiable physical condition with unique characteristics. Absent a showing that distinctions involving pregnancy are mere pretexts designed to effect an invidious discrimination against the members of one sex or the other, lawmakers are constitutionally free to include or exclude pregnancy from the coverage of legislation such as this on any reasonable basis, just as with respect to any other physical condition.[56]

This position was effectively reaffirmed in *General Electric* v. *Gilbert*,[57] in which the exclusion of pregnancy from General Electric's disability program was upheld in the face of a challenge under Title VII of the Civil Rights Act.

Similarly, the present Court finds differential treatment justified by women's special circumstances, even when those circumstances reflect legislatively[58] or socially imposed burdens.[59] In *Parham* v. *Hughes*,[60] a plurality of the Court upheld a Georgia statute that allowed an unwed mother to sue for the wrongful death of her child, but disallowed such suits by an unwed father unless he had procured a court order legitimating the child. The Court found that treating men and women differently in this fashion did not constitute impermissible sex discrimination because the two sets of parents were not similarly situated in two respects. First, under Georgia law, unwed fathers, but not unwed mothers, could legitimate their children by a unilateral act. This difference is, of course, imposed by law, not by biological necessity. Second, the Court pointed to the difficulty in ascertaining the father's identity. Here the difference in situation results primarily from socially imposed differences in child-rearing patterns, since, as a physiological matter, unless the woman is observed giving birth, there is little reason to put more faith in a woman's claim to be a particular child's parent than in a man's claim to be that child's parent. The Court's reliance on these societally imposed differences reflects its present willingness to uphold distinctions that are generally accurate though unfair to individuals and likely to perpetuate existing sex roles.

The most recent expression of the Court's current ideology of equality is a 1981 Supreme Court case, *Michael M.* v. *Sonoma County*,[61] upholding California's statutory rape law, challenged by a seventeen-year-old male, which punished males having sex with a female under eighteen. The thrust of his attack on the statute was that it denied him equal protection since he, not his partner, was criminally liable.

Statutory rape laws have rested historically on the legal fiction that young women are incapable of consent. They exalt female chastity and reflect and reinforce archaic assumptions about the male initiative in sexual relations and the weakness and naïveté of young women.[62] Nevertheless, the Court in *Michael M.* found no violation of equal-protection guarantees and upheld the differential treatment as reasonably related to the goal of eliminating teenage pregnancy.

Although the Court in *Michael M.* cited its prior decisions rejecting sex-based classifications without proof of a "substantial relationship" to "important governmental objectives," it did not, in fact, apply them. No legislative history was produced in California or elsewhere to show that the purpose of the sex-based classification was to eliminate teenage pregnancy. Moreover, the experience of other jurisdictions showed that the criminalization of male, but not female, conduct bore little relation to the goal of eliminating teenage pregnancy. Instead, the Court simply stated that because females become pregnant and because they bear the consequences of pregnancy, "equalization" via differential punishment is reasonable.

We need not be medical doctors to discern that young men and young women are not similarly situated with respect to the problems and risks of sexual intercourse. Only women may become pregnant and they suffer disproportionately the profound physical, emotional and psychological consequences of sexual activity.[63]

Thus, the Court asserts, the sex-based classification, which "serves roughly to 'equalize' the deterrents on the sexes,"[64] realistically reflects the fact that the sexes are not similarly situated.

Justice Potter Stewart's concurring opinion in *Michael M.* develops the crux of this new ideology of realistically based classifications:

The Constitution is violated when government, state or federal, invidiously classifies similarly situated people on the basis of the immutable characteristic with which they were born. . . . [W]hile detrimental gender classifications by government often violate the Constitution, they do not always do so, for the reason that there are differences between males and females that the Constitution necessarily recognizes. In this case we deal with the most basic of these differences: females can become pregnant as the result of sexual intercourse; males cannot. . . .

"[A] State is not free to make overbroad generalizations based on sex which are entirely unrelated to any differences between men and women or which demean the ability or social status of the protected class." Gender-based classifications may not be based upon administrative convenience or upon archaic assumptions about the proper role of the sexes. . . . But we have recognized that in certain narrow circumstances men and women are *not* similarly situated and in these circumstances a gender classification based on clear differences between the sexes is not invidious, and a legislative classification realistically based upon these differences is not unconstitutional. . . .

Applying these principles to the classification enacted by the California legislature, it is readily apparent that [the statute] does not violate the Equal Protection Clause. Young women and men are not similarly situated with respect to the problems and risks associated with intercourse and pregnancy, and the statute is realistically related to the legitimate state purpose of reducing those problems and risks.[65]

Yet, the classification at issue in *Michael M.* had very little to do with biological differences between the sexes. As is seen from the total absence of supportive legislative history, the statute was not designed to address the problem of teenage pregnancy. Moreover, as Justice John Paul Stevens points out, if criminal sanctions are believed to deter the conduct leading to pregnancy, a young woman's greater risk of harm from pregnancy is, if anything, a reason to subject her to sanctions. The statute instead embodies and reinforces the assumption that men are always responsible for initiating sexual intercourse and females must always be protected against their aggression. Nevertheless, the

Court's focus on the physical fact of reproductive capacity serves to obscure the social bases of its decision. Indeed, it is striking that the Court entirely fails to treat pregnancy as sex discrimination when discrimination really is in issue, while using it as a rationale in order to justify differential treatment when it is not in issue.

Like *Bradwell* and *Muller*, *Michael M.* affirms that there are differences between the sexes, both the physical difference of childbearing capacity and women's social role, which should result in differential legal treatment. However, because this affirmation comes at the same time as the Court claims to reject "overbroad generalizations unrelated to differences between men and women or which demean [women's] ability or social status," the Court's approval of differential treatment is especially pernicious. The fact of and harms caused by teenage pregnancy are used by the Court to avoid close analysis of the stereotypes involved and careful scrutiny of the pregnancy rationale. The role that the challenged statute plays in reinforcing those harms is never examined. The Court accepts as immutable fact that men and women are not similarly situated, particularly when pregnancy is involved. The Court then appears to favor equal rights for women, but for one small problem—pregnancy.

As an ideological matter, the separation of pregnancy and childbearing capacity, social discrimination, and even legally imposed discrimination from "invidious" discrimination, in which differential treatment is unrelated to "real" differences between men and women, perform an important function of legitimizing discrimination through the language of equality.[66] Although its doctrinal veneer is different, the Court's current approach has the same effect as *Bradwell* and *Muller*. If both pregnancy and socially imposed differences in role always keep men and women from being similarly situated—thereby excluding sex-based differences from the purview of equal protection —then the real substance of sex discrimination can still be ignored. Childbearing capacity is the single greatest basis of differential treatment for women—it is a major source of discrimination in both work and family life, and the critical distinction on which the ideology of both separate spheres and physical differences rests. Yet, by appearing to reject gross generalizations about proper roles of the sexes exemplified by both *Bradwell* and *Muller*, current ideology attempts to maintain credibility by "holding out the promise of liberation."[67] By emphasizing its reliance on a reality that appears more closely tied to physical differences and the hard facts of social disadvantage, e.g., the consequences of teenage pregnancy for young girls, the Court appears sensible and compromising. Indeed, the message of the Court's approach is merely to reject "ultra feminist" androgyny while favoring equality generally. However, by excluding the core of sex discrimination, the Court is effectively removing women entirely from the reach of equal protection.

This new ideological approach must be viewed, as were *Bradwell* and *Muller*, in its historical context. Although the women's movement provided the triggering change in consciousness, and an understanding of the nature and forms of sex stereotyping on which the sex-discrimination challenges of this period have been based,[68] many of the sex-discrimination cases decided by the Supreme Court have not arisen from feminist struggles and have been presented to the Court by men, not women. As a result, these cases, including *Michael M.*, did not always develop the harm perceived by women for the Court, either as a factual or legal matter. Moreover, in the absence of a sustained mass movement, the Supreme Court has been able to use feminist formulations to justify the status quo. Over the last several years, with the advent of a visible right-wing, anti-feminist, and anti-abortion movement, the women's movement appears to be garnering less public support. Indeed, a strategy of these groups to separate superficial claims for parity, such as equal pay, from more fundamental demands, such as the Equal Rights Amendment and reproductive control, has already had some impact on the women's movement, where issues of reproductive control have not always been viewed as sex discrimination.[69] The Court's new approach tends to strengthen this separation of issues within the women's movement and reward the most conservative tendencies.

Although the legal ideology of equality shows some progression from *Bradwell* to *Michael M.*, there is less than might be expected. Certainly the Court's view of women, and the ways in which it sees the sexes, has moved from an overt view of women's separate roles to a more subtle view of limited differences, but this new view is more dangerous precisely because it appears so reasonable. The Court's perception of differences that suffice to justify discrimination has altered somewhat, but it remains equally fixed. The Court continues to validate inequality by legitimizing differential treatment.

NOTES

1. As David Kairys explains in the introduction to this book, American legal doctrine distinguishes sharply between the public and the private sectors. Focusing on the question of governmental versus private control, the distinction plays an important role in disguising the very limited nature of the rights afforded people in general. A distinction between public and private spheres also characterizes the law relating to women, but in this context

"public" has a much broader and "private" a much narrower meaning. "Public" refers to governmental and market matters, while "private" refers to the domestic or family realm.

2. There is some evidence that during colonial times, when the household was the unit of production, the law intervened more directly in the home. Thus, it may be more appropriate to speak of the law's withdrawal rather than its absence from the domestic sphere.

3. This section draws heavily on Kathryn Powers's article "Sex Segregation and the Ambivalent Directions of Sex Discrimination Law," 1979 *Wisconsin Law Review* 55 (1979).

4. Eleanor Flexner, *A Century of Struggle*, rev. ed. (Cambridge, Mass.: Harvard University Press, 1975).

5. Hoyt v. Florida, 368 U.S. 57, 61 (1961). In Taylor v. Louisiana, 419 U.S. 522 (1975), a case involving a male rape defendant, the Supreme Court tacitly overruled *Hoyt* but avoided the question of equal protection for women, relying instead on the defendant's Sixth Amendment right to a fair trial.

6. 10 U.S.C. §6015; 10 U.S.C. §8549 (Navy and Air Force). The Army and Marine Corps preclude the role of women in combat as a matter of established policy; Rostker v. Goldberg, 101 S. Ct. 2646, 2657 (1981) (upholding the all-male draft registration scheme).

7. *Id.*

8. There is a dispute as to whether women's actual status during the colonial period corresponded to the position accorded them by law. Initial research suggested that women were able, as a practical matter, to function as managers, traders, artisans, and even attorneys. Thus, despite their exclusion from formal political processes, they were granted a basic and integral, though subservient, role in the community. The same research suggested that women's position declined with the growth of commercial capitalism and specialization. Subsequent research, however, argues that women's crucial economic role failed to translate into power and influence, and that sex roles were far more rigidly defined than had been thought. Cf. Mary Ryan, *Womanhood in America*, 2d ed. (New York: New Viewpoints, 1979) and Albie Sachs and Joan Hoff Wilson, *Sexism and the Law* (New York: The Free Press, 1978) *with* Mary Beth Norton, *Liberty's Daughters: The Revolutionary Experience of American Women* (Boston: Little, Brown, 1980).

9. By 1978, 56 percent of all women over sixteen worked at least part of the year, while in 1950 the figure was below 30 percent. Excluding farm workers, before 1900, less than 20 percent of all women were in the paid labor force. Alice Kessler-Harris, *Women Have Always Worked: A Historical Overview* (Old Westbury: The Feminist Press, 1981), pp. 70, 147.

10. *See, e.g.*, the discussion of Myra Bradwell's exclusion from the Illinois bar, and of protective legislation, *infra*.

11. The Equal Pay Act of 1963 and Title VII of the Civil Rights Act of 1964 provided civil remedies for employment discrimination, while private discrimination in the housing and credit markets was prohibited in 1974.

12. *See* Dothard v. Rawlinson, 433 U.S. 321, 336 (1977). *See also* Phillips v. Martin Marietta Corp., 400 U.S. 542 (1971), suggesting that a company could legally deny jobs to women with preschool children if it could show that such children interfered more with female workers as a group than male workers as a group.

13. *See* Vorchheimer v. School District of Philadelphia, 430 U.S. 703 (1977) (affirmed by an equally divided court).
    By contrast, the doctrine of separate but equal was rejected in the racial context in 1954. *See* Brown v. Board of Education, 347 U.S. 483 (1954).

14. *See, e.g.*, Weinberger v. Wiesenfeld, 420 U.S. 636 (1975); Califano v. Goldfarb, 430 U.S. 199 (1977); Califano v. Westcott, 443 U.S. 76 (1979).

15. *See* Barbara A. Babcock et al., *Sex Discrimination and the Law: Causes and Remedies* (Boston: Little, Brown, 1975), pp. 782–800.

16. United States v. Nicholas, 97 F.2d 510 (2d Cir. 1938); *see generally*, Linda Gordon, *Woman's Body, Woman's Right* (New York: Penguin Books, 1977).

17. Griswold v. Connecticut, 381 U.S. 479 (1965).

18. Eisenstadt v. Baird, 405 U.S. 438 (1972).

19. Roe v. Wade, 410 U.S. 113 (1973).

20. *Id.* Doe v. Bolton, 410 U.S. 179 (1973).

21. Maher v. Roe, 432 U.S. 464 (1977); H. L. v. Matheson, 450 U.S. 398 (1981).

22. *See* note 11 *supra.* On the federal level, for example, discrimination on the basis of race but not sex is forbidden by the Civil Rights Act of 1964.

23. *See* Powers, *supra* note 3, at 76, for a similar analogy.

24. Recent limitations on interspousal immunity may be due in part to the recognition of the role played by insurance, a factor that removes the situation from the private sphere and places it in the public realm.

25. The law's absence from the realm of personal relationships is even more conspicuous when the relationships lack official sanction. Lesbians, for example, are not barred from relief by intrafamily immunity doctrines only because the law does not allow them to solemnize or otherwise gain public recognition of their relationship.

26. *See* Meyer v. Nebraska, 262 U.S. 390 (1923); Pierce v. Society of Sisters, 268 U.S. 510 (1925).

27. *See* in particular chapter 4.

28. The Supreme Court is by no means the exclusive source of legal ideology. Indeed, it is arguable that in the area of women's rights, Supreme Court opinions are not the best or most accurate source of prevailing views of women, since few Supreme Court cases prior to 1970 involved assertions of equal rights by women.

29. Much of the material regarding the first two cases has been drawn from Babcock et al., *supra* note 15.

30. Bradwell v. Illinois, 83 U.S. (16 Wall.) 130 (1873).

31. Arabella Mansfield, in Iowa, had become the first woman regularly admitted to practice law in the United States in 1869.

32. *See* Ryan, *supra* note 8; Nancy F. Cott, *The Bonds of Womanhood* (New Haven: Yale University Press, 1977); Kessler-Harris, *supra* note 9.

33. Only about 10 percent of all women worked in the paid labor force in the mid–1840s. The percentage did not rise above 20 percent before 1900. Kessler-Harris, *supra* note 9, at 61, 70.

34. *See* Cott, *supra* note 32, at 197–99.

35. *See generally* Ellen C. DuBois, *Elizabeth Cady Stanton and Susan B. Anthony: Correspondence, Writings and Speeches* (New York: Schocken, 1981).

36. 83 U.S. (16 Wall.) 130 (1873).

37. *Id.* at 141–42.

38. Lochner v. New York, 198 U.S. 45 (1905).

39. Babcock et al., *supra* note 15, at 28.

40. Muller v. Oregon, 208 U.S. 412 (1908).

41. This brief has mistakenly come to be known as the first Brandeis brief, since Louis Brandeis actually filed it, although Josephine Goldmark, Florence Kelly, and other volunteers assembled the data. Babcock et al., *supra* note 15, at 29.

42. Muller v. Oregon, 208 U.S. at 421–22.

43. Sex-based protective legislation was considered valid until a series of court decisions between 1968 and 1973 invalidated such statutes. A few statutes, however, remain on the books today.

44. *See* Heidi Hartmann, "Capitalism, Patriarchy and Job Segregation by Sex," 1 *SIGNS* 137 (1976).

45. *See, e.g.,* Hoyt v. Florida, 368 U.S. 57 (1961).

46.   Reed v. Reed, 404 U.S. 71 (1971).
47.   *See generally* Joseph Tussman and Jacobus TenBroek, "The Equal Pro-
      tection of the Laws," 37 *California Law Review* 341 (1949).
48.   Reed v. Reed, 404 U.S. at 75.
49.   Most of these cases have involved assumptions built into government benefit
      statutes that the male was the breadwinner and the female the dependent at
      home. *See* Frontiero v. Richardson, 411 U.S. 677 (1973); Weinberger v.
      Wiesenfeld, 420 U.S. 636 (1975); Califano v. Goldfarb, 430 U.S. 199 (1977);
      and Califano v. Westcott, 443 U.S. 76 (1979).
50.   Frontiero v. Richardson, 411 U.S. 677 (1973).
51.   *Id.* at 684.
52.   Stanton v. Stanton, 421 U.S. 7 (1975).
53.   *Id.* at 14–15.
54.   In Craig v. Boren, 429 U.S. 190, 197 (1976), the Court articulated the stand-
      ard that "to withstand constitutional challenge, . . . classifications by gender
      must serve important governmental objectives and must be substantially re-
      lated to achievement of those objectives."
55.   Geduldig v. Aiello, 417 U.S. 484 (1974).
56.   *Id.* at 496, n.20.
57.   General Electric v. Gilbert, 429 U.S. 125 (1976). The Supreme Court's view
      of pregnancy expressed in *Gilbert* was promptly rejected by Congress. The
      Pregnancy Discrimination Act, 26 U.S.C. §3304(a) (12) (1976), was passed
      by Congress to overturn the *Gilbert* decision. This suggests that the Supreme
      Court's ideology concerning pregnancy as a permissible basis for differential
      treatment in employment was not widely accepted. It underscores the
      tenuousness of relying on Supreme Court opinions as a source of prevailing
      views on women. *See* note 28 *supra*.
58.   For example, in both Schlesinger v. Ballard, 419 U.S. 498 (1975), and
      Rostker v. Goldberg, 101 S. Ct. 2646, the Supreme Court rejected equal-
      protection challenges to sex discrimination in the military on the grounds
      that since sex-based differential treatment already existed in the military,
      men and women were not "similarly situated" to begin with. In *Rostker*, the
      Court particularly emphasized that since the perpetuation of this differential
      treatment was fully considered by Congress and not "unthinking," it was
      permissible. *Supra* at 2655.
59.   Ironically, despite his actual vote, Justice Potter Stewart's dissent in Caban v.
      Mohammed, 441 U.S. 380, 398 (1979), at least gives lip service to the need
      to differentiate between inherent physical differences and societally im-
      posed differences in roles.
60.   Parham v. Hughes, 441 U.S. 347 (1979).
61.   Michael M. v. Sonoma County, 450 U.S. 464 (1981).
62.   Note, "The Constitutionality of Statutory Rape Laws," 27 *UCLA Law
      Review* 757, 761 (1980); Michael M. v. Sonoma County, 159 California Re-
      porter 340, 601 P.2d 572 (1979); (Mosk, J., dissenting). Leigh Bienen,
      "Rape III: National Developments in Rape Reform Legislation," 6 *Women's
      Rights Law Reporter* 170, 189 (1981). However, as Bienen points out, the
      women's movement has sometimes been ambivalent as to whether these laws
      helped or hurt women. Bienen, *supra* at 180.
63.   Michael M. v. Sonoma County, 450 U.S. at 471.
64.   *Id.* at 473.
65.   *Id.* at 477–79.
66.   *See* in particular, chapter 5; Alan Freeman, "Legitimizing Racial Discrimina-
      tion Through Antidiscrimination Law: A Critical Review of Supreme Court
      Doctrine," 62 *Minnesota Law Review* 1050 (1978).
67.   *Id.* at 1052.
68.   Indeed, feminist legal strategies are still evolving. For a thorough presenta-
      tion of the principle that each person is entitled to equal treatment based on
      equal performance without regard to sex, *see* Barbara Brown et al., "The
      Equal Rights Amendment: A Constitutional Basis for Equal Rights for

Women," 80 *Yale Law Journal* 871 (1971). Concern that the equal-rights approach allows a few exceptional women to satisfy the criteria for success and thus escape subordination while their individual success serves to justify the reality that most women remain in an inferior position has been expressed in Powers, *supra* note 3; Catherine MacKinnon, *Sexual Harassment of Working Women: A Case of Sex Discrimination* (New Haven: Yale University Press, 1979); and Ann E. Freedman, "Housework, Childcare and the Limits of Equality Theory" (Paper presented at the Critical Legal Studies Conference, Minneapolis, Minnesota, May 1981). For a discussion of alternate formulations, see these sources and Nadine Taub, Book Review, 80 *Columbia Law Review* 1686 (1980).

69. *See* Mary Dunlap, "Harris v. McRae," 6 *Women's Rights Law Reporter* 165 (1981).

7
FREEDOM OF SPEECH
David Kairys

Contemporary court decisions, legal scholarship, and law school classes on freedom of speech typically communicate the shared views that the history of freedom of speech is legal rather than social or political in nature, and that the attainment and enforcement of speech rights are based in the Constitution and are the concern of the courts rather than the people. Many historians and legal scholars acknowledge that there have been incidents and periods in our history in which freedom of speech has been denied, but these events are described as aberrations and blamed on some overzealous individual or group that was out of step with American traditions. The law is further relieved of any responsibility for these transgressions by the commonly accepted notion that there were no court decisions on freedom of speech before the First World War, and that shortly thereafter speech was legally protected by the Supreme Court and has remained so ever since. Popular literature extends these views posited in the legal literature to embrace the idea that freedom of speech is a legal right, a cornerstone of the Constitution, that has been faithfully enforced by the courts throughout our history.

However, the history and reality of free speech in the United

I appreciate the helpful comments on early drafts of this chapter provided by Thomas Emerson, Marge Frantz, Victor Rabinowitz, David Rudovsky, and James Weinstein.

States are entirely different. Despite the persistent but nonspecific references to "our traditions" in legal and popular literature, no right of free speech, either in law or practice, existed until a basic transformation of the law governing speech in the period from about 1919 to 1940. Before that time, one spoke publicly only at the discretion of local, and sometimes federal, authorities, who often prohibited what they, the local business establishment, or other powerful segments of the community did not want to hear.

Although there was a popular belief in freedom of speech at the time it was guaranteed on paper in the First Amendment, the extent and depth of that belief have significantly fluctuated throughout our history. The primary periods of stringent enforcement and enlargement of speech rights by the courts, the 1930s and the 1960s, correspond to the periods in which popular movements demanded such rights.[1]

From the adoption of the First Amendment (1791) to the beginning of the basic legal transformation (1919), social and religious activists, almost all of them left or progressive, demanded recognition of freedom of speech. The most significant of these—the Abolitionists, the anarchists, the Industrial Workers of the World (IWW, or Wobblies), the Socialist Party, and the early labor and women's movements—were sometimes successful in speaking, gathering, and distributing literature publicly. Federal and state courts, however, repeatedly refused to protect any form of speech.

The transformation of the law of free speech between 1919 and 1940 resulted primarily from the activities of the labor movement, the first mass-based movement posing a credible challenge to the existing order that demanded freedom of speech. The labor movement viewed free speech as a necessary component of the right to organize unions; and the seminal Supreme Court decisions constitutionally protecting free speech came in the late 1930s as part of a general social, political, and legal shift in favor of labor that included, in the legislative arena, the adoption of the National Labor Relations Act (NLRA).

Since 1940, the courts have continued the pattern of stringent enforcement and enlargement of speech rights only in periods when a mass movement has demanded them, and have withdrawn from the commitment to freedom of speech during times of popularly based repression, including the capitulation in the 1950s and the withdrawal in recent years. Further, the contemporary scope and reality of our speech rights are commonly exaggerated, and the concept of free speech has been used ideologically to support and legitimize social inequity and injustice, and to mask a lack of real participation and democracy.

This history and the social role and functioning of the law regarding freedom of speech are discussed below, first, in a brief history of the law and practice from 1791 to 1940; second, in an analysis of legal decision making in two Supreme Court cases that best illustrate the basic change in speech law; and, third, in a discussion of the contemporary social and ideological role of freedom of speech.

A BRIEF HISTORY OF FREE SPEECH IN THE UNITED STATES, 1791 TO 1940

Liberty . . . does not reside in laws, nor is it preserved by courts. Yet the ordinary citizen is so neglectful of the protection of his [or her] own liberties that the legal profession almost alone concerns itself with their interpretation. This is unfortunate—for lawyers are not commonly lovers of liberty.

—Leon Whipple (1927)[2]

For all that has been written about freedom of speech, there is little that acknowledges the pre–World War I history or recognizes the profound change in the law in this century, and even less that attempts to analyze the change. But many primary and secondary sources document the specific incidents, practices, and court rulings that comprise this history.[3] The incidents and periods discussed here, while they concern a variety of speech, press, and religious activities, do not constitute a comprehensive treatment of speech. A particular aspect— speaking, gathering, and distributing literature in public places—has been emphasized because it is the subject of the Supreme Court cases that best illustrate the transformation in the law and because this aspect played a major role in the events leading to the transformation.

The Transformation in Legal Doctrine

In 1894, the Reverend William F. Davis, an evangelist and long-time active opponent of slavery and racism, attempted to preach the Gospel on Boston Common, a public park. For his first attempt, Davis was incarcerated for a few weeks in the Charles Street Jail; the second time, he was fined and appealed the sentence.

The hostility of the Boston authorities toward Davis probably stemmed from his espousal of the Social Gospel, a popular religious trend of the time that emphasized social responsibility and often condemned the corruption of city officials. In any event, Davis believed there was a "constitutional right of citizens to the use of public grounds and places without let or hindrance by the City authorities."[4]

The Supreme Court of Massachusetts disagreed.[5] In an opinion by Oliver Wendell Holmes—later a justice of the Supreme Court of the United States known for his decisions protecting freedom of speech—the court upheld Davis's conviction based on a city ordinance that prohibited "any public address" on public grounds without a permit from the mayor. Holmes, like almost all state and lower federal court judges,[6] viewed such an ordinance as simply a city regulation of the use of its park, which was within the city's rights as owner of the property. Davis had no basis, in the Constitution or elsewhere, to claim any limits on this property right:

That such an ordinance is constitutional . . . does not appear to us open to doubt. . . . For the Legislature absolutely or conditionally to forbid public speaking in a highway or public park is no more an infringement of the rights of a member of the public than for the owner of a private house to forbid it in his house.

The Supreme Court of the United States unanimously affirmed, quoting Holmes's analogy to a private house.[7] In the only reference to the Constitution, the Court said it "does not have the effect of creating a particular and personal right in the citizen to use public property in defiance of the Constitution and laws of the State." Nor did the Court find any constitutional or other limit on the mayor's authority to deny permission selectively or for any reason: "The right to absolutely exclude all right to use, necessarily includes the authority to determine under what circumstances such use may be availed of, as the greater power contains the lesser."

Forty years later,* the labor movement, like Reverend Davis, believed that the government should hold and maintain public streets, sidewalks, and parks for the use of the people. Labor organizers had regularly been denied freedom of speech, except in cities with progressive or socialist mayors. After Congress passed the NLRA in 1935, the Congress of Industrial Organizations (CIO) sought to explain its provisions and the benefits of unions and collective bargaining to working people throughout the country. Nowhere was their reception more hostile than in Jersey City, New Jersey, the turf of political boss Frank Hague.

The CIO planned to distribute literature on the streets and host outdoor meetings, but permits for these activities were denied by Hague. Hague was an early supporter of the less militant American Federation of Labor (AFL) and of the New Deal, which provided him

---

* There were intervening related decisions; these cases and the process of change are discussed in later portions of this chapter.

with resources for distribution to local communities and political allies, but by the mid–1930s he had firmly allied himself with the manufacturing and commercial establishments. He made it clear that labor organizers were not welcome in Jersey City, and many were cast out of town, usually by being put on a ferry to New York. Local businesses were promised that they would have no labor troubles while he was mayor; his response to the CIO was: "I am the law."[8]

The CIO brought suit against Hague, the outcome of which was a Supreme Court ruling in favor of the CIO.[9] The Court said:

Wherever the title of streets and parks may rest, they have immemorially been held in trust for the use of the public and, time out of mind, have been used for purposes of assembly, communicating thoughts between citizens, and discussing public questions. Such use of the streets and public places has, from ancient times, been a part of the privileges, immunities, rights, and liberties of citizens.

This was a direct repudiation of both the doctrinal basis and the result in *Davis*, and it first established the basic concept of free speech now taken for granted. However, the Court did not explicitly overrule *Davis*,[10] discuss the lack of free speech prior to its decision, or even acknowledge that it had made a fundamental change in legal doctrine. Rather, the opinion was an inspiring exposition of a right to freedom of speech based on natural law, and, like all natural-law-based principles, it is essentially timeless and without a social context.

In the quoted passage, the streets and parks have "immemorially" been held for the people and used for speech "time out of mind," and the right of free speech stems "from ancient times." The Court apparently was somewhat defensive and wished to emphasize this point, since it repeated it three times in the crucial passage of the opinion. But there is no indication as to what time or place the Court was referring; it certainly had never been so in the United States before this very case, as the Court had itself ruled in *Davis*. One can almost feel sorry for poor Boss Hague: like most of his contemporaries, even those who never reached the level of boss, and city administrators throughout American history, Hague prohibited speech he or the local establishment did not want to hear, surely unaware that he was tampering with rules "from ancient times."

The Court made an essentially political and social judgment to change the law, but it was presented as based solely on required, preexisting, and legal principles, and directed at a scapegoat rather than at a systematic social practice.

Before the Transformation

Davis is the only Supreme Court decision addressing these basic free-speech issues before the transformation began, but state and lower federal court decisions, as well as the practice throughout the country, confirm that there was no tradition of or legally protected right to free speech prior to the transformation. The supposed existence of such a tradition is a longstanding myth.

The Constitution and the Early Popular Understanding of Freedom of Speech. The Constitution, as ratified in 1787, does not mention freedom of speech, although historians and legal scholars generally agree that the Constitution was popularly understood to embody basic notions of political freedom. The Bill of Rights, in the form of amendments adopted four years later, was promised and necessary to secure ratification. The First Amendment right of expression restricted only the federal government. but most state constitutions had similar provisions, and the federal government was seen as posing the major danger to free speech.[11]

However, the experience of revolution and the emergence of the new nation generated a wave of intolerance immediately before and after the adoption of the Constitution. To some extent this is understandable and typical of revolutions that have occurred elsewhere: after a violent struggle and in the wake of victory, there is a yearning for consensus, or at least conformity that appears to reflect consensus. But the very nature of the new nation—its unprecedented emphasis on individual freedom—seems to have accentuated rather than restrained this process. Belief and pride in the attainment of freedom was turned against itself; nonconformity and dissent were greeted with extreme, legally sanctioned, and sometimes violent intolerance.

Although the issue of the relationship of the colonies to England was hotly and publicly debated before and during the war, any subsequent sign of even an early questioning of independence tended to be viewed as disloyalty. Many people had sentimental, familial, and economic allegiances to England, which was often also their birthplace. Because they believed differences could be settled without war, they were treated as traitors, regardless of whether they had actually acted or sided with England during the Revolution. They were subjected to special taxes, loyalty oaths, banishment, and violence; and laws in most states prohibited them from serving on juries, voting, holding office, buying land, or practicing certain designated professions. At this same time, the pacifism of the Quakers was also regarded as treasonous. Their religious services were banned, and they were frequently imprisoned, banished, and subjected to mob violence.[12] This pattern of repression based on a false equation of disloyalty with ancestry, religion, or expression of opposition to established policy would be repeated throughout this history.

The Federalists—Our First Party.   While the ink on the First Amendment was barely dry, the Federalist Party attempted to silence its opponents with prosecutions for the common-law offense of seditious libel. This offense, based on the conception of a monarch and government as divine and above reproach, essentially rendered criticism of the government or its officials a criminal act. Republicans who differed with Federalist policies were prosecuted; some were convicted and imprisoned. In a turnabout, the Republicans used the same device to prosecute Federalists, including a minister who criticized Jefferson in a Thanksgiving Day sermon.[13]

The Federalists, undaunted by the First Amendment to their Constitution, became dissatisfied with the ineffectiveness of these seditious libel prosecutions, due to doubts raised about whether federal courts have common-law jurisdiction. In 1798, they pushed through Congress, by a narrow margin, the Sedition Act, which made it a crime to

. . . write, print, utter or publish . . . any false, scandalous and malicious writings against the government of the United States, or either House of Congress . . . or the President with the intent to defame . . . or to bring them into contempt or disrepute . . .[14]

Although the act also contained two protective devices—truth was made a defense, and the jury was to decide whether the words were seditious—Federalist judges quickly negated their effect. They refused to distinguish between statements of fact and opinion, and they ruled that the defendant must prove the truth of every minute detail to establish the truth defense. Overall, they treated the First Amendment as if it only codified preexisting law and prohibited only prior censorship, although prior censorship had been prohibited in England since 1695 and in the colonies since 1725.[15]

The most prominent person prosecuted under the Sedition Act was Matthew Lyon, a member of Congress critical of the Federalists. Lyon was imprisoned and his house sold to pay his fine (nevertheless he was reelected in the next election). The longest prison term, two years, was served by a laborer for erecting a sign on a post that read, in part, "NO STAMP ACT, NO SEDITION . . . DOWNFALL TO THE TYRANTS OF AMERICA, PEACE AND RETIREMENT TO THE PRESIDENT." The act was "never invoked against alien enemies, or possible traitors, but solely against editors and public men whom the Federalists under President Adams desired to silence or deport in order to suppress political opposition."[16]

The act and consequent prosecutions were extremely unpopular, and convictions were difficult to obtain without manipulation of the composition of juries (which, as a result, were comprised almost entirely of Federalists) and active bias by Federalist judges. "Popular indignation at the Act and the prosecutions wrecked the Federalist Party,"[17] further indication of the popular understanding and belief in freedom of expression at that time.

Jefferson pardoned all those convicted, and the government repaid their fines. The Supreme Court never reviewed any of the common-law or statutory sedition cases, but several legal doctrines that restricted expression were adopted by the lower courts and would be repeatedly resurrected later. The two foremost were the "indirect-causation" or "bad-tendency" doctrine, which allowed prosecution for words that could, in however remote or indirect a fashion, contribute to disorder or unlawful conduct sometime in the future; and the "constructive-intent" doctrine, which ascribed to the speaker or writer the intent to cause such remote and indirect consequences. Perhaps most important, in this infancy of the First Amendment, the law proved to be a willing partner in repression.

The Mob as an Expression of Public Opinion, 1830–1860. During the early 1800s, the relatively new and abstract ideas of liberty and democracy that had fueled the Revolution seemed less important than pressing social problems primarily related to urban centralization and immigration. Democracy came to be viewed as sanctioning, or even requiring, the use of any means necessary to thoroughly and quickly implement the will of the majority. Again, the perceived righteousness of American democracy became its undoing, as the majority claimed "their final right to settle with the minority."[18] Any person who differed from the majority—by ancestry, religion, appearance, or disagreement with majority positions—was suspect and blamed for social problems, which usually took the heaviest toll on them. The goal was to eliminate differences, which were perceived as the cause of social disorders; the means was mob violence. "The early governing autocrats had tried to limit liberty by stifling interpretation of the Constitution or by appeals to English precedents. The people simply appealed to force."[19] And the government, including the courts, offered no protection.

Discrimination against minorities was not unusual. In New York, Masons were prohibited from serving on juries until 1927; in many states Jews were excluded from juries, professions, and public office until the mid–1800s; and blacks were still slaves. But the broad range of "Native American" movements during this period unleashed a ferocious reign of terror against each wave of new immigrants and, not coincidentally, cheap labor. In this nation of immigrants, "native" was defined, it would appear, not as the original population (American Indians) but on a continuum, so that groups could claim nativity vis-à-vis all other groups of more recently immigrated ancestry.

Among the Native American persecutions,[20] none was more ferocious than the persecution of Irish Catholics, which included the random killings and raids of the Know-Nothing Party. The Irish, as so many other minorities, absorbed the Native American ideology rather than develop a tolerance born of experience. Later, when they ascended to power in parts of California, they persecuted the Chinese.

The Mormons, seen as dangerous first for their savvy land purchases and later for their practice of polygamy, were banished, randomly beaten, and killed in several states. In Missouri the governor ordered them "exterminated," and men, women, and children were massacred in a series of pogroms. They moved to Illinois, where their leader, Joseph Smith, was murdered by a mob while in jail. They then moved to Utah, where they became the natives and proceeded to persecute others, including blacks.

Social reformers of this period, including people favoring abolition of slavery, free education, birth control, and temperance, were treated similarly.[21] Statutes in every southern state forbade any speech or writing that questioned slavery. These were uniformly enforced by the courts; such speech or writing was held possibly to lead to slave insurrections and was therefore prohibitable based on the bad-tendency doctrine.

Alongside this legal suppression, citizens' committees and vigilante activities were widespread and unchecked by legal authorities. There were many lynchings and beatings of abolitionists, and the citizens' committees kept track of even the mildest expression of antislavery views. A slaveholder in Grayson County, Virginia, who defended a minister's sermon against slavery, was tarred and feathered by the local committee. When he sought warrants for the arrest of some committee members he recognized, the committee threatened his lawyers and the judge, and disrupted a hearing. Subcommittees were subsequently formed throughout the county to report any "suspicious opinions," and the courts were instructed not to act in cases of crimes against abolitionists. It became common in the South after 1840 to repudiate the notion of natural rights and the Declaration of Independence, which were both seen as based on Jefferson's "radicalism."[22]

There were no similar statutes and few lynchings in the North, but mobs accomplished the same goals. Most notable were riots in

Philadelphia and Illinois, where Elijah Lovejoy, the editor of an anti-slavery newspaper, was murdered by a mob.[23]

In 1837, after a series of lengthy and embarrassing petitions against slavery were presented to Congress, it banned presentation of all such petitions in order that "the agitation of this subject should be finally arrested, for the purpose of restoring tranquillity to the public mind."[24] Basic notions of freedom and democracy—and the First Amendment right "to petition the Government for redress of grievances"—were, it seems, secondary in importance to the tranquility of a public mind that apparently was undisturbed by widespread mob violence and slavery.

The Early Labor Movement. The labor movement was accustomed to hostility from the legal system; in the early 1800s, the courts generally regarded unions and strikes as criminal conspiracies. By the 1870s, the labor movement began to focus on freedom of speech, which it viewed as a necessary component of the right to organize. Peaceful labor demonstrations were regularly and often violently broken up by the police. For example, during the depression of 1873–1874, a large group of unemployed workers demonstrating in New York were attacked by police. The city had granted a permit but revoked it minutes before the demonstration. Demonstrators, unaware of the revocation, were beaten with clubs by platoons of police, who rushed into the crowd. Two meetings in a private hall called to protest the police action at the demonstration were also broken up by the police. By a contemporary account, "the aggrieved working men and their sympathizers felt as though they had no rights which the municipality was bound to respect."[25] They were correct.

The Anarchists. Beginning in 1897, Emma Goldman and other anarchists toured the country speaking on a range of topics, from politics to literature and the arts. They were regularly prohibited from speaking, on streets or in public or private halls, or limited to certain topics. The process became so routinized that Goldman, who called it a struggle for "liberty without strings," incorporated it into her condemnations of governmental power and coercion. Usually, radicals, liberals, and some conservatives would rally to support her right to speak.

For example, in 1909 Goldman was to deliver a lecture entitled "Henrik Ibsen as the Pioneer of Modern Drama" at Lexington Hall in New York City. The police, present in the hall, said she could speak so long as she addressed the topic. However, the first time she mentioned "Ibsen," a police sergeant mounted the speaker's platform and said she was deviating from the topic. Her protestations that she must mention

Ibsen's name to discuss Ibsen and drama were to no avail. The large crowd, at first amused by the absurdity of the police order, was roughly cleared from the hall with the use of clubs.[26]

The "Free-Speech Fights" of the IWW. From 1909 to 1915, the IWW conducted a nationwide campaign to challenge denials of the right to speak on public streets, sidewalks, and parks.[27] Seeking to reach mainly migratory workers in the only places possible, the Wobblies saw themselves in a "struggle for the use of the streets for free speech and the right to organize." This struggle became the focal point for employer resistance to the Wobblies' organizing efforts.

The strategies for the free-speech fights derived from earlier successful efforts by members of the IWW, Socialist Party, and Socialist Labor Party. In 1908, they had together won the repeal of a ban on street speaking in Los Angeles by repeatedly violating the ban until the jails were filled. This was systematized in 1909 by drawing on hundreds, and sometimes thousands, of workers from around the country with announcements in the Wobbly newspaper, *Industrial Worker*.

Each person would mount a soapbox and begin a speech with the usual Wobbly greeting, "Fellow workers and friends." These four words ordinarily sufficed to result in arrest, after which the next person would mount the soapbox. The jails would soon be filled, as would schools and other buildings used for the overflow. The struggle was seen as political, not legal, and early on elected committees decided not to "waste" their limited resources on lawyers' fees.

The first major fight, in Missoula, Montana, was led by Elizabeth Gurley Flynn. In 1909, the Wobblies were speaking on the streets and distributing literature to protest employment agencies that charged unemployed workers a fee for nonexistent jobs. When the agencies and local businesses persuaded the city council to pass an ordinance banning street speaking, the *Industrial Worker* issued a national call, and a "steady stream of Wobblies flocked into Missoula, 'by freight cars—on top, inside and below.'" As the jails filled, the Wobblies received support from a variety of sources, including Senator Robert LaFollette, university professors, and townspeople worried about the costs of incarcerating so many persons. The authorities eventually relented: all of the criminal charges were dropped, and, as Flynn later wrote, "We returned to our peaceful pursuit of agitating and organizing the I.W.W."[28]

Beginning the next year, twelve hundred people were arrested in a Spokane, Washington, free-speech fight that lasted several months. In response to Wobbly street speaking, also directed primarily against corrupt employment agencies (which had, for example, sent five thousand fee-paying workers to a company that employed only one hundred), the city council prohibited "public meetings on any of the streets, sidewalks, or alleys." A local court upheld the ban while carving out an exception for the Salvation Army. The free-speech prisoners were beaten in jail, and some were placed in chains and forced to work on a rock pile. Three died in an unheated school that was used after the prisons had been filled. When the police shut down the *Industrial Worker* office and arrested Flynn (then noticeably pregnant) though she had not violated the ordinance, the fight became "front-page news in every newspaper in the country,"[29] and hundreds more headed for Spokane. The ordinance was repealed, the *Industrial Worker* was allowed to publish, nineteen employment agencies lost their licenses, and two particularly brutal prison guards were fired. After another successful fight the following year in Fresno, California, the Wobblies were often able to win the de facto right to speak and organize with only a threat of a national call in the *Industrial Worker*.

Employers on the West Coast then organized the Merchants and Manufacturers Association to oppose free speech for the Wobblies, and they openly advocated a tactic that was first widely used in the Fresno fight: vigilantes, working with the police, would routinely beat the street speakers and throw them out of town. This became the regular practice, with the vigilante mobs usually composed of and headed by leading business and banking figures. The most brutal actions occurred in San Diego in 1912, where anti-Wobbly vigilantes included leading members of the chamber of commerce and real-estate board, as well as a variety of merchants and bankers. These vigilantes regularly attacked the Wobblies as they entered town on freight trains, and made them kiss the flag and walk through gauntlets of men swinging clubs. One Wobbly was shot to death; others were tarred and feathered or had "IWW" branded on their bodies. However, throughout this and other, frequent attacks, the Wobblies persisted nonviolently and were almost always successful, including major victories in Cleveland, Denver, Detroit, Philadelphia, Omaha, Kansas City, Des Moines, San Francisco, Vancouver, Hawaii, and Alaska.

The *Industrial Worker* summed up the Wobbly experience with the legal system: "A demonstration of working men in the interests of the constitutional right of freedom of speech is judged a 'riot' by the courts; but violence and terrorism on the part of the capitalists and their tools is 'law and order.' "[30] While the Wobblies did not achieve widespread or legal protection of the freedom to speak, they did achieve major successes and brought the issue to the public consciousness. They also made it quite clear that continued refusal to allow and protect free speech would lead to major confrontations into which significant segments of society would be drawn to support the labor movement as well as free speech.

The Women's Movement. Advocates of women's rights were particularly harassed by local and federal officials. In the early 1900s,
Margaret Sanger and Emma Goldman were frequently arrested and
sometimes fined or imprisoned for distributing leaflets with information on birth control. Newspapers that offended the postmaster—
which included almost anything on the subject of sex or women—were
denied the use of the mails. The publisher of a socialist newspaper in
Oklahoma received a six-month sentence, under a federal obscenity
statute, for publishing an ad for a pamphlet that criticized the popular
view of women as sex objects and explained "why the Socialists believe
women are human beings."[31] This conviction was affirmed on appeal,[32] and in a later case federal censorship of the mails was approved
by the Supreme Court.[33]

In 1917 participants in the women's suffrage movement, harassed
locally for some time, came to the White House seeking President
Wilson's endorsement of a constitutional amendment granting women
the right to vote. When their efforts failed, they set up a picket of six
women with banners at the White House gates. The women were
convicted of "obstructing traffic," which they had not done, and imprisoned for three days after refusing to pay fines. During the weeks
that followed, others were similarly convicted and sentenced for obstructing traffic or disorderly conduct, and some were sent to a distant
prison. Months later, more women were arrested in a public park
across from the White House, many of whom were mistreated in jail
and staged hunger strikes in protest.[34]

The repressive measures of this period were investigated by the
U.S. Commission on Industrial Relations, a body with business and
labor representatives established by Congress in 1912 to investigate the
conflict between labor and capital and related causes of social unrest.
The commission, which was drawn into the free-speech issue because
it was repeatedly raised as a major problem by workers and organized
labor, concluded that

[O]ne of the greatest sources of social unrest and bitterness has been the
attitude of the police toward public speaking. On numerous occasions in
every part of the country, the police of cities and towns have either arbi-
trarily or under the cloak of a traffic ordinance, interfered with, or prohibited public speaking, both in the open and in halls, by persons connected
with organizations of which the police or those from whom they receive
their orders, did not approve. In many instances such interference has been
carried out with a degree of brutality which would be incredible if it were
not vouched for by reliable witnesses.
     . . . [The] long list of statutes, city ordinances, and military orders
abridging freedom of speech and press . . . have not only not been interfered

with by the courts but whenever tested have almost uniformly been upheld by State and Federal courts.[35]

The courts justified these decisions with both an expanded notion of the "police power," which gave the states enormous powers of repression in the name of preservation of safety and order, and the bad-tendency doctrine, whereby almost any expression of a different view was depicted as undermining law and order. Leon Whipple, a leading historian of civil liberty in the U.S., described this mode of thought well:

It proceeds from preserving the peace to preserving the status quo. This force for safety soon translates safety into "law and order" and this into "the established order." It changes health into comfort, and comfort into peace of mind, which means no agitation, no freaks, no tampering with things as they are.[36]

The Transformation: 1919–1940

The Espionage Act of 1917 made it a federal crime to "willfully make or convey false reports or false statements with intent to interfere with the operation or success of the [armed forces of the United States] or to promote the success of its enemies," to "willfully cause or attempt to cause insubordination, disloyalty, mutiny, or refusal of duty," or to "willfully obstruct . . . recruiting or enlistment."[37] The next year, more offenses were added, including "uttering, printing, writing, or publishing any disloyal, profane, scurrilous, or abusive language, or language intended to cause contempt, scorn, contumely or disrepute as regards the form of government of the U. S., the Constitution, the flag, the uniform of the Army or Navy, or any language intended to incite resistance to the U. S. or promote the cause of its enemies."[38]

These acts, designed for use against opponents of American participation in World War I, constituted yet another example in this repressive history. However, for the first time, they prompted some justices of the Supreme Court to raise First Amendment problems with the criminalization of dissent; and, in so doing, they ushered in the beginning of the transformation of speech law, which proceeded case-by-case over the course of the next twenty years.

The judicial response to the Espionage Acts began with business as usual. A Second Circuit decision, *Masses Publishing Co.* v. *Patten*,[39] approved of the postmaster's refusal to deliver a newspaper to its subscribers because it expressed negative opinions about the purposes and conduct of the war. This and over two thousand criminal prosecutions were justified with the bad-tendency and constructive-intent doctrines. Zechariah Chafee, Jr., a Harvard law professor, examined these prosecutions in detail and concluded that

[T]he courts treated opinions as statements of fact and then condemned them as false because they differed from the President's speech or the resolution of Congress declaring war. . . . [I]t became criminal to advocate heavier taxation instead of bond issues, to state that conscription was unconstitutional . . . , to urge that a referendum should have preceded our declaration of war, to say that war was contrary to the teachings of Christianity. Men have been punished for criticizing the Red Cross and the Y.M.C.A. . . .[40]

None of the Espionage Act convictions was reversed by the Supreme Court on First Amendment grounds, but the first signs of change came in the opinions of Justices Louis Brandeis and Oliver Wendell Holmes. In 1919 Justice Holmes articulated his "clear-and-present-danger" test in *Schenck* v. *United States*.[41] This was seemingly at least a partial repudiation of the bad-tendency doctrine, and it was set out in a unanimous opinion.

However, the *Schenck* test, which is still with us today, hardly provides a precisely defined or objectively applicable standard. It is open to many interpretations; there were and are a wide range of opinions about when and under what circumstances a danger is of sufficient importance or sufficiently clearly or presently posed. While the *Schenck* opinion was widely hailed by liberal commentators,[42] its exaggerated importance was evident in the decision itself. All that Schenck, a Socialist Party leader, had done was distribute a leaflet to draftees criticizing the war, challenging the draft as unconstitutional, and urging them to challenge their conscription on legal grounds and by legal means. There would seem to be no danger, since the courts could adjudicate such challenges, and whatever consequences there might be were neither clear nor present. Yet, Holmes's opinion affirmed the conviction, and it would be regularly cited in later cases to justify convictions for mere dissent.[43]

Holmes's votes with the majorities in two subsequent affirmances of convictions further undercut the meaning and importance of the *Schenck* test: one involved the author of critical articles on the constitutionality of the draft and the purposes of the war, and the other sent Eugene Debs to prison on a ten-year sentence for a speech at a socialist rally in which he mildly condemned the war as a contest between competing capitalist classes.[44] The *Debs* case raised a public outcry because of the stature of Debs and the fact that his supposed crime was an attempt to cause insubordination in the military and to obstruct recruiting, although he did not speak to soldiers or urge resistance to the draft. While in prison, Debs received more than 920,000 votes for president as the Socialist Party candidate in the election of 1920, more than he had received in any of four prior elections.

Holmes and Brandeis began their famous series of dissents in *Abrams* v. *United States*.[45] In that case, the conviction of mainly Russian-born and Jewish defendants for aiding the Germans was based on a leaflet that condemned U. S. military intervention in the Soviet Union in 1918. The majority of the Court held that the actions advocated, such as a general strike, would affect the war effort against Germany even though that intent, as required by the Espionage Act, was clearly not present. In this and subsequent cases,[46] Brandeis and Holmes masterfully set out in dissents and concurrences the fundamental social, historical, and political bases for free speech that have survived to this day. Quoting Justice Brandeis:

Those who won our independence believed that the final end of the State was to make men free to develop their faculties; and that in its government the deliberative forces should prevail over the arbitrary. They valued liberty both as an end and as a means. They believed liberty to be the secret of happiness and courage to be the secret of liberty. They believed that freedom to think as you will and to speak as you think are means indispensable to the discovery and spread of political truth; that without free speech and assembly discussion would be futile; that with them, discussion affords ordinarily adequate protection against the dissemination of noxious doctrine; that the greatest menace to freedom is an inert people; that public discussion is a political duty; and that this should be a fundamental principle of the American government. They recognized the risks to which all human institutions are subject. But they knew that order cannot be secured merely through fear of punishment for its infraction; that it is hazardous to discourage thought, hope and imagination; that fear breeds repression; that repression breeds hate; that hate menaces stable government; that the path of safety lies in the opportunity to discuss freely supposed grievances and proposed remedies; and that the fitting remedy for evil counsels is good ones. Believing in the power of reason as applied through public discussion, they eschewed silence coerced by law—the argument of force in its worst form. Recognizing the occasional tyrannies of governing majorities, they amended the Constitution so that free speech and assembly should be guaranteed.[47]

After World War I and the Russian Revolution, various forms of American radicalism blossomed, and there was a period of hysterical reaction, usually referred to as the "Red Scare." On the state level, there were new sedition, criminal anarchy, and syndicalism laws; thirty-two states forbade the flying of a red flag; and the New York legislature expelled five socialists. Socialist Victor Berger was twice denied a seat in the House of Representatives; the federal government deported many aliens for their beliefs; and in 1920 the attorney general (assisted by a young federal agent named J. Edgar Hoover) conducted the infamous Palmer raids. Private institutions and individuals, often acting with the government, engaged in similar repression. Harvard alumni and Justice Department officials sought to have Professor Chafee fired for his criticism of the *Abrams* decision in a law review article; charges that he was "unfit as a law school professor" were rejected, but only after a hearing at the Harvard Club.[48]

Holmes and Brandeis continued their articulation of a broad-based right of expression, although, as in *Schenck*, the votes they sometimes cast affirming convictions conflicted with their eloquence.[49] In 1925 a majority finally said the First Amendment was applicable to the states.[50] However, the breakthrough in results came in 1931 in *Stromberg* v. *California*,[51] where the Court reversed a state conviction for displaying a red flag at a Young Communist League summer camp. That same year the Court first prohibited prior restraints by the states on the press.[52]

Subsequently, freedom of expression was enlarged throughout the decade. The leading decisions spanned only five years (1936–1940), during which time the Court (in addition to *Hague*): invalidated a state tax on the press, reversed a conviction for a peaceful assembly, reversed a conviction for an attempt to promote "resistance to lawful authority" by distribution of a pamphlet advocating a separate black nation in the South, invalidated the conviction of a Jehovah's Witness for violating an ordinance requiring a permit for distributing literature, invalidated an ordinance banning all leafletting, protected a Jehovah's Witness's right to solicit door-to-door without a permit, and protected the right to picket.[53] Probably the most libertarian decision in the Court's history, in its reasoning if not also in its result, came in 1943, when it invalidated a state compulsory flag-salute law.[54]

In these cases, the bad-tendency and constructive-intent doctrines were repudiated, and a multifaceted right of expression was established. As the decade wore on, the natural-law-based rationale of *Hague* was emphasized, and the rich history of the struggle for free speech was transformed into a natural right from ancient times, guaranteed by the Constitution and enforced, with some unfortunate exceptions, by the courts.

The Free-Speech Movement

It is so common to view free speech as a legal rather than political issue that we tend to overlook the fact that there was—and is today—a free-speech movement that played an important role in the struggle for free speech.

While the political and religious groups and activists who were denied freedom of expression usually viewed it as secondary in importance to their substantive demands, they and many others organized efforts to more effectively raise the free-speech issue. There were a number of ad hoc groups, such as the Free Speech Committee, which held a meeting of two thousand people in 1909 following a series of incidents highlighted by the refusal to allow Emma Goldman to speak on Ibsen's writings in New York. About the same time, the IWW started its free-speech fights, which combined labor organizing with the free-speech demand, and Theodore Schroeder formed the Free Speech League, which primarily produced theoretical writings. In the early 1930s, the International Labor Defense focused on various civil liberties issues predominantly in the South (and brought national and international attention to the Scotsboro case).

Though undeniably significant, none of these efforts was broadly based, able to command consistent national attention, or systematic in its strategies or approach to the free-speech issue. What the free-speech movement lacked was a mass base, a national organization, and an effective organizer; it found all three in the labor movement, the National Civil Liberties Bureau (which became the American Civil Liberties Union in 1920), and Roger Baldwin.[55]

Baldwin, whose upper-middle-class family could claim an ancestor on the *Mayflower*, was a pacifist with a strong commitment to personal freedom and social justice. His philosophic and political thinking was deeply affected by Emma Goldman and other anarchists, although he did not oppose all forms of government. He also differed from the anarchists in his approach; as he told me, "I was essentially a pragmatist. I did things that I thought would work. Emma was essentially an idealist, and she did things that she thought were right."

In 1917 Baldwin and Crystal Eastman, a leader of the American Union Against Militarism (AUAM), convinced the board of AUAM to form an adjunct, called the Civil Liberties Bureau, that would be primarily concerned with the prosecutions and treatment of conscientious objectors during World War I. The Bureau was generally greeted with hostility, including a denunciation in *The New York Times* for "antagonizing the settled policies of our government,"[56] which caused controversy within AUAM and resulted in its separation from AUAM a few months later. As an independent entity, the NCLB was headed by Baldwin and included on its board several nationally known reformers, socialists, and lawyers, including Clarence Darrow and Norman Thomas.

The NCLB immediately took on the toughest civil liberties issues of the day: protection of conscientious objectors and the Espionage Act prosecutions. The federal government responded by raiding the

NCLB office and seizing all its files. Also in this initial period, Baldwin served a year in jail for draft resistance, after which he remarked, "I am a graduate of Harvard, but a year in jail has helped me recover from it."[57]

When he returned to the NCLB, Baldwin insisted on a new approach that emphasized labor-related civil liberties issues and an alliance with the labor movement. The NCLB issued a pamphlet on the IWW, which, though containing a rather weak disclaimer, clearly indicated where the organization stood on the conflict between labor and capital:

[There have been] deliberate misrepresentations by employing interests opposed to organized labor, who have . . . paint[ed] the I.W.W. as a terrorist organization of "anarchists." They thus frighten the public into an alliance with them instead of with labor. . . . [V]iolence has been much more commonly used against the I.W.W. than by it; . . . the violence used by employers is open, organized, deliberate and without any excusable provocation; . . . the I.W.W. have almost never retaliated even in the face of outrages ranging from murder to mass deportations. . . . [The disloyalty and treason charges against the I.W.W. are based on] simply the ordinary activities of labor-unions struggling to get better wages and conditions. . . .[58]

This pamphlet was banned from the mails and almost led to an Espionage Act prosecution, but, in one of the few successful legal challenges of the period, the NCLB won a court order overturning the ban.[59]

Baldwin led the NCLB through a reorganization in 1920 that emphasized the alliance with labor. The NCLB had long tried to unite liberal and left groups around the free-speech issue, but many identified the NCLB with pacifism or even disloyalty, and its strong image provoked criticisms from the left and right. The reorganized NCLB, to be named the American Civil Liberties Union, would, according to the reorganization memorandum written by Baldwin,[60] institute a "dramatic campaign of service to labor" with a National Executive Committee composed of a core of labor leaders and labor sympathizers. One major tactic would be IWW-type free-speech fights where employers or local governments denied labor organizers free speech. "A few well-known liberals, for instance, going into the strike districts of western Pennsylvania and exercising their right to speak in defiance of sheriff-made law ought to dramatize the situation effectively." And so it did; there were successful labor-related free-speech fights sponsored and supported by the ACLU in the 1920s and 1930s in Connecticut, New Jersey, Pennsylvania, and West Virginia.[61]

The new National Executive Committee, all of whose members were pro-labor, consisted of a core of labor leaders and many well-known socialists, communists, and liberals.[62] They had succeeded in uniting a coalition of labor and the left, which sought and found support from all levels of society.

Baldwin told me he viewed the free-speech issue as primarily political and only secondarily legal, and as inseparable from the rights of workers to organize and bargain collectively. The reorganization scheme was aimed at increasing the power and political effectiveness of the ACLU.

Organization was the basis of our service in the ACLU. We as an organization were powerless and therefore had to attach ourselves to the defense of movements that had power. . . .

If we had been a legal aid society helping people get their constitutional rights, as such agencies do their personal rights, we would have behaved quite differently. We would have stuck to constitutional lawyers and arguments in courts. We would not have surrounded [the NCLB and the ACLU] with popular persons. But we did the opposite thing. We attached ourselves to the movements we defended. We identified ourselves with their demands . . . [and] we depended on them for money and support.

Thus constituted and directed,[63] the ACLU proceeded to challenge and organize around, for example, anti-evolution statutes in the *Scopes* case, the Espionage Act prosecution of communist Benjamin Gitlow, the Sacco-Vanzetti prosecutions—and, in 1937, the antilabor and antifree-speech actions of Boss Hague.

LEGAL DECISION MAKING:
EXPLAINING THE TRANSFORMATION

The fundamental conflict between the *Davis* and *Hague* decisions raises the basic questions about legal decision making: How do judges make decisions? How and why does the law change?*

---

* These questions present a methodological problem. It is difficult to decipher the motivation or reasoning of individuals and institutions, or to assess the causative role of individuals, groups, and movements in historical and social developments. Often, credit or blame is casually ascribed to an individual or group when deeper social and historical forces or other factors are clearly involved, or some force or factor is described as being almost mystically translated into reality without a need for social actors. One cannot *prove* (or disprove) such matters; a certain amount of personal, and therefore subjective, judgment is inevitable. Indeed, often what would seem to be the best proof—the motivation and reasoning offered by key social actors—is of no help or is even misleading.

My perspective is, briefly, that historical and social developments are accomplished and implemented by people, who are affected, but not mystically or otherwise governed, by social and political forces and the events and people around them; that the thought processes of these people are usually understandable and

An appropriate starting point is the explanations given by the justices themselves: that their decisions were determined by legal reasoning and analysis. Indeed, if the law is separate from political and social forces, as it purports to be, there should be a coherent *legal* explanation. The primary source of law in these cases was, of course, the Constitution, but the operative constitutional provisions, the First and Fourteenth Amendments, were identical in both cases. *Hague* held that the First Amendment, prohibiting any "law abridging freedom of speech" and operating against the states through the Fourteenth Amendment, establishes an individual right to speak on public streets, sidewalks, and parks; *Davis*, with the same provisions in effect, held the opposite.

It might be argued that there was a legal barrier to enforcement of the First Amendment against the states prior to the Supreme Court's incorporation of the First Amendment into the Fourteenth Amendment in 1925. But this only begs the question; the same provisions were in effect since the Civil War, and thereafter an incorporation decision could have been made whenever the Court chose to make it. In fact, the Court had clear opportunities and discussed the issue even before the *Davis* case.[65] The incorporation of the First Amendment was not a legally required or determined phenomena; rather, it was, chronologically and actually, a manipulation of legal doctrine that was part of the transformation, more an effect than a cause.

Another possible legal explanation might be found in the prior decisions that interpreted the general language of the First Amendment. However, in both periods there were precedents and reasoning supporting each side. Moreover, since precedents and reasoning can be

---

are not much different from those of the rest of us; that the effect of social and political forces and of individuals, groups, and movements struggling to change things is typically underplayed or ignored in historical analyses; and that credit or blame is routinely individualized and ascribed to key people in positions of power regardless of their actual roles. Thus, since Brandeis and Holmes were the first Supreme Court justices to embrace the concept of freedom of speech, a common explanation of the change in speech law (by those who recognize and are pleased with the change) has been that Brandeis and Holmes, and/or lawyers and legal scholars who persuaded them, caused the change because they were smarter, wiser, or better researchers than other judges.[64] At its crudest and most obviously inadequate, this mode of historical analysis would contend that Lincoln freed the slaves. I also focus on the individuals responsible—in this case the judges—but within the context of "regular people" whose values and priorities depend on such factors as their socialization, experience, goals, and self-perception, and who act and make decisions based on sometimes complex but usually understandable considerations. So viewed, one can use the best available historical evidence to assess the options open to them, the various factors affecting each option, their explanations for their actions, and the relative merits of all explanations. I have adopted this approach, and it has pointed in the direction of the conclusions I have drawn here, which are further validated by their ability to explicate the major expansions and contractions of free-speech rights during other periods.

distinguished, modified, or discarded, they do not require any particular rule or result. This is particularly clear in *Hague*, since *Davis* was a direct precedent that the Court chose to avoid. There is no legal explanation for that choice; the law merely provides a variety of bases for justifying choices made on other grounds. This would still be true had the Court decided to follow *Davis*, because that would also be a choice nowhere required in the law, and the question would still be why the Court made that choice.

There is no legally required rule or result, and despite endless attempts by judges and legal scholars to find transcendent legal principles, there simply are none. But one can make sense of these decisions by examining the social and political contexts in which they were made, and by viewing legal decision making and law as political processes.[66]

Davis asked the Court to overturn a longstanding local practice sanctioned by many lower federal and state court decisions; and the Supreme Court, without even a dissent, simply repeated the result and doctrine developed by the lower courts. But society underwent fundamental changes between *Davis* and *Hague*. Industrialization, the First World War, the Depression, the New Deal, and the left and labor movements led to basic shifts in consciousness and social and power relations. These shifts affected judges as well as society generally, and some of the judges, though from the same strata of society as the judges of the *Davis* era, came to see the justice of at least some left demands. Justice Holmes's reassessment of speech rights would seem to exemplify this kind of change. In the early 1920s, he revised his thinking about freedom of speech, and the author of the *Davis* opinion in the Massachusetts Supreme Court became the U. S. Supreme Court's foremost spokesman for free speech. This was not the result of more legal research or any legal principle but of his and society's altered state of consciousness.

Such a social change is transmitted to and affects individuals in various ways—through mass media, public and private associations, professional groups, peer pressures, and in the case of Holmes, by a particularly critical meeting with Chafee, who was very upset about the *Debs* decision.[67] The judges, like Holmes, who came to place considerable value on freedom of speech (and it was surely not all of them) did so not because they were more in touch with the framers of the Constitution or were more competent judges, but because they, as people living and working in society, were affected by historical and social changes and the events and people surrounding them. Due to the peculiar nature of our legal system and the socialization, education, and experience of our judges, these judges would generally express this new consciousness in legal terms, and many of them would honestly deny its newness and honestly believe it stemmed from legal analysis.

Furthermore, Davis was an isolated individual, while the left and labor movements were broad-based, national, and politically powerful. A significant measure of sympathy, understanding, and legitimacy flows from power; demands and speakers that were once regarded as extremist become legitimate as they crystallize into a movement that gains numbers and power. Whipple, in his examination of freedom of speech as practiced from colonial days to the First World War, concluded that "whoever has power, economic or political, enjoys liberty."[68]

The power of such a movement also places judges in a bind. Though most were likely to be hostile or ambivalent toward the labor and left movements and their demands, the demand for free speech had clear historical roots and was seen as appropriate by many people. To deny this demand, a judge would have to risk fomenting a major confrontation in a period already fraught with the possibility of revolution. Moreover, it would be clear that if labor could not speak and organize legally, it would do so illegally and perhaps adopt a strategy similar to the IWW free-speech fights, which won considerable support for the IWW as well as for the Constitution. Although some judges might welcome the confrontation, others—even those born and raised on Wall Street—would find it preferable to bring these activities within and under the control of the system, as Congress had done with the NLRA.

The power of this movement and the precedents favoring local control over speech would also raise institutional concerns. To uphold the right of free speech would require contradicting longstanding precedents and widespread practice. On the other hand, to deny a demand so long promised on paper and so widely supported would raise a public outcry, undermine the Court's authority, and perhaps stimulate support for Roosevelt's court-packing scheme announced in 1937.

As I described in the introduction, the courts are nonmajoritarian institutions that rely for their legitimacy on myths about the objectivity and nonpolitical nature of judicial decision making. This, in turn, lends a broader legitimacy to social and power relations that are reflected, articulated, and enforced by the courts. Within this context, these institutional concerns amount to a choice between rejecting (or avoiding) a precedent and widespread practice and ruling against the mainstream of political thought. That the latter would be a major concern is clear from the widespread controversy about the courts in this period; the Court's recent trend in the direction of the mainstream of society in several related decisions;[69] the belief in some upper-class circles that the law's blatant pro-business slant was undermining its power and authority; congressional enactment of the NLRA in 1935; and an *amicus* brief filed by the American Bar Association favoring the CIO's position.[70] Moreover, in 1936 Congress established a committee to investigate "violations of the right of free speech and assembly and undue interference with the right of labor to organize and bargain collectively," reflecting the fact that these two rights were widely viewed as inseparable.[71]

The various factors discussed here would not necessarily operate intentionally or even consciously, nor would the justices necessarily see themselves as engaged in anything other than a legal analysis. Rather, they would be quite accustomed to expressing social and political concerns and values as legal arguments and to implementing changes expressed in legal terms and not necessarily even self-understood as changes. Their socialization, education, and experience, their perception of their role, and their understanding of the needs of the society they serve would lead to this change in the law. Probably at least some would see it for what it was: a revision of the rules of the game to stabilize and preserve the system of social and power relations we know as capitalism.

SINCE THE TRANSFORMATION: THE REALITY AND IDEOLOGY OF FREE SPEECH

The basic principle that individuals and groups have the ability to express different and unpopular views without prior restraint or punishment is a necessary element of any democratic society. To the extent that we have enforced this principle in the roughly forty years since the transformation—which we have, to an unprecedented degree, since the early 1960s—we can and should be proud. I do not question the principle, its realization in recent years, or its importance and validity under any system of social relations.

However, freedom of speech means much more than this in the United States. We have developed an ideology of free speech that has become a basic element of our national identity, and, as in earlier periods, our unprecedented emphasis on individual freedom and democracy has been turned against itself.

In capitalist countries, a sharp distinction is drawn between a person's "private" and "public" life. In the public sphere, which includes selection of government officials and political expression, basic concepts of freedom, democracy, and equality are applicable. However, in the private sphere, which encompasses almost all economic activity, we allow no democracy or equality and only the freedom to buy and sell.

For the vast majority, this essentially amounts to the ability to buy a variety of goods and services, and the necessity to sell their labor in competition with others for a limited number of jobs and on terms usually dictated by a more powerful individual or institution. Fundamental social issues, such as the use of our resources, investment, the energy problem, the work of our people, and the distribution of our goods and services, are all left to "private"—mainly corporate—decision makers.

The ideology of free speech, basic to this public/private split, is used to validate and legitimize existing social and power relations and to mask a lack of real participation and democracy. Whatever the state of our economy and people, this ideology tells us that we are free and our society is democratic—and therefore better than other societies that place more emphasis, for example, on feeding the hungry, healing the sick, caring for the aged, and educating the illiterate, or on improving the quality of the lives of its working people—because we can all buy and sell, we can vote, and we have free speech.

Like all effective ideology, the ideology of free speech reflects as well as distorts reality. Thus, while freedom of speech is essential to any free and democratic society, so is the ability to participate meaningfully in the formulation of social policies and priorities. Moreover, this ideology exclusively defines freedom of speech by a historically and culturally specific set of speech rights whose scope and importance are exaggerated.

The struggle for free speech up to the transformation, waged largely by leftists and finally realized by the labor and left movements, has been falsely redefined as a set of preexisting, natural rights whose essence and history are legal rather than political. A false pride in the legal system has displaced a source for genuine pride in the people, who fought business interests and the government—including the courts—to achieve recognition of free speech.

Since the transformation, the basic approach set out in *Hague* and other cases of that era has been more or less followed with variations depending mostly on the historical context. Thus, during the 1960s, the civil rights movement demanded and obtained stringent enforcement and enlargement of speech rights. This is best exemplified by the Supreme Court decisions expanding the right to picket, protecting the press, and protecting even a demonstration with signs inside a public library.[72]

However, in the most repressive period since the transformation—the 1950s, when Senator Joe McCarthy, the House Un-American Activities Committee, and many others resurrected the pretransformation tradition—the judiciary essentially collapsed.[73] Unpopular ideas and associations again became illegal, and the courts abdicated their tenuously held position in the face of a reactionary media blitz, leading Justice Hugo Black to say, "It has been only a few years since there was a practically unanimous feeling throughout the country and in our courts that this could not be done in our free land. . . . [The ultimate question is] whether we as a people will try fearfully and futilely to preserve democracy by adopting totalitarian methods, or whether in accordance with our traditions and our Constitution we will have the confidence and courage to be free."[74] Thus, in the only period of extreme and popularly based repression since the transformation, the courts provided no meaningful protection,[75] and the political shift to the right in recent years has already been accompanied by a judicial retrenchment of First Amendment protections.[76]

Moreover, the ability of our people to communicate meaningfully based on First Amendment rights has been exaggerated. There is, as in almost all areas of the law, a difference between rights in law and rights in practice, and legal standards in speech cases are particularly vague, allowing judges even broader-than-usual discretion. While the rules governing many commercial transactions are set out in minute detail, the speaker, demonstrator, and writer must cope with the clear-and-present-danger standard and First Amendment balancing tests. The inadequacy of the clear-and-present-danger standard was apparent in the opinions that first articulated it: it can easily be used to justify repression and punishment of dissent—to allow the bad-tendency doctrine in by the back door—and it is more open than most legal standards to the subjective notions and whims of judges.[77] Similarly, First Amendment balancing tests, while purporting to require particular, legally determined results, provide, in the words of Professor Thomas Emerson, only "various considerations [that can] be enumerated but not weighed. There [is] no standard of reference upon which to base a reasoned, functional determination. Ultimately, the decision rest[s] upon vague judgments, most of them unexpressed."[78]

Further, the clear-and-present-danger standard and First Amendment balancing tests are examples of a variety of speech rules that allow expression only if it is abstract and ineffective. Since the scope of the dangers referred to has never been meaningfully defined (or even limited to unlawful activities), the clear-and-present-danger formulation amounts to the notion that speech loses its protection when it becomes persuasive or effective concerning something a judge views as dangerous.[79] Similarly, the balancing test often reduces to a question of whether the speech at issue, given all the circumstances, will likely or potentially cause disruption, which means "harmless" and "futile" speech is protected while speech that is effective, persuasive, or apt to provoke a response is not.[80] Another example of such a rule concerns labor picketing: workers can picket concerning a labor dispute, but when many do it—and therefore the strength of their message has the potential of being effective—the courts regularly impose a limit on the number of pickets, even where the picketing has been wholly non-obstructive and peaceful.[81]

The effectiveness and usefulness of our speech rights is also diminished by the reality that effective communication is expensive, which means it is virtually limited to those with substantial wealth. It is the powerless, and therefore usually moneyless, who most need and must rely on the Constitution for a means of communication and organization. What the system basically allows is a display of displeasure, which often will not even gain a spot on the local news unless some violation of the law, injury, or destruction of property accompanies it. People with power and money do not need to picket, demonstrate, or distribute leaflets on the street. The mass media continuously express their perspectives, both explicitly and implicitly; they have the connections and resources to communicate their messages by other, "more respectable"—and more effective—means.

Essentially, the law has frozen the scope and nature of our speech rights at levels appropriate to the 1920s and 1930s, when specific audiences, like factory workers, were geographically centered, and speaking, gathering, and distributing literature in public places were the primary means of communication. Technological, social, and cultural changes have rendered the fruits of the free-speech struggle somewhat obsolete. Television, radio, newspapers (increasingly concentrated and limited in number and diversity), and direct mail now constitute the battleground, but in the absence of mass-based demands, the law has allowed no meaningful inroads into these media for people or groups without substantial money or power. Indeed, accompanying the recent rightward political trend, there will likely be a decrease in popular access to these media and an increased "privatization" of the means of communication, exemplified by the attacks on the already weak "fairness doctrine" and the apparent acceptance of a highly privatized conception of cable television.

The scope and reality of our speech rights as a means of communication and persuasion are thus limited by these legal, economic, and practical barriers. I would not relinquish these rights—with considerable patience and persistence, they can and have been meaningful, and often they are all we have. But the ordinary person or group of ordinary persons has no means, based in the Constitution or elsewhere, to engage meaningfully in that dialogue on the issues of the day that the First Amendment is so often heralded as promoting and guaranteeing.

Finally, speaking and voting are presently the only ways to participate in the decisions that influence our lives. Wider participation already exists in a variety of forms in many countries. For example, in West Germany a company cannot move to a new location without the approval of a board that includes community and worker representation, and if it does move, it must do extensive retraining of the employees left without a job, the expense of which becomes one of the costs of moving; and in Yugoslavia, worker councils have considerable say in the management of the industries that employ them. Such proposals run into ideological barriers in the United States, primarily based on the public/private split that restricts economic issues to the "private" sphere and thereby insulates them from popular participation or scrutiny. The ideology of free speech plays an important role in this: it is used to confine notions of freedom and democracy to the "public" sphere and to mask the lack of real participation and democracy.

The ideological development and use of free speech in the United States have rendered this hard-won principle of liberation also an instrument of delusion: its reality is far less impressive than its rhetoric; its attainment and continued vitality depend more on popular movements than judges or courts; and its seeming embodiment of individual power and democracy masks powerlessness and society's refusal to allow real participation in the decisions by which our lives are governed. Every society should have a mechanism for enforcement and protection of the ability of individuals and groups to express non-majoritarian and unpopular views, and in the United States that mechanism has been the courts and the juridical concept that certain activities are not subject to majority approval. The courts should be encouraged to fulfill this promise of "our traditions." This can be most effectively accomplished—and broader notions of freedom and democracy can most effectively be introduced—if we acknowledge the history of and limits on freedom of speech, if we recognize its essentially political nature, and if we separate the reality from the ideology.

NOTES

1. Looking only at higher court decisions and placing them in their historical contexts, I suggested a few years ago that "[t]he periods of stringent protection and enlargement of civil rights and civil liberties correspond to the periods in which mass movements posing a credible challenge to the existing order have demanded such rights." David Kairys, "Book Review," 126 *University of Pennsylvania Law Review* 930, 942 (1978).
2. Leon Whipple, *Our Ancient Liberties*, vol. 8 (New York: DeCapo Press, 1972).
3. *See generally* Leon Whipple, *The Story of Civil Liberty in the United States* (Westport, Conn.: Greenwood Press, 1927); Zechariah Chafee, Jr., *Free Speech in the United States* (Cambridge, Mass.: Harvard University

Press, 1941); Norman Dorsen, Paul Bender, and Burt Neuborne, *Emerson, Haber and Dorsen's Political and Civil Rights in the United States* (Boston: Little, Brown, 1976), 1:20–51; Thomas Emerson, *The System of Freedom of Expression* (New York: Random House, 1970); John Roche, *The Quest for the Dream* (New York: Macmillan, 1963); Jerold Auerbach, *Labor and Liberty* (New York: Bobbs-Merrill, 1966); Jerold Auerbach, "The Depression Decade," in *The Pulse of Freedom,* ed. Alan Reitman (New York: W.W. Norton, 1975); Paul Murphy, *World War I and the Origin of Civil Liberties in the United States* (New York: W.W. Norton, 1979); David Rabban, "The First Amendment in Its Forgotten Years," 90 *Yale Law Journal* 514 (1981).

4. *Boston Globe,* May 11, 1897.
5. Commonwealth v. Davis, 162 Mass. 510, 511 (1895).
6. The leading cases are collected and discussed in Rabban, *supra* note 3.
7. Davis v. Massachusetts, 167 U.S. 43 (1897).
8. Dayton McKean, *The Boss* (Boston: Houghton Mifflin, 1940); Irving Bernstein, *The Turbulent Years* (Boston: Houghton Mifflin, 1970); Richard Connors, *A Cycle of Power* (Metuchen, N.J.: Scarecrow Press, 1971).
9. Hague v. CIO, 307 U.S. 496 (1939). Of the seven justices participating, five concurred in the substantive aspects of Justice Owen Roberts's plurality opinion, which is considered the opinion of the Court for present purposes.
10. The Court said it did not have to "determine whether . . . the *Davis* case was rightly decided" because Davis did not apply for a permit and the purpose of the *Davis* ordinance was not "directed solely at the exercise of the right of speech and assembly" but also included regulation of the park for the "public convenience." However, while these facts are correct, the *Davis* court clearly based its decision on the property rights of the city, a basis the *Hague* court rejected. Moreover, both ordinances set up permit systems that the Court had already invalidated only months earlier, Lovell v. Griffin, 303 U.S. 444 (1938), and the *Hague* ordinance was ruled void on its face because individuals have a constitutional right to speak and assemble on public streets, sidewalks, and parks. The decisions are inconsistent. *See also* Jamison v. Texas, 318 U.S. 413 (1943).
11. *See generally* Whipple, *supra* note 2; Whipple, *supra* note 3; Zechariah Chafee, Jr., *How Human Rights Got into the Constitution* (Boston: Boston University Press, 1952); Chafee, *supra* note 3. This conclusion has been challenged. *See, e.g.,* Leonard Levy, *Legacy of Suppression: Freedom of Speech and Press in Early American History* (Cambridge, Mass.: Harvard University Press, 1960).
12. Claude Van Tyne, *Loyalists in the American Revolution* (New York: Macmillan, 1902); John Fiske, *The Critical Period of American History* (Boston: Houghton, 1896); Whipple, *supra* note 3, at 10–11.
13. Whipple, *supra* note 3, at 19–22; James Stephens, *Digest of the Criminal Law,* 6th ed. (New York: Macmillan, 1904), pp. 96–99.
14. Act of June 25, 1798, 1 Stat. 570; Act of July 14, 1798, 1 Stat. 596.
15. Frank Anderson, "The Enforcement of the Alien and Sedition Laws," *Annual Report of the American Historical Association* (1912), pp. 113–26; Whipple, *supra* note 3, at 25–27; Chafee, *supra* note 3, at 18.
16. Whipple, *supra* note 3, at 21, 26–27.
17. Chafee, *supra* note 3, at 27.
18. Whipple, *supra* note 3, at 49.
19. *Id.* at 51.
20. *Id.* at 57–63, 71–73.
21. *Id.* at 73–75, 90; Russell Nye, *Fettered Freedom* (Lansing: Michigan State University Press, 1963), pp. 154–57, 174–76.
22. Nye, *supra* note 21, at 187, 227–29.
23. Whipple, *supra* note 13, at 93–100; Nye, *supra* note 21, at 145–50.
24. XII Register of Debates 28 (1837); Nye, *supra* note 21, at 41–85.

25. Quoted in Whipple, *supra* note 3, at 222.
26. Richard Drinnon, *Rebel in Paradise* (Chicago: University of Chicago Press, 1962), pp. 121–42.
27. This description is drawn from Philip Foner, *History of the Labor Movement in the United States* (New York: International Publishers, 1965), 4:172–213; Whipple, *supra* note 3, at 223–24; Paul Brissenden, *The I.W.W.* (New York: Russell & Russell, 1957), pp. 262–66; Joyce Kornbluh, *Rebel Voices* (Ann Arbor: University of Michigan Press, 1964), pp. 94–126; Edwin Witte, *The Government in Labor Disputes* (New York: McGraw-Hill, 1932), p. 202.
28. Foner, *supra* note 27, at 176–77.
29. *Id.* at 183.
30. *Industrial Worker*, February 1, 1912.
31. Whipple, *supra* note 3, at 277–80.
32. Coomer v. United States, 213 Fed. 1 (8th Cir. 1914).
33. *Ex parte* Jackson, 96 U.S. 727 (1877).
34. Whipple, *supra* note 3, at 312–17.
35. *Final Report of the U.S. Commission on Industrial Relations*, at 98, 49 (1915). The commission recommended "that Congress forthwith initiate an amendment to the Constitution securing these rights against encroachment by Federal, State, or local governments or by private persons and corporations." *Id.* at 50.
36. Whipple, *supra* note 3, at 267.
37. Act of June 15, 1917, c. 30, I, § 3, 50 U.S.C. 33 (Repealed 1948).
38. Act of May 16, 1918, c. 75, §1, 40 Stat. 553, 1359–60.
39. 245 F. 102 (2d Cir. 1917). The court reversed a ground-breaking libertarian ruling by District Judge Learned Hand.
40. Chafee, *supra* note 3, at 51.
41. 249 U.S. 47 (1919).
42. *E.g.*, Zechariah Chafee, Jr., "Freedom of Speech in War Time," 32 *Harvard Law Review* 932 (1919).
43. *See, e.g.*, Abrams v. United States, 250 U.S. 616, 619 (1919); Schaefer v. United States, 251 U.S. 466, 477 (1919).
44. Frohwerk v. United States, 249 U.S. 204 (1919); Debs v. United States, 249 U.S. 211 (1919).
45. 250 U.S. 616 (1919).
46. *See* Schaefer v. United States, 251 U.S. 466 (1919); Peirce v. United States, 252 U.S. 239 (1920); Gilbert v. Minnesota, 254 U.S. 325 (1920); United States *ex rel.* Milwaukee Social Democratic Publishing Co. v. Burleson, 255 U.S. 407 (1921); Gitlow v. New York, 268 U.S. 652 (1925).
47. Whitney v. California, 274 U.S. 357, 375–76 (1927) (footnote omitted).
48. Chafee, *supra* note 3; Dorsen, Bender, and Neuborne, *supra* note 3, at 39–46; Robert Murray, *Red Scare: A Study of National Hysteria, 1919–1920* (Minneapolis: University of Minnesota Press, 1955); William Preston, *Aliens and Dissenters: Federal Suppression of Radicals, 1903–1933* (Cambridge, Mass.: Harvard University Press, 1963); Donald Johnson, *The Challenge to American Freedoms, World War I and the Rise of the American Civil Liberties Union* (Lexington: University Press of Kentucky, 1963), pp. 119–48; Peter Irons, "Fighting Fair: Zechariah Chafee, Jr., The Department of Justice, and the 'Trial at the Harvard Club,'" 94 *Harvard Law Review* 1205 (1981).
49. *See* Whitney v. California, *supra.*
50. Gitlow v. New York, 268 U.S. 652 (1925). Technically, this was dictum, since it was not necessary to the decision.
51. 283 U.S. 359 (1931).
52. Near v. Minnesota, 283 U.S. 697 (1931).
53. Grosjean v. American Press Co., 297 U.S. 233 (1936); DeJonge v. Oregon, 299 U.S. 353 (1937); Herndon v. Lowry, 301 U.S. 242 (1937); Lovell v.

Griffin, 303 U.S. 444 (1938); Schneider v. Irvington, 308 U.S. 147 (1939); Cantwell v. Connecticut, 310 U.S. 296 (1940); Thornhill v. Alabama, 310 U.S. 88 (1940).

54.   West Virginia State Board of Education v. Barnette, 319 U.S. 624 (1943). The justices were probably affected by the widespread news in this period (withheld from the public earlier) of the Holocaust in Germany, to which they seemed to refer: "Those who begin coercive elimination of dissent soon find themselves exterminating dissenters. Compulsory unification of opinion achieves only the unanimity of the graveyard." *Id.* at 641.

55.   *See generally* Johnson, *supra* note 48; Drinnon, *supra* note 26; Auerbach, *Labor and Liberty* and "The Depression Decade," both *supra* note 3; Peggy Lamson, *Roger Baldwin: Founder of the American Civil Liberties Union* (Boston: Houghton Mifflin Co., 1976). In this account, I have also relied on a personal interview with Baldwin. At ninety-seven, he still exhibited the clarity and vigor he brought to bear on the free speech issue. The interview was conducted on May 5, 1981, at Baldwin's home in New Jersey. I appreciate the assistance of my friend Candace Falk, who had me invited to an interview of Badlwin originally planned to cover only her forthcoming book on Emma Goldman.

56.   *The New York Times*, July 4, 1917, p. 8, col. 4.

57.   Johnson, *supra* note 48, at 48.

58.   NCLB, *The Truth About the I.W.W.* (April 1918).

59.   Johnson, *supra* note 48, at 74–78.

60.   NCLB memorandum, "Proposed Reorganization of the Work for Civil Liberty," December 31, 1919, quoted *id.* at 146.

61.   *See* Auerbach, *Labor and Liberty*, *supra* note 3. *See also* Paul Murphy, "Communities in Conflict," in Reitman, *supra* note 3.

62.   The labor leaders included James Maurer (president of the Pennsylvania Federation of Labor), Henry Linville (president of the Teachers Union of New York), Duncan McDonald (president of the Illinois Federation of Labor), A. J. Muste (National Organizer for the Amalgamated Textile Workers Union), Julia O'Connor (National Organizer for the Telephone Operators Union), and Rose Schneiderman (Women's Trade Union League). Not all of organized labor was part of this effort; generally, the more progressive unions participated. Many unions also used their own lawyers instead of or in addition to the ACLU lawyers. Other committee members included Jane Addams, Albert DeSilver (co-director with Roger Baldwin), Elizabeth Gurley Flynn, Felix Frankfurter (then a professor of law at Harvard), Helen Keller, Walter Nelles (attorney), and Norman Thomas.

63.   Since the transformation, the ACLU has had a very different posture: it emphatically does not identify with, or care about, its clients' substantive demands or politics. But that position was adopted and tenable only after the political process that led to the transformation.

64.   *See* Rabban, *supra* note 3.

65.   *See* Spies v. Illinois, 123 U.S. 131 (1887); United States v. Cruikshank, 92 U.S. 542 (1875). Another good opportunity was lost in Patterson v. Colorado, 205 U.S. 454 (1907).

66.   The law is, to some extent, politicized by the judge-selection process. Since many presidents appoint judges based on their political perspectives, and presidents are, of course, politically chosen, there is, in theory, a built-in mechanism for the law to reflect political shifts. However, this mechanism is seldom an explanatory factor because vacancies occur only haphazardly (President Nixon appointed four justices, while President Carter appointed none); the timing of appointments, elections, and political shifts is also haphazard; there is seldom the possibility of creating a majority; and many judges do not turn out as expected (for example, Earl Warren). While Roosevelt's appointments had some effect in the late 1930s, none were seated until 1937, when the transformation was almost completed, and they were

never a majority. This mechanism, though itself political, does not explain this or most other important changes.

67. Fred Ragan, "Justice Oliver Wendell Holmes, Jr., Zechariah Chafee, Jr., and the Clear and Present Danger Test for Free Speech: The First Year, 1919," 58 *Journal of American History* 24, 43 (1971); Irons, *supra* note 48, at 1211–12. Holmes apparently was also affected by Judge Learned Hand, with whom he corresponded, and an article in *The New Republic. See* Robert Cover, "The Left, The Right and The First Amendment: 1918–1928," 40 *Maryland Law Review* 349 (1981).

68. Whipple, *supra* note 2, at vi.

69. *E.g.,* N.L.R.B. v. Jones & Laughlin Steel Corp., 301 U.S. 1 (1937).
The ABA *amicus,* and the list of its prestigious signatories, is summarized at 307 U.S. at 678.

71. Pursuant to the resolution, S. Res. No. 266, 74th Cong., 2d Sess. (1976), the Senate Committee on Education and Labor created its Subcommittee on Violations of Free Speech and the Rights of Labor. The subcommittee, as its title and the resolution suggest, viewed freedom of speech and the right of workers to organize and bargain collectively as inseparable. *See S. Rep. No.* 1150, 77th Cong., 2d Sess. (1942); S. Rep. No. 398, 78th Cong., 2d Sess. (1944). *See generally* Auerbach, *Labor and Liberty, supra* note 3.

72. *See* Cox v. Louisiana, 379 U.S. 536 (1965); *New York Times* v. Sullivan, 376 U.S. 254 (1964); Brown v. Louisiana, 383 U.S. 131 (1966).

73. *See, e.g.,* Barenblatt v. United States, 360 U.S. 109 (1959); Uphaus v. Wyman, 360 U.S. 72 (1959); Dennis v. United States, 341 U.S. 494 (1951); American Communications Association v. Douds, 339 U.S. 382 (1950); Lawson v. United States and Trumbo v. United States, 176 F.2d 49 (D.C. Cir. 1949), *cert. denied,* 339 U.S. 934 (1950) (the Hollywood 10 case). The courts also capitulated to a wave of hysterical reaction only a few years after the transformation. *See* Korematsu v. United States, 323 U.S. 214 (1944), approving the imprisonment of all Japanese-Americans on the West Coast.

74. Barenblatt v. United States, 360 U.S. at 147 (dissenting).

75. The ACLU and Baldwin also succumbed. Baldwin played a leading role in the ACLU's expulsion of Elizabeth Gurley Flynn from the ACLU board because of her membership in the Communist Party. Auerbach, "The Depression Decade," *supra* note 3; Corliss Lamont, *The Trial of Elizabeth Gurley Flynn by the American Civil Liberties Union* (New York: Horizon Press, 1968); Lucille Milner, *Education of an American Liberal* (New York: Horizon Press, 1954). The ACLU has recently rescinded and repudiated this action.

76. *E.g.,* Heffron v. Intern. Soc. for Krishna Consciousness, 101 S. Ct. 2559 (1981); Hudgens v. N.L.R.B., 424 U.S. 507 (1976) (discussed in chapter 1).

77. *See* Dennis v. United States, 341 U.S. 494 (1951); Emerson, *supra* note 3, at 112–21.

78. Emerson, *supra* note 3, at 117. *See also* Dorsen, Bender, and Neuborne, *supra* note 3, at 58.

79. *See* Alexander Meiklejohn, *Political Freedom* (New York: Harper & Brothers, 1960), pp. 29–50; Dorsen, Bender, Neuborne, *supra* note 3, at 57–58.

80. *See, e.g.,* Heffron v. Intern. Soc. of Krishna Consciousness, 101 S. Ct. 2559 (1981); Roseman v. Indiana University of Pennsylvania, 520 F. 2d 1364 (3d Cir. 1975), *cert. denied,* 424 U.S. 921 (1976). *See also* Richard Harris, *Freedom Spent* (Boston: Little, Brown & Co., 1976).

81. *See, e.g.,* N.L.R.B. v. United Mineworkers of America, 429 F.2d 141 (3d Cir. 1970).

8
CONTRACT LAW
AS IDEOLOGY
Peter Gabel and Jay M. Feinman

The recent rise of right-wing forces in the United States has been brought about in large part through the shaping and manipulation of collective fantasies. Among the most powerful of these fantasies is a resurgence of what one might call the utopian imagery of freedom of contract. As Reagan "lifts the government off of our backs," we are told that we all will once again be able to stand as free and equal individuals, ready to take whatever action serves our respective self-interests. The image conveys a sudden release of personal power, as if it had only been "government" that had been obstructing the realization of our individual desires. At the same time, the image also conveys a new feeling of social solidarity, a feeling that once that obstruction is removed, we Americans will return to a time when a deal was a deal, when as plain-speaking people we could hammer out our collective destiny through firm handshakes enforceable in a court of law.

For this resurgent ideology to enjoy a temporary measure of success, it makes no difference that it is based upon a lie. The truth is that those of us living in the United States today cannot actually achieve our desire for increased personal power, for freedom, and for genuine social connection and equality so long as we are trapped within ubiquitous hierarchies that leave us feeling powerless, alienated from one another, and stupefied by the routines of everyday activities. And the truth also is that this reduction of our humanity will be overcome only by our own sustained efforts to abolish these hierarchies, to take control over the whole of our lives, and to shape them toward the satisfaction of our real human needs. This sort of concrete, practical movement would embody the *realization* of the utopian content of "freedom of contract," but no such movement is needed for the utopian imagery of the present period to have a profound catalytic effect; instead, the imagery can tap the suppressed needs that people feel as they are numbed into quasi-oblivion in front of industrial machines, word-processors, and television sets, and can jettison those needs into fantasies of fulfillment. The efficacy of the imagery, in other words, derives precisely from the fact that people experience little possibility of achieving personal power, freedom, or genuine social connection in the concrete context of their everyday lives.

A principal vehicle for the transmission of such ideological imagery has been and continues to be "the law." In order to understand the present and historical function of the legal system, and of contract law as a part of this system, one must grasp the relationship between the utopian images transmitted through legal ideas and the socioeconomic context that these ideas serve to justify. In this essay, we provide a brief introduction to a method for understanding this ideological power of law by tracing the relationship between the history of contract law and the development of capitalism over the last two hundred years.

CONTRACT LAW IN THE EIGHTEENTH CENTURY

Eighteenth-century contract law would be barely recognizable to the modern lawyer. The vision of eighteenth-century contract law was not the enforcement of private agreements but the implementation of customary practices and traditional norms. Indeed, in his *Commentaries on the Law of England*, written in the 1760s, Sir William Blackstone did not consider contracts to be a separate body of law at all.

In part, contracts was that portion of the law of property concerning the transfer of title to specific things from one person to another—the process by which "my horse" became "your horse." Because of this present-oriented title theory, legal enforcement of an executory agreement (an agreement under which the parties promised to render their performances at some time in the future) was almost unknown. Contract law also concerned customary obligations between people related to status, occupation, or social responsibilities. For example, a patient was "contractually" obligated by custom to pay for a physician's services whether or not he actually had promised to pay prior to the rendering of the services. In all types of contracts cases, the substantive fairness of the agreement or relation was subject to scrutiny by a lay jury applying community standards of justice. If a physician sued for his fee or a seller of goods for her price, the jury could decide that even an amount agreed to by the parties was excessive and inequitable, and so award a smaller sum instead.[1]

Thus, eighteenth-century contract law was hostile to commercial enterprise. The traditional image of the world presented by contract law regarded the enforcement of market transactions as often illegitimate, so a seller could never be guaranteed the price he or she had bargained for, and liability might be imposed in the absence of agreement when required by popular notions of fairness. Such a system could exist because the development of a system of production founded upon universal competition in national and world markets had not yet fully emerged, and the political world-view that justified the relatively static property relations of traditional, precapitalist society had not yet been entirely overturned.

Between the latter part of the eighteenth century and the middle of the nineteenth century, both the economic and political foundations of eighteenth-century contract law were, in Marx's phrase, "burst asunder." In this period the system of economic and social relations known as free-market capitalism achieved a full development begun several centuries earlier, and the political climate was explosively transformed in the service of those social and economic developments with the aid of violent revolutions in America and Western Europe. These changes dramatically transformed the life situations of people in Western society and brought about an equally dramatic transformation in contract law.

CONTRACT LAW IN THE NINETEENTH CENTURY

In the nineteenth century, the key changes in society were its split into capital-owning and nonowning classes, and the dissolution of traditional patterns of social relations. As to the first, the social and economic positions of those who owned capital in the form of land, money, and machinery, and those who, having been thrown off the land or out of their traditional crafts, owned only their minds and bodies, increasingly diverged. Both groups became subject to the pressures of the capitalist form of social organization. Capitalists were driven irrespective of their personal will or greed to compete with one another for markets for their products and to extract, with the assistance of a developing mechanical technology, the greatest possible production from their workers at the lowest possible cost. Workers were forced to sell their labor power to owners for a wage in order to survive and thereby to subject much of their daily lives to the owners' control; at the same time, competition among them drove wages down to bare survival levels.

The second great change in society was the dissolution of many of the traditional bonds among people that had characterized the social relations of earlier periods. The social meaning of work, property, and community were increasingly fragmented as socioeconomic processes based on competition and individual self-interest reorganized the social universe. Traditional social environments had hardly been idyllic and certainly embodied forms of alienation and class domination that ought not to be idealized. But the rise of capitalism—with its universal market in which people and things were everywhere made subject to the exigencies of money exchange—generated a dramatic and dislocating social upheaval. Within a short stretch of historical time, people experienced and were forced to adapt to the appearance of the factory and the slum, the rise of the industrial city, and a violent rupture of group life and feeling that crushed traditional forms of moral and community identity in favor of that blend of aggression, paranoia, and profound emotional isolation and anguish that is known romantically as the rugged individual.

How could people have been persuaded or forced to accept such massive disruptions in their lives? One vehicle of persuasion was the law of contracts, which generated a new ideological imagery that sought to give legitimacy to the new order. To speak of "ideological imagery" is to imply that there is a reality behind the image that is concealed and even denied by the image. The reality was the new system of oppressive and alienating economic and social relations. Contract law denied the nature of the system by creating an imagery that made the oppression and alienation appear to be the consequences of what the people themselves desired.

Denial and legitimation were accomplished by representing reality in ideal terms, as if things were the way they were because the people wished them to be so.[2] This representation was not the product of conspiratorial manipulation by power-mad lawyers and judges. Instead, the legal elites tended to identify with the structure of the social and economic order because of what they perceived to be their privileged position within it, and they expressed the legitimacy of that structure when arguing and deciding cases in their professional roles. During this period important members of the bench and bar associated themselves emotionally and intellectually with the capitalist transformation and became imbued with the "logic" of the new system. In arguing and deciding cases, they fit the situation presented within that logic to resolve the conflict represented by the dispute at issue. Those resolutions tended to legitimate the basic social relations, no matter how unjust, oppressive, and alienating they actually were. In the process of resolving many cases, legal concepts were built up that embodied the new social relations. The result was a system of contract law that appeared to shape economic affairs according to normative principles but that was, in fact, only a recast form of the underlying socioeconomic relations.

The legitimating image of classical contract law in the nineteenth century was the ideal of free competition as the consequence of wholly voluntary interactions among many private persons, all of whom were in their nature free and equal to one another. From one point of view this was simple truth, for the practical meaning of the market system was that people conceived of as interchangeable productive units ("equality") had unfettered mobility ("freedom") in the market. From another point of view, however, this was denial and apology.[3] It did not take account of the practical limitations on market freedom and equality arising from class position or unequal distribution of wealth. It also ignored other meanings of freedom and equality having to do with the realization of human spirit and potential through work and community. The legitimation of the free market was achieved by seizing upon a narrow economic notion of freedom and equality, and fusing it in the public mind with the genuine meaning.

The legal consequences of this legitimating mystification were the separation of contract law from the law of property and the law of nonconsensual relations, the representation of all social relations as deriving from the free and voluntary association of individuals without coercion by the state, and the allocation of responsibility for the coercion worked by operation of the market to personal merit or luck. In an economy founded upon the accumulation of capital through exchange transactions occurring in a competitive market, the proper role of the state was conceived to be that of the relatively passive enforcer of the "free will" of the parties themselves, of their "freedom of contract." As a result, the nineteenth-century law of contracts consisted of a series of forms ostensibly designed solely to realize the will of free and equal parties, as that will was objectively manifested in agreements.[4]

Some leading contracts cases taught to first-year law students illustrate the power and effects of this mystification. The rules for contract formation and performance were extensions of the principle of objectively manifested free will. A son and his wife worked for his father on the father's farm for some twenty-five years without pay, in the expectation that the father would will the farm to him on his death. When the father died without a will, the farm was divided among all his heirs. Could the son, like the eighteenth-century physician, recover in contract, if not for the farm, at least for the value of his services? No, because there was no clear expression of an agreement between father and son, without which the court would be invading the freedom of the parties if it imposed liability.[5] On the other hand, where the parties had made a definite agreement, it bound them absolutely. Thus, a builder contracted to build a schoolhouse; the partly finished building was blown down by a windstorm; and after being rebuilt, it collapsed again due to soil conditions that could not be remedied. Was the builder liable for failure to build a third time? Indeed he was, for "where a party, by his own *contract*, creates a duty or charge upon himself, he is bound to make it good if he may, notwithstanding any accident by inevitable necessity."[6]

The most important and in some ways the most peculiar rules of classical contract law concerned the doctrine of "consideration," which grew out of the principles of freedom and equality. Since the market was the measure of all things, only those promises were enforceable that represented market transactions—those for which the person making the promise received something, a "consideration," in return. Thus, a promise to make a gift was not enforceable because it was gratuitous.[7] Further, if a person offered to sell his house to another and agreed to give the other person until Friday to decide whether to buy or not, he could change his mind and revoke the promise because it was, like a gift, a gratuity.[8] Conversely, when a bargain had been struck, it was firm, and the courts would not inquire into the "adequacy of consideration," *i.e.*, the fairness of the bargain. If a person promised to pay a large sum of money in return for a worthless piece of paper, the nineteenth-century court, unlike the eighteenth-century jury, would "protect" the exercise of free will between supposedly equal parties and bind him without weighing the substantive fairness of the transaction.[9]

The results in these cases may seem unfair or irrational today, but to the judges of the time they were neither. The courts could not easily have intervened to protect a party or to remedy unfairness without violating the ideological image that the source of social obligation rests only upon the bargain that the parties themselves have evinced, not upon the community's version of justice. This imagery, drawn as it was from the exigencies of competitive exchange, served to deny the oppressive character of the market and the lack of real personal liberty experienced by people in their private and work lives. Most important, it served to deny that there was a system at all that was coercively shaping and constricting the social world, because the

imagery made it appear that this world was simply the perpetual realization of an infinite number of free choices made by an infinite number of voluntary actors.

CONTRACT LAW IN THE TWENTIETH CENTURY

Today judges applying contemporary contract law would probably
reach different results in these cases. The son might receive a recovery
for the value of the services conferred on the father. Liberalized doctrines of excuse for nonperformance might relieve the builder. In many
circumstances, a "firm offer," such as the offer to sell the house upon
acceptance before Friday, is binding without consideration; in other
cases, the court might not enforce the offer but would at least compensate the buyer for expenses incurred in reliance on the offer. And,
purportedly, courts today will in extreme cases correct any gross unfairness in a bargain.

Contemporary contract law views these cases differently not because twentieth-century judges are wiser or smarter than their
nineteenth-century counterparts, or because a new and more equitable
style of legal reasoning has somehow sprung into being through a
progressive maturation of the judicial mind. The old rules disintegrated for the same reason they were conceived: there has been a
transformation of social and economic life that has brought about a
parallel transformation in the ideological imagery required to justify
it.

The transformation from the nineteenth-century to the twentieth-
century forms of American capitalism was the consequence of a variety of factors that can only be summarized here: competition among
businesses produced ever larger concentrations of capital within fewer
and fewer companies; workers organized in response to their collective
dependence on these emerging monopolies and challenged in a revolutionary way the myths of freedom and equality; exploitation of the
Third World, advancing technology, and efficient organization of
production facilitated the partial assimilation of the American labor
movement, allowing for the payment of higher wages while deflecting
more radical labor demands; this increase in the level of wages, the use
of part of the economic surplus for unemployment insurance, Social
Security, and other types of welfare benefits, and the greater psychological control of consumer purchases through the mass media helped
to alleviate the system's persistent tendency toward underconsump-
tion. The basic requirement for understanding contemporary contract

law is to look at the socioeconomic system thus produced and to observe its transposition, through the medium of law, into an imaginary construct that attempts to secure the system's appearance of legitimacy.

The essential characteristic of contemporary capitalism is the substitution of integration and coordination in the economy for the unbridled competition of the free market. Coordination is accomplished first by monopolistic corporations that are vertically and horizontally integrated (meaning there are but a few "horizontal" corporations at the top of the major industries that own the capital that controls "vertically" production and distribution in each industry); and second, by a massive involvement of the state in regulating and stabilizing the system. In place of the unrestricted mobility of productive units that characterized the operation of the market in the nineteenth century, we now have integration, coordination, and cooperation to above all maintain systemic stability through an ever more pervasive and efficient administration.

A brief look at the dominant American industry, the automobile industry, will illustrate. The industry is composed of three giant companies and one smaller firm, which account for three fourths of the vehicles sold annually. The firms are vertically integrated in fact; every step of the production and distribution process, from raw material production to retail sales, is accomplished either within the company itself, by basic industry firms such as the steel companies, which are closely allied in interest with the automakers, or through legally independent entities, such as parts suppliers and dealers, which are actually subject to the economic control of the manufacturers.[10] Although General Motors, the largest of the "Big Three," may have the capital and market power to significantly increase its market share at the expense of some of its competitors, it has not usually done so, preferring a relatively predictable shared monopoly to cutthroat competition. State intervention occurs to support the industry through massive purchases of its products for civilian and military use, and the provision of highways as public goods for the use of cars; to coordinate the production of goods that market forces alone do not produce, such as safety devices; and even to ensure the continued existence of the firms, as in the federal welfare scheme to bail out Chrysler.

The rise of the coordinated economy has created a major problem for the law—how to transform the ideology of "freedom and equality" and its adjunct, "freedom of contract," into a new image that might retain the legitimating power of the older images while modifying them to conform more closely to the actual organization of daily life in the era of monopoly capitalism. The strategy for solving this problem has been to transform contract law into a relatively uniform code for business transactions that is predominantly defined not by the individualist principle of unregulated free competition but by the more collective principle of competition regulated by trade custom.[11] Since most "trades" (whatever nostalgia for a bygone era that term may evoke) are actually integrated production networks subject to supervision by dominant firms, the modern law of contracts is able to retain the legitimating features of private agreement while effectuating the regulatory and stabilizing component that is a central principle of the contemporary economy.

The principle of regulated competition leads to different results in the kinds of cases mentioned earlier. The twentieth-century counterpart to the case of the son who could not recover from his father's estate because of the absence of an express promise is the 1965 Wisconsin case of *Hoffman* v. *Red Owl Stores*.[12] The Hoffmans were small-town bakers who were induced to sell their bakery and move to a new town in reliance on the promises of an agent of the Red Owl supermarket chain that they would be granted a franchise, which never came. Under classical contract law, the Hoffmans would be without a remedy because the formal franchise contract had never been executed; in the twentieth century, however, the Wisconsin court discarded that restricted notion of agreement and held that they could recover because their reliance on the agent's representation had been commercially reasonable. The strict nineteenth-century requirement of bargain was rejected in favor of a broader standard of social obligation more expressive of the realities of the late-capitalist economy.

Hoffman v. *Red Owl* is a leading case for the principle that atomistic, concrete agreement is no longer the sole principle of contract law; people's tendency to act in reliance on less formal representations must be protected as well. It also illustrates the doctrine that private economic actors have a duty to act in "good faith." Both principles embody the ethic of cooperation and coordination reflective of the modern economy.

These principles apply in other cases also. The promise to keep open until Friday an offer to sell a house would now frequently be enforced because that is recognized as an appropriate and necessary way to do business today.[13] In rare cases, courts can even be moved to inquire into the fairness of a bargain—into the adequacy of consideration—under the recently developed doctrine of unconscionability. While this doctrine has more theoretical significance than practical effect, sometimes consumers and other parties with little economic power can be protected from the more outrageous excesses of economic predators.[14] In sum, people are conceived to be partners in a moral community where equity and the balancing of interests according to standards of fair dealing have supplanted the primitive era, when every moral tie was dissolved in "the icy waters of egotistical calculation."[15] And the state as passive enforcer of private transactions has become the state as active enforcer of the newly conceived notion of the general welfare.

CONCLUSION

The chart on page 182 may help to summarize this three-stage transformation of the economic and legal world. It shows how at each stage in our history the ideological imagery of contract law served to legitimate an oppressive socioeconomic reality by denying its oppressive character and representing it in imaginary terms.

    This is a very different explanation of the role of contract law from liberal or leftist instrumental analyses, which suggest that particular rules of law or particular results "helped" capitalists by providing a framework for legal enforcement of market activity. Instrumental analyses of contract law confuse the role of direct force with the role of law in the development of sociohistorical processes. Social processes like "free-market capitalism" do not get "enforced" by "laws." Rather, these processes are accepted through social conditioning, through the collective internalization of practical norms that have their foundation in concrete socioeconomic reality. Since these norms are alienating and oppressive, the process of collective conditioning requires the constant threat of force and the occasional use of it. For example, if you fail to perform your part of a bargain, it *may* be the case that a sheriff with a gun will attach your bank account to pay the aggrieved party his or her damages. The occasional deployment of direct force serves to maintain the status quo as well as to get people to accept its legitimacy.

    "The law" does not enforce anything, however, because the law is nothing but ideas and the images they signify. Its purpose is to justify practical norms (and in so doing to help constitute them by contributing to the collective conditioning process). One important way that this justification process occurs is through judicial opinions. Judicial opinions "work" as ideology by a rhetorical process in which oppressive practical norms are encoded as "general rules" with ideological content; these "rules" then serve as the basis for a logic ("legal reasoning") that supposedly determines the outcome of the lawsuit. The key social function of the opinion, however, is not to be found in the outcome and the use of state power which may follow from it, but in the rhetorical structure of the opinion itself, in the legitimation of

	Socioeconomic Reality	*Ideological Imagery*
Eighteenth Century	The social order is organized through traditional statuses and hierarchies, creating relations of class domination determined primarily by distribution of landed wealth, fixed occupation, and inherited social position.	The social order is oganized through hierarchies based upon "natural" class position, which exist prior to human intervention; and the legal system implements customary moral and religious principles, which support the natural hierarchies.
Nineteenth Century	The social order is organized through free competition, made coercive through the operation of an unregulated market, creating relations of class domination determined primarily by the ownership of capital	The social order is organized through the formation of voluntary contracts among free and equal citizens, with whose choice the state will not interfere, creating a classless society where everyone has equal opportunity for personal gain and happiness.
Twentieth Century	The social order is organized through the predominant control by monopolies of all aspects of production, with the help of regulatory planning and "stabilization" by the state, creating relations of class domination determined primarily by the ownership of capital.	The social order is organized through the voluntary cooperation of different groups in the economy (big business, labor, franchisees, the unemployed, etc.) whose good-faith cooperation the state seeks to coordinate purposively toward the general administration of a fair society where class inequalities are compensated for through regulation and redistribution.

the practical norm that occurs through the application of it in the form of a "legal rule." That enforcement of bargains was much more likely to occur under nineteenth-century contract law than under eighteenth-century law is, of course, true; but this does not mean that the function of nineteenth-century contract law was to "enforce bargains." The reverse expresses the truth more accurately—that the enforcement of bargains functioned to permit the elaboration of contract law as legitimating ideology.

The central point to understand from this is that contract law today constitutes an elaborate attempt to conceal what is going on in the world. Contemporary capitalism bears no more relation to the imagery of contemporary contract law than did nineteenth-century capitalism to the imagery of classical contract law. Contemporary capitalism is a coercive system of relationships that more or less corresponds to the brief description given here. The proof of this statement inheres in the situations we all face in our daily lives in the functional roles to which we are consigned: lawyer, secretary, student, tenant, welfare recipient, consumer of the products and services of Exxon, Citibank, and Sears. Despite the doctrines of reliance and good faith, large business corporations daily disappoint our expectations as to how they should behave. Despite the doctrine of unconscionability, unfairness is rampant in the marketplace. In this reality our narrow functional roles produce isolation, passivity, unconnectedness, and impotence. Contract law, like the other images constituted by capitalism, is a denial of these painful feelings and an apology for the system that produces them.

Most of the time the socioeconomic system operates without any need for law as such because people at every level have been imbued with its inevitability and necessity. When the system breaks down and conflicts arise, a legal case comes into being. This is the "moment" of legal ideology, the moment at which lawyers and judges in *their* narrow, functional roles seek to justify the normal functioning of the system by resolving the conflict through an idealized way of thinking about it.

But this also can be the moment for struggle against the narrow limits imposed in law on genuine values such as freedom, equality, moral community, and good faith. By questioning whether the legal system helps or hinders the actual realization of those values in a meaningful sense in everyday life, the critical approach permits us to expose the illegitimacy of the system and to explore the possibility of a different order of things.

NOTES

1. Morton Horwitz, *The Transformation of American Law, 1780–1860* (Cambridge, Mass.: Harvard University Press, 1977), chap. VI.
2. *See* Peter Gabel, "Reification in Legal Reasoning," 3 *Research in Law and Sociology* 25 (1980).

3.   *See* Duncan Kennedy, "The Structure of Blackstone's *Commentaries*," 28 *Buffalo Law Review* 205 (1979).

4.   *See* Friedrich Kessler and Grant Gilmore, *Contracts: Cases and Materials*, 2d ed. (Boston: Little, Brown, 1970), pp. 2–6.

5.   Hertzog v. Hertzog, 29 Pennsylvania State Reports 465 (1857).

6.   School Trustees of Trenton v. Bennett, 27 New Jersey Law Reports 513 (1859).

7.   Kirksey v. Kirksey, 8 Alabama Reports 131 (1845).

8.   Dickinson v. Dodds, 2 English Law Reports, Chancery Division (Court of Appeal 1876). For the way in which American contract theorists manipulated this and other English precedents to support their ideas, *see* Grant Gilmore, *The Death of Contract* (Columbus: Ohio State University Press, 1974).

9.   Haigh v. Brooks, 113 English Reports 119 (Queen's Bench 1839, Exchequer 1840).

10. Stewart Macaulay, "The Standardized Contracts of United States Automobile Manufacturers," *International Encyclopedia of Comparative Law* (New York: Oceana Publications, 1974), vol. 7, chap. 3, secs. 21–55.

11. *See* Eugene Mooney, "Old Kontract Principles and Karl's New Kode: An Essay on the Jurisprudence of Our New Commercial Law," 11 *Villanova Law Review* 213 (1966).

12. 26 Wisconsin Reports 2d 683, 133 Northwestern Reports 2d 267 (1965).

13. New York General Obligations Law, §5–1109 (McKinney 1978); Uniform Commercial Code, §2–205; Restatement (Second) of Contracts, §87(2) (1981).

14. *See* Arthur Leff, "Unconscionability and the Code: The Emperor's New Clause," 115 *University of Pennsylvania Law Review* 485 (1967).

15. Karl Marx and Friedrich Engels, *The Communist Manifesto* (New York: Washington Square Press, 1964), p. 62.

9
TORTS
Richard L. Abel

A tort is a wrong (*i.e.*, not mere discourtesy) done to one person by another for which the law provides a remedy. It includes such disparate events as a car accident, a worker who suffers lung damage through handling asbestos insulation, a parent who beats a child, a detergent that damages clothes, and a school that unlawfully detains a student.

Tort law is not a coherent body of doctrine that can logically be deduced from fundamental principles. Its content is best defined by reference to the boundaries of adjacent areas of the law. Tort law prescribes remedies for wrongs or injuries whether or not inflicted intentionally. Unlike criminal law, however, its purpose is to compensate the victim, though punitive damages are simultaneously a penalty and an incentive to the victim to seek redress. Tort law rectifies damage to property but does not adjudicate ownership; the taking of personal property is the tort of conversion, and the tort concept of nuisance combines elements of tort and property law. Contract remedies, not tort, are appropriate where the duty breached is found in a preexisting agreement. However, this distinction is blurred if the agreement is implied by law, as when a seller is held to warrant the fitness of a

I owe an enormous debt to colleagues in critical legal studies, too numerous to name here, who offered invaluable criticism and suggestions; this essay is very much a collective product.

consumer good; and tort damages are sometimes granted for breach of contract, as when an insurer willfully refuses to pay a valid claim to its insured. Although tort is largely the product of our gradually evolving case law, violation of a statute, and even of the Constitution, can provide the basis for a tort action.

TORT LAW AND CAPITALISM

Contemporary tort law is intimately related to the rise of capitalism, as both cause and effect. In earlier periods, law was largely preoccupied with personal status, control over resources (primarily land), and the development of contractual relations (mercantile capitalism). Industrial capitalism transformed the entire social structure, engendering urbanization, which enormously increased the frequency of interaction among strangers. This is significant because strangers, unlike acquaintances or intimates, have less incentive to exercise care not to injure one another inadvertently and find it more difficult to resolve the differences that arise when such injury occurs. Both problems are aggravated by class and racial differences within the modern capitalist city. At the same time, interaction among friends and relatives becomes progressively limited, ultimately to the confines of the nuclear family. This is significant because intimates commit most intentional torts. Indeed, inadvertent injuries that cannot be forgiven are often interpreted as intentional, by reference either to witchcraft beliefs in tribal societies or theories of unconscious ambivalence since Freud. Yet intentional torts within the nuclear family are rarely resolved by the legal system, both because the process frequently would destroy the relationship that generated the tort and because those who commit the torts—men against women, parents against children—are sufficiently powerful to obstruct legal redress.

Industrialization also conferred on capitalist enterprise the ability to effect extensive damage, first through dominion over unprecedented amounts of physical force (e.g., factories, railroads) and more recently through the proliferation of toxic chemicals. Individuals—car drivers, for instance—acquired comparable power only much later, and even then individual behavior and its consequences were fundamentally shaped by the capitalist enterprise that created the instrumentality. Concentration of capital and mass production increased the number of workers, consumers, and others who might be harmed by capitalist indifference or miscalculation. Capitalism and technology also distanced from their victims those who made the "decision for accidents," so that the acts at issue in tort law have increasingly come to resemble modern warfare.

A separate but related development altered the legal response to intentional torts: the growth of the state apparatus as an essential precondition of capitalism. The state, in the form of police, criminal courts, and the penal system, expropriates interindividual conflict and invites, indeed requires, passivity and dependence (consider the invisibility of the victim in most criminal prosecutions). Crime virtually supplants intentional tort; civil remedies are largely limited to unintentional behavior.

Capitalism also shapes the experience of injury. First (and this enumeration is not chronological) capitalism creates a proletariat that must sell its labor for wages in order to live. It simultaneously destroys the obligations of mutual support outside the nuclear family and pays those within it who are gainfully employed a level of wages too low to support nonproductive members. Because inability to work thus becomes tantamount to destitution or dependence upon charity, the core of damages is compensation for loss of earning capacity. Second, capitalists, petty bourgeois, and more recently unionized workers are able to accumulate consumer goods, which require protection against inadvertent destruction. Just as there is greater power to destroy, so there is more to be destroyed. The capitalist process of commodification and the industrial process of mass production make one chattel as good as another (indeed, the newer the better) and money the equivalent of all; hence, money damages come to be seen as adequate compensation. Third, the family (now reduced to a nucleus) is no longer able to care for illness or injury, partly because its members must seek employment outside the home, partly because care itself has been commodified and monopolized by the emergent medical profession. Since this monopoly allows professionals to command high fees, injuries come to "cost" a great deal more. Finally, the logic of the commodity form is progressively extended to nonproductive experience (damages for pain and suffering, emotional distress) and intimate relationships (damages for wrongful death, loss of consortium). Thus, tort law under capitalism equates money with labor, possessions, care, emotional and physical integrity, and ultimately love.

Capitalist tort law exploits and alienates tort victims in ways that parallel the exploitation and alienation of labor by the capitalist mode of production. In precapitalist society, injury, like work, creates use value: it elicits care from intimates who are motivated by concern, and it prompts a demand for an apology backed by the threat of retribution by those who belong to the same community as the victim and are therefore also injured. The capitalist state, which asserts its monopoly of force to obstruct this latter response, simultaneously creates a market for injuries in the form of tort law and the legal system (just as it constitutes the market for the sale of labor, capital, land, and commodities). Where capitalism separates the worker from the means of production, the legal profession separates tort victims from the means of redressing their wrongs and the medical profession disables victims and intimates from caring for illness and injury. In each instance, a fraction of the dominant class mobilizes the power of the state in its own interests—to protect the property of the capitalist and the monopoly of expertise of the lawyer and physician. The lawyer then combines legal expertise with the victim's injury (as the capitalist combines capital with the worker's labor) to produce a tort (a commodity) that has exchange value both in the state-created market (the court) and in the dependent markets it spawns (negotiated settlements). The lawyer (like the capitalist) exercises total control over this process; the victim (like the worker) has virtually no say over which torts are produced or how. When the transaction is complete, the victim receives the bare minimum (or less) necessary for survival, and the lawyer takes the rest as a fee (the capitalist expropriation of surplus value), some of which may be shared with physicians.

Because capitalism separates those who produce from those who own the means of production, workers lose control over their own safety. Because capitalists have to maximize profit in a competitive market, they *must* sacrifice the health and safety of others—workers, consumers, those affected by environmental dangers. Capitalism fosters injury for still another reason: it must constantly expand its markets and increase consumption; torts contribute to this end, just like planned obsolescence and warfare. Tort doctrine has reflected this dynamic in many ways: the choice of negligence over strict liability; doctrines of contributory negligence, the fellow-servant rule, and assumption of risk; exculpatory clauses; and the lower standard of care for (precapitalist) landowners and (late-capitalist) professionals.

CRITIQUE OF CAPITALIST TORT LAW

Discrimination on the Basis of Class, Race, and Gender

Liberal legalism, the dominant political philosophy under capitalism, decries explicit, de jure discrimination. Therefore, tort law gradually eliminated distinctions between patients who were injured in charitable and profit-making hospitals, fee-paying automobile passengers and gratuitous guests, business and social guests injured by landowner negligence, those injured by medical malpractice, and other tort victims. But the focus on superficial equality hides the persistence of numerous invisible inequalities.

First and foremost, there is inequality in the incidence of injury and illness: capitalists, professionals, white-, pink-, and blue-collar workers are exposed to vastly different hazards in the workplace; consumers (of household goods, foods, automobiles, medical care, etc.) suffer different risks of injury depending on the quality of the products and services they buy (necessarily a reflection of class); residential segregation by class determines the level of environmental pollution that members of a household will endure. For the same reasons, ethnic differences in employment, consumption, and residence will produce racial inequalities in incidence. Women are exposed to more dangers in the home than are men but conversely may be "protected" from hazards at work by being excluded from dangerous jobs that enjoy higher pay and status.

Second, class, race, and gender will affect the extent to which and the way in which the experience of injury is transformed into a claim for legal redress: the sense of entitlement to physical, mental, and emotional well-being (women only recently began to resist abuse by their husbands; textile workers are just now coming to view chronic shortness of breath as unnatural); the feeling of competence to assert a claim and to withstand retaliation; the capacity to mobilize the legal process, which includes choosing and controlling a lawyer and preparing evidence; and financial and emotional resources, which will affect the quality of legal representation obtained and the ability of the claimant to overcome opposition and delay in order to pursue negotiation or litigation to a satisfactory conclusion.

Third, the law discriminates in the availability and generosity of the remedies it offers. The greatest difference is between tort damages and other compensation systems. An injured blue-collar worker is far more likely to be injured at work than is someone from another occupational category; such injuries are relegated to workers' compensation, which pays only a fraction of tort damages and rejects altogether some claims that would be valid in tort. But other oppressed categories —women, children, the elderly, the poor, and ethnic minorities—are also excluded from tort recovery. They are more frequently the victims of violent crimes, whose assailants are either unidentifiable, unavailable, or financially irresponsible; the only remedy is compensation schemes that exist in only half the states, reach very few victims, and pay insufficient amounts. Women and children who are injured by intimates are left without any remedy. The poor and minorities, who either cannot evade the draft or enlist in the military as an alternative to structural unemployment, are dependent on inadequate veterans'

benefits when injured in war; and when they are victims of governmental misconduct—police violence; abuse in prisons, schools, and
mental institutions—they may be completely remediless either because
of sovereign immunity or because officials possess substantial tactical
advantages in defending against such claims.

Another form of remedial discrimination is internal to the tort
system: the quantum of damages preserves and, indeed, amplifies the
present unequal distribution of wealth and income. Imagine a car crash
between A, who is unemployed and drives a worthless jalopy, and B,
who owns a Rolls-Royce and earns a high income. If A is negligent and
B nonnegligent, A will have to pay for the damage to the Rolls and to
B's earning capacity. But if B is negligent and A nonnegligent, B will
have to pay almost nothing. This inequality is exaggerated by the fact
that damages for pain and suffering are often expressed as a multiple of
pecuniary damages (usually two to one). If we make the hypothetical
more realistic by taking account of the liability insurance each party is
likely to have, the inequality remains: A's insurance premium will have
to reflect the possibility of injury to B and be higher than would be
necessary to protect A and others like her, whereas B's premium will
reflect the possibility of an injury to A and be lower than would be
necessary to protect a world of Bs. A thus pays part of the cost of
protecting the privileges of B.

Producing Illness and Injury

Capitalist tort law systematically encourages unsafety. The dynamic of
capitalism—competitive pursuit of profit—impels the enterprise to
endanger the workers it employs, the consumers of its products and
services, and those who inhabit the environment it pollutes. The cost
of safety almost always diminishes profits. The capitalist, therefore,
must be as unsafe as he can get away with being.

Tort law purports to curb these destructive consequences of capitalism. The legal-economic rationale that presently dominates and
shapes tort principles is market deterrence, which argues that the most
efficient way to promote an optimum level of safety is to internalize
accident costs by making those who negligently cause accidents legally
liable for their consequences. But there are fundamental theoretical
and empirical reasons why market deterrence does not and cannot
work. First, the very name is deceptive: there cannot be market deterrence because there is no market for injury and illness. The determination of what an accident costs can only be decided collectively,
whether by a judge, a jury, or a legislature. Furthermore, the decision
necessarily introduces a large margin of error, since it must not only

value intangibles but also make predictions about an *individual* future: lost earnings, career, change in number of dependents, life expectancy, prognosis for recovery, possible medical discoveries, etc.

Second, a court is required to decide whether a particular injury was negligently inflicted; but the economic conceptualization of negligence as suboptimal safety (epitomized in Learned Hand's formula weighing the cost of accident avoidance against the cost of injury discounted by its probability)[1] can be meaningfully applied only to an ongoing activity. Thus the inevitable errors in determining negligence will result in inadequate safety.

Third, a court is required to determine whether or not a particular actor caused a given injury or illness. But we know that causation is probabilistic and that for any event there are a multiplicity of contributing causes.[2] The imposition of liability on one party (or even several) necessarily fails to internalize the accident costs in other causal activities.

Fourth, there is an inescapable tension between promoting safety through accident-cost internalization and spreading these costs—another goal of tort law. The most important mechanism for spreading costs is liability insurance, which has become so widespread and which discriminates so crudely among the insured in setting premiums that it alone virtually destroys the capacity of tort liability to optimize safety.

Fifth, in order for liability costs to alter the behavior of entrepreneurs, the latter must be unable to pass these costs on to consumers; but this condition will not be satisfied if liability costs are an insignificant percentage of the price of the good or service, if demand is relatively price inelastic (the good or service is a necessity), or if the market is highly oligopolistic.

Sixth, market deterrence assumes that all actors who "cause" accidents are economic maximizers; consequently, it argues that victims must be *denied* compensation, in whole or in part, in order to be motivated to protect themselves. This can only diminish the concern of capitalists for the safety of others.

Seventh, and most important, market deterrence assumes that the legal system fully internalizes *all* the costs of negligent accidents. Yet we have just seen in the previous section that capitalist tort law systematically denies compensation for injury and illness and does so in a highly discriminatory manner. Therefore, the theory of market deterrence logically compels the conclusion that capitalist tort law encourages unsafety and subjects the most oppressed sectors of the population to the greatest danger. It motivates the entrepreneur to reduce liability costs, not accident costs, and to seek to evade the consequences of carelessness, not to enhance safety. Thus, we have Ford producing a Pinto with a gasoline tank it knows to be explosive,

Johns-Manville continuing to subject its workers to asbestos for decades after it learns they will suffer lung damage and cancer, McDonnell-Douglas producing and American Airlines flying the DC-10 that crashed in Chicago when both knew of the faulty pylon and other design defects. The capitalist response to the threat of tort liability is to strive to externalize accident costs by concealing information (denying workers access to their medical records), threatening retaliation against those who seek compensation, and using the enormous resources of the enterprise (and of its liability insurer) to coerce victims into accepting inadequate settlements, to overwhelm them in litigation, and to pass legislation that immunizes the enterprise from liability costs (as the nuclear-energy industry has done with the Price-Anderson Act). We know from studies of the deterrent effect of criminal sanctions that certainty is more important than severity; because it is so unlikely that damages will ever be paid, tort liability is often an empty threat, incapable of promoting safety.

If market deterrence worked the way it claims it does, state regulation of danger would be wholly unnecessary. The capitalist enterprise would balance the cost of safety against the cost of accidents; and whatever level of danger it chose would, by definition, be optimally efficient. Indeed, the mythical efficiency of the market is often invoked to oppose all regulation, or at least to require agencies to conform to the fictitious criteria of cost-benefit analysis, as in the attacks on the Occupational Safety and Health Administration (OSHA) by capitalists, the Supreme Court,[3] and now the Reagan administration. Yet surely the failure of tort as a means of control is visible in the proliferation of regulation in such areas as food and drugs; environmental pollution; toxic wastes; pesticides; air, rail, and road transportation; nuclear energy; consumer products; professional services; and the workplace. Virtually everyone concedes the need for rules in at least some of these areas, e.g., traffic laws or the testing of medicines. Indeed, capitalists often welcome regulation as a protection against the competitive market. But we also know that these agencies fail to achieve acceptable levels of safety because, when compared to the capitalist enterprises they seek to regulate, they are inadequately funded, more restrained by legal formalism, denied effective sanctions, and readily captured by the industries they purport to control.

The most insidious consequence of dependence upon market deterrence and state regulation has been the undermining of collective efforts by those endangered to protect their own safety. Critics have often noted that the regulatory agency can lull citizens into a false sense of security, and hence into passivity, by appearing vigorously to champion public interests. The politics of safety are transformed into the administration of safety, thereby obscuring the political interests the administrative apparatus continues to serve. But if the bankruptcy of government regulation is a familiar tale, the effect of dependence on market deterrence is less widely recognized, and yet such dependence is even more dangerously seductive. Market deterrence, by mandating the payment of money damages to the injured person, subverts collective efforts to exert control over safety. Damages are paid only to individuals (not collectivities) because the injury, like the individual, is viewed as unique; group reparations and class actions are unavailable to those who share the experience of having been injured by the same polluter, manufacturer of a defective produce, or employer. Damages are paid only for an injury caused by the defendant's act. This means both that unsafe conduct causing no injury is not deterred and that legal attention is focused on the temporally delimited act of an individual rather than on the ongoing activity of a collectivity. Capitalist tort law, like capitalist medicine, is obsessed with individual cure at the expense of collective prevention because (among other reasons) capitalism creates a market only for the former. Money damages undermine the sense of a collective interest in safety both by conveying the false impression that they adequately compensate for the injury, so that greater safety is unnecessary, and by arousing jealousy of the victim, thereby dividing those who might be injured in the future from the unfortunate victim who has suffered already.

At the same time that the class of victims, actual and potential, is individualized, those responsible for creating the danger and potentially liable for damages are collectivized—by the corporate form, the doctrine of *respondeat superior*, an expansive interpretation of proximate cause, and the spread of liability insurance. This aggregation is necessary because tort damages have grown too large to be paid by the individual (again the subversion of control in the name of spreading costs). But the inequality between individual victim and collective tortfeasor is also constructed by the legal system: although the collective liability insurer can aggressively badger the victim for a release, the personal injury lawyer cannot solicit the victim for authority to represent him in suing the insurer;[4] group legal service plans, originally created by automobile owners to provide lawyers for accident victims, were long illegal;[5] corporations often refuse to bargain with unions over safety practices, claiming these as "management prerogatives"; and of course most workers, consumers, and citizens are not organized collectively. Thus, the legal structure of the struggle over safety pits the individual victim—or potential victim—against a collectivity in the legislature, the regulatory agency, the court, and at the negotiating table.

Reproducing Bourgeois Ideology

It would be a mistake to interpret legal phenomena solely in terms of their instrumental effect upon material conditions. Tort law is also significant in the reproduction of bourgeois ideology. The fault concept upon which that law was built reinforces a central element of bourgeois ideology: individualism. Predicating liability upon the defendant's fault and denying recovery because of the victim's fault perfectly express the bourgeois belief that each person controls his or her fate. And indeed the bourgeoisie experience this control in their own lives—in their work, their consumption, and their environment—an experience epitomized in the contemporary *sauve qui peut* obsession with personal physical, mental, and emotional well-being.

But the nineteenth-century concept of fault is too moralistic for today's tastes and too patently inconsistent with the reality that collective consequences are caused by the confluence of multiple, ongoing, collective activities. As a result of these tensions, strict liability has progressively displaced negligence, and the defenses of contributory negligence and assumption of risk have been eroded through doctrinal change and jury nullification. Yet individualism has been saved, if in a modified form. The triumph of economic analysis has redefined fault as the efficient allocation of resources, a concept that appears scientific and apolitical rather than mushy and moralistic. And economic efficiency portrays everyone as potentially capable of avoiding accidents, thereby equating the car driver with the automobile manufacturer, the worker with the boss. Fault translated into the language of economics has once again infiltrated strict liability under cover of the requirement of a defect; fault has revived contributory negligence in the guise of doctrines of comparative negligence and unforeseeable use; and it has answered the problem of concurrent causation by comparing the fault of multiple tortfeasors. Individualism also survives in the rejection of affirmative duties, a rejection that asserts that each man is an island, sole unto himself.

Tort law offers symbolic support for inequality as well. By compensating owners for property damage, it upholds the notion of private property and its concomitant, *i.e.*, that a person's worth, as a tort plaintiff, is proportional to the value of the property he owns. By preserving the income streams of those who suffer physical injury, and of their dependents, tort law affirms the legitimacy of the existing income distribution. By excluding certain categories of people from tort recovery, the law suggests that their injuries, and therefore they themselves, are less highly valued. Furthermore, by relegating injured employees to workers' compensation, which is limited to a fraction of lost wages in most jurisdictions, the law treats workers like pure labor value, implicitly denying that they suffer the pain for which we compensate tort victims or enjoy the pleasures whose loss is often a significant element of tort damages. Tort law proclaims the class structure of capitalist society: you are what you own, what you earn, and what you do.

Finally, tort law responds to intangible injury by extending that fundamental concept of capitalism—the commodity form—from the sphere of production to the sphere of reproduction. Damages for pain and suffering extrapolate the Benthamite hedonic calculus to its ultimate extreme, insisting that for every pain suffered there is some equivalent pleasure that will erase it—a pleasure that can be bought with money—and that the jury therefore must simulate a market in sadomasochism by asking themselves what they would charge to undergo the victim's misfortune. Tort thus extracts an involuntary present sacrifice in exchange for future gain (damages), thereby reproducing bourgeois notions of delayed gratification, an instrumental view of the self, characteristics that Weber stressed in his identification of capitalism with the Protestant ethic. Damages commodify our unique experience by substituting the universal equivalent, money—as when a plaintiff's attorney asks the jury to assign a monetary value to each second of the victim's pain and then aggregate it over a lifetime of suffering. This dehumanization is particularly striking in two extreme (and opposite) situations: when injuries shorten a victim's life expectancy so that money damages are rationalized as enhancing present pleasure in lieu of later years foregone—a secular variation on the Faustian compact; and when the guardian of a child born illegitimate or deformed sues for wrongful life, arguing that money is necessary to compensate the child for the net detriment of a disadvantaged life over nothingness. Giving the victim money damages for pain and suffering, especially when the injury is severe and the award proportionately large, has several additional consequences: it salves the guilt the rest of us feel at having been spared such torment (the survivor syndrome); it justifies us in succumbing to the selfish desire to have nothing further to do with the disabled and disfigured; indeed, rather than stimulating compassion for the victim, large awards incite envy for what is seen as a windfall and convey the erroneous impression that the compensation system is working well—too well, if anything.

If damages for pain and suffering commodify experience, the recent expansion of tort remedies for injuries to relationships commodifies love. Damages are now paid for loss of the society and companionship of a parent in wrongful death actions; for loss of consortium of an injured spouse, lover, parent, or child; for witnessing or learning about an injury to a loved one; for mistreatment of the corpse of a loved one; for negligent misinformation about the death of a loved one; even for injury to loved objects.[6] Such compensation affirms several symbolic messages. All relationships have a monetary value and hence can be bought and sold. The value of a relationship varies with the extent to which the attributes of the other partner approximate societal ideals of physical beauty, mental acuity, athletic ability, emotional normality, etc. (rating-dating among teenagers in the fifties carried to its logical extreme—a single scale of desirability along which everyone can be ranked). If the other partner is impaired, the relationship should be discarded—like any other consumer product in our throwaway society—and a replacement purchased with the money damages received—the tort counterpart of no-fault divorce, in which successful middle-aged men cast off their devalued wives and use their accumulated wealth and status to buy new ones who are younger and therefore more valuable. In effect, all relationships are treated as a form of prostitution—the semblance of love exchanged for money; tort law thus generalizes the feminist critique of marriage. Just as society pays pain and suffering damages to the injured victim who is shunned (so he can purchase the commodified care and companionship that will no longer be volunteered out of love and obligation), so it pays damages to those who loved him, compensating them for their lost "investment" in the relationship (so they can invest in other human capital). There is a striking analogy to precapitalist customs of bride-price and dowry, antenuptial agreements, and post-divorce settlements—all of which seek to equalize the value of partners in a marriage market by transferring money or commodities—an analogy that reveals the patriarchal origins of contemporary tort law.

A SOCIALIST APPROACH TO INJURY AND ILLNESS

Just as capitalism expropriates from workers, consumers, and citizens the power to control their own health and safety, offering only an inadequate level of compensation in exchange, so the primary concern of a socialist alternative must be to ensure that those at risk regain control over the threat of injury and illness. Compensation must be subordinated to safety, although the former goal remains important. This reversal of priorities simply reflects our spontaneous response to danger: surely we think first about the safety of those we love and not about whether they will be compensated if they are injured. We do not accept injury—or, even more perversely, welcome it—just because it is accompanied by damages. Furthermore, compensating victims by imposing liability on the causal actor cannot achieve an acceptable level of safety. Even if we remedied all the defects in the capitalist compensation system—raising damages to adequate levels and increasing rates of recognition, claim, and recovery to 100 percent (each of which reforms would require a fundamental transformation of bourgeois society)—we would have devised a social-democratic rather than a socialist solution to the problem of injuries, a solution that preserves the essential structures of capitalism and therefore contains two irremediable and fatal flaws.

First, we would have spread the cost of accidents across society through a social-welfare scheme, whereas what we must do is spread the risk of accidents more equally. True, accidents would then cost the same, regardless of the victim, and there would be no economic incentive to inflict them on a particular class, race, or gender. But those with greater resources would still be able to buy more immunity from risk and would undoubtedly do so, just as they do now under capitalism. For every social democracy preserves differences of wealth and income that allow the privileged to obtain superior education, health care, cultural and physical amenities—and safety. The social-democratic program might better promote the capitalist criterion of allocative efficiency, but it would not realize the distributional goal of equality.

Second, the social-democratic solution remains paternalistic (like capitalist law, whatever its pretensions to protect individual freedom). The valuation of illness and injury (and the converse, health and safety) is still performed by the state—whether by a legislature, regulatory agency, judge, or jury—and not by the person or group who suffers (or enjoys) it. Respect for personal autonomy demands that the person at risk decide what it is worth to undergo that danger—even bourgeois economics concedes this, which suggests that the bourgeois ideal of optimal efficiency can be realized only under socialism and may not be all that different from the principle "to each according to his needs."

The two requirements of a just approach to illness and injury— equalizing risk and restoring control to those who undergo danger— cannot be satisfied without radical change: in the division of labor, *i.e.*, (a reduction in specialization and perhaps rotation between handwork and headwork, as occurred during the Chinese Cultural Revolution and in many intentional communities; and in control over the means of production, which must be transferred from capitalists to workers.[7] The first steps might be forms of cooperative enterprise and worker involvement in improving health and safety in the workplace—*not* nationalization of industry, which simply substitutes the state for capital. Since both reforms would threaten capitalist control, vigorous

resistance can be expected and is already visible in the Reagan administration's decision to withdraw funding from the national cooperative
bank and in its attacks on OSHA. The strength of capitalist opposition
may also explain the timidity of unions. But for precisely these reasons,
occupational health and safety is an excellent issue for rank-and-file
activists and for organizing unorganized workers. It is harder to see
how to equalize exposure to the risks posed by consumer goods and
services, and by residence (although economic equality and its political
and social consequences would advance this goal); and how to empower those exposed to such risks to control their own safety (increased self-reliance may be necessary, since consumers are a diffuse
category, unlike those who share the same workplace or residential
area).

The socialist approach to the problem of safety will still require a
response to illness and injury, since these misfortunes will also occur
under socialism, though their frequency and distribution will be radically altered. Furthermore, because full attainment of the socialist program will have to await the overthrow of capitalism, it is essential to
identify other short-run goals that progressives can pursue, as long as
there is no reason to believe that these detract from safety or come to
be seen as substitutes for prevention.

Historically, and perhaps inevitably, there has been a tension between efforts to extend recovery to new victims or new forms of
misfortune and efforts to increase the amount of compensation paid to
each. Thus, both workers' compensation and no-fault insurance for
automobile accidents protect more victims but are less generous than
tort damages. I believe this is the right choice on grounds of both
equity and political tactics. The paramount criterion for a just compensation system should be equality: it should respond to all victims if
it responds to any, and the response to each should be equal. The first
requirement mandates equality among victims whether or not their
misfortunes were caused by fault (their own or that of others) or by
human actors at all; those who suffer from tort, unavoidable accident,
illness, and congenital disability should be treated alike. After all, that
is how we respond to the misfortunes of those we love. The second
requirement argues that inequalities of wealth and income should not
be reproduced in the level of compensation, for this would maintain
those inequalities materially and reaffirm them symbolically. Thus,
there should be no compensation for damage either to property or to
individual earning power above a minimum level: those who enjoy
privileges of wealth or income should pay to protect them against loss.
But if the present system of compensating pecuniary loss treats equals
unequally (all people are created equal), compensation for intangibles
treats unequals equally (human experience is unique). I advocate an

end to compensation for nonpecuniary loss, both for this reason and because I believe that damages for intangible injury dehumanize by substituting money for compassion, arousing jealousy rather than expressing sympathy, and contributing to a culture that views experience and love as commodities. We need, instead, to re-create a society that responds to misfortune with personal care rather than by relegating the victim to the scrap heap of welfare and custodial institutions—nursing homes, hospitals, "special" schools, and ghettos for the aged and the mentally ill—the sanitized and less visible skid rows of our society.

Implementing these latter recommendations might also enhance our ability to provide a remedy for all—the first and primary meaning of equality. By reducing the amount of compensation paid to any one victim—*i.e.*, by excluding property damage, loss of income above some minimum level, and intangible injury—we would free resources that could be distributed to additional victims. Even more important, the extraordinarily high transaction costs of the present system would be virtually eliminated because there would no longer be any need to adjudicate causation, fault, defenses, or even damages. For the same reason, lengthy delays would disappear and victims would no longer be dependent on, or exploited by, lawyers. The politics of injury would be replaced by the administration of care.

To this end I propose that the state provide comprehensive medical care and a guaranteed minimum income. The first would be broadly defined to include all forms of therapy, rehabilitation, physical aids, special education, etc. The second would ensure a minimum standard of living for all members of society regardless of why their incomes were otherwise inadequate. Both state responsibilities are mandated by the fundamental requirements of human dignity; they are a response to all forms of misfortune, not just to traumatic injuries. But this proposal, too, will have its opponents who benefit from the status quo: most personal injury lawyers (whose greed and hypocrisy have become notorious), the private insurance industry (endowed with enormous assets and substantial political clout), and those who presently enjoy privileges of wealth and income. These adversaries are less formidable than the capitalist class that will resist the reallocation of risk and worker control over safety (indeed, capitalists might well favor some of these changes); but they are not insignificant enemies, as the dismal history of recent reform efforts shows.

It is essential to recognize the limitations of this plan. It would not greatly alter the existing distribution of wealth and income, since the privileged would protect themselves by insuring their property and income expectations. It would not itself encourage greater compassion for the victims of misfortune, although they would less likely become the objects of misplaced envy. It would not express societal outrage at the victim's wrong, for which purpose a criminal penalty is necessary. And it would do nothing to enhance safety (if there is also little persuasive evidence that externalizing accident costs presently internalized through the tort system would reduce safety). Nevertheless, the proposed response to misfortune would be more humane and just and might allow us to concentrate on safety the energies that are presently dissipated in simultaneously pursuing the often inconsistent goals of compensation and the punishment of moral fault.

NOTES

1. Conway v. O'Brien, 111 F.2d 611 (2d Cir. 1940); U. S. v. Carroll Towing Co., 159 F.2d 169 (2d Cir. 1947).
2. *See* chapter 10.
3. *See* Industrial Union Department v. American Petroleum Institute, 100 S. Ct. 2844 (1980); *but see* American Textile Manufacturers Institute, Inc. v. Donovan, 101 S. Ct. 2478 (1981).
4. H. Laurence Ross, *Settled Out of Court* 2d ed. (Chicago: Aldine, 1980); Reichstein, "Ambulance Chasing: A Case Study of Deviance and Control Within the Legal Profession," 13 *Social Forces* 3 (1965); Ohralik v. Ohio State Bar Association, 436 U. S. 447 (1978).
5. Lillian Deitch and David Weinstein, *Prepaid Legal Services: Socioeconomic Impacts* (Lexington, Mass.: Lexington Books, 1976), pp. 16–17.
6. Zaninovich v. American Airlines, Inc., 26 App.Div.2d 155, 271 N.Y.S.2d 866 (1966); Rodriguez v. Bethlehem Steel Corp., 12 Cal.3d 382 (1980); Bulloch v. U. S. (D.N.J. 1980); Berger v. Weber, 82 Mich.App. 199, 267 N.W.2d 124 (1978); Shockley v. Prier, 225 N.W.2d 495 (Wis. 1975); Dillon v. Legg, 68 Cal.2d 728 (1968); Corrigal v. Bail and Dodd Funeral Home, Inc., 89 Wash.2d 959 (1978); Johnson v. State, 37 N.Y.2d 378 (1975); Rodrigues v. State, 52 Hawaii 156 (1970).
7. I have developed these proposals in a recent article, "A Socialist Approach to Risk," 41(3) *Maryland Law Review* (1982).

10 THE DOCTRINE OF OBJECTIVE CAUSATION
Morton J. Horwitz

When the first-year law student is taught to distinguish sharply between "actual" or "but for" causation and "proximate" or "legal" cause, the student is learning a system that did not crystalize until the 1920s. Before the successful attack of Legal Realism on the objectivity of causation, judges and lawyers thought in terms only of "actual" causes, of "chains of causation," which could be "broken" by "intervening" or "supervening" events. This historical essay is about how this paradigm of objective causation came into being and was challenged during the late-nineteenth century.

THE EARLY CONCEPTUALIZATION AND CHALLENGE

At the conceptual center of all late-nineteenth-century efforts to construct a system of private law free from the dangers of redistribution was the idea of objective causation. In tort law especially, where the dangers of social engineering had long been feared, the idea of objective causation played a central role in preventing the infusion of "politics" into law.

If tort law was to be private law, legal thinkers reasoned, its central legitimating function had to be corrective justice, the restoration of the status quo that existed before any infringement of a person's right. The plaintiff in a tort action should recover only because of an unlawful interference with his right, not because of any more general public goals of the state.

The idea of vindication of individual rights was intimately connected with the notion of objective causation. Only if it was possible to say objectively that A caused B's injury would courts be able to take money from A and give damages to B without being charged with redistribution. Without objective causation a court might be free to choose among a variety of possible defendants in order to vindicate the plaintiff's claim. If the question of which of several acts "caused" the plaintiff's injury was open to judicial discretion, how could private law stay clear of the dangers of the political uses of law for purposes of redistribution?

There were two basic metaphors used by legal thinkers to express the idea of objective causation. The first was the notion of there being a distinction between "proximate" cause and "remote" cause. The idea had worked its way into the common law from Lord Bacon's *Maxims of the Law*, the first of which was: "In law, look to proximate, not remote, causes." The second, related notion, taken over from the natural sciences, was that there were objective "chains of causation" from which judges could scientifically determine which acts, in a complicated series of events, really "caused" the plaintiff's injury. A number of related legal doctrines also sought to classify situations in which separate acts constituted "intervening" or "supervening" causes sufficient to break the "chain" and hold another defendant liable. But, above all, it was necessary to find a single "scientific" cause and thus a single responsible defendant, for any acknowledgment of multiple causation would open the floodgates of judicial discretion.

The earliest attacks on this system of causation can be traced back to the 1870s and to efforts of young American philosophers to counter a growing movement in America toward philosophical idealism.

Along with his fellow members of the informal Metaphysical Club, Oliver Wendell Holmes, Jr., "had come very early to share their deep distrust and antagonism to the *a priori* categories of Kant and the conceptual dialectic of Hegel. A philosophy of law, an analysis of legal history, which was built on Kantian or Hegelian foundations must be repudiated and cast aside."[1] Together with future Harvard philosophers William James and Chauncey Wright, Holmes shared membership in the Metaphysical Club with a young instructor at Harvard Law School named Nicholas St. John Green.

In the midst of his Metaphysical Club speculations in 1870, Green published an article in the recently established *American Law Review* on "Proximate and Remote Cause," which, so far as I know, was by far the earliest direct challenge to orthodox legal notions of objective causation, and was not to be repeated for another fifty years. Green disputed the fundamental Baconian maxim that the law could objectively distinguish between "proximate" and "remote" causes in order to assign legal liability in a nondiscretionary manner. "The phrase 'chain of causation,' . . . embodies a dangerous metaphor," wrote Green.

It raises in the mind an idea of one determinate cause, followed by another determinate cause, created by the second, and so on, one succeeding another till the effect is reached. The causes are pictured as following one upon the other in time, as the links of a chain follow one upon the other in space. There is nothing in nature which corresponds to this. Such an idea is a pure fabrication of the mind.

There is no single objective "proximate" cause, Green argued. "To every event there are certain antecedents. . . . It is not any one of this set of antecedents taken by itself which is the cause. No one by itself would produce the effect. The true cause is the whole set of antecedents taken together."

In a passage typical of those that have led historians to see the roots of pragmatism and skepticism in these early speculations of the Metaphysical Club, Green declared: "When the law has to do with abstract theological belief, it will be time to speculate as to what abstract mystery then may be in causation; but as long as its concern is confined to practical matters it is useless to inquire for mysteries which exist in no other sense than the sense in which every thing is a mystery."[2] "When a court says this damage is remote, it does not flow naturally, it is not proximate," he wrote four years later, "all they mean, and all they can mean, is, that under all the circumstances they think the plaintiff should not recover. They did not arrive at that conclusion themselves by reasoning with those phrases, and by making use of them in their discussion they do not render that decision clear to others."[3]

It is important to note nevertheless that Green did not dispute the possibilities of objective causation in the physical sciences, where "there is a search for what may with some propriety, perhaps, be called proximate cause." In the sciences, he conceded, it was possible to use causation as "not an absolute but a relative term," signifying "the nearest known cause considered in relation to the effect, and, in contrast to some more distant cause."

Green surveyed the uses of causation in various fields of law to demonstrate how courts manipulated the terms "proximate" and "remote" to accomplish other purposes. In contract cases, courts employed these terms to determine what damages might "reasonably be supposed to have been contemplated by the parties." In negligence cases, "misconduct is called the proximate cause of those results which a prudent foresight might have avoided." But above all, there is "no settled rule" in tort because the determination of causation "often varies in proportion to the misconduct, recklessness or wantonness of the defendant."[4] In law, moral conceptions constantly intruded upon scientific ones.

Green thus not only anticipated Holmes's famous "prediction theory" of law. He also previewed[5] what a half-century later would be the most powerful argument of the legal realists against the continued insistence of legal orthodoxy on the objective character of causation in law: that because judges and jurists inevitably imported moral ideas into their determinations of legal causation, they were making discretionary "policy" determinations under the guise of doing science.

There are many reasons why the later legal realists' critique of causation doctrine largely succeeded while Green's challenge seems to have been ignored.[6] In the realm of ideas, however, one important difference between the two periods stands out. While Green was prepared to concede that the notion of objective causation "may with some propriety" be used in the physical sciences, his legal realist successors were to witness an internal challenge to causation in the natural sciences themselves. Without its pretensions to scientific foundations, legal conceptions of objective causation became increasingly vulnerable.

THE POLITICS OF CAUSATION: ENTREPRENEURIAL LIABILITY AND ECONOMIC GROWTH

The underlying political issues in the controversy over legal causation were directly confronted in 1874, four years after Green wrote, by the orthodox treatise writer Francis Wharton. The recent appearance of John Stuart Mill's *Autobiography*, Wharton wrote, had "revived . . . the controversy on causation" originally stirred up by the publication of Mill's *Logic* (1843).[7] "The doctrine advocated by . . . Mill that the cause of an event is the sum of all its antecedents," Wharton argued, was "irreconcilable with the principles of Roman and of Anglo-American law." Besides, he maintained, the inevitable result of a doctrine of multiple causation was "communism."

Wharton's major argument was that the theory of causation was different in law than it was in the natural sciences. "[P]hysicists who treat all antecedents as causes, and who can only judge of material forces, can afford no aid to jurisprudence when it undertakes to distinguish those conditions of which are material, and therefore merely consecutive, from those which are moral and causal." Given the fact that the scientific definition of causation "has not, with rare exceptions, been considered, by Anglo-American courts, to call even for discussion, this shows that so far as concerns practical life, the materialists' view of causation has no ground on which to stand."

Thus far, it should be noticed, Wharton's main strategy was simply to dissociate legal causation from scientific causation. There was not yet an attempt to argue that the claims of legal "science" can or should be grounded on those of the natural sciences. For Wharton, the distinctively legal emphasis on "moral" causation was connected with the search for a "free agency" among the multiple antecedent causes. By the "levelling of all antecedents to the same parity," by failing both to "distinguish . . . between physical and moral forces" and to "require . . . that physical forces be directed in conformity with moral law," Mill was "denying man's moral primacy over and responsibility for nature. . . ."

The result was "the practical communism which this theory of the causal character of all antecedents promotes."

Here is a capitalist among these antecedents; he shall be forced to pay. The capitalist, therefore, becomes liable for all the disasters of which he is in any sense the condition, and the fact that he is thus held liable, multiplies these disasters. Men become prudent and diligent by the consciousness that they will be made to suffer if they are not prudent and diligent. If they know that they will not be made to suffer for their neglects; if they know that though the true cause of a disaster, they will be passed over in order to reach the capitalist who is a remoter condition, then they will cease to be prudent. . . . No factory would be built. . . . Making the capitalist liable for everything, therefore, would end in making the capitalist, as well as the non-capitalist, liable for nothing; for there would be soon no capitalist to be found to be sued.[8]

One will be startled at the seemingly sudden leap that Wharton makes from the technical question of legal causation to his warnings of destruction of capitalism only if he or she fails to understand the systemic character of legal thought in the later nineteenth century.

Mill himself had attacked the existing doctrine of objective causation because it was associated with German idealist metaphysics, which he later noted was, "in these times, the great intellectual support of false doctrines and bad institutions. . . . There never was such an instrument devised for consecrating all deep-seated prejudices. And the chief strength of this false philosophy in morals, politics, and religion, lies in the appeal which it is accustomed to make to the evidence of mathematics and of the cognate branches of physical science."[9]

Wharton's defense of objective causation and his insistence on a single responsible legal cause were repeated by all late-nineteenth-century treatise writers. For Wharton's generation the ideas of "moral" causation and of "free agency" were still regarded as intelligible and objective a priori categories. That Nicholas St. John Green alone could argue that the confusion of scientific and moral notions was precisely what made legal doctrines about causation unintelligible is evidence of his premature skepticism. In the 1870s few were yet prepared to agree that the infusion of moralism into law made it political. Indeed, it was the "amoral" that Wharton identified with communism. By the end of the nineteenth century, however, orthodox legal thinkers would begin to downplay the "moral" element in causation while emphasizing the scientific basis of objective causation in law. But as they thereby implicitly conceded their own growing skepticism about the objectivity of moral categories, they laid themselves open for the final assault on causation by the legal realist heirs of Nicholas Green, who would now not only show the illicit moralism of legal causation but also the collapse of causation in the natural sciences as well.[10]

There were few occasions before the twentieth century when the political problems underlying the question of objective causation burst forth with the clarity of a Green or a Wharton. By and large, orthodox judges and jurists continued to invoke the metaphors of "chains of causation" and "natural and probable consequences" as if these were concepts capable of objective determination.

But the skepticism of Green found another channel: the prediction theory of law articulated by Oliver Wendell Holmes. There are two separate elements in Holmes's theory. The first, expressed by his famous aphorism from "The Path of the Law" (1897), is that "the prophecies of what courts will do in fact, and nothing more pretentious, are what I mean by the law." Indeed, as early as in his Harvard University lectures of 1871–1872, Holmes first expressed a similar idea virtually contemporaneously with Green's, which does suggest a reciprocal influence between Green and Holmes. Above all, Holmes's emphasis on the probabilistic nature of prediction was an effort to deny the claims of the legal system to logical or "mathematical" certainty.[11]

But there was another similar but far more practically significant shift to a prediction theory in Holmes's thought: his emphasis on foresight in the law of torts. Not only is Green's influence quite clear but, as we shall see, the function of foresight in both Green and Holmes was to avoid the problems inherent in any claims to objectivity in legal cause.

A shift to "foresight" as a substitute for "natural sequence" had begun to appear in the case law of the 1860s. By the early 1870s, there were already "two views," Wharton noted, concerning liability for negligence.

The first view is that a person is liable for all the consequences which flow in ordinary natural sequences from his negligence; the second, that he is liable for all the consequences that could be foreseen as likely to occur.[12]

Wharton opposed the foreseeability view and insisted on "ordinary natural sequence" as the basis for determining causation and hence liability. "If the consequence flows from any particular negligence according to ordinary natural sequence, without the intervention of any independent human agency, then such consequence, whether foreseen as probable or unforeseen, is imputable to the negligence."[13]

More than any other writer, Wharton was responsible for clearly formulating the orthodox view of objective causation that would continue to dominate late-nineteenth-century legal thought. Only a half-century later would legal critics derisively refer to this formula as "negligence in the air."[14]

By that time, the idea of negligence as a "relational" concept had completely triumphed, and the notion of objective causation had begun to disintegrate. While he himself was something of a transitional figure with respect to the moralistic foundations of negligence, Wharton basically continued to draw on the earlier notion that it was simply just to hold an immoral actor liable for the proximate consequences of his act.

For the late nineteenth century, one judicial decision stood out as a radical rejection of the idea of objective causation; and every treatise writer, including Wharton, was forced to take a stand on its merits. In *Ryan* v. *New York Central Railroad* (1866),[15] the New York Court of Appeals had held that a railroad that negligently caused a fire was liable only to the owner of an adjacent house and not to subsequent owners whose houses were destroyed in the path of the spreading fire.

The court had employed traditional language in rejecting the claim of the second-house owner. Only the destruction of the first house was the "proximate" result of the railroad's negligence; all of the remaining injuries were "remote," the court declared. Yet, even the use of traditional language offered little comfort to believers in the nondiscretionary and self-executing character of the orthodox categories. The result, limiting liability to the first house, seemed contrary to any common-sense understanding of the difference between proximate and remote consequences. And even more importantly, the court

spent far more time explaining why any other result "would . . . create
a liability which would be the destruction of all civilized society."[16]

The New York court, Judge Thomas Cooley contemptuously
noted, was "apparently . . . more influenced in their decision by the
fact that the opposite doctrine 'would subject to a liability against
which no prudence would guard, and to meet which no private for-
tune would be adequate,' than by a strict regard to the logic of cause
and effect."[17]

The decision in *Ryan* is one of many in the period after 1840
limiting the liability of the agents of economic growth, especially the
railroad. Yet, the typical judicial strategies for extending entrepreneurial immunity had rarely dealt so cynically with the idea of causation. While virtually all judges and jurists of the nineteenth century
had also promoted doctrines limiting entrepreneurial liability, the
Ryan decision nevertheless remained an outcast through the entire
period.[18]

The explanation gives us some insight into the relative autonomy
of legal ideas. The conception of objective causation was too central to
the legitimation of the entire system of private law for it to be abandoned even in the interest of erecting another barrier to entrepreneurial liability. Many judges, to be sure, manipulated the
proximate-remote distinction in other cases to limit entrepreneurial
liability, but few did so as brazenly as *Ryan*, threatening to bring the
entire intellectual system into disrepute.

Wharton seems to have come closer than any treatise writer to
defending the *Ryan* decision. While never explicitly endorsing it, he
did cite it as illustrative of the slightly different orthodox principle that
the intervention of an "independent responsible human agency" re-
lieves a negligent defendant from liability. "If a house is properly built,
if it is properly watched, if a proper fire apparatus is in operation, it
can be prevented, when a fire approaches from a neighboring detached
house, from catching the fire."[19] From this Wharton seems to have
concluded that the owner of the second house was, in effect, con-
tributorily negligent and thus produced a break in the chain of causation. But unlike the court in *Ryan*, even Wharton recognized a
Michigan court's assertion that without an intervening cause, "the
principle of justice, or sound logic . . . is very obscure, which can
exempt the party through whose negligence the first building was
burned from equal liability for the burning of the second."[20]

Wharton thus sought to absorb the *Ryan* case into his own orthodox paradigm of objective causation. Indeed, he devoted considerable
energies to demonstrating the terrible consequences of failing to relieve entrepreneurs of liability when an "intervening cause" broke the
negligent "chain of causation."

"Whether a railroad company is to be liable for all fires of which its locomotives are the occasion," he wrote, "is a question so important to the industrial interests of the land. . . ." Unless abutting landowners are "held to be personally responsible for the consequences of placing combustible materials by the side of a railroad," the "noncapitalists" will be "skipped over" and "the rich corporation" will be "attacked."

Capital, by this process is either destroyed, or is compelled to shrink from entering into those large operations by which the trade of a nation is built up. We are accustomed to look with apathy at the ruin of great corporations, and to say, "well, enough, they have no souls, they can bear it without pain, for they have nothing in them by which pain can be felt." But no corporation can be ruined without bringing ruin to some of the noblest and most meritorious classes of the land. Those who first give the start to such corporations are men of bold and enterprising qualities, kindled, no doubt, in part by self-interest, but in part also by the delight which men of such type feel in generous schemes for the development of public resources, and the extension to new fields of the wealth and industry of the community. Those who come in, in the second place, to lend their means to such enterprises after these enterprises appear to be reliable objects of investment, are the "bloated bond-holders," consisting of professional men of small incomes, and widows and orphans whose support is dependent on the income they draw from modest means left to them by their friends. Nor is it these alone who are impoverished by the destruction of the corporations of which I here speak. The corporation may itself be soulless, and those investing in it may deserve little sympathy, but those whom it employs are the bone and sinew of the land. There is no railroad, no manufacturing company that does not spend three-fourths of its income in the employment of labor. When the corporation's income ceases, then the laborer is dismissed. We hear sometimes of the landlord's caprice. But there are no evictions which approach in vastness and bitterness to those which are caused by the stoppage of railway improvements or of manufacturing corporations; in few cases is there such misery to the laboring classes worked, as when one of these great institutions is closed. I think I may, therefore, safely say that the question before us relates eminently to the industrial interests.[21]

It was the doctrine of independent, intervening causes on which Wharton staked his entire hopes for limiting entrepreneurial liability within the orthodox paradigm of objective causation. And it was here that the emerging doctrine of foreseeability seemed to him to pose the greatest danger. "The consequence" of any foreseeability test, Wharton wrote, "would be that the capitalist would be obliged to bear the burden, not merely of his own want of caution, but of the want of caution of all who should be concerned on whatever he should produce." If courts could argue that even intervening causes of an injury were foreseeable, the result "would be traced back until a capitalist is reached. . . . If this law be good, no man of means could safely build a steam engine, or even a house."[22]

But whether or not the choice between "natural sequence" and "foreseeability" tests had, in fact, any real effect on aggregate levels of liability, it is clear that any formulation of causation in terms of foresight presented major dangers.

We have already seen that Wharton regarded the "natural sequence" idea as a major intellectual barrier against multiple causation, which he identified as leading to "communism." But Wharton also saw an entirely different threat emanating from any reliance on a foreseeability test: the potential of redistribution through a theory of strict liability.

There existed

certain necessary though dangerous trades, of which we can say statistically that in them will be sacrificed prematurely the lives not merely of those who voluntarily engage in them, but of third persons not so assenting. Yet in such cases (e.g., gas factories and railroads), we do not hold that liability for such injuries attaches to those who start the enterprise foreseeing these consequences.[23]

In a statistical world, Wharton saw, any foreseeability test would lead to the conclusion that all risks were predictable in the aggregate. Indeed, though he was not alarmed at the prospect, Green saw similar results from a shift to a prediction theory and noted that "[w]ith events of this kind underwriters deal."[24]

In a world of randomness, where there is no necessary connection between particular causes and effects, all we can hope to do is to statistically correlate acts and consequences in the aggregate. Wharton's individualistic notions of "moral causation" and "free agency" had begun to yield to a world of probabilities and statistical correlations.

When, in 1897, Holmes declared that in law "the man of the future is the man of statistics, and the master of economics,"[25] he already clearly understood the implications that flowed from the radical change in the conception of responsibility that a prediction theory entailed.

Earlier, in The Common Law (1881), Holmes had opposed turning the state into "a mutual insurance company against accidents" that would "distribute the burden of its citizens' mishaps among all its members." Not only was "state interference . . . an evil, where it cannot be shown to be a good"; more importantly, "the undertaking to redistribute losses simply on the ground that they resulted from the defendant's act" would "affront the sense of justice," since it was based on "the coarse and impolitic principle that a man acts always at his peril."[26]

Now, however, he recognized both the pressure of organized labor for workmen's compensation laws and "the inclination of a very large part of the community . . . to make certain classes of persons insure the safety of those with whom they deal." For Holmes, the issue of strict liability versus negligence had become, by the turn of the century, simply "a concealed, half conscious battle on the question of legislative policy," which could not "be settled deductively." Most injuries

with which our courts are kept busy today are mainly incidents of certain well-known businesses. They are injuries to person or property by railroads, factories, and the like. The liability for them is estimated, and sooner or later goes into the price paid by the public. The public really pays the damages, and the question of liability, if pressed far enough, is really the question how far it is desirable that the public should insure the safety of those whose work it uses.[27]

Without objective causation, the problem of assigning liability had become simply a question of the fairness of the distribution of risks, "a concealed half-conscious battle on the question of legislative policy." Liability for injury had become just another cost of doing business, which could be "estimated," insured against, and ultimately included in "the price paid by the public." The individualistic world of Wharton's "moral causation" and "free agency" had begun to be transformed into a world of liability insurance in which the "legislative" question of who should pay would ultimately undermine the self-contained, individualistic categories of private law.

NOTES

1. Mark DeWolfe Howe, *Justice Oliver Wendell Holmes: The Proving Years* (Cambridge, Mass.: Belknap Press, 1957), p. 151.
2. Nicholas St. John Green, "Proximate and Remote Cause," 4 *American Law Review* 201 (1870). Reprinted in *Essays and Notes on the Law of Tort and Crimes* (Menasha, Wis.: G. Banta, 1933).
3. Book Review in 8 *American Law Review* 508; *Essays*, p. 82.
4. Green, *supra* note 2, at 213–15.
5. Jerome Frank edited an edition of Green's writings, *Essays and Notes on the Law of Tort and Crimes*, *supra* note 2.
6. Though we may pay tribute to Green's prescience and originality, his direct influence on legal doctrine seems to have been nonexistent. If we are to find Green's influence, we must trace it through a more indirect process by which a number of his perceptions were taken up by others and gradually

accumulated into a critical whole. Brilliant and original as Green was, if he is to be allowed any measure of immortality, it must be either specifically, through his effect on Holmes, or more generally, because of his contributions to the development of pragmatism.

7.   John Stuart Mill's challenge to orthodox ideas of causation was first presented in his *System of Logic* (1843), Book VI, ch. 11, and his *Examination of Sir William Hamilton's Philosophy* (1865). Mill's ideas on causation came to Wharton's attention through Rowland G. Hazard's *Letters on Causation and Freedom in Willing* (London: Longmans, 1869), which contests Mill's ideas. *See* Francis Wharton, *A Treatise on the Law of Negligence*, 2d ed. (Philadelphia: Kay, 1878), p. 137, n. 1. The issue was apparently revived for Wharton by the posthumous publication of Mill's *Autobiography* (1873). The significance of Mill's epistemology for American philosophy is discussed in Bruce Kuklick's *The Rise of American Philosophy: Cambridge, Mass., 1860–1930* (New Haven: Yale University Press, 1977), pp. 16–21.

     Just as Wharton's *Treatise on the Law of Negligence* (Philadelphia: Kay & Brother, 1874) was about to be published, he wrote a separate pamphlet, *A Suggestion as to Causation* (Cambridge, Mass.: Riverside Press, 1874), which he intended as an appendix to his *Treatise*. In addition to his *Treatise*, his ideas on causation are elaborated in "Remote and Proximate Fires," 1 *Southern Law Review* (n.s.) 729 (1875).

8.   Wharton, *A Suggestion as to Causation, supra* note 7, at 11.

9.   John Stuart Mill, *Autobiography* (Indianapolis: Liberal Arts Press, 1957), p. 145.

10. We may consider Judge Benjamin Cardozo's famous 1928 decision in the *Palsgraf* case as the culmination of Legal Realist attacks on the objectivity of causation. I hope, on another occasion, to spell this out. You should refer to G. Edward White's excellent discussion of *Palsgraf* in *Tort Law in America: An Intellectual History* (New York: Oxford University Press, 1980), pp. 92–102.

     It is important to see that the collapse of causation in the natural sciences was occurring at virtually the same time as *Palsgraf* was decided.

When Friedrich Waissman lectured at Oxford University on the subject "The Decline and Fall of Causality," he pinpointed 1927 as the year that "saw the obsequies" of causality in contemporary science. The deathblow, for Waissman, came with Heisenberg's enunciation of the uncertainty principle in 1927.

See William A. Wallace, *Causality and Scientific Explanation*, vol. 2 (Ann Arbor: University of Michigan Press, 1972), p. 163.

     Moving beyond the natural sciences, Thomas L. Haskell, in *The Emergence of Professional Social Science* (Urbana, Ill.: University of Illinois Press, 1977), points to a general decline of causal analysis in American social thought beginning around the turn of the century. The attack on formalism, he argues, was, at bottom, an attack on causation by a new generation of thinkers who "from their concrete social experience in an urbanizing, industrializing society" understood the world as radically more interdependent. "Where all is *inter*dependent," Haskell writes, "there can be no *in*dependent variables. To insist on the interconnectedness of social phenomena in time and in social space is to insist on the improbability of autonomous action" (p. 13). Haskell continues (p. 40):

Things near at hand that had once seemed autonomous and therefore suitable for causal attribution were now seen as reflexes of more remote causes. Those factors in one's immediate environment that had always been regarded as self-exacting, spontaneous entities—causes: things in which explanations can be rooted—now began to be seen as merely the final links in long chains of causality that stretched off into murky distance. One's familiar institutions were drained of causal potency and made to appear merely secondary and proximate in their influence on one's life.

In law, the contemporary distinction between "actual" and "legal" cause emerged under these influences.

11. Max Frisch, "Justice Holmes, The Prediction Theory of Law, and Pragmatism," 39 *Journal of Philosophy* 85 (1942); Howe, *supra* note 1, at 74–76; Kuklick, *supra* note 7, at 48–50.
12. Wharton, *Treatise on the Law of Negligence, supra* note 7, at 112.
13. *Id.* at 63.
14. Cardozo quoting Pollock, *Torts* in Palsgraf v. Long Island Rail Road, 248 N.Y. 339 (1928): "Proof of negligence in the air, so to speak, will not do."
15. 35 N.Y. 210 (1866).
16. 35 N.Y. at 217.
17. Thomas M. Cooley, *A Treatise on the Law of Torts*, vol. 1 (Chicago: Callaghan & Co., 1906), pp. 116–17.
18. The decision was rejected in England and most American states. Cooley, *supra* note 17, at 117–18. Only in New York and Pennsylvania, Pennsylvania Rail Road v Kerr, 62 Penn. St. 353 (1869), adopted the *Ryan* rule. Even in New York, the case was "limited and explained away" by subsequent cases: Thomas G. Shearman and Amasa A. Redfield, *A Treatise on the Law of Negligence*, 4th ed. (New York: Baker, Voorhis, 1888), p. 32, n. 4; Cooley, *supra* note 17, at 117, n. 13, and "the weight of this case as a precedent was somewhat diminished" by subsequent Pennsylvania decisions as well. *Id.* at 117–18, n. 14.
19. Wharton, *supra* note 7, at 125.
20. *Id.* at 135, quoting Judge Christiancy in Hoyt v. Jeffers, 30 Mich. 181 (1874).
21. "Liability of Railroad Companies for Remote Fires," 1 *Southern Law Review* (n. s.) 729 (1875).
22. Wharton, *supra* note 7, at 114–15.
23. *Id.* at 63.
24. Green, *supra* note 2, at 215.
25. Oliver Wendell Holmes, "The Path of the Law," in *Collected Legal Papers* (New York: Harcourt, Brace & Howe, 1920), p. 187.
26. Oliver Wendell Holmes, *The Common Law* (Boston: Little, Brown, 1963), pp. 77–78, 124.
27. Holmes, *supra* note 25, at 182–83.

CRIMINAL LAW
THE ORIGINS OF CRIME AND CRIMINAL VIOLENCE
Mark Kelman

This chapter consists of three essays. The first two set out different perspectives on the origins of crime and the third discusses the criminal justice system and the role of the police.—Ed.

Criminal law, crime, and criminal violence are among the most difficult issues for critical commentators to face. The essential problem is that there is no developed critical understanding of crime and criminal violence. This essay is intended to set out an agenda for a critical criminology that escapes the flaws of both standard pictures of crime —the traditional mainstream view and the traditional left view.

THE MAINSTREAM PARADIGM: THE DOMINANT VIEW OF CRIME

Mainstreamers tend to believe in one or a combination of three general approaches to the origin of crime: (1) a variety of economic theories that correspond in the philosophical literature to arguments justifying punishment as necessary to deter crime; (2) the "bad-man" theory, which corresponds in its current, pessimistic mode to an incapacitationist justification for punishing and which was associated in its optimistic, enlightenment mode with a reformationist view of punishment; and (3) the "wicked-choice" theory, which corresponds to a retributionist view of the justification of punishment.

Economic Theory[1]

In this view, criminals are treated pretty much like other rational economic actors: they have a positive taste—or demand—for property, for causing pain, for killing their real or imagined enemies. They tend to be people whose taste for property is more readily satisfied through taking than through other means: the demand for their services in the "straight" world is limited, so they are rational in finding crime a relatively attractive career. Often, right-wing economists of crime will sound like the most vulgar pseudo-Marxist materialist determinists, tracing each criminal career exclusively to economic circumstances.

The demand for crime,* like the demand for most activities and goods, is thought to be sensitive to the price of the activity. As it gets more "expensive" to assault, for instance, would-be assaulters will be less prone to do so. The "price" of crime is predominantly set by explicit state practices: while one "price" of crime is the risk of victim retaliation, the risk of paying money fines and/or going to jail (which economists tend to view as an imperfect in-kind substitute for fines) are the predominant costs the would-be criminal faces when he decides to violate the law. The amount of prison time the criminal will expect to serve when he commits a crime is largely a function of the state's ability to catch criminals and convict them; but it is also influenced by the severity of penalties, which is, in turn, a function of nominal legislative punishments and charging, sentencing, and parole practices. An increase in apprehension or conviction rates, and/or lengthening of sentences ought to make crime more "expensive" and therefore reduce its incidence. Of course, the state ought not to see reducing the incidence of crime as its sole goal; penalties for a violation ought to match the "social cost" of the violation (adjusted to account for the fact that the state will not be able to punish every violator)—the "optimal" amount of crime is committed when criminals, facing the penalty structure based on the social costs of violation, make a series of rational calculations based on whether their criminal activity is still worthwhile to them.

---

* Although it may sound odd to speak of a "demand" for crime, in the economic model the quantity of potential criminal acts, when considered from the criminal's vantage point, is termed the demand.

Politically, the central message of the economic view of crime has focused less on optimal criminality than on the observation that we can reduce crime by upping its price. While it is easiest to raise nominal prison terms, most mainstreamers tend to feel that this is less effective than to increase the certainty of punishment.* Increasing the certainty of punishment—by "unshackling" the police and the courts —is a longstanding rallying cry of the traditional Right.[2] Mainstream liberals are more likely either to view the problem of increasing certainty as insoluble (if the problem is viewed as one of apprehension, which may well, after a crime is no longer in progress, be next to impossible) or to view potential solutions as politically unacceptable (if the problem of uncertainty is deemed to be caused by the fact that police can successfully apprehend and prosecute only by the use of constitutionally impermissible means).

Traditional deterrence-oriented utilitarian justifications for punishment obviously resonate in this view of criminality. The notion that clearly harm-causing punishment is justified because, looking forward in time, it will diminish the future amount of suffering that would-be criminals would inflict unless dissuaded by their knowledge of the punishment that awaits them is grounded in a conception of criminal activity as rationally weighed economic activity.[3]

"Bad-Man" Views[4]

Many mainstreamers, perhaps all to a limited extent, doubt that the practice of punishment effectively reduces crime, except to the extent that particular dangerous people are incapacitated or isolated in prison (and thus can harm only other incarcerated criminals) during their dangerous periods. They tend to believe that at least the most violent recidivists are incorrigible criminal *types*. The criminal type may be defined quasi-technologically, particularly during periods when the cultural prestige of hard science is high; he can be seen as a genetically defective individual (e.g., XYY chromosome males are violence-prone) or as "going through a stage of violence" (e.g., criminal teenage males have not yet "burned out" the violence in "their systems"). The criminal type may also be understood as a product of

---

* If criminals were perfectly "risk neutral," they would treat the prospect of a 10 percent chance of a ten-year prison term and a 100 percent chance of a one-year term identically—the "expected prison term" *ex ante* (before the decision is made to break the law) is one year in either case. If, as mainstreamers believe, criminals tend to be risk preferrers when it comes to gambling on the "loss" of being imprisoned, the subjectively perceived disutility of the 10 percent risk of a ten-year term will be lower than the disutility of the certainty of the one-year term.

adverse environmental or cultural influences (e.g., present-oriented lower-class life makes people oblivious to punishment, since the threat of punishment is always in the future while the desire to act criminally is always in the present). The quasi-technological views invariably correspond to an incapacitationist view of the justification of punishment; the cultural views are by no means inconsistent with incapacitationist rationales, but historically they were originally associated with reformationism in more optimistic periods, when the environmentalists believed that job training, psychological counseling, etc., could overcome prior experience and remake the bad man.

"Wicked-Choice" Theories[5]

A third strand of mainstream theory, grounded in large part in moralistic and religious traditions, views the criminal as an ordinary person who has simply chosen evil. The vengeful anger that many feel at criminals—in part perhaps a result of the desire simply to counterbalance the fact that the perpetrator is entwined with and therefore tainted by the harm that befell the victim—is doubtless in large part rooted in a genuine sense of outrage at wrongful behavior. Whether one feels this at all traditional criminals (as the Moral Majoritarian might) or at, say, rapists, there is certainly a powerful tendency to focus blame on individual wrongdoers within this culture. The formal retributionist justifiers of punishment, who believe that punishment must be inflicted because a wrong has been done in the past, regardless of the future-regarding consequences of punishment, must ultimately predominantly understand the social fact of crime as the simple sum of a series of unacceptable individual choices.

TRADITIONAL RADICAL CRIMINOLOGY

There are a number of related propositions that have traditionally been articulated by critics of the mainstream approach: some deny the existence of a reasonably universal category of criminal behavior or insist that the current social definition of both crime and noncrime is unacceptable; some focus on the degree to which the core of universally condemnable criminality is an overstated social problem; some focus on the excusability of conduct that is harmful, some on its justification.

Categorization of Crime[6]

Radical criminologists have traditionally argued that the definition of offenses is historically contingent, a function of the needs of the dominant class at any point in history. Many activities that seem totally unexceptionable on their face (for instance, hunting in England on medieval common grounds) turns into the capital offense of poaching as the ascending bourgeoisie wants to consolidate its control over land as a commercial factor of production and to proletarianize the peasantry by denying it sources of sustenance other than wages for hired work. In addition, the state will criminalize, or explicitly repress, activities that threaten state function or the hegemony of the ruling class in civil society in any of its local spheres of domination.[7] For example, labor unions, which may in their early stages have threatened bourgeois control of the workplace, have been treated as criminal conspiracies, and the scope of sedition varies with the solidity of the political regime. At times, depending on the theorist, the basic laws against theft —which certainly help to ratify the existing distribution of income— are treated as a historically contingent, illegitimate instance of class-biased crime definition; at times, they are treated as unexceptionable instances of a more universally valid protective law.

At the same time, as activities harmless to all but the rulers are outlawed, obviously harm-causing activities that are routinely performed by the dominant classes (e.g., spewing carcinogens into the air and water) tend to be noncriminal or, even when criminalized (e.g., white-collar crimes like embezzlement and price fixing), punished trivially and rarely.

Overstatement[8]

Radicals have often argued that what's left of criminality when one removes the class-biased nonharms, while regrettable, is an overrated social problem. They have tended to argue that the incidence of criminal violence, except criminal violence against women (which is generally presented as *understated* in a male-dominated culture), is overstated, largely to divert attention from the serious day-to-day problems of decaying capitalist systems and to fuel divisive racism.

Excusability[9]

Like many traditional mainstream liberals, radicals have often emphasized the degree to which it is preposterous to *blame* the core criminal, as if his conduct were a product of deliberation and evil will rather than a more predictable, less freely chosen reflection of adverse socio-economic background. I will come back to explore in some more detail later a critical view of excusability; suffice it to say that sharpening the content of the "adverse background" conditions that may contribute to violent behavior is, in my view, one of the key tasks for a radical criminologist.

Justifiability[10]

Picturing the outlaw as a self-conscious rebel is a not uncommon rhetorical tactic in dealing with the universally condemnable core of criminal violence. Unlike the critical theorist operating in his "excusing" mode, who focuses on not ascribing blame to someone who has performed acts that are definitely reprehensible as acts, the critical theorist in his "justification" mode will feel certain that, while the criminal caused suffering, like any revolutionary fighter would, the long-term result of this conduct will be a better world. Once more, there is a more complex mode of the justification argument that we must explore, that does not require ascribing politically revolutionary ends to muggers.

CRITIQUES OF THE MAINSTREAM AND TRADITIONAL RADICAL VIEWS

Economic View

To a considerable extent, the economic view is wrong in its own terms. It is almost laughable that some economists believe that the criminal justice system as constituted is designed to generate an "optimal" level of criminality: the notion that a rapist willing to pay the "full price" of his rape has performed a socially beneficial act is doubtless foreign to all but the most entrenched neoclassical economists. Professor Richard Posner's supposition that premeditated murder is punished more severely than unpremeditated murder because one is more likely to get away with it, and thus the expected punishment would be lower unless the nominal punishment is set higher, is as implausible a hypothesis as one can imagine.

More significantly, one can readily exaggerate the effectiveness of deterrence-oriented measures; for instance, some of the economists' estimates of the effect of the death penalty on homicide rates are unfathomably confident and exaggerated.[11] One can also very readily overstate the degree to which crime is unacceptably common because people too easily "get away" with it. It is far easier to get away with a particular crime than to sustain an even vaguely long-term criminal career without getting jailed. Moreover, the Right's fear that the liberal criminal-procedure rulings of the Warren Court era have eroded police functions seem suspect; except in drug cases, which are relatively problematic proscriptions to begin with, there seems to be little evidence that exclusionary rules have hurt the state's case-making ability.[12]

Far more interesting, though, the economists' tendency to take the taste for, say, rape or assault as an exogenous given, and then focus policy on adjusting the price of the crime to spin out the "proper" amount, is preposterous; the taste for criminality and violent domination is not just an input into social-policy design but is clearly one of the most significant outputs of a social system. Ignoring the degree to which this "mysterious taste" varies historically is to ignore the only issue of real interest.

"Bad-Man" Theories

Without joining the rich debate about genetic predispositions in character, it seems indisputable that the rapidity of the fluctuations in crime rates makes it practically unthinkable that the practice of criminality is not at least dominantly mediated by society and culture, that few criminals are people who commit the particular offenses that they do because they are irresistibly disposed to do so. Moreover, while it is often difficult to see one's own scientific accounts as fairy tales, the long history of obviously crazy searches to identify born offenders makes one prone to be suspicious of the validity of the latest round of accounts of the inexorability of deviance.[13]

"Wicked-Choice" Theories

Like any completely free-will-oriented or intentionalistic account of behavior, these highly individualistic theories simply ignore the degree to which we must all feel at least partly drawn to deterministic accounts of conduct, including criminal conduct. Pure-choice theorists must at least be quite bothered by the disproportionate number of criminals who were victims of racism, poverty, and unstable and abusing families; and must wonder about the meaningfulness of blaming those whom we can so readily understand.[14]

Radical Theories of Distorted-Crime Definition

It is certainly the case that definitions of criminality are neither cross-culturally universal nor intraculturally uncontroversial. One form or another of witchcraft is doubtless the crime that most women have historically been punished for; within our culture, it is quite difficult even to fathom the offense. The other dominant woman's crime—prostitution—is, in the eyes of a large portion of Americans, a victimless "noncrime," hypocritically punished to satisfy religious pressure groups. It is also certainly true that behavior that is classed as criminal in certain periods will objectively favor certain forms of economic development; whether particular members of the bourgeoisie explicitly "conspire" to dominate the legal apparatus or whether legal consciousness simply corresponds and responds to emerging class and productive relations, it remains unquestionable that, say, the enforcement of criminal vagabondage in early industrial England helped create a larger base of more willing industrial workers than would have existed otherwise. Finally, state power is clearly used to overtly crush a regime's opponents; focused pressure for radical transformation is almost invariably criminalized.

Still, one must wonder whether a critical commentator, here and now in the 1980s, can seriously expect people to be interested in his work if he explains much about the contemporary problem of crime by telling street-terrified urban dwellers that the definition of crime is socially contingent. With the exception of the so-called victimless crimes—mostly laws about drugs and consensual sex, which liberal mainstreamers already tend to oppose and which seem to be socially based not in the haute bourgeoisie but the religious petite bourgeoisie —one would be hard-pressed to argue that the standard index crimes (like murder, rape, robbery, burglary, aggravated assault, and theft) proscribe behavior that is, in a practical or political sense, problematically categorized as unacceptable. While, as I will argue below, criminality may be excusable or, at a certain level, not unjustified, the particular criminal acts that are of political interest in this culture cannot meaningfully be dismissed as creatures of ruling-class control.

The flip side of the crime-definition argument—that corporate harm-causing is unduly ignored—is a bit more complex. It is doubtless the case that more deaths are more or less proximately caused by the proliferation of practices that employ less than feasible safety or pollution-prevention devices than are caused directly by incidental homicides, and that various more or less legal consumer frauds redirect more money from those who were entitled to it than does traditional stealing. Still, the mainsteam instinct that the polluter (who kills) and the murderer (who kills) are different is not simply a victory for mystified bourgeois ideology (though in discussing justification, I will try to indicate that there is a significant rhetorical mystification going on). The polluter, in fact, does not act solely in his own interest, and radical attempts to imply that he does have deservedly fallen on increasingly deaf ears. Economists who remind us that there is a real resource cost to, say, abating pollution, that a wide range of us (not just corporate fat cats) can get more of other goods if we pollute more, are not simply spreading ideology. The relevance for criminal law is reasonably direct—to the extent that there is more nearly universal implication in the "crime" of pollution, it is less an act of deviance, ascribable to the party who happens to have physical control over pollution at the source, than a perhaps misconceived social policy. Even when a particular manufacturer violates existing policy (or influences existing policy in a direction that is unduly favorable to his private interests), one would be hard-pressed to see the activity as so discontinuous and distinct from our continued practice of not attaining maximum safety that to label the violator a criminal killer seems extraordinary. And the traditional white-collar thief—the embezzler whose conduct is formally criminalized but rarely seriously punished —is, once more, not simply benefitting from class bias (though he doubtless benefits from a somewhat correct nonegalitarian sense that, within this culture, the capacity of middle-class and upper-class citizens to tolerate our inhumane prisons is even lower than the typical criminal's, since the typical criminal has been more continuously exposed to inhumane conditions). He is also benefitting from a perfectly reasonable belief that the incidental thief is far more likely to confront, ultimately violently, his victim than the person who fidgets with the computer to take a thousand strangers' bank interest away.

Nonetheless, we should question even the culture's near-universal acceptance of the harms routinely tolerated and its condemnations of those that seem incidental or disruptive. A woman may ultimately be just as abused and exploited by the sexual harasser as the rapist; the fact that the sexual harasser so closely resembles the boss in his ordinary mode—demanding deference, favors, etc., because the worker has little choice but to take it—should ultimately be used by radicals to undermine the legitimacy of power, not to defend harassers as obviously noncriminal.

Radical Views of the Overstated Crime Problem

It is doubtless true that crime statistics are, like most social scientific data, significantly uninterpretable. To name just a handful of problems: (1) Comparing even the supposedly most straightforward figure

—the homicide rate—cross-culturally is very difficult because American police are much more prone than Europeans to class any violent death as murder, even if conviction under prevailing legal definitions of murder is impossible. (2) The index crimes we refer to in summarizing crime rates encompass incidents of wildly different degrees of severity. Much of what is called assault is also called fighting, only some assaults involve strangers pummeling the unsuspecting; much larceny consists of the failure to recover property that was left around in public or involves disputes between people who both believe they have rightful claims to items. (3) Except for the problematic homicide figures, rates of crime in large American cities are not so distinct from those in other large cities around the world as most Americans are apt to believe. Do more than one in a hundred know that Oslo, Norway, has a higher rate of assaults with and without injury than does New York City?

Still, the bottom line on the incidence of crime is that people are hardly duped into worrying an awful lot about it. Each year, 2 percent of Americans are the victims of a serious crime, and 10 percent are the victims of some crime. Over a ten-year period, then, odds are that nearly one of five people will be the victim of a serious crime—that nearly everyone will know someone intimately who has been—and that the chance for some people (e.g., poor, urban blacks) are even worse. For critical theorists to minimize the centrality of the experience of terror and victimization—a far more overt feeling of impotence than most people feel in any other social setting, including hierarchical and dominating work relations—seems both politically inept and counterfactual.

Excusability

Perhaps the greatest challenge for critical commentators on criminality is to clarify their conception of the nature of the social conditions that are associated with crime. In part, efforts on this score to distinguish traditional and radical positions have been purely rhetorical. Mainstream liberals are likely to put an individualist and voluntarist slant on the adverse background material that explains and therefore excuses bad conduct (e.g., criminals are apt to have abusive parents—who themselves chose to abuse—or criminals are apt to be poor—because they have remained uneducated, unskilled), while critical theorists will socialize and collectivize the same background materials (e.g., frustrated, hierarchically suppressed workers are prone to abuse their wives and children, lack of state funding for child care puts single parents under enormous stress).

The central issue to deal with in excusing crime, of significant political importance, is the widespread existence of noninstrumental criminal violence, *i.e.*, violence that is predominantly expressive rather than necessary to the seizure of property. It is, of course, important to remember that there is a great deal of property crime *and* that one must recall that property crime may be reasonably attributed simply to widespread resentment at relative poverty, massive unemployment,[15] the relative attractiveness of theft as a job compared to secondary labor-force jobs that are available to many poor youth, a desire to escape the boredom of dead-ended personal lives and stagnant communities,[16] and to the cycle of drug abuse and the need for drug money. Still, the most politically central aspect of crime today is non-instrumental violent crime.

The existence of a frighteningly (though uncertainly) large group of relatively unremorseful violent criminals is one of the truly night-marish outcomes of a variety of social breakdowns within our culture, and any serious critical commentary must try to address the formation of this asocial group. To attribute the extreme dissociation from norms of sociability that we observe to simple poverty would be quite mis-taken; crime was significantly higher in the sixties and seventies than during the Depression.[17] Critical commentators must develop more complex notions about marginalization—about, in essence, the dissocia-tion of growing sectors of the American population from the standard work force and hierarchical ladders. A satisfactory theory of mar-ginalization would require:

(a) an account of what it is to be marginalized, divorced from hopes of benefitting in significant ways by submitting to or adopting dominant cultural norms. In this regard, one must penetrate the con-nection—if, indeed, there is a connection—between divorce from the more problematic norms (like submission to work discipline, deferen-tial behavior to those with economic power) and more universally necessary ones (like a fundamental understanding of the humanness of those that surround the individual). It is by no means obvious that the deep attitudes of asociality, manifest most visibly in the thorough absence of remorse at brutality in a number of criminals, are best described as part of a generalized syndrome of disconnectedness from the social fabric rather than, say, rage or resentment or bluntness of affect.

(b) an account of the connection between marginalization and violence. It might seem, at first blush, that a "marginalization" theory of criminality simply assumes that people are naturally violent in the absence of the inhibitions created by socially integrating contacts with the dominant economy. If this were the case, the failure to be so-cialized would simply serve to remove the block most of us have to near-universal desire for domination and control. A more complex "marginalization" thesis, though, might conceivably try to account for violent criminality in part as an alternative subculture, symbiotic with and in conflict with the dominant culture, rather than view disconnectedness as a simple anti-inhibitant. It would be interesting to investigate the extent to which violent, outwardly directed rage, an excessive tendency to blame others for all one's suffering, serves as an effective subcultural counter to the distorted tendency of the dominant meritocratic capitalist culture to hold the victims of elitism, racism, and limited opportunities accountable for their condition. In this regard, the growth of an "ideology" of rage alongside the strengthening of the hegemony of the myths of formal legal egalitarianism and "affirmative action" would be particularly interesting. Further, one would want to see whether marginalized populations are more prone to behave violently when, as in hierarchical capitalist cultures, the "straight" culture exalts domination as a personal goal. Violence in this light is simply the nonlegitimate means to a socially vaunted end.

(c) an account of the origin of violence-inducing marginalization. One partly true theory—more grounded in mainstream liberalism—is that a portion of the population is somehow inevitably "left behind" by modernity, by ascending technological capitalism. The condition of this group is further worsened by inept state welfare and foster-care/adoption rules, which help break up the family, a possible island of stability and ongoing social contact. In the right-wing version, state regulations (minimum wages, union-supporting legislation) preclude the relatively uneducated or naturally untalented and unproductive from participating in the labor force, and create a cycle of increased disconnection from work and sociability.

Another partly true theory—more grounded in Marxist economics —is that a marginal population is both a necessary outcome of and a critical input into late-capitalist labor markets. All the advanced capitalist countries seem to have great difficulty filling both the pretechnical service-sector jobs that still loom reasonably large in providing the amenities of bourgeois life and the low-skill remnants of mechanical production. The characteristics of jobs like restaurant dishwashers, gardeners, piecework assemblers, etc., are that they are episodic, there are no ascending skills or internal job hierarchies, and the labor markets for these jobs are competitive rather than union-dominated or otherwise semi-monopolized because the training periods are so short as to allow for rapid replacement of workers. These characteristics are incompatible with the socialized desires of now-schooled proletarian workers, and the jobs are rarely filled by members of the dominant race and gender. Generally, in Western Europe, these jobs are filled by guest workers from abroad, socialized outside the host country, then explicitly legally marginalized and forced to live unsettled and episodic lives while they work. In the United States, legal and illegal immigrants indeed have begun to dominate these jobs, but they were traditionally filled—in the era in which "senseless violence" began to blossom—by hangers-on, street-corner society people who, as their jobs required, worked in short fixes, dropped out, and roamed. Whether the creation of a pool of short-fix, episodic, socially unrooted workers is associated with the creation of a socially troublesome, episodic, asocial culture is a problematic contention. The relationship between those persons who episodically participate in the secondary labor market and those who drop out into thoroughly marginal and violent lives is uncertain. Still, the contention that marginality is central to an advanced capitalist culture, which isolates many of its "full-fledged citizens" from its worst jobs, seems to me a crucial one that critical commentators must explore.

Justification

Any critical account of criminality that depends on the politically progressive self-consciousness of criminals seems to be doomed. One of the key points about criminality seems to be that it is perfectly well integrated into the worst aspects of capitalistic culture. Criminals are, by and large, selfish, appropriative, materialistic; they treat others as simple barriers to their own ends who are to be respected only insofar as they—or the state backing them up—have the power to resist domination. Nonetheless, the general practice of criminality—if not the intentions of particular criminals—may well make this a more humane polity than it would otherwise be. It seems arguable that the benign aspects of the welfare state are, in significant part, responsive to fears of violence and takings. Part of the balance of power in this society—a balance of power grounded in ownership, skills, access to state and private force that culminates in the existing distribution of benefits and burdens—is the disruptive potential of those generally excluded from the mainstream of the economy, a potential that is highlighted by existing criminals.

Rhetorically, a significant move that mainstream defenders of corporate misconduct have always used in justifying the harm that their darlings do is to generalize rather than particularize. The marketing of a dangerous product is interpreted as a part of a generally justified system of producing and exchanging goods, not as the more particular sale of the unsafe good, which is a departure from the generally justified system of exchanging and distributing only reasonably safe goods. When mainstreamers—in their self-righteous anticriminal mode—look at the traditional incidental criminal, like the thief, they view each act of theft as a particular departure from whatever normatively justified general system of property rights has been pre-ordained rather than as a part of the establishment of a normatively justified general system. Each instance of theft, unlike each sale of a good, whether safe or not, must be justified on its own for the mainstreamer; it is not enough to recognize that the distributive scheme that would exist in a world without thieves would be normatively less desirable than the one that has emerged in part because of crime. Clarifying this rhetorical shift is a way around the easy legitimation of corporate crime, as well as a more reasonable approach to "justification" of criminality than one that requires romanticizing people who frequently deserve little praise.

CONCLUSION

One ought not to trivilize criminality; it is a real problem, a central item on the political agenda, because it actually affects people's lives. Yet one ought not to let it seem unduly exceptional; people are victims not just of muggers but of daily, unexceptional, routinized exploitation, domination, and physical abuse.

One ought not to pretend that there is a rigidly determined formulaic equation for criminality, that misconduct can be traced in a straightforward fashion to particular correctable features of a capitalistic state. But one ought not to ignore that crime is not a historically constant, contextless given; criminals are more likely to be people who have been subject to certain forms of oppression, and these forms of oppression are not inevitable. The ways in which oppression is transformed into criminality are likewise ambiguous—an abusive parent may more directly cause violence than unemployment per se—but we must not ignore the political content of the origins of crime because the most immediate causes seem, at the first level, personal. Ours is a society in which there are pressures to abuse, as well as few outlets for the abused.

We ought not to pretend that criminals are heroes; but we must be aware that the world is not unambiguously worse for their presence. Finally, while it is no doubt the case that some forms of isolation of the imminently dangerous will indeed be part of our social world for the foreseeable future, an attitude of smug moral superiority toward those who are often as victimized as victimizing is an attitude incompatible with a proper devotion to the alleviation of both criminally and noncriminally rooted suffering.

NOTES

1. For good summaries of the economic theory, *see* Richard Posner, *Economic Analysis of Law*, 2d ed. (Boston: Little, Brown, 1977), sec.7.1–2; Isaac Ehrlich, "Participation in Illegitimate Activities: A Theoretical and Empirical Investigation," 81 *Journal of Political Economy* 521 (1973); Frank Zimring and Gordon Hawkins, *Deterrence: The Legal Threat in Crime Control* (Chicago: University of Chicago Press, 1973), pp. 158–72.

2. *See, e.g.* James Q. Wilson, *Thinking About Crime* (New York: Basic Books, 1975).

3. *See, e.g.*, Glanville Williams, *Criminal Law: The General Part*, 2d ed. (London: Stevens, 1961).

4. For bad-man views of criminality, *see* Edward Banfield, *The Unheavenly City* (Boston: Little, Brown, 1970); Barbara Boland and James Q. Wilson, "Age, Crime and Punishment," 52 *Public Interest* 22 (1978).

5. *See, e.g.*, George Fletcher, *Rethinking Criminal Law* (Boston: Little, Brown, 1978); Herbert Fingarette, *The Self in Transformation: Psychoanalysis, Philosophy, and The Life of The Spirit* (New York: Basic Books, 1963), pp. 162–69; Joel Feinberg, *Doing and Deserving* (Princeton: Princeton University Press, 1970); Thomas Szasz, *Law, Liberty and Psychiatry* (New York: Macmillan, 1963).

6. *See, e.g.*, Edward P. Thompson, *Whigs and Hunters* (New York: Pantheon, 1975); Douglas Hay et al., *Albion's Fatal Tree* (New York: Pantheon, 1975); Richard Quinney, *Class, State and Crime* (New York: Longman, 1977).

7. *See, e.g.*, Denis Pritt, *Law, Class and Society, Book One: Employers, Workers and Trade Unions* (London: Lawrence and Wishart, 1970), and *Book Three: Law and Politics and Law in the Colonies* (London: Lawrence and Wishart, 1970), pp. 11–81; Michael Ignatieff, *A Just Measure of Pain* (London: Macmillan, 1978); Jim Arnison, *The Shrewsbury Three* (London: Lawrence and Wishart, 1974); Edwin Powers, *Crime and Punishment in Early Massachusetts, 1620–1692* (Boston: Beacon Press, 1966), pp. 400–05.

8. *See* William J. Chambliss, "Toward a Radical Criminology," pp. 230–41 *infra*.

9. *See, e.g.*, David Gordon, "Capitalism, Class and Crime in America," 19 *Crime and Delinquency* 163 (1973); Krohn, "Inequality, Unemployment and Crime: A Cross-National Analysis," 17 *Sociological Quarterly* 303 (1976); paralleling quite closely the more mainstream positions of the President's Commission on Law Enforcement and the Administration of Justice, *The Challenge of Crime in a Free Society* (1967) to the effect that a reduction in inequality of income and power was necessary to lessen crime.

10. *See, e.g.*, Richard Quinney, "Crime and the Development of Capitalism," *Current Perspectives on Criminal Behavior*, 2d ed., ed. A. Blumberg (New York: Alfred A. Knopf, 1981), pp. 68–71.

11. *See* Lawrence Klein, Brian Forst, and Victor Filatov, "The Deterrent Effect of Capital Punishment: An Assessment of the Estimates," *Deterrence and Incapacitation*, ed. A. Blumstein, J. Cohen, and D. Nagins (Washington, D.C.: National Academy of Sciences, 1978); William Bowers and Glenn Pierce, "The Illusion of Deterrence in Isaac Ehrlich's Research on Capital Punishment," 85 *Yale Law Journal* 187 (1975).

12. *See, e.g.*, Charles Silberman, *Criminal Violence, Criminal Justice* (New York: Random House, 1978), pp. 201, 264–65.

13. *See* Ysabel Rennie, *The Search for Criminal Man* (Lexington, Mass.: D. C. Heath, 1978). This describes methods ranging from Hubert Lauvergne's phrenology to Cesare Lombroso's elaborate characterizations of "born criminals" as possessing everything from a desire to be tattooed to a tendency to epilepsy and large ears.

14. For a summary of studies showing a strong relationship between class and

crime, *see* John Braithwaite, *Inequality, Crime, and Public Policy* (London: Routledge and Kegan Paul, 1979), pp. 24–32, 58–62.

15. *See* note 8 *supra*.

16. *See* David Matza, *Delinquency and Drift* (New York: John Wiley & Sons, 1964) for a good discussion of powerlessness, the desire to "make a mark," boredom, and the criminal career.

17. It seems to be the case that poverty itself within the United States has next to no relationship to criminality though income inequality does. *See, e.g.,* John Marlin, "City Crime: Report of the Council on Municipal Performance," 9 *Criminal Law Bulletin* 557 (1973). Whether inequality itself causes crime (through, e.g., the mechanism of stirring resentment) or whether those municipalities that have economic structures associated with atypically high inequality (service-oriented, nonindustrial, highly mobile populations) engender crime for other reasons is obviously problematic.

TOWARD A RADICAL CRIMINOLOGY
William J. Chambliss

THE UNDOING OF TRADITIONAL CRIMINOLOGY

Sir Francis Bacon pointed out long ago that the questions we ask shape our knowledge far more than do the theories we propose.[1] Traditionally, criminology asked, "Why is it that some people commit crime while others do not?"[2] In the face of civil rights demonstrations, antiwar protests, civil disobedience, the invasion of middle-class leisure by marijuana and cocaine, and blatant criminality by political leaders and giant corporations, criminologists began to wonder if that question was sufficient for an understanding of crime.

Whereupon criminology and the sociology of law wedded. The sociology of law traditionally asked, "Why are some acts defined by law as criminal while others are not?" and "Why, given the definition of acts as criminal, are some people arrested, convicted, sentenced, and kept in confinement while others are not?" and "What effect does punishing people have, generally, on the society and, specifically, on the person punished?"[3]

The new questions forced a reappraisal. Studies of the lawmaking process discovered that many acts come to be defined as criminal because of the interplay of power and political struggles reflecting

economic conditions. Other studies showed that those arrested, prosecuted, sentenced, and confined were not always the most serious
violators but were almost always the poorest; and the imposition of
punishment apparently deterred some types of crime but not necessarily crimes of violence or thievery, the ones for which it was most
likely to be imposed. Finally, it was noted that official and public
definitions of crime ignore white-collar, corporate, governmental, and
organized crime, and distort the actual danger of criminality to people, the seriousness of even major offenses, and the degree to which
we are in fact experiencing a "crime wave" and "soaring crime
rates."[4]

    These revelations were not particularly new, but they were none-
theless sufficient to create what the philosopher of science T. S. Kuhn
refers to as a "paradigm revolution."[5] Until this revolution criminologists proposed a panoply of social psychological theories to account for
why some people committed crime and others did not.[6] Cultural
transmission theories argued that criminality was normal for some
people because they learned crime from their peers, parents, or subculture. Psychoanalytic theories proposed the explanation that family
relations, which were either overly strict or overly permissive, were
at the root of criminal behavior. Personality theories argued that criminals were different from noncriminals in their possession of psycho-
pathic or sociopathic traits. Biological explanations argued that genes
led some to crime and others away from it. Collective behavior was
seen as the cause by some whereby juveniles and, in later years, adults
created delinquency out of the pressures and prospects of a particular
moment. For a while in the 1950s almost everyone was arguing that it
was "differential opportunity" to achieve status, wealth, and power
that led some (those with few opportunities for the goodies) to commit crime and others to be able to succeed without it. Labeling theory
argued that everyone committed crime (primary deviance they called
initial acts of crime) but that some were labeled by their peers, the
community, or themselves, and that this led them to continue in their
criminality as their self-image changed to reflect the labels attached to
them.

    These social psychological theories seemed plausible in the affluent
society of the 1950s, and fared well until their logical structure and
empirical foundation were subjected to close scrutiny by radical
criminology.[7] Seen in the light shining from the cultural, political, and
economic revolutions of the 1960s, it was clear how these theories fell
headfirst into the logical traps Karl Popper warned against:[8] relying on
auxiliary hypotheses (e.g., not ALL people must be labeled "criminal" by
others to become criminal, SOME are criminal because they so label
themselves even though others do not) and tautologies (e.g., sociopathic

people are those who show antisocial attitudes by committing criminal acts; and crime, which by definition expresses antisocial attitudes, is a result of sociopathic personalities). The synthesis of sociolegal studies and criminology dovetailed with the critical assessment of the scientific utility of the social psychological approach. Studies of criminal law in action revealed systematic biases in the criminal-law process that tainted the value of research data gathered on institutionalized juveniles.[9]

Moreover, when Martin Luther King, Jr., was jailed for protesting discrimination on buses, in lunchrooms, and in schools; when black children were murdered and the murderers went unindicted; when war protestors were arrested, prosecuted, and shot (e.g., Kent State and Jackson State); when the vice-president of the United States (Spiro Agnew) was indicted and found guilty of accepting and soliciting bribes and kickbacks; and when the Central Intelligence Agency, with the approval of the president of the United States, planned assassinations of political leaders of foreign countries, it became impossible to explain violations of the criminal law in terms of sociopathic personalities, differential opportunity, labeling, or lower-class culture.

Before pleading *nolo contendre*, Spiro Agnew helped fuel the flames of the incipient paradigm revolution with his diatribes favoring a campaign of "law and order," which went even further in its myopic vision of criminality than the criminological establishment:

When I talk about troublemakers, I'm talking about muggers and criminals in the streets, assassins of political leaders, draft evaders, and flag burners, campus militants, hecklers and demonstrators against candidates for public office and looters and burners of cities.[10]

Agnew was putting the sons and daughters of criminologists and businesspeople in a category with "muggers" and "criminals." That made some realize what the acceptance of the view of crime generated by the government and police really implied.

Problems with the narrowness and limitations of the traditional view were further exacerbated by the rediscovery of widespread criminality by the powerful.[11] A traditional criminologist, Edwin Sutherland, pointed the way to bringing "white-collar" (which is now called corporate) crime under the purview of social science, but in the early 1950s his observations were not very well synthesized into the field.[12] When the assassinations of President John Kennedy and his brother Robert were alleged to be linked to political struggles; when Penn Central executives were found blatantly tapping the till for millions of dollars and still the federal government bailed the corporation out of bankruptcy; when President Richard Nixon was forced to resign for criminal acts against his political and business competitors; when the most powerful multinational corporations of the world hired private detectives to intimidate competitors and critics, and when those same corporations engaged in wholesale bribery of foreign governments and local politicians; when, to end with only one of an endless array of possible examples, organized crime was discovered to be not a Mafia but a network of apparently law-abiding businessmen, politicians, and law-enforcement officers welded together by their desire for gain and power, then criminological research and theory *had* to change or become an anachronism.

Sociolegal studies of the social, political, and economic forces that led to the definition of some acts as criminal and others not raised serious questions about theoretical paradigms that took the definition of behavior by the state as a given. Vagrancy, drug use, homosexuality, public intoxication, drunkenness, and disorderly conduct were discovered to be the offenses for which 75 to 80 percent of all the arrests are made each year in the presumably crime-infested cities of the world. Historical analyses revealed the political and economic forces behind the creation of criminal law. Research shows that the law of theft arose to protect the interests and property of mercantilists against the interests and property of workers; vagrancy laws reflected the tensions in precapitalist England among feudal landlords, peasants, and the emergent capitalist class in the cities; "machine smashing" in rural England was a rational response of workers seeking to defy the trend toward boring, monotonous industrial production, but the state came down on the side of the capitalist class and criminalized such acts; rights of rural village dwellers to hunt, fish, and gather wood were retracted and such activities became acts of criminality punishable by death as a result of the state's intervention on the side of the landed gentry in opposition to the customs, values, and interests of the majority of the rural population; indeed, even murder came to be defined as an act against the state (that is, as a crime) as a result of political and economic struggles in which the majority of the people were simply powerless to have their views represented at law. Laws that were acknowledged by everyone as serious violations of personal freedom and security—laws prohibiting murder, rape, vandalism, and theft—were found, on closer scrutiny, to be based on contradictory values and to have emerged as a result of political and economic forces. C. Ray Jeffrey notes that:

State law and crime came into existence during the time of Henry II as a result of [the] separation of state and church, and as a result of the emergence of a central authority in England which replaced the authority of feudal lords.[13]

The English historian A. L. Morton elaborates the point, making it abundantly clear how what had formerly been a personal matter to be settled amongst the offended parties was, for political and economic reasons, taken over by the crown of England and defined as a crime:

Henry developed a process which was in time to take the administration of justice out of the hands of private individuals and make it solely the affair of the State. In earlier times, a crime had been first of all an offense against the victim or his family, and was therefore to be settled by suitable payment to the sufferers. Now crime came more and more to be regarded as an offense against the King's peace, for which it was the right and duty of the State to exact punishment. The conception of the King's peace, which emerged in later Anglo-Saxon times, grew stronger with each addition to the power of the State.[14]

In the face of these findings and the contradiction between the reality of the criminal law in action and the abstract distortion of "the crime problem" in criminological theory, it was—it is—simply impossible for criminology to continue with "business as usual."

RADICAL THEORIES OF CRIME

Knowledge reflects its historical context, whether it is knowledge about the sun's movement relative to the earth or the causes of crime. In the late 1960s, when blacks were protesting against oppression, exploitation, official violence, and racism, it was quite predictable that someone would suggest that all criminality of the lower classes was merely a manifestation of a rational response to class oppression. Even rape was accounted for as an attack on property held by others.[15] The blatant manipulation of the law by the rich and powerful to protect themselves and the obviousness with which the criminal law was employed to suppress political dissent also predictably led to theories claiming that "all law" was merely a tool for protecting the interests of the ruling (read "capitalist") class.[16]

Those theories were short-lived even on the fringes of the Left. The saving grace of science is that theories must eventually come face to face with facts. "Facts kick," as John Dewey put it. And the fact is that much criminality simply cannot reasonably be attributed to class oppression—even the criminality of the oppressed; this we know from studies of persons in prison, many of whom clearly articulate the pecuniary or expressive nature of their criminal acts.[17] The problem cannot be solved by taking refuge in the broad brush of argument that it was oppression that created the pecuniary motive or the impulsive action in the first place. That refuge is as tautological as the social psychologists' attempt to explain criminal behavior by people's "association" or by their "marginality," when the definition of whether or not the association with criminality is "intense" enough is evidenced mainly by whether or not the person committed a crime, or whether or not a person is "marginal" is evidenced mainly by the fact that the person committed a crime that is, by definition, a "marginal" act.

Nor did the "ruling-class" theory of law fare much better. Doubtless much law derives directly from ruling-class participation in and influence over the lawmaking process. Furthermore, even when not the direct result of ruling-class intervention, criminal laws often support ruling-class interests at the expense of everyone else.[18] Unfortunately for ruling-class theory, however, many laws have a history that clearly contradicts the ruling-class hypothesis: factory health-and-safety legislation criminalizes an owner's refusal to comply with official orders to rectify unsafe conditions at work; laws against bribing public officials (at home or abroad); laws against interfering in the political struggles of other nations; even Karl Marx's early study of the laws limiting the length of the working-day goes against the interests of the capitalists and thus contradicts ruling-class theory.[19] Furthermore, it is also abundantly clear that many laws emerge out of a divided ruling class.[20]

Ruling-class theory, like any theory, can be defended against these empirical exceptions by creating a tautology: laws that derive from interclass conflict or that are not apparently in the interests of the ruling class are, in fact, in their interest "in the long run" because these laws have a legitimizing function and thus protect the system from revolutionary change. Absent a revolution, this move is a clever tautology because so long as the system survives (and it took even feudalism eight hundred years to destroy itself), then the laws must, logically, be in the interest of the ruling class. This is a nice way of making a polemical point, but it hardly suffices as an adequate logical structure for a scientific theory.

Early shots at developing a radical alternative to criminological *theory* were thus wanting. Note, however, that the expansion of empirical studies of criminal-law creation and the law in action; a conscious and consistent awareness of the criminality of the rich and powerful; a sensitivity to the political economy of crime—all these and many other changes from the social psychological approaches of the 1950s are profound and important in the working paradigm of the criminology of the 1970s and 1980s. They represent a shift in focus, perspective, and conceptualization from which a return to "marginality" theories focusing only on the criminality of some mythical and empirically unrecognizable class of "violent and dangerous" criminals is simply untenable.[21]

Radical criminology, emerging in the 1960s and 1970s, was first and foremost a reaction *against* the dominant wisdom. It sought a wider arena for research and a broader conceptualization of the problem. The study of criminal-law creation and implementation became a cornerstone of criminological inquiry. The broader sociohistorical role of political and economic forces was scrutinized as a potential source of explanations of crime and delinquency. Social class was reconceptualized as a social relation characteristic of a particular economic form within a historically determined political organization rather than, as had earlier been the case, translated into a social psychological experience. Criminology came, as Ralf Dahrendorf had advised it should, "out of Utopia" and down to earth with a more realistic view of the widespread nature of serious criminality and the impossibility of explaining it with simplistic theories.[22]

Critics of radical criminology often ignore its effect on the dominant assumptions of the discipline and focus almost exclusively on its failure to adequately "explain" crime. It would be foolhardy to defend radical criminology from this criticism. As with all social science, the value of the endeavor is more clearly found in the perspective it provides than in its ability to generate empirically valid generalizations. Judged by the standard of producing valid generalizations that meet even minimal scientific requirements, all social science is a failure. Judged by the standard of forcing us to own up to our biases and myopic visions, radical criminology has succeeded despite the fact that critics grossly distort and misunderstand what is being said.

The failure of radical criminology to come up with a palatable explanation leads some to seek a return to the social psychology of the past. That, in my view, is the worst possible alternative, not because it is ideologically conservative, which it invariably is, but because it leads us to ask the wrong questions.

We cannot find an answer to why some people commit crime while others do not in a world where almost everyone does. We cannot reasonably assume that there is a discoverable difference between those who commit crime and those who do not. We cannot, we should not, ignore the problem of street crime. But we cannot hope to increase our knowledge by stepping back into the trap of thinking that these acts can be understood without also understanding how the Ford Motor Company can calculate the cost of lawsuits if someone is killed by faulty engineering and decide, on the basis of cost-effective calculations, to go ahead and produce a dangerous automobile; how employers can refuse to spend the money necessary to reduce work hazards; how government officials reward Green Berets for murder;

how the CIA hired organized-crime figures to assassinate another nation's president; or how the FBI instigated violence by and committed violence against political dissidents. Recognizing the need to reaffirm the importance and prevalence of violent offenses may be a necessary reminder to a criminology focusing on corporate crime, organized crime, and political misfeasance and malfeasance; but to forget the character of criminality in all social classes, or to ignore or relegate to a mere curiosity the historical roots of criminal law, is to take a giant step backward.

The theoretical perspective that follows from asking why some people commit crime leads one to see culture—norms, values, beliefs— as fundamental in shaping behavior, and thereby to ignore the political and economic structure. It was precisely the dead end of this too narrow social psychological question focused on a very minute segment of crime and criminality that gave rise to radical criminology in the first place. To seek once again a theory of crime that ignores what we have learned in the past two decades about the political and economic forces underlying criminalization is to neglect the most important shift in theoretical perspectives on crime in the last fifty years.

The challenge for radical criminology is to link the study of crime with political and economic forces shaping our institutions and our social relations. This problem gave rise to the birth of a radical perspective; it remains a major unresolved challenge. My solution to this problem is to employ the methodology of the dialectic and the theory of structural contradictions as a starting point for an integrated, critical criminology.[23] Briefly, this position argues that in every political and economic system there are fundamental contradictions. People acting consciously, albeit with a substantial handicap of inherited traditions, beliefs, and institutions, attempt to deal with these contradictions. The range of reactions is finite but diverse. How one responds to and deals with the contradictions—and, more importantly, how classes of people respond to and deal with the contradictions inherent in their historical moment—determine the shape and contours of the world at that time. Capitalism is thus not a predetermined system and lower-class criminality is not a predetermined response to capitalism; rather, both are solutions to certain structural contradictions of the political economy, which generate conflicts, dilemmas, and attempts at resolution.

There is a fundamental contradiction in capitalist societies, for example, between the maximization of profits (which leads capitalists to want to pay low wages) and the necessity for a large class of consumers (who must have money from wages to buy the products). Capitalists fight to keep wages down; workers fight to raise them. Criminal law enters into the resultant conflict stemming from this contradiction by trying to force people to work at jobs not of their choosing and to make it a crime to expropriate the property of others. The law-enforcement establishment selectively enforces laws in a manner that reduces conflicts for their agencies with those who have the power to cause them strain, while workers and the unemployed seek to resolve the problems created for them by these laws through criminal acts, from illegal strikes to theft and violence. The process, in a word, is dialectical. It is a process of people writing their own history out of the conflicts and dilemmas generated by structural contradictions written on the slate they inherited as their birthright.

CONCLUSION

We must reject the plea that if the people whose vision of crime is unfailingly determined by law-enforcement and media distortions view crime fearfully and apprehensively, then criminology must study, explain, and try to solve the problem, not quibble over its accuracy. One way to counteract the public apprehension is to provide a more accurate description of precisely how dangerous the streets really are. For example, the likelihood is very low that a person living in a middle-class neighborhood will be victimized even in the societies with the highest crime rates. Furthermore, it is revealing that a comparison of assaults as evidenced by victim surveys shows the rate of assault in Oslo, Norway, New York, and Atlanta to be just about the same. Murder is also greatly overestimated in official statistics as witnessed by the comparison of murder rates from victim surveys and the murder rates reported by police to the FBI, rates which, obviously, it is in the interests of the police and the media to exaggerate in order to enhance the standing and position of the former and the sales of the latter.[24] To justify perpetuating and not qualifying the official, self-interested view of crime thrust at the public by the law-enforcement/media establishment is to fail in one of our principal obligations as scholars. Should we have studied the Communist threat in the 1950s because Richard Nixon and Joseph McCarthy were confusing the public with scare stories about the danger to life, limb, security, and safety posed by the Red Menace? No. Then as now it is our responsibility to put the problem into perspective, not buy into the hype.

Not only radical criminology but all criminological and legal scholarship should be committed to correcting the law-enforcement/media definition of crime. A scientific criminology, whether Marxist or behaviorist, must commit itself to understanding the full range of criminality and not accept blindly the pictures given by the Uniform

Crime Reports or *Time*. Explanations of crime must be broad-brushed, not narrowly (and I believe fruitlessly) in pursuit of social psychological theories to answer the impossible question of why some people commit crime while others do not. Criminology must, as radical criminology has unquestionably demonstrated, understand and explain the entire range of phenomena called crime. We must understand the political, economic, and social forces leading to differences in crime rates in different historical periods as well as differences between countries in the same period. We must explore the differences between crime in capitalist and socialist societies. We must look carefully at the historical roots of criminal laws and the legislative and appellate court processes that define acts as criminal to understand the larger issues and enlighten the public as to exactly what crime is and what kind of a threat it poses to their well-being. We must continue to examine the legal process to see why some laws are enforced and others are not; why some people are arrested, prosecuted, and sentenced, while others are not.

These are some of the advances made by radical criminology in the 1960s and 70s. These are the promises all criminological inquiry holds and must fulfill. It will be an incredible run backward if we return to the criminology of the 1940s and close our eyes to our wider responsibility. The power of radical criminology as a consciousness-raising force, the ameliorative effect it has on a traditional view of crime, and the degree to which it has, in fact, fulfilled its promise to turn traditional criminology around are all too apparent to even the most conservative, hidebound spokesperson for the law-enforcement definition of reality for us to revert to the Agnew days of criminology.

NOTES

1. F. Bacon, *The Philosophical Works*, ed. J. Robertson (London: George
    Routledge & Sons, 1905). *See also* S. Langer, *Philosophy in a New Key*
    (Cambridge, Mass: Harvard University Press, 1951).
2. E. Sutherland and D. R. Cressey, *Principles of Criminology*, 10th ed. (Philadelphia: J. B. Lippincott, 1978); W. J. Chambliss, *Crime and the Legal Process* (New York: McGraw-Hill, 1969).
3. J. Hall, *Theft, Law and Society*, 2d ed. (Indianapolis: Bobbs-Merrill, 1952);
    C. R. Jeffrey, "The Development of Crime in Early English Society," 47
    Journal of Criminal Law and Criminology 537 (1957); A. Turk, *Criminality and Legal Order* (Chicago: Rand McNally, 1969); W. J. Chambliss and
    R. Seidman, *Law, Order and Power* (Reading, Ma: Addison-Wesley, 1971);
    R. Quinney, *Crime and Justice in America* (Boston: Little, Brown, 1969);
    R. Quinney, *The Problem of Crime* (Boston: Little, Brown, 1970); R.
    Quinney, *The Social Reality of Crime* (Boston: Little, Brown, 1970); J.

Andeneas, "Deterrence and Specific Offenses," *38 University of Chicago Law Review* 532 (1971); W. J. Chambliss, "Types of Deviance and the Effectiveness of Legal Sanctions," 1969 *Wisconsin Law Review* 703 (1969); W. Bailey, "Murder and Capital Punishment," *Criminal Law in Action*, ed. W. Chambliss (New York: John Wiley, 1975), pp. 480–20; C. Tittle and C. Logan, "Sanctions and Deterrence," *Law and Society Review* 371 (Spring 1973).

4. Hall, *supra* note 3; E. P. Thompson, *Whigs and Hunters* (New York: Pantheon Books, 1976); D. Hay, "Property, Authority and Criminal Law," in D. Hay et al., *Albion's Fatal Tree* (London: Allen Lane, 1975); W. J. Chambliss "A Sociological Analysis of the Law of Vagrancy," *Social Problems* 45 (Summer 1964); W. J. Chambliss, "On Lawmaking," *6 British Journal of Law and Society* 149 (1979); P. Wald, "Poverty and Criminal Justice," in Chambliss, *supra* note 3, at 98–110; W. J. Chambliss, "The Saints and the Roughnecks," 11 *Society* 24 (1973).

5. T. S. Kuhn, *The Structure of Scientific Revolutions* (Chicago: University of Chicago Press, 1962).

6. Key works advocating each of the theoretical traditions sketched in this paragraph are: (1) Cultural transmission/differential association tradition, *see* Sutherland and Cressey, *supra* note 2; T. Sellin, *Culture Conflict and Crime* (New York: Social Science Research Council, 1938); C. Shaw and H. D. McKay, *Juvenile Delinquency and Urban Areas* (Chicago: University of Chicago Press, 1969); W. Miller, "Lower Class Culture as a Generating Milieu of Gang Delinquency," 15 *Journal of Social Issues* 5 (1959). (2) The psychoanalytic tradition, *see* A. Aichhorn, *Wayward Youth* (New York: Viking Press, 1936); K. R. Eissler, ed., *Searchlights on Delinquency* (New York: International Universities Press, 1956); K. Freidlander, *The Psychoanalytic Approach to Juvenile Delinquency* (New York: International Universities Press, 1947); D. Abrahamsen, *The Psychology of Crime* (New York: Columbia University Press, 1960); R. Andry, *Delinquency and Parental Pathology* (London: Methune, 1960); as an example of personality theory, *see* H. Eysenck, *Crime and Personality* (London: Paladin, 1970). (3) The collective-behavior tradition is represented in the works of A. Cohen, *Delinquent Boys* (Glencoe, Ill.: The Free Press, 1955); D. Matza, *Delinquency and Drift* (New York: John Wiley, 1964). (4) Theories employing the "differential opportunity" tradition include R. Merton, "Social Structure and Anomie," 3 *American Social Review* 672 (1938); R. Cloward and L. Ohlin, *Delinquency and Opportunity* (New York: The Free Press, 1960). (5) Labeling or societal reaction theory is articulated in F. Tannenbaum, *Crime and the Community* (New York: Columbia University Press, 1938); E. Lemert, *Social Pathology* (New York: McGraw-Hill, 1951); H. Becker, *Outsiders* (New York: The Free Press, 1963).

7. Quinney, *The Social Reality of Crime*, *supra* note 3; A. Turk, "Prospects for Theories of Criminal Behavior," 55 *Journal of Crime Law and Criminology* 454 (1954); S. Cohen, *Images of Deviance* (London: Hammondsworth Penguin, 1971); I. Taylor, P. Walton, and J. Young, *Critical Criminology* (London: Routledge and Kegan Paul, 1975); H. Schwendinger and J. Schwendinger, "Defenders of Order or Guardians of Human Rights," 5 *Issues in Criminology* 123 (Summer 1970); H. Schwendinger and J. Schwendinger, *Sociologists of the Chair* (New York: Basic Books, 1974).

8. K. Popper, *The Logic of Scientific Discovery* (New York: Basic Books, 1959); Kuhn, *supra* note 5; Langer, *supra* note 1.

9. *Supra* note 6 no. 5; Chambliss, "The Saints and the Roughnecks," *supra* note 4; A. Porterfield "Delinquency and Its Outcome in Court and in College," 49 *American Journal of Sociology* 199 (1943); W. J. Chambliss and R. Nagasawa, "On the Validity of Official Statistics," *Journal of Research on Crime and Delinquency* 71 (January 1969).

10. S. T. Agnew, *The Wisdom of Spiro T. Agnew* (New York: Ballantine, 1969), p. 40.

11. D. M. Gordon, "Class and the Economics of Crime," 3 *The Review of Radical Political Economy* 51 (1971); F. Pearce, *Crimes of the Powerful* (London: Pluto Press, 1976); W. G. Carson, *The Other Price of Britain's Oil* (London: Martin-Robertson, 1981); M. Levi, *Phantom Capitalists* (London: Heinemann, 1982); M. B. Clinard and P. Yeager, *Corporate Crime* (New York: The Free Press, 1981); G. Geis and R. Meier, *White-Collar Crime: Offenses in Business, Politics and Professions* (New York: The Free Press, 1977); W. J. Chambliss, *On the Take* (Bloomington: Indiana University Press, 1978); A. Block and W. J. Chambliss, *Organizing Crime* (New York: Elsevier, 1981).

12. E. Sutherland, *White-Collar Crime* (New York: Holt, Rinehart and Winston, 1949).

13. C. R. Jeffrey, *supra* note 3 at 649.

14. A. L. Morton, *A People's History of England* (London: Lawrence & Wishart, 1938), p. 70. *See generally* W. J. Chambliss, *Crime and the Legal Process* (New York: McGraw-Hill, 1969); W. J. Chambliss, "The State, the Law and the Definition of Behavior as Criminal or Delinquent," *Handbook of Criminology*, ed. D. Glasser (Chicago: Rand McNally, 1974), pp. 7–43. *See also* Chambliss and Seidman, *supra* note 3; Chambliss, "On Lawmaking," *supra* note 4; Thompson, *supra* note 4.

15. S. Griffin, "Rape: The All-American Crime," *Ramparts*, September 1971, at 26–35; E. Cleaver, *Soul on Ice* (New York: McGraw-Hill, 1968).

16. D. Danielski, "The Chicago Conspiracy Trial," *Political Trials*, ed. T. Becker (Indianapolis: Bobbs-Merrill, 1971).

17. H. King, *Boxman*, ed. William J. Chambliss (New York: Harper and Row, 1971); E. Sutherland, *The Professional Thief* (Chicago: University of Chicago Press, 1974).

18. Laws that appear inimical to ruling-class interests often result from ruling-class participation in the lawmaking process. For the hidden agenda contained in the law, *see* G. Kolko, *The Triumph of Conservatism* (New York: The Free Press, 1963). *See also* A. McCormick, "Dominant Class Interests and the Emergence of Anti-Trust Legislation," 3 *Contemporary Crises* 399 (1979); R. Quinney, *Critique of Legal Order: Crime Control in Capitalist Society* (Boston: Little, Brown, 1974).

19. K. Marx, *I Capital* (New York: International Publishers, 1967), pp. 272ff.

20. K. Calavita, "U.S. Immigration Law and the Control of American Labor," 5 *Contemporary Crises* 341 (1981).

21. As illustrated by the article in this volume by Mark Kelman, "The Origin of Crime and Criminal Violence."

22. R. Dahrendorf, "Out of Utopia: Towards a Re-orientation of Sociological Theory," 64 *American Journal of Sociology* 115 (1958).

23. For a more complete formulation of this theory, see Chambliss, "On Lawmaking," *supra* note 14; Block and Chambliss, *supra* note 11; W. J. Chambliss and R. B. Seidman, *Law, Order, and Power*, 2nd ed. (Reading, Mass.: Addison-Wesley, 1982).

24. W. J. Chambliss, *Crime Rates, Crime Myths and Official Smokescreens* (Stockholm: Institute of Criminology, 1976).

THE CRIMINAL JUSTICE
SYSTEM AND THE ROLE
OF THE POLICE
David Rudovsky

There is a widely held perception that the criminal justice system is too lenient, that it "coddles" criminals and interferes with law enforcement. This claim is surely curious in a society that sends a higher proportion of its people to prison for longer periods of time than any country other than South Africa and the Soviet Union. (In 1981, over 500,000 persons, or 250 for every 100,000 in the general population, were in our prisons and jails; the rates in Britain and West Germany, for example, were each less than one-third of the American rate.[1]) Nevertheless, in a turnabout that deflects attention from our social and economic inequities and cultural glorification of violence, aspects of the criminal justice system that, in principle, secure fairness and equality often are *blamed* for creating or exacerbating the problem of crime and violence.

The most significant social impact of the constitutional principles of due process and equal protection is not their effect on crime, which is minimal or nonexistent, or even the basic fairness they can and do provide in some circumstances. Rather, it is the appearance of fairness they lend the criminal justice system, as well as their legitimation of a class- and race-biased judicial process. Indeed, a critical view of each aspect of the criminal justice system, including the criminalization of conduct, police investigation, arrest, prosecution, and incarceration, reveals the very significant degree to which these protections are un-realized promises.

In this essay, I will first briefly identify some of the discriminatory aspects of the criminal justice system. I will then focus in some detail on judicial decisions concerning the police, which provide a good il-lustration of these biases and of the social role of the criminal justice system. I will argue that the police are not subject to meaningful legal restraints and that the courts have legitimized police conduct that protects prevailing social and power relationships rather than impose the kinds of legal restraints that should exist in a democratic society.

First, at the definitional and enforcement levels, criminal proscrip-tions are not class-neutral. Some crimes, such as vagrancy, disorderly conduct, public drunkenness, and certain drug offenses, are primarily aimed at the lower economic classes. These laws provide the police with convenient and largely unreviewable tools to control and punish certain persons and lifestyles.

Moreover, laws forbidding robbery, theft, assault, and homicide are vigorously enforced against "street criminals" but rarely applied to comparable corporate conduct. For example, prosecutions are seldom brought where an employer's failure to comply with health and safety regulations has resulted in the injury or death of workers or con-sumers. This differential treatment has been raised to the definitional level in the proposed new federal criminal code, which initially in-cluded an "endangerment provision" that would have criminalized violations of certain environmental and safety laws. The provision was directed at corporate decisions that would "knowingly place a person in imminent danger of death or serious bodily injury"—the same stan-dard presently applied to the rest of us. The Business Roundtable, an organization of some two hundred major corporations, successfully lobbied to delete the provision, as well as virtually every other sanction against corporate crimes.[2] While provisions prohibiting life-threaten-ing corporate activity have been excluded, those that would undermine the rights of workers, dissidents, and persons accused of crime have been included.

Second, even fair criminal proscriptions and procedures operate unfairly due to the inequity of our social structure.[3] The quality of counsel, investigative efforts, and other critical aspects of the defense are greatly dependent on the wealth of the defendant. Furthermore, institutional restraints operate to overload public defenders, and the system offers incentives and imposes retributions aimed at discourag-ing jury trials and not-guilty pleas (including the common court-sanctioned practice of imposing longer sentences for those who are convicted by a jury). While the public perception of fairness is largely molded by widely publicized show trials, over 80 percent of all criminal cases are disposed of by guilty pleas, many of which are questionable both from a legal and social perspective.[4]

Third, the vagueness of our substantive and procedural rules gives broad discretion to police officers, prosecutors, and judges, and results in the manipulation and misuse of their powers on both the conscious and unconscious levels. For example, the trial judge who deliberately credits false police testimony is able to mask and insulate his action with a fact-finding process that provides no meaningful standards and allows no meaningful review; and the judge who deliberately sets excessive bail can legally punish a defendant without proof of guilt.[5] On an unconscious level, police, prosecutors, and judges tend to see the world in terms of a mainly white, male, upper-middle class culture. Because their unspoken and sometimes unconscious values deeply affect decision making at all stages of the process, it is hardly surprising that their judgments have a disproportionately negative impact on the liberty and rights of the poor and minorities, whose very lifestyles and beliefs are frequently viewed with hostility and fear.

Finally, while affirmative civil suits are generally available to remedy unlawful conduct, in the area of criminal law and constitutional rights, the courts have created a series of procedural obstacles that enable them to avoid passing judgment on, and thereby sanction, constitutionally suspect policies and practices. Time and again, the Supreme Court has ruled that an aggrieved party does not have "standing" to bring the suit, or that the case is "moot," or does not present a "controversy" that can be resolved by a court, or that the federal courts should "abstain" from resolving the issue.[6] The Court has also interpreted constitutional provisions in a way that restricts the reach of basic due process, privacy, and free-speech principles.[7] These procedural devices and substantive limitations, which prevent inquiry into serious abuses and insulate governmental officials from judicial review, reflect political judgments as to the appropriate hierarchy of values in our justice system.

The courts' handling of the police function clearly illustrates the operation of these discriminatory processes: the state, through a combination of discretionary and often unreviewable delegation of power to police officers, repressive policies, and unenforced constitutional promises, has been able to rationalize race and class discrimination and the perpetuation of existing social and power relations.

Historically, the police have used a variety of tactics, from lynching and other forms of physical brutality to petty harassment, against blacks and other racial minorities.[8] Although a principal purpose of the Thirteenth, Fourteenth, and Fifteenth Amendments to the Constitution and the accompanying federal Civil Rights Acts was to combat these kinds of abuses, those laws were almost immediately gutted by the judiciary and ignored by law-enforcement and other officials. One hundred years after their passage, the Kerner Commission found:

To some Negroes, the police have come to symbolize white power, white racism, white repression. And the fact is that many police do reflect and express white supremacist attitudes. The atmosphere of hostility and cynicism is reinforced by a widespread belief among Negroes in the existence of police brutality and in a "double standard" of justice and protection—one for Negroes and one for whites.[9]

The police have consistently sided with powerful economic interests against strikers and working-class movements. The Haymarket protesters, the Molly Maguires, the "Bread and Roses" strikers, farm workers, striking miners in Harlan County, and innumerable less publicized workers' actions and movements have suffered from police repression, as have the civil rights, women's, gay, and antiwar movements.

Moreover, police abuse, while less overtly political, is found in the routine performance of police duties aimed at nonpolitical crime. Our society simply lacks the elementary social cohesiveness, sense of shared purpose, and fundamental social and economic fairness to make possible a solution to the problem of crime without a radical restructuring of our entire social system. The police are asked to perform an impossible task; their attempts to impose order out of the reality of social chaos are fruitless. Personal fear and pressure to protect by any means society's short-run interest in order inevitably leads to state-sanctioned brutality and violations of individual rights. This is not to suggest, of course, that police do not have or do not exercise a legitimate role in this or any other society. Fair enforcement of equitable social and political norms is no less important than (and a corollary to) freedom from governmental oppression. Unfortunately, in this society law enforcement, obedience to law, and survival are often mutually exclusive goals for the police.

Viewed this way, police misconduct, aside from some particularly sadistic actions, is integral to our political system. The public's understandable fear of crime has been used to support a "free hand" for the police. Indeed, so ingrained is the institutional toleration of police abuse that it takes particularly egregious incidents to spark any substantial public reaction. However, when these incidents occur[10] or systemic studies are conducted, the depth of the problem is clearly visible.[11]

Some people remain silent about police abuse for fear of weakening law enforcement's hand in dealing with crime. Others openly support illegal police tactics to preserve their own social and political privileges. Testimony by the president of the Philadelphia Chamber of Commerce before the United States Commission on Civil Rights provides a good example:

[M]ost businessmen feel that the protection which business receives in this city is so outstanding that they are willing to put up with instances which *had they occurred to somebody in their own family or in their employment they would consider unbearable.*

It's not difficult to differentiate between something that happens to either you or somebody with whom you're very close where police brutality is involved, and where you have righteous indignation and you want instant action, and something that happens to somebody else, where you shrug your shoulders and say, "Well, I'm afraid that's something we just have to accept in return for adequate police protection." The average businessman does feel that he is willing to put up with "a little brutality" in return for what he considers adequate protection.

The chairman of the board of the largest corporation in Pennsylvania agreed: "I think that most of the members of the business community that I know and speak to me candidly on the subject feel that there is a kind of tradeoff. Whether that's right or wrong, that's the perception. . . ."[12]

Despite such examples, the popular perception is not of an uncontrolled police force but rather of police who are handcuffed by the courts, thus allowing the crime rate to spiral. I will briefly examine three aspects of purported judicial control over the police: exclusion of evidence in criminal cases, civil suits against the police, and criminal prosecution of police.

The most pointed criticism of judicial limitations involves decisions like *Miranda* v. *Arizona*[13] and *Mapp* v. *Ohio*,[14] which require the suppression of evidence obtained by illegal methods. Together with other Supreme Court decisions in the 1960s that constitutionalized criminal procedure, these cases at least implicitly acknowledged widespread police and prosecutorial abuse, and articulated a sense of equal justice and due process of law that was lacking in the criminal process. However, the police, prosecutors, and courts easily found the means to dilute their impact, and the current Burger Court has made serious doctrinal inroads on their basic premises.[15]

Almost immediately, the mandate of these cases was circumvented at trial. Most suppression claims involve factual disputes, and these basic protections are undermined by a fact-finding process that slants decision making in favor of particular classes of litigants. For example, the implementation of these protections hinges on such questions as: Were the *Miranda* warnings given? Did the suspect waive his right to counsel? Did the defendant act in a manner that gave the police officer "probable cause" for his arrest? In many situations police simply lie about such facts. Thus, it is quite easy for an officer to assert that *Miranda* warnings were given or that the defendant was acting in an illegal or suspicious manner, thus justifying a frisk. Judges regularly choose to accept even blatantly unbelievable police testimony. After the *Mapp* decision, which required courts to exclude from trial illegally seized evidence, defendants who had previously submitted to police searches apparently altered their behavior patterns such that, upon seeing an officer, they felt compelled to toss away incriminating evidence. Judicial acceptance of such testimony allows the police to circumvent *Mapp* with a technicality: one who throws away evidence has "abandoned" it and cannot claim that he was unlawfully searched; however, he can be convicted of having possessed it.

The enormous controversy surrounding the exclusionary rule is somewhat curious, since it has only the most minimal impact on conviction rates.[16] The General Accounting Office has concluded that only 2 percent of all federal cases are lost because of exclusion of evidence. Of course, if the exclusionary rule is seen as a symbolic law-and-order issue, one can readily understand why some urge its demise, although the message such a repeal would send to largely uncontrolled police officers is troublesome to contemplate. In fact, the acceptance by police and other government officials of widespread illegal police practices demonstrates that it is the underlying constitutional principles and not the exclusionary rule that is the primary target of the police establishment. Whether or not evidence is excluded at trial is not the significant issue; rather, it is the power of the police to act in an unbridled and uncontrolled fashion. Nevertheless, because the Constitution is politically more difficult to attack, enforcement mechanisms become the target.

The attack on the exclusionary rule is an example of the way the public's perception of the criminal process has been consciously manipulated. The distortion of the actual impact of this rule on conviction rates and (if, in fact, any relationship exists) on public safety diverts the focus from the illegal police conduct and leads the public to believe that constitutional principles are too dangerous to enforce.

While an individual can sue police officers who violate constitutional rights under the federal Civil Rights Acts,[17] the legal system has provided few effective civil remedies for police misconduct. A person whose rights have been violated must face the reality of costs of litigation, the difficulty of finding lawyers willing to handle such cases, and the most difficult problem of convincing juries and judges to hold police accountable. These factors operate to deter legal action against the police.

There are also doctrinal impediments, an interesting example of which is the qualified immunity or "good-faith" defense.[18] The standard rule in civil law is that a violation of another's rights or the failure to adhere to prescribed standards of conduct constitutes grounds for liability. The vantage point is usually that of the victim rather than the perpetrator; and questions of the defendant's good faith, intent, or knowledge of the law are irrelevant.[19] In civil rights actions, however, government officials have either an "absolute" or "qualified" immunity from suit. Some officials, like judges and prosecutors, cannot be sued for their official acts regardless of how malicious or unconstitutional they may be, while others, including police officers, may avoid liability by proving that they acted in good faith. For example, many instances of arbitrary police behavior occur in the arrest and searching of suspects. Under the Fourth Amendment, police may arrest or search if there is probable cause to believe a crime has been committed; absolute proof of guilt is not required. However, in civil damage actions asserting a lack of probable cause, the courts have ruled that even if probable cause did not exist—and there is, therefore, no reasonable basis for the police action—no liability attaches if the officer in "good faith" believed it to exist. Compensation for the victim of a constitutional violation is thereby given a subordinate position in the hierarchy of values. Moreover, by virtue of the fact that relief is refused, even though a constitutional violation has occurred, the constitutional right itself is diminished. As discussed elsewhere in this book,[20] the fact that such a policy decision is made in the legal arena does not make it any less political in nature.

Were individual damage suits and suppression of evidence in criminal cases successful, they would have some impact on systemic police abuses. However, police defendants are represented without charge to them by city attorneys; they do not pay the judgment; and they are not subject to discipline because of civil liability. Only if a municipality is required to pay significant damage awards, or if publicity about such abuses becomes a focal point of local politics, is it possible that internal change will result. Overall, however, police practices are not substantially changed.

It might seem that class-action injunctive suits aimed at forcing broad-scale changes in police practices would offer a more realistic process for reform. But, as noted above, the courts have applied an array of procedural impediments to constitutional adjudication.[21] In one classic example, the Supreme Court ruled that a federal court did not have the power to order a city to set up formal internal administrative procedures to handle citizen complaints of police brutality.[22] The Court based its decision on principles of "federalism," thereby ignoring the evidence both of a practice and policy of police harassment and abuse of citizens, and of the refusal of top officials to take action to prevent these constitutional violations. The failure of the Court to draw the most obvious of inferences—that police officials are aware of and responsible for brutality of systemic proportions—is grounded more in the political judgment that police departments should be free from judicial or other restraints than in any legal or constitutional principle.

Finally, while the police are, in theory, subject to criminal prosecution, few charges against them are ever pressed. Local and state prosecutors, who must rely on their relationship with the police, usually are opposed to restrictions on police conduct. Because they view allegations of police misconduct as efforts to undermine the social order they ordinarily disregard them. Even egregious police crimes tend to be rationalized as technical violations of the law in the course of good-faith efforts at law enforcement. Federal prosecutors have similar attitudes; in addition, they are restricted by administrative regulations (unique to police abuse cases) that require Department of Justice approval of prosecutions, and by a criminal statute requiring proof that an officer acted with a "specific intent" to deprive the victim of his or her civil rights.[23]

An extreme but not isolated example of the nonprosecution policy occurred with regard to the 1971 Attica prison uprising. Contrary to initial media reports that played on racist stereotypes and fears, all of the 128 inmates and hostages injured during the retaking of the prison (while negotiations were still in progress), 39 of whom died, were shot by the state police and prison guards.[24] Although New York Governor Nelson Rockefeller said the troopers had done a "superb job," an investigation by the state's prosecuting attorney disclosed numerous police crimes that were covered up by the Rockefeller Administration. An assistant prosecutor involved in the cases has written that among the crimes the state refused to prosecute were:

a police shooting of hostage John D'Archangelo through the abdomen. The police tried to convince the medical examiners that an inmate had killed him with a spear; . . . a trooper admitted shooting inmate Kenneth Malloy, who was lying on the pavement, because Mr. Malloy managed to give a "fish kick," thereby convincing the trooper that he was about to attack. Another trooper had already put four bullets from his .357 magnum into Mr. Malloy. The troopers shot his eyes out. Another trooper complained later of nightmares about seeing brains; . . . a trooper fired a load of buckshot into the neck of inmate James Robinson, killing him instantly, as Mr. Robinson lay bleeding to death from a police rifle bullet.[25]

When prosecutions of police are brought, pro-prosecution judges suddenly seem to become extreme advocates of defendants' rights; constitutional provisions they had criticized as loopholes for criminals are transformed into the bedrock of the criminal justice system. In

Philadelphia, for example, where years of extreme police abuse culminated in widespread demands for accountability, the following
criminal projections of police officers were terminated by judges based
on largely unprecedented "technicalities": a mistrial was declared
when a detective correctly identified himself as assigned to the district
attorney's "police brutality" unit (the judge ruled that the mere mention of the term "brutality" was prejudicial); a judge reversed a jury's
guilty verdict when, in post-trial motions, a new defense lawyer alleged that the original attorney had not interviewed all possible
witnesses, even though the additional witnesses' statements were not
helpful to the defendant; a judge ruled that police defendants were not
guilty just before jury deliberations were to start in a nationally publicized case in which videotape evidence clearly showed an officer
kicking and stomping on a handcuffed member of a black militant
organization (the judge stated that he wanted to spare the community
further anguish); a judge ruled that a prosecutor's delay in filing
charges against an officer violated his right to a fair trial, although the
statute of limitations had not run and there was no evidence of deliberate delay or prejudice to the preparation of the defense; and a judge
suppressed a routine police incident report because the officer was not
given *Miranda* warnings, although the officer was not then a suspect or
in custody, an explicit precondition for the application of *Miranda*.

When confronted by indisputable evidence of police abuse or the
refusal of the courts to restrain illegal police activities, many people
take solace in the "bad apple" theory and thereby ignore the institutional causes of police misconduct. No one can dispute the fact that
there are some particularly abusive police, but the failure of the criminal
justice system to provide meaningful controls on the exercise of state-
sanctioned force should be understood as a deliberate political judgment to free the police to control the streets and enforce the status
quo. This policy in turn results in the subordination of equality and
fairness to the preservation of order.

NOTES

1. National Institute of Justice, *American Prisons and Jails* (Washington, D.C.:
   U. S. Government Printing Office, 1980); Benjamin H. Renshaw, Department of Justice Press Release, July 2, 1981; American Institute of Criminal
   Justice, *Just the Facts* (Philadelphia, 1890); Elliot Currie, "Crime and Ideology," *Working Papers*, May 1982.
2. *See* Colman McCarthy, "Crime Is a Matter of Class," *Philadelphia Inquirer*,
   October 6, 1981, p. 15–A; Paul Savoy, "Legalizing Corporate Murder," *The*

Nation, June 20, 1981, p. 745; Marshall B. Clinard and Peter Yeager, *Corporate Crime* (New York: The Free Press, 1980). *Cf.* Fenner v. General Motors Corp., 657 F.2d 647 (5th Cir. 1981) (GM was aware of potentially fatal defects in Oldsmobile but failed to correct or to warn purchasers).

3. See, *e.g.,* John Hope Franklin, *From Slavery to Freedom*, 4th ed. (New York: Alfred A. Knopf, 1974); Richard Kluger, *Simple Justice* (New York: Alfred A. Knopf, 1975); C. Van Woodward, *The Strange Career of Jim Crow*, 3d ed. (New York: Oxford University Press, 1974); Regents of University of California v. Bakke, 438 U.S. 265, 387 (Marshall, J., dissenting).

4. The Presidents's Commission on Law Enforcement and the Administration of Justice, *Task Force Report: The Courts* (Washington D.C.: U.S. Government Printing Office, 1967), p. 9; Jerome H. Skolnick, *Justice Without Trial* (New York: John Wiley & Sons, 1966); Albert W. Alschuler, "The Defense Attorney's Role in Plea Bargaining," 84 *Yale Law Journal* 1179 (1975); David L. Bazelon, "The Defective Assistance of Counsel," 43 *University of Cincinnati Law Review* 1 (1973). *See also* ABA Project on Minimum Standards Relating to Pleas of Guilty (Chicago: American Bar Association, 1968) (estimates that 95 percent of convictions in some localities are by plea); William F. McDonald and James A. Cramer, eds. *Plea Bargaining* (Lexington, Mass.: Lexington Books, 1980), p. 22.

5. On the inequities of the money bail system, *see* Ronald Goldfarb, *Ransom* (New York: Harper & Row, 1965); Daniel J. Freed and Patricia M. Wald, *Bail in the United States* (Washington D.C.: U.S. Dept. of Justice, 1964); Caleb Foote, "The Coming Constitutional Crisis in Bail," 113 *University of Pennsylvania Law Review* 1125 (1965); Commonwealth *ex rel.* Hartage v. Hendrick, Pa., 268 A.2d 451 (1970).

    For a discussion of the related issues concerning conditions in prison, *see* David Rudovsky, Alvin J. Bronstein, and Edward I. Koren, *The Rights of Prisoners* (New York: Avon Books, 1978; to be republished, 3d ed., New York: Bantam Books, 1983); David J. Rothman, *The Discovery of the Asylum* (Boston: Little, Brown, 1971); American Friends Service Committee, *Struggle for Justice* (New York: Hill & Wang, 1971); Herbert L. Packer, *The Limits of the Criminal Sanction* (Stanford: Stanford University Press, 1968); Charles E. Silberman, *Criminal Violence, Criminal Justice* (New York: Random House, 1978); Elizabeth Alexander, "The New Prison Administrators and the Court: New Directions in Prison Law," 56 *Texas Law Review* 963 (1978); Jones v. North Carolina Prisoner's Union, 433 U.S. 119, 139 (Marshall, J., dissenting); Bell v. Wolfish, 441 U.S. 520 (1979).

6. See, e.g., Rizzo v. Goode, 423 U.S. 362 (1976); Warth v. Seldin, 422 U.S. 490 (1975); O'Shea v. Littleton, 414 U.S. 488 (1974); Laird v. Tatum, 408 U.S. 1 (1972); Younger v. Harris, 401 U.S. 37 (1971).

7. See, *e.g.,* Parratt v. Taylor, 101 S. Ct. 1908 (1981); Baker v. McCollan, 443 U.S. 147 (1979); Paul v. Davis, 424 U.S. 693 (1976); Laird v. Tatum, 408 U.S. 1 (1972).

8. See note 3, *supra. See also* W. Haywood Burns, chapter 5, *supra.*

9. *Report of the National Advisory Commission on Civil Disorders* (New York: Bantam Books, 1968), p. 11.

10. See, *e.g.,* Robles v. City of McAllen, C.A. No. B–81–58 (S.D. Texas) ($400,000 settlement of several police-abuse cases where police station videotapes showed regular, unprovoked beatings of prisoners); Jonathan Neumann and William K. Marimow, "The Homicide Files," *The Philadelphia Inquirer*, April 24–27, 1977.

11. United States Commission on Civil Rights, *Who Is Guarding the Guardians?* (Washington, D.C.: U.S. Government Printing Office, 1981).

12. *Id.* at 3–4 (emphasis added).

13. 384 U.S. 436 (1966).

14. 367 U.S. 643 (1961).

15. See, *e.g.,* United States v. Salvucci, 448 U.S. 83 (1980); Rakas v. Illinois,

439 U.S. 138 (1978); United States v. Ceccolini, 435 U.S. 368 (1978); Stone v. Powell, 428 U.S. 475 (1976); South Dakota v. Opperman, 438 U.S. 364 (1976); Kirby v. Illinois, 406 U.S. 682 (1972); Kastigar v. United States, 406 U.S. 441 (1972); Harris v. New York, 401 U.S. 22 (1971).

16.   For studies on the exclusionary rule, see Michael Wald, et al., "Interrogation in New Haven: The Impact of Miranda," 76 Yale Law Journal 1519 (1967); Dallin H. Oaks, "Studying the Exclusionary Rule in Search and Seizure," 37 University of Chicago Law Review 665 (1970); Anthony G. Amsterdam, "Perspectives on the Fourth Amendment," 58 Minnesota Law Review 429 (1974); John Kaplan, "The Limits of the Exclusionary Rule," 26 Stanford Law Review 1027 (1974); Bradley C. Canon, "Is the Exclusionary Rule in Failing Health? Some New Data and a Plea Against a Precipitous Conclusion," 62 Kentucky Law Journal 681 (1974); Critique, "On the Limitations of Empirical Evaluations of the Exclusionary Rule," 69 Northwestern University Law Review 740 (1974).

17.   42 U.S.C. §§1981, 1983, 1985, 1986, and 1988. Suits may also be brought under state tort law. See generally Michael Avery and David Rudovsky, Police Misconduct Law and Litigation (New York: Clark Boardman Co., 1980); Paul Chevigny, Police Power (New York: Pantheon Books, 1969).

18.   See Harlow v. Fitzgerald, — U.S. —, 50 U.S.L.W. 4797 (U.S., June 24, 1982); Procunier v. Navarette, 434 U.S. 555 (1978); Imbler v. Pachtman, 424 U.S. 409 (1976); Wood v. Strickland, 420 U.S. 308 (1975).

19.   See Alan Freeman, chapter 5, supra.

20.   See David Kairys, chapter 7, supra.

21.   See note 4, supra, and accompanying text.

22.   Rizzo v. Goode, 423 U.S. 362 (1976).

23.   18 U.S.C. §§424, 243. See Screws v. United States, 325 U.S. 91 (1945).

24.   This account is drawn from Tom Wicker, A Time to Die (New York: Quadrangle-The New York Times Book Co., 1975); Attica: Official Report of the New York State Commission on Attica (1972). The initial reports from Attica, instigated by a deputy warden, were that inmates had "slit throats" and "castrated" hostages. This was completely false. In addition to the failure to prosecute the police, the state prosecuted the inmates for the deaths and injuries that occurred during the retaking of the prison under the "felony-murder" rule (which hold a felon criminally responsible for any death, no matter who is at fault, that occurs during the course of a felony). These prosecutions were halted after several acquittals by juries.

25.   Malcolm Bell, "Ten Years After Attica," The New York Times, September 12, 1981 (Op-Ed column by the assistant prosecutor).

12

CORPORATIONS AND FREE SPEECH
Mark Tushnet

Corporations dominate the media through which we interpret the world beyond our personal experience. They establish committees to collect money that supports right-wing candidates; they transform themselves through institutional advertising from oil companies into energy companies, thus justifying their control over coal and nuclear power. They purchase space in newspapers for propaganda against "excessive regulation"; they advertise in ways that tell us how our material and spiritual well-being will improve only if we consume more. The major communications media themselves all operate in the corporate form.

Since 1970, the question of corporate speech has become a central issue of constitutional law. Until then governments had been allowed to regulate corporate speech—for example, by banning cigarette advertising on television—without serious hindrance. Within a relatively short period of time, the constitutional picture has changed dramatically so that today governments find it extremely difficult to regulate corporate speech. In 1980, the Supreme Court held that a state could not prohibit a heavily regulated electrical utility from engaging in advertising that would promote the use of electricity, despite the acknowledged interest in controlling energy use, nor could it prohibit utilities from using mailings to customers as a forum for advocating increased reliance on nuclear energy.[1]

The example above suggests one source of the new concern for corporate speech. With few exceptions, before the 1970s governments had regulated only the speech of corporate actors well outside the core of capitalist enterprise; it mattered little that advertising by fly-by-night sales operations might be prohibited or regulated. The consumer and antinuclear movements of the 1970s, coupled with popular revulsion at corporate involvement in the crimes of the Nixon administration and in overseas bribery, contributed to occasional legislative successes that cut more deeply into the heart of monopoly capitalism. Following a well-worn path, corporations moved from the legislative arena, in which they had lost, to the judicial arena, where they succeeded in persuading the judges to rule that constitutional interests were at stake.

But we cannot understand the development of constitutional protection for corporate speech in any simple conspiratorial way. One indication of the complexity of the issue is that Justice William Rehnquist, the present Court's most reactionary member, has consistently opposed the new developments, while the Court's liberals, Justices William Brennan and Thurgood Marshall, have supported them, albeit with some misgivings. Of course, justices who are conventionally called liberal need not be antibusiness. Indeed, one interpretation of "liberal" jurisprudence is precisely that it has had the effect of shoring up the foundations of American capitalism, sometimes against the strenuous objections of many American capitalists. This interpretation, though, is usually most plausible when capitalism has been threatened enough to require some modest ameliorative steps. In contrast, protection of corporate speech has directly conferred obvious benefits on corporations, which is not what we would ordinarily expect of reforms designed to quell protests against corporate power. Further, although there were some anticorporate initiatives in the 1970s—in the movement against nuclear power, for example—those initiatives were relatively modest. Corporate leaders may have thought that they were under serious attack, but they were not.

Rather, the legislative initiatives of the 1970s, modest though they were, acted as a kind of catalyst. They themselves did not threaten serious harm to monopoly capitalism, and no direct response was essential to the survival of that system. But they did serve to focus constitutional concern in a way that made it easy to articulate in the area of corporate speech a deep structure of capitalist ideology.

That deep structure is the treatment of all products of human activity as commodities, which are subject to trade in markets and which take their primary meaning from their location in markets. The corporate-speech cases do no more and no less than treat speech as a commodity like any other. Three apparently independent doctrines, taken together, reveal the deep structure. For convenience, we can call these doctrines: (1) the corporation as person; (2) the free market-place of ideas; and (3) money talks.

THE CORPORATION AS PERSON

The commercial corporation emerged as a legal form in England during the seventeenth and eighteenth centuries. Initially, commercial corporations received privileged status—monopoly powers in some markets and limitations on the liability of their participants for corporate wrongdoing—because they were engaged in some promotional activity that the monarchy and Parliament regarded as particularly valuable. For many years, concern that corporate privilege be received only when public benefit would result led to stringent legislative control over the creation of corporations: special acts of the legislature were required to create each corporation.

By the nineteenth century, difficulties with special incorporations had appeared. Legislatures faced pressures of two kinds. The corporate form, especially with its provision for limited liability,* proved enormously useful as a device for amassing the capital needed for large-scale industrial enterprise of the sort that was becoming common. Entrepreneurs therefore sought incorporation in such numbers as to overwhelm legislative capacity. In addition, corporations had traditionally been associated with monopoly and, in any event, certainly had competitive advantages flowing from limited liability. Those advantages provided opportunities for corruption, since entrepreneurs would bribe legislators with part of the anticipated gains from incorporation. Consumers, who suffered from the high prices that monopolies could charge, and competitors joined to secure the enactment of general incorporation statutes, under which incorporators simply had to file various documents to obtain corporate status.

The spread of general incorporation statutes led to widespread use of the corporate form. But states still retained substantial power to regulate corporations. The adoption of the Fourteenth Amendment in 1868 gave corporations a vehicle for loosening the bonds of state regulation. The Amendment provided that "no person" should be deprived of various rights. Although it could have been held that under the Fourteenth Amendment corporations were not "persons," the first

---

* Limited liability meant that the entrepreneurs who pooled their resources in one corporation risked only what they invested; if the corporation failed, as many did, those persons who were owed money by the corporation could not obtain it from the personal assets of the investors.

time an attorney attempted to discuss the issue before the Supreme
Court he was interrupted by the justices, who said that they regarded
the issue as closed: corporations were persons.[2] This meant, most
notably, that corporations could not be deprived of property without
due process. Thus, the Court converted an amendment primarily designed to protect the rights of blacks into an amendment whose major
effect, for the next seventy years, was to protect the rights of corporations. But some rights, such as the right to be free of self-incrimination,
were thought to be so peculiarly personal that they could not be held
by corporations.[3]

Some views of the First Amendment would lead one to treat free-
speech rights too as unavailable to corporations. In 1978 the Supreme
Court firmly rejected that position, with only Justice Rehnquist asserting it.[4] For several years the Massachusetts legislature had placed on
the ballot a referendum that would establish a state personal income
tax, and each time massive lobbying by banks and corporations led to
the defeat of the proposals. Finally, the legislature tried another approach. It barred such corporations from spending money to influence
referenda that did not materially affect their business, and stated that
a referendum on establishing a personal income tax fell into that category. Justice Rehnquist reverted to older ideas about corporations,
asserting that corporations were created by the state, which could
impose conditions on their operations. Thus, in his view, Massachusetts
offered a tradeoff: the corporate form could be used to advantage, and
the state could prohibit the form from making the desired expenditures. Both Justice Lewis Powell, who wrote the majority opinion, and
Justice Byron White, who dissented because he thought the prohibition a permissible regulation of protected speech, disagreed with Justice Rehnquist's analysis. Justice Powell wrote, "If a legislature may
direct business corporations to 'stick to business,' it may also limit
other corporations—religious, charitable, or civic—to their respective
'business' when addressing the public."

One might have responded "So what?" But there was another
concern. If the state could regulate what banks could say, could it
not also regulate what newspapers and television stations doing
business in the corporate form could say? Justice Rehnquist would
have prohibited regulations of activities "necessarily incidental to the
purposes" for which the corporation was created; but even apart from
problems of deciding what is "necessarily incidental," the test was
inconsistent with his premises.

The proper response to concern about regulation of media corporations ought to have been that they too could be regulated. Indeed,
one could have argued that the framers of the Constitution wanted to
protect the individual pamphleteer or publisher, someone who stood

apart from the government and had no economic or political power, rather than corporations that had considerable power and relied on the government for certain benefits. But corporations have reached such a position of dominance in legal thought about American society that that response was unthinkable. Instead, the First Amendment, usually thought of as a vehicle by which otherwise powerless people can gain power, became another one of the assets held by the powerful.

THE FREE MARKETPLACE OF IDEAS

The referendum case contained another theme. In addition to considering the rights of corporations as speakers, the Court considered the rights of citizens as recipients of the messages. Significantly, the Court had only a few years before deprecated the rights of recipients when it upheld the State Department's refusal to permit Ernest Mandel, a European Marxist theorist, to visit the United States to speak to various interested audiences.[5] Yet this theme has been developed forcefully in cases that give constitutional protection to some kinds of commercial advertising.

The present law derives from *Bigelow* v. *Virginia*.[6] There a newspaper distributed to students at the University of Virginia had published an advertisement that announced that abortions were legal in New York, as they were not in Virginia at the time, and offered the services of a referral agency. The publisher was convicted of violating Virginia's prohibition on encouraging or promoting abortions, but the Supreme Court reversed the conviction. *Bigelow* posed a problem for those who would distinguish between political and commercial speech. On the one hand, the advertiser was motivated exclusively by commercial considerations. On the other, the availability of abortions was then a matter of intense public controversy. It is surely not irrelevant that the advertisement was published in a student newspaper, whose acts might be considered statements of political opposition to Virginia's restrictions on the availability of abortions. Yet treating *Bigelow* as a case of political speech, while perhaps seeming to allow significant regulation of commercial advertising, would have been quite troubling on the conceptual level. The political content of the advertising was something like, "We think that abortions should be more readily available than they are." But any commercial advertising can be given a similar political content. An advertisement for an automobile that stresses its ability to get the purchaser away from tedium has political content too: "We know that your daily life is dreary, and we think that its dreariness should be relieved by our cars." If one politicized the advertisement in *Bigelow*, one might find it hard to avoid politicizing all commercial advertising. That result undermines the distinction between public and private life that characterizes the political philosophy of capitalism and liberalism.

It is thus not surprising that the Court pursued the other path and differentiated *Bigelow* as a case of commercial advertising. The Court was then committed to protecting some commercial advertising, and it next concluded that price advertising for prescription drugs could not be banned.[7] Consumers challenged the prohibition, leading the Court to emphasize the interests of recipients of speech. In an inversion that would have surprised some of the framers of the Constitution, a consumer's interest in receiving accurate price information was said to be "as keen, if not keener by far, than his interest in the day's most urgent public debate." The penetration of market-oriented ways of thinking into constitutional law, which that inversion illustrates, was even clearer when the marketplace of information and ideas was explicitly linked to the marketplace of goods. Advertising, Justice Harry Blackmum said, communicates information about goods and their prices. "So long as we preserve a predominantly free enterprise economy, the allocation of our resources in large measure will be made through numerous private economic decisions. It is a matter of public interest that those decisions, in the aggregate, are well informed. To this end, the free flow of commercial information is indispensable."

Those on the political Right have noted how the constitutional defense of the free market has shifted from some general notion of due process to the specifics of the First Amendment. Those on the political Left should read the case as standing for the proposition that the Constitution precludes legislative action that would remove some goods from allocation according to market principles. In some ways, though, the result should not be surprising. After all, one of the classic statements of free-speech theory is found in Justice Oliver Wendell Holmes's dissent in *Abrams* v. *United States*: "[W]hen men have realized that time has upset many fighting faiths, they may come to believe even more than they believe the very foundations of their own conduct that the ultimate good desired is better reached by *free trade in ideas*—that the best test of truth is the power of thought to get itself accepted in the *competition of the market*. . . ."[8] If free speech was defended with the metaphor of the market, it was only a matter of time and political circumstance before the market was defended with the metaphor and the substance of free speech.

MONEY TALKS

Another metaphor has played its part in the law of corporate speech. The essential message of the Supreme Court's decisions on campaign expenditures is that money talks, and that the First Amendment is implicated whenever legislatures attempt to limit the role of large private expenditures in political campaigns. *Buckley* v. *Valeo*[9] involved the Federal Election Campaign Act, which limited the amounts individuals could contribute to candidates or spend independently on a candidate's behalf. The Court upheld limitations on contributions because there the money spoke to two audiences: the public, who would hear the candidate's message; and the candidate, who would hear the contributor's hints for favored treatment. But it held unconstitutional the limitations placed on independent expenditures because they did not threaten "real or apparent corruption" and because there was no overriding interest in "restrict[ing] the speech of some . . . in order to enhance the relative voice of others. . . ."

Buckley v. *Valeo* means that economic advantages, frequently secured through manipulation of the state apparatus, can be preserved and enhanced by reinvesting the gains from political activity. We have seen in the 1980 presidential campaign season how frequently nominally independent expenditures are made by committees linked to candidates by friendship and ideological congruence. Even more significant, because *Buckley* protects the advantages of wealth, nominally independent expenditures are made with a heavy tilt toward the right wing. In addition, the constitutional protection given to independent expenditures has contributed to the erosion of the party system, which has been one of the political mechanisms by which the reactionary tendencies in American capitalism have been forced to engage in compromises so that a broad-based party could be held together. *Buckley* did uphold expenditure limitations imposed on candidates who accepted public financing under a system that, as Justice Rehnquist put it, "enshrined the Republican and Democratic parties in a permanently preferred position" by providing subsidies according to criteria that only those parties could satisfy. All that the limits on those who accepted public financing meant, though, was that candidates forced by law to limit their own expenditures would welcome independent offers, again with the effect of reducing the candidates' dependence on the party.

Though not all of these cases deal expressly with speech by corporations, their conceptual and practical implications are sufficiently clear. Corporations have substantial power in contemporary society regardless of the dictates of constitutional law governing corporate speech. But on occasion corporate domination of society comes under attack; and when those challenges reach the political arena, corporations are able to use the additional weapons that constitutional law provides. Why has such a state of affairs come about? Corporations and their lawyers are, of course, always seeking to protect and enhance their operations. However, when the recent cases were decided, there were few truly substantial threats to corporate power. A simple instrumental explanation—the Court, behaving as it often does, gave corporations what they really needed—is inadequate. That kind of explanation must be augmented by emphasizing the sense of naturalness that the significant metaphors have.

The market metaphor and "money talks" are powerful precisely because they capture important aspects of life in capitalist society, where nearly everything, from food to friendship, seems to be a commodity available for sale and purchase. But then it seems only sensible to treat speech as a commodity as well. Indeed, it may be peculiar that the Court came so late to the recognition that the governing metaphors of free-speech theory and of life in capitalist society supported constitutional protection of corporate speech. Here, however, the unnaturalness of the metaphor of the corporation as person must be emphasized. Our language and its metaphors give lawyers structured ways of thinking about social problems; however, some metaphors are trite and obvious while others are forced and unnatural. People walk around, converse, feel deeply or shallowly about their experiences. Corporations do not. Though for some purposes we may want to treat corporations as persons, the metaphor is forced; and on issues that matter, its artificiality is likely to be troublesome. The commodity metaphor, which can be drawn from the recent cases involving corporate speech, is both obvious and unnatural. Someday a political movement may be able to recapture the older sense of corporations as creations of public power and as subject to public control. It might then exploit the artificiality of the commodity metaphor to bring corporate power to heel despite the depressing state of contemporary constitutional law on the issue.

NOTES

1.   Central Hudson Gas v. Public Service Commission, 447 U. S. 557 (1980); Consolidated Edison v. Public Service Commission, 447 U. S. 530 (1980).
2.   Santa Clara County v. Southern Pacific Rail Road, 118 U. S. 394 (1886).
3.   See, e.g., Wilson v. United States, 221 U. S. 361 (1911). (Fifth Amendment privilege against self-incrimination); California Bankers Association v. Schultz, 416 U. S. 21 (1974) (privacy).

4.   First National Bank of Boston v. Bellotti, 435 U. S. 765 (1978).
5.   Kleindeinst v. Mandel, 408 U.S. 753 (1972).
6.   421 U. S. 809 (1975).
7.   Virginia Board of Pharmacy v. Virginia Consumers Council, 425 U. S. 748
     (1976).
8.   250 U. S. 616 (1919).
9.   424 U. S. 1 (1976).

13

LEGAL ENTITLEMENT AND WELFARE BENEFITS
Rand E. Rosenblatt

Lawyers who entered the legal profession in the 1960s were confronted more explicitly than their predecessors had been with the problem of law and social inequality. It was a time "when it was virtually impossible to feel comfortable with the status quo . . . when it was not so easy to dismiss a 'radical' critique . . . [and] when hope for a newer world came naturally."[1] Central to that hope was the belief that law could and should play a major role in changing relationships of highly unequal power: between government, corporations, and other powerful institutions on the one hand, and the dispossessed and unorganized on the other. Among the powerless were numerous groups traditionally subordinated by law and political practice: blacks and other minorities, women, the poor, the elderly, political dissenters, criminal defendants, and the mentally and physically handicapped. Paradoxically, the "legal system" that had played a prominent part in oppressing these groups was looked to as a major tool for their achievement of full citizenship.

One area in which this hope was particularly strong was social-welfare programs for the poor. By the late 1960s, the United States had developed a complex web of income-assistance programs directed

---

I wish to thank Gary Bellow, Edward Sparer, Ann Freedman, Karl Klare, Stephen Gold, and David Kairys for helpful comments on earlier drafts of this essay.

toward a variety of beneficiary groups, administered by different levels of government, and financed by numerous types of taxes.[2] Some of these programs, such as Social Security, had won wide public acceptance. The social consensus that elderly workers had "earned" their retirement, symbolized (but hardly financed) by payment of federal payroll taxes, made it relatively easy to design and administer a national system of entitlement to benefits based on clear rules of employment and age.[3]

Other programs, however, generated sharper social conflict. Where benefits are available to persons normally expected to work, American policy makers and the public have traditionally restricted eligibility so as to maintain economic need as an "incentive" for low-wage work. The classic examples of such programs are aid to single-parent families with children under eighteen (AFDC), aid to two-parent families with an unemployed wage earner (AFDC-U), and aid to low-income adults without children, often termed "general assistance."[4] Unlike the Social Security system, these programs were only partly financed by the federal government and were administered by the states with few federal restrictions. The states in turn exercised their discretion to achieve two primary goals: (1) maintaining a labor supply for low-wage work; and (2) minimizing the costs of welfare benefits to the taxpayers. To be sure, other goals, such as care for needy children, have been part of the programs but always within the context of labor supply and budget limitations.[5]

Prior to the mid–1960s, recipients of benefits under programs such as AFDC were not seen as having "rights" to benefits or even to a fair process for deciding individual cases. During the late 1960s, the tradition of restrictive political discretion in public-assistance programs was challenged by organized welfare recipients assisted, for the first time in American history, by significant numbers of publicly funded lawyers.[6] A major part of this campaign, in which the lawyers were heavily involved, sought to reduce state and local political discretion and to "legalize" welfare programs in ways that would favor recipients.

At first, this legalization strategy achieved some notable victories. Many federal courts, including the Supreme Court, issued unprecedented decisions recognizing recipients' legal entitlement to welfare benefits, and invalidating particular substantive and procedural restrictions. Congress and the federal executive branch, although more ambivalent than the federal courts about the desirability of legalizing welfare, also supported this trend in a number of important ways.[7]

But beginning in the early 1970s, a strong countermovement to welfare rights developed among the voters and in all branches of the federal and state governments. Expansion of recipients' rights was

halted and then increasingly reversed. Under the Reagan administration and the 97th Congress, concepts of legal entitlement took on an
entirely different meaning, not as a basis for expanding welfare benefits
but as a means of reducing federal expenditures, authorizing and requiring restrictive state discretion, and denying eligibility to large
numbers of recipients.[8] Of course, the question of "legalizing" welfare
benefits was not the only, or even the central, issue on the political
agenda; the ebb and flow of recipients' rights occurred within a
broader debate about the aims of welfare policy as a whole.

As is common in judicial opinions, the Court majorities supporting
these decisions (in both directions) did not admit that major changes
were taking place. In each case, the prevailing justices attempted to
explain their decision as resulting from application of settled rules of
law. However, these explanations are not convincing. Rather, the
shifting development of welfare law can be best understood as part of
a more complex social and political process. First, the traditional analogy of public welfare to private charity had lost its persuasive force by
the mid–1960s. Second, the unprecedented mobilization of minorities
and the poor created considerable pressure for recognition of welfare
recipients' rights and human dignity. But third, recognition of recipients' rights ran counter to the labor-supply and budget-restriction
goals of the traditional welfare system. The Court's doctrinal shifts in
the late 1960s and early 1970s reflected the difficulties of reconciling
these pressures, as well as the genuine disagreements between liberal
and conservative justices—again echoing a larger social debate—over
the extent to which courts should attempt to regulate relationships of
social inequality.

This essay seeks to explore the strengths and weaknesses of legalization as a strategy for redistributive change. It first summarizes different perspectives that contributed to the legalization strategy and the
ways that concepts of entitlement were recognized by the federal
courts. It then examines the theoretical difficulties of the legalization
effort suggested by critical legal theory and the ways those difficulties
emerged in three important contexts: (1) the relationship between
welfare recipients and the welfare bureaucracy; (2) the problem of
work; and (3) the political isolation of the poor from other social
classes.

TRADITIONAL WELFARE DOCTRINE AND THE CONCEPT OF LEGAL ENTITLEMENT TO WELFARE BENEFITS

The traditional view was that welfare benefits were "charity" or a "privilege," and therefore subject to virtually any restrictions that officials might wish to impose. The most extreme version of this view —often termed the right/privilege distinction—denied welfare recipients judicial remedies for any official illegality, no matter how blatant. Thus, in 1966, when welfare recipients sought a federal court injunction to prevent Washington, D.C., welfare officials from using "harsh, illegal and humiliating methods" of investigating individuals' eligibility, District Judge Alexander Holtzoff dismissed the complaint in part because

[P]ayments of relief funds are grants and gratuities. Their disbursement does not constitute payment of legal obligations that the government owes. Being absolutely discretionary, there is no judicial review of the manner in which that discretion is exercised.[9]

The less extreme version of the traditional view conceded that recipients could have access to the courts to challenge welfare officials' actions, but defined the role of the courts so narrowly, and the legitimacy of political discretion so broadly, as to ensure judicial approval of virtually any rule or practice.[10]

The traditional view was rooted in the structure and policies of the welfare system, and also in the prevailing categories and modes of legal thought.[11] Several structural and policy characteristics of the nineteenth- and early-twentieth-century welfare system, all designed to maintain a labor supply for low-wage work and to limit welfare expenditures, were inconsistent with recognition of recipients' rights. First, the system was intensely localistic in structure and financing; under most American statutes prior to the federal Social Security Act of 1935, the question of whether to have any relief program, and of what sort, was effectively left to the discretion of local units of government.[12] Second, the poor were the objects of overt and extreme hostility. An early Supreme Court opinion upheld the constitutionality of state legislation prohibiting the poor entry into New York City as a reasonable measure to guard against "the moral pestilence of paupers."[13] Third, relief itself was regarded as a kind of dangerous addiction that sapped the recipient's self-respect and will to work. For the recipient's own sake, as well as that of society, nineteenth-century reformers set out to make welfare assistance as onerous and degrading as possible, and thereby to discourage needy persons from seeking it. Social opprobrium was ensured by depriving recipients of ordinary civil rights, including the right to vote and to marry without consent. By the 1960s, many of the harsher elements had been mitigated by state and federal reforms. Nevertheless, much of the basic structure remained in place, notably length-of-residence requirements, pervasive invasion of privacy, and unregulated state discretion over eligibility conditions and the dollar amounts of grants.[14]

The prevailing categories and modes of legal thought in the late-nineteenth and early-twentieth centuries reinforced the discretionary power of welfare officials by drawing a sharp line between a small "public" or "political" sphere, in which "equality before the law" was the ideal, and a large "private" or "social" sphere, in which inequality was considered the legitimate and necessary outcome of individual liberty and "natural" racial and gender differences. In the public sphere, for example, blacks could not be categorically excluded from jury service or the right to vote.[15] Conversely, a state could require racial segregation on railroads, in part because such separation was said to violate no "public" or "political" rights, but merely ratified "private" desires and "social" custom.[16] Indeed, under the Supreme Court's interpretation of the due process clause, legislatures were not *permitted* to reduce or regulate inequality in the private sphere because such regulation infringed on individuals' "liberty." On this basis, legislative efforts to regulate labor contracts for the benefit of workers and to prohibit racial discrimination in privately owned public accommodations were held unconstitutional.[17]

Within this general legal perspective, two concepts were particularly relevant to the area of welfare benefits: property ownership and constitutional obligation. Owners of private property were seen as having a very broad scope of legitimate power, both against other private individuals and against the government. One of the strongest justifying theories of *governmental* power was thus—paradoxically—the metaphor of private ownership. When government could be characterized as acting as an owner of property, the courts accorded it the same kind of broad powers as were granted to private owners.[18]

The metaphor of private ownership, reasoned the courts, applied equally to the welfare system. The government had no constitutional "obligation" to provide welfare benefits; on the contrary, it could decide to have no such program at all. "If I have no ground for complaint at being denied a privilege absolutely," the argument went, "it is difficult to see how I acquire such a ground merely because the state, instead of denying me a privilege outright, offers me an alternative, however harsh."[19] The "harsh alternative" at stake was usually the relinquishing of a constitutional right—such as freedom of speech —in order to obtain a government job or benefit.

The weakness of this reasoning had been exposed at least as early as 1916.[20] The fact that a city need not, under the federal Constitution, have any public park or welfare program, does not "logically" mean that having such a service, it can exclude from its benefits (for example) blacks, Jews, or socialists. The first decision—whether to have a public service at all—normally rests on a complex evaluation of competing social claims on scarce resources. The second decision—to exclude particular groups or penalize particular beliefs or actions— involves a much more focused judgment about worthiness and hierarchy. Despite the obvious fallacy of equating these two types of decisions, the right/privilege distinction was invoked by courts for decades, probably because most judges agreed with both the principle of unreviewable ownership discretion and with the particular judgments of worthiness being made.

Beginning in the 1950s and early 1960s, in the wake of the McCarthy era, the growing civil rights movement, and the nascent War on Poverty, an increasing number of legal scholars and social-welfare advocates began to perceive that unreviewable government power of this sort was dangerous to individuals' liberty and economic security.[21] In the context of welfare benefits, their arguments generated three variations on the concept of "entitlement."* The most modest version simply held the government to its own rules: if a recipient satisfied the conditions of eligibility in the statute and regulations, he had a legally enforceable right to receive the appropriate benefits. This represented a marked change from the traditional view, under which eligibility rules were seen as *excluding* persons who could not satisfy them and leaving the further question of selection among the "eligibles" to the discretion of welfare officials.[22]

A second version of the entitlement argument was that since welfare benefits were a legal right defined by statute, they should not be used by government to "buy up" recipients' constitutional rights. For

---

*The legal concept of entitlement should not be confused with the concept of entitlement used by philosophers such as Robert Nozick. According to Nozick, a person is "entitled" to possess something when he has acquired it in ways consistent with general principles of justice. Although Nozick does not specify the precise content of such principles, he does argue that they are limited to two general types: (1) acquiring something not already held by another human being; and (2) transferring holdings among human beings, apparently by gift or voluntary exchange. *See* Robert Nozick, *Anarchy, State, and Utopia* (New York: Basic Books, 1974), pp. 150–53. In contrast, the legal concept of entitlement is based on legal *sources* for the definition of rights, such as constitutions, statutes, and judicial precedents. These sources may refer to the methods of acquisition mentioned by Nozick, but they also include many other types of rights and ways of acquiring them.

example, the fact that needy persons accepted welfare benefits should not be interpreted to mean that they had "consented" to waive their normal constitutional right to be free from home searches without warrants or probable cause. The major reasons offered in support of this position were functional. Contrary to the position implicit in the right/privilege distinction, manipulation of benefits does undermine constitutional rights, and the apparent "consent" of the beneficiary is usually given under duress. The same reasons that justify protection of "private" property against unconstitutional conditions—respect for individual liberty and constitutional rights—support protection of "new property" as well.[23]

These two versions of entitlement were designed to put the welfare recipient—or other government grantee—on an equal footing with the average citizen, *i.e.*, to ensure that she is treated no *worse* than an owner of private property under the ordinary rules of law. A third version of entitlement went further in recognizing affirmative claims by needy citizens against the government. According to Professor Charles Reich,[24] many types of government subsidies "are essentials, fully deserved, and in no sense a form of charity." Seeing poverty as caused largely by social forces that virtually "compel" sacrifices by the poor, Reich argued that welfare benefits were a social obligation. From this perspective, "[t]he idea of entitlement is simply that when individuals have insufficient resources to live under conditions of health and decency, society has obligations to provide support, and the individual is entitled to that support as of right."*

THE CONCEPT OF LEGAL ENTITLEMENT IN THE SUPREME COURT

In three landmark cases decided between 1968 and 1970, the Supreme Court repudiated the right/privilege distinction as applied to welfare and recognized recipients' entitlement in the first two senses, *i.e.*, to protect both their statutory and constitutional rights.

---

* Something like this concept of entitlement has also been used, although for different political purposes, in debates about the federal budget. In this context the phrase "entitlement program" refers to a budget item that is no longer within the control of the yearly appropriations process. Rather, the legislature has made a long-term and somewhat open-ended commitment to fund benefits for everyone who meets certain eligibility criteria. One of the major policy objectives of the Reagan administration has been to reduce the number of programs that fall into this category and to subject a larger number of programs to budgetary restrictions based not on the program's objectives but on yearly government spending policy.

The first of the three cases, *King* v. *Smith*,[25] involved an Alabama rule that defined any man with whom a recipient mother had sexual relations as the "substitute father" of all her children, regardless of whether he was actually the father of any of them, contributed to their support, or even lived in the home. Since eligibility for the AFDC program depends on the fact of being a *single*-parent family, the effect of this rule was to make needy children and mothers ineligible if the mothers had sexual relationships. The Supreme Court justified its decision in favor of the recipients—the first one in its history—on statutory grounds. Congress, reasoned Chief Justice Earl Warren, could not have intended the states to tell "destitute children to look for their food to a man who is not in the least obliged to support them. . . ." The Alabama rule was thus inconsistent with definition of "parent" in the federal Social Security Act and illegally denied benefits to families who had a federal statutory right to receive them.

In *Shapiro* v. *Thompson*[26] and *Goldberg* v. *Kelly*,[27] recipients challenging state and federal laws could not rely on a superior federal law to make an argument of statutory entitlement, and instead turned to the concept of fundamental rights embodied in the text and structure of the Constitution. In both cases, the Court summarily rejected the traditional right/privilege distinction and held that denial of welfare benefits could not infringe fundamental rights without substantial justification. In *Shapiro* the Court decided that a one-year waiting period before new state residents could obtain welfare penalized the fundamental constitutional right to interstate travel and thereby denied equal protection of the law. In *Goldberg*, the Court held that because an erroneous termination of benefits might imperil a recipient's health or even life, welfare agencies were required to offer recipients an opportunity for a hearing that met "minimal due process standards" before benefits were terminated. Minimal due process included advance notice to the recipient of the proposed agency action and the opportunity to confront adverse witnesses, present oral argument, and be represented by counsel before an impartial decision maker.

Cases such as *King*, *Shapiro*, and *Goldberg* benefitted recipients in both tangible and intangible ways. In *King*, for example, the Supreme Court had estimated that about 20,000 persons, including 16,000 children, had been excluded by the substitute-father rule in Alabama alone. Similar rules in other states were thought to exclude over 500,000 children. More broadly, the reasoning of the *King* decision—that states could not exclude persons who met federal eligibility standards, at least not by rules inconsistent with the federal act—led to numerous lower court decisions striking down other state exclusionary rules.[28] In these ways, judicial decisions recognizing recipients' rights expanded eligibility for welfare benefits and, together with legislative, administrative, and social and economic changes, contributed to a doubling of the AFDC rolls between 1966 and 1970.

What recipients perceived as recognition of their "rights" appeared to others, however, as undermining the two central goals of traditional welfare policy: holding down the costs of welfare to the taxpayers and ensuring that welfare benefits are not more "attractive" than low-wage work. Assertion of these goals by the states successfully blocked judicial recognition of the third and most important variant of entitlement: the right to adequate benefits to meet important living needs. In *Dandridge* v. *Williams*[29]—decided shortly after the recipients' procedural victory in *Goldberg*—the Supreme Court upheld a state rule limiting monthly family grants to a maximum of $250 regardless of family size, thereby leaving some large families with less than 60 percent of the state-determined "minimum need." The state justified its policy in part as a means of encouraging employment. But this "employment incentive" was of a particularly brutal kind: denying subsistence benefits to children—including newborn infants—in order to give a single parent (almost always a mother) an "incentive" to work. Moreover, the state apparently conceded that "only a very small percentage of the total universe of welfare recipients are employable"[30] and offered no evidence as to how many of them were in the large families burdened by the family maximum. In other words, an extremely harsh "incentive," in the form of threatening subsistence, was being imposed on a group most of whose members could not respond even if they wished to. Yet the *Dandridge* court found the rule, with almost no discussion, to be "rationally based and free from invidious discrimination."[31]

A similar solicitude for state discretion and "work incentives" quickly undermined the less controversial versions of entitlement based on rights contained in the Social Security Act and federal Constitution. In *Wyman* v. *James*,[32] the Court weakened Fourth Amendment protection against home searches without warrants or probable cause by ruling that a state could terminate welfare benefits because a recipient refused to allow a caseworker entry into her home. In *New York State Department of Social Services* v. *Dublino*,[33] the Court weakened the concept of federal statutory rights by upholding more restrictive state work requirements than those contained in the federal law.

LEGALIZATION AND SOCIAL INEQUALITY

As a general matter, concepts of law and rights can interact with social inequality in four different ways. First, laws can promote *formal inequality*, or hierarchy, by embodying concepts of group superiority and inferiority as the basis of legal rights. Legally required racial discrimination in the southern states or in contemporary South Africa are familiar examples. Second, legal concepts can establish *formal equality*, or laissez-faire competition, by treating all persons *as if* they were equal, and enforcing contracts and legislation *as if* they resulted from free and consensual agreement. From this perspective, the weak (such as racial minorities or the poor) cannot be formally disadvantaged by law or "intentional" discrimination but may be legitimately burdened by competition among unequals. Third, legal concepts can attempt to achieve *procedural equality* by regulating the economic or political "bargaining process." Procedural due process, freedom of speech, labor law, and administrative procedure are related to this ideal. Finally, legal concepts can promote *substantive equality* by encouraging egalitarian distribution of power and resources. Legal disapproval of employment practices with discriminatory racial or gender effects is a major example.[34]

The legalization strategy of the welfare advocates can be seen as an attempt to apply the values of procedural and substantive equality to the welfare system. Procedural equality would be promoted in individual cases through requirements of notice and fair hearings, and in policy making through recipient participation in the administrative rule-making process.[35] Substantive equality was sought through a variety of doctrines and arguments, primarily that persons in equal financial need be treated the same, that categorical or irrebuttable presumptions of income be eliminated, and that penalties on the exercise of constitutional rights (such as travel or privacy of the home) be prohibited.[36]

Despite the undeniable short-term benefits of such arguments, a growing body of experience and scholarship suggests that they are likely to be counterproductive in significant ways. Procedural equality is a favorite legalization strategy because it appears to do nothing more than increase the "fairness" of bargaining or decision making, and thereby avoid the more controversial value of equality of results. But precisely because procedural equality tends to ignore the actual inequalities of the parties, it may perpetuate inequality in much the same way as concepts of laissez-faire competition. Elaboration of procedures creates new structures or rules in which the struggle between stronger and weaker parties will continue to take place, and in which the

stronger parties will normally prevail.[37] Moreover, the very existence
of formalized procedures may enhance the illusion of fair participation
while guaranteeing the dominance of more powerful interests. For
example, legalization of collective bargaining has narrowly channeled
workers' influence and confirmed the legitimacy of managerial control.
Elaboration of federal administrative procedure has arguably had a
similar impact on the influence of weak consumer groups and strong
corporations in many areas of regulatory policy.[38]

Legal concepts based on substantive equality do directly address
issues of distributive justice. For this very reason, however, they are
perceived less as "legal" than as "political" concepts, particularly in a
society, such as the United States, which is not committed to egalitarian distribution. For example, the federal courts have gone to
elaborate lengths to portray occasional distributive awards to blacks as
"remedies" for fault-based discrimination.[39] The inability to construct
such limiting theories for most welfare cases, and the clear tension
between substantive rights and the restrictive goals of welfare policy,
led the Supreme Court to retreat from *King* and *Shapiro*, and to ratify
most state efforts to limit welfare expenditures through discretionary
restrictions.*

The dilemmas of welfare legalization suggested by general theory
have in fact appeared in the form of what Edward Sparer terms
Gordian Knots, or seemingly inescapable contradictions.[40] Without
procedural and substantive rights, and legal advocates to assert them,
recipients are at the mercy of local officials, who range from decently
competent to ignorant to harshly oppressive. A perhaps extreme but
not atypical example of what occurs when legal rights are effectively
suspended was uncovered by a law school study of five Virginia
counties in 1970.[41] In three of the counties, federal and state law in
effect did not exist; as one local official put it, "[t]here's the law and
then there's how you do things." What was done included blanket
denial of benefits to illegitimate children and to "newcomers" (some of
whom had lived in the county for a *generation*), refusal to take applications and grant awards to eligible recipients, refusal to award any
Medicaid benefits, and refusal to inform recipients of their right to

---

* The tendency to define "entitlement" solely in terms of legislatively declared
rights, and then to use the absence of such rights as the reason for *denying* individuals' claims, has been apparent in other areas of constitutional litigation. *See,*
e.g., Paul v. Davis, 424 U.S. 693, 711–12 (1976) (since state law does not require
police to follow any procedures before publicly labeling a person a criminal, a
person so labeled has not been deprived of "liberty" under the federal Constitution); Arnett v. Kennedy, 416 U.S. 134, 154–55 (1974) (opinion of Rehnquist, J.)
(where federal law defines substantive reasons for termination of employment and
procedures for applying them in individual cases, employee has no other constitutional right to fair procedure, and "must take the bitter with the sweet").

appeal. The result was people who were "near starvation" because of the illegal administration of the program.

So the argument for asserting legal rights is compelling. Moreover, there is little doubt that many recipients—numbering hundreds of thousands or even millions—have benefitted concretely from welfare-rights litigation. Yet—and this is the tension of the Gordian Knot—the very assertion of such rights *also* tends to undermine or work against recipients' interests. First, because welfare programs are unpopular with taxpayers (in part because they are substantially financed by regressive state and local taxes that bear heavily on low- and moderate-income workers, some themselves not far above the eligibility line), legal victories expanding welfare benefits often generate a political backlash. For example, extensive litigation in the 1970s blocking illegal reductions in the state Medicaid programs increased budgetary pressure on the states to make further cutbacks and caused Congress to authorize restrictive state discretion. Similarly, legal victories such as *King* v. *Smith*, which expanded eligibility for AFDC benefits, have led to state reductions in the amount of the grant.[42]

Second, the reality of welfare policy is strongly influenced by the day-to-day attitudes and practices of the caseworkers who deal directly with recipients. At a minimum, many recipients could benefit from caring or merely competent assistance from welfare caseworkers. But a series of administrative reforms associated with legalization—notably the reduction or elimination of discretionary "special needs" grants, the adoption of mechanical "flat grants," and the separation of social services from eligibility determination—has further "routinized" and undermined the caseworker-client relationship. Without suggesting that there was an earlier "golden age," the need of both recipients and caseworkers for human relations with each other is not served, and may well be undermined, by the categorical and bureaucratic requirements associated with rules and legal procedures. To exacerbate the problem, higher-level welfare officials have used concepts of legal entitlement as a negative weapon to exclude persons who cannot prove their eligibility in the prescribed way, and to control lower-level workers through "quality-control" devices that check only for incorrect grants rather than incorrect denials.[43]

Third, procedural due process does not function to secure generally accurate decisions. The vast majority of adverse decisions are never appealed, not because they are correct, but because the poor lack the information, resources, and advocacy assistance needed to confront the complex welfare bureaucracy. When agency actions are appealed, the resulting decisions do not function as a system of internal control, because no discernible pattern of appellate policy is developed and communicated to the line caseworkers. The result is a system of procedural rights that may help a small number of aggressive or fortunate recipients, but which functions largely as a legitimating symbol of fairness for a generally unchanged system.[44]

Fourth, contradictions of legalization also appear with respect to the central issue of work. Here, as in other areas, assertion of legal rights has been one of the few methods available to protect recipients against exploitation. In one successful case, welfare recipients challenged the practice of terminating all welfare grants at "harvest time," regardless of whether agricultural labor was actually available, whether an individual was capable of doing it, or whether it paid a living wage.[45] By themselves, however, such cases provide only sporadic negative protection, and the poor (as well as many others) remain in urgent need of adequately paid and decent work. The political failure to adopt a full-employment policy, or even to protect existing limited public-employment programs, has had the effect of isolating the poor as a socially superfluous "underclass."[46] The consequences of this isolation for both the poor and moderate-income workers have been tragic. In part because of these political divisions, it has been possible for the Reagan administration and the 97th Congress to enact massive reductions in benefits and legal rights not only in AFDC and Medicaid, but also in Food Stamps, Unemployment Insurance, Legal Services, public employment, Social Security, and numerous specialized social-welfare programs. The motivation for these reductions can be plausibly explained not as balancing the federal budget (because the amounts are too small) but as an effort to "discipline" the low- and moderate-income labor force.[47]

The existence of hostile political or bureaucratic reaction to welfare rights does not mean, however, that legal rights should not be asserted. One can argue that such conflicts are inevitable and that the poor must struggle with the tools they have. Moreover, whatever other initiatives might be taken, most poor persons will remain unorganized and vulnerable, and hence in desperate need of the protection afforded by legal rights and remedies.

At the same time, the predictable negative consequences of legalization for the poor argue strongly for a broader strategy of redistributive change. The poor—as well as other disadvantaged groups—need concrete benefits and protection now, so legal rights must be asserted and defended. But the poor also need much more: programs and advocacy efforts that help them establish alliances with other social groups to work together for common interests and ends. Possible candidates for such alliances are the workers in institutions serving the poor—the caseworkers, teachers, health workers, public-housing staff, and legal-services workers—whose relations with their clients have often been so ambivalent and so mutually dissatisfying. Alliances of this sort are obviously hindered by class, race, and ethnic divisions, and further complicated by work structures and concepts of professionalism. At the same time, these workers have significant interests and values in common with the poor. In addition, the poor may, as they indeed have, look to organized labor and to minority and women's groups as important potential allies.

If such cross-class cooperation is ever to exist—and I do not mean to understate the difficulties—I suspect that the legal concept of entitlement will play a transitional but secondary role. At the beginning, when all the participants are mutually distrustful, entitlement will have an important role to play in safeguarding existing prerogatives and benefits. But if these benefits are to be maintained and extended, their legal protection will have to be transformed into a more cooperative, less legalistic, and therefore more secure form. A change of this magnitude will not, of course, occur in this area alone but would have to be part of, and contribute to, a broader process of social change.

NOTES

1. Richard Parker, "The Past of Constitutional Theory—And Its Future," 42 *Ohio State Law Journal* 223, 257 (1981).
2. For overviews of American income maintenance programs, *see, e.g.,* Gilbert Steiner, *The State of Welfare* (Washington: Brookings Institution, 1971); "Poverty Amid Plenty: The American Paradox," Report of the President's Commission on Income Maintenance Programs, November 1969.
3. I do not mean to suggest that the issues of eligibility and benefits in Social Security have been free from controversy. *See, e.g.,* Califano v. Goldfarb, 430 U.S. 199 (1977) (widowers); Mathews v. Lucas, 427 U.S. 495 (1976) (illegitimate children); Mathews v. Eldridge, 425 U.S. 319 (1976) (disability termination procedures); Flemming v. Nestor, 363 U.S. 603 (1960) (alien deported because of membership in the Communist Party). My point is rather that the central or "core" purpose of Social Security—retirement income for eligible workers—has been relatively free of legal difficulty.
4. *See* 42 U.S.C. §§601 *et seq. See generally* Winifred Bell, *Aid to Dependent Children* (New York: Columbia University Press, 1965); Joel Handler, *Reforming the Poor* (New York: Basic Books, 1972), pp. 21–24; Califano v. Westcott, 443 U.S. 76 (1979).
5. For example, the states often pay substantially less—on the order of 25 to 50 percent—than the state-determined "minimum" amounts needed for subsistence. Cases upholding grant levels set below minimum need on the basis of budgetary restrictions and work incentives include Dandridge v. Williams, 397 U.S. 471 (1970), and Jefferson v. Hackney, 406 U.S. 535 (1972).
6. No comprehensive history of the Legal Services Program or the welfare rights movement yet exists. Useful sources include Frances Piven & Richard Cloward, *Regulating the Poor* (New York: Pantheon Books, 1971); Frances Piven and Richard Cloward, *Poor People's Movements* (New York: Pantheon Books, 1977); Comment, "The New Public Interest Lawyers," 79

Yale Law Journal 1069 (1970); Joel Handler, Ellen Hollingsworth, and Howard Erlanger, *Lawyers and the Pursuit of Legal Rights* (New York: Academic Press, 1978).

7. Congress supported legalization of welfare benefits by specifying conditions on federal grants to the states, by not excluding welfare recipients from access to the federal courts, and by funding the Legal Services Program. For discussion of how congressional grant conditions generated legal claims by recipients, *see* Rand Rosenblatt, "Health Care Reform and Administrative Law: A Structural Approach," 88 *Yale Law Journal* 243 (1978).

8. *See, e.g.*, Omnibus Budget and Reconciliation Act of 1981 §§547, 671, 901, 2191, 2351 (enlarging state discretion over five major "block grants" in education, health care, and social services), and §§308(a), 555–58, 332(i) (3) (1981) (eliminating beneficiary participation and grievance procedures). *See also* John Dooley and Alan Houseman, "Legal Services in the '80s and Challenges Facing the Poor," 15 *Clearinghouse Review* 704 (1982); Philadelphia Citizens in Action v. Schweiker, 527 F.Supp. 182 (E.D. Pa. 1981) (injunction against federal and state regulations implementing welfare reductions), rev'd., 669 F.2d 877 (3d. Cir. 1982).

9. Smith v. Board of Commissioners of District of Columbia, 259 F. Supp. 423, 424 (D.D.C. 1966), *aff'd on other grounds*, 380 F.2d 632 (D.C. Cir. 1967).

10. *See, e.g.*, Flemming v. Nestor, 363 U.S. 603 (1960); People *ex rel.* Heydenreich v. Lyons, 374 Ill. 557, 30 N.E.2d 46, 50–51 (1940).

11. "Categories" of legal thought include such familiar distinctions as "contract" and "tort," or "public" and "private." The overlapping concept of a "mode" of legal thought refers to the characteristic *types* of arguments used to create and manipulate categories, e.g., "balancing," "functionalism," and "formalism." *See* Duncan Kennedy, "The Structure of Blackstone's Commentaries," 28 *Buffalo Law Review* 209, 214–15 (1979).

12. The policy of local, as opposed to regional or national, financing and administration of relief to the poor had been established in centuries of English practice codified in the Elizabethan Poor Law of 1601, 43 Eliz. 1, c.2. *See generally* Jacobus TenBroek, "California's Dual System of Family Law: Its Origin, Development and Present Status," Part I, 16 *Stanford Law Review* 257, 258–91 (1964); Karl de Schweinitz, *England's Road to Social Security* (New York: A. S. Barnes & Company, 1943); J. M. Wedemeyer and Percy Moore, "The American Welfare System," 54 *California Law Review* 326 (1966).

13. The Mayor of the City of New York v. Miln, 11 Pet. 102, 142 (1837).

14. *See, e.g.*, Edward Sparer, "Welfare Reform: Which Way Is Forward?" 35 NLADA Briefcase 110, 110–11 (1978). *See also* Edward Sparer, "The Role of the Welfare Client's Lawyer, 12 *U.C.L.A. Law Review* 361, 366–71 (1965).

15. *See, e.g.*, Strauder v. West Virginia, 100 U.S. 303 (1880); Guinn v. United States, 238 U.S. 347 (1915). Women, both white and black, were not granted even this degree of equality in the public sphere. *See, e.g.*, Minor v. Happersett, 88 U.S. (21 Wall.) 162 (1875) (voting); Hoyt v. Florida, 368 U.S. 57 (1961) (jury service).

16. *See* Plessy v. Ferguson, 163 U.S. 537 (1896).

17. *See, e.g.*, Coppage v. Kansas, 236 U.S. 1 (1915); Lochner v. New York, 198 U.S. 45 (1905); The Civil Rights Cases, 109 U.S. 3 (1883).

18. *See, e.g.*, Commonwealth v. Davis, 162 Mass. 510, 39 N.E. 113 (1895), *aff'd* 167 U.S. 43 (1897) (legislature has as much power to restrict or condition speaking in publicly owned parks as the owner of a private house does in his own home).

19. Robert Hale, "Unconstitutional Conditions and Constitutional Rights," 35 *Columbia Law Review* 321, 322–23 (1935).

20. *See* Thomas Reed Powell, "The Right to Work for the State," 16 *Columbia Law Review* 99 (1916).

21. The major expressions of this view included Harry Jones, "The Rule of

Law and the Welfare State," 58 *Columbia Law Review* 143 (1958); Jacobus TenBroek and Richard Wilson, "Public Assistance and Social Insurance: A Normative Evaluation, 1 *U.C.L.A. Law Review* 237 (1954); Charles Reich, "The New Property," 73 *Yale Law Journal* 733 (1964); Charles Reich, "Individual Rights and Social Welfare: The Emerging Legal Issues," 74 *Yale Law Journal* 1245 (1965); Sparer, "The Role of the Welfare Client's Lawyer," *supra* note 14.

22. *See, e.g.,* Sparer, "Welfare Reform," *supra* note 14.

23. *See, e.g.,* Reich, "The New Property," *supra* note 21, at 756–64, 771–74.

24. Reich, "Individual Rights and Social Welfare," *supra* note 21, at 1255.

25. 392 U.S. 309 (1968).

26. 394 U.S. 618 (1969).

27. 397 U.S. 254 (1970).

28. *See* Edward Sparer, "The Right to Welfare," *The Rights of Americans,* ed. Norman Dorsen (New York: Pantheon Books, 1971), pp. 65, 70.

29. 397 U.S. 471 (1970).

30. *Id.* at 525 (Marshall, J., dissenting).

31. *Id.* at 487. *See also* Jefferson v. Hackney, 406 U.S. 535 (1972).

32. 400 U.S. 309 (1971).

33. 413 U.S. 405 (1973).

34. For a general discussion of these themes, *see* Roberto Unger, *Law in Modern Society* (New York: The Free Press, 1975), pp. 192–216.

35. *See* Goldberg v. Kelly, 397 U.S. 254 (1970) (procedural due process in individual cases); National Welfare Rights Organization v. Mathews, 533 F.2d 637 (D.C.Cir. 1976) (recipient participation in agency rule making). *Cf.* National Welfare Rights Organization v. Finch, 429 F.2d 294 (D.C.Cir. 1970) (recipient participation in HEW compliance proceedings against state agencies).

36. *See, e.g.,* Dandridge v. Williams, 397 U.S. 471 (1970); Jefferson v. Hackney, 406 U.S. 535 (1972) (rejecting argument that persons in equal financial need receive equivalent grants); King v. Smith, 392 U.S. 309 (1968) (affirming injunction against irrebutable presumption of parental relationship and support); Shapiro v. Thompson, 394 U.S. 618 (1969) (prohibiting penalty on exercise of constitutional right of interstate travel); *but see* Wyman v. James, 400 U.S. 309 (1971) (permitting penalty on assertion of Fourth Amendment right to be free from home search without warrant or probable cause).

37. For an excellent general discussion, *see* Marc Galanter, "Why the 'Haves' Come Out Ahead: Speculations on the Limits of Legal Change," 9 *Law and Society Review* 95 (1974).

38. On labor relations, *see* Karl Klare, chapter 4, *supra.* On administrative law, *see* Richard Stewart, "The Reformation of American Administrative Law," 88 *Harvard Law Review* 1667, 1776–77 (1975); Rosenblatt, *supra* note 7, at 261–62.

39. *See* Alan Freeman, "Legitimizing Racial Discrimination Through Anti-Discrimination Law: A Critical Review of Supreme Court Doctrine," 62 *Minnesota Law Review* 1049 (1978).

40. Edward Sparer, "Gordian Knots: The Situation of Health Care Advocacy for the Poor Today," 15 *Clearinghouse Review* 1 (1981).

41. J. L. Mashaw, "Welfare Reform and Local Administration of Aid to Families with Dependent Children in Virginia," 57 *Virginia Law Review* 818 (1971).

42. For a detailed analysis of the Medicaid litigation and tax impact of Medicaid costs on different income groups, *see* Sparer, *supra* note 40. On the impact of *King, see* Sparer, "Welfare Reform," *supra* note 14, at 113.

43. On the impact of legalization on the welfare bureaucracy, *see* William Simon, "Critical Legal Theory and the Social Science Tradition: Legality, Bureaucracy, and Class in the Welfare System" (Legal Services Institute Working Paper, 1981); Michael Lipsky, *Street-Level Bureaucracy* (New

York: Russell Sage Foundation, 1980). On the "quality-control" program, *see* Evelyn Brodkin and Michael Lipsky, "Entitlement Programs at the Local Level: Quality Control in AFDC as an Administrative Strategy" (Paper presented at the Annual Meeting of the American Political Science Association, September 1981). Although the quality-control program purports to check for incorrect denials, Brodkin and Lipsky argue persuasively that the system effectively fails to monitor and correct erroneous denials. *Id.* at 32–33, 39–40.

44. On the inadequacy of procedural due process in individual cases as a check on administrative errors in welfare, *see* Jerry Mashaw, "The Management Side of Due Process: Some Theoretical and Litigation Notes on the Assurance of Accuracy and Fairness in the Adjudication of Social Welfare Claims," 59 *Cornell Law Review* 772 (1974).

45. Anderson v. Schaefer, 300 F. Supp. 401 (N.D. Ga. 1968).

46. *See, e.g.*, John Low-Beer, "Perspectives on Social Inequalities," 84 *Yale Law Journal* 1591, 1594–95, 1600–02 (1975).

47. *See* Frances Piven and Richard Cloward, "Keeping Labor Lean and Hungry," *The Nation*, November 7, 1981, at 466–77.

III

ALTERNATIVE PROGRESSIVE APPROACHES

This concluding part consists of four short essays that briefly introduce and discuss a variety of progressive approaches to the law more generally than the substantively focused writings in Part 2. There are substantial differences among the authors concerning both the issues considered significant and the approaches advocated. The essays are intended to provide a basis for further discussion and development; and they reflect the reality that, at this early stage, our critiques of the law and traditional legal theory are more fully developed than our formulations of a coherent alternative theory. The major trends and some basic terminology are described in the first essay.—Ed.

14

NEW DEVELOPMENTS IN LEGAL THEORY
Robert W. Gordon

The current preoccupations of many left-wing writers on law may seem at best baffling or at worst pointlessly academic and obscure. At every meeting of the Conference on Critical Legal Studies, one can sense these barriers of puzzlement or irritation being raised between political allies who see themselves for the occasion mainly as "theorists" or "practitioners." It is not—not at all—that the "practitioners" are against theory. They are hungry for theory that would help make sense of their practices; that would order them meaningfully into larger patterns of historical change or structures of social action; that would help resolve the perpetual dilemma of whether it is or is not a contradiction in terms to be a "radical lawyer," whether one is inevitably corrupted by the medium in which one works, whether one's victories are in the long run defeats or one's defeats victories; or that would suggest what tactics, in the boundless ocean of meanness and constraint that surrounds us, to try next. But what they get back from some "theorists" is not that kind of theory—indeed, to some extent, it is a rejection of that kind of theory—but rather essays with names like "The Structure of Blackstone's *Commentaries*" and "Reification in Legal Reasoning," and even "The Importance of Normative Decision-making: The Limitations of Legal Economics as a Basis for Liberal Jurisprudence As Illustrated by the Regulation of Vacation Home Development,"[1] very technical and seemingly far off the point of any

281

common commitment. My hope here is not to try to explicate or even summarize this body of work, which is dense and difficult and often inaccessible, but rather to suggest why the people who do this work are going about it as they are, how we could think that it might be a useful way of acting on our political commitments.

As one way of showing how someone could have come to adopt this kind of theoretical project, I will try to describe the intellectual biography of such a person. This will be a composite biography, partly imaginary and partly autobiographical. It will not tell the story of any particular person involved in the "critical legal studies" movement; nor could it, because we have come from so many different starting points —some of us law teachers with humanist intellectual concerns and liberal (civil rights and antiwar) political involvements in the 1960s and 1970s; others radical activists of the 1960s who identified with neo-Marxist versions of socialist theory or feminism or both; still others primarily practitioners, many of whom are associated with the National Lawyers Guild and who work in collective law practices, legal-services offices, or a variety of other progressive jobs. Yet for all the diversity in background of this collection of people, and the perpetual, sharp conflicts over issues of method within it, there is an amazing amount of convergence in the work of this group, which suggests that there may be some common features to our common disenchantment with liberal legalism.

So, imagine someone who first started thinking seriously about law as a student in law school in the late 1960s. There, he or she would have been struck by the amazing contrast between the preoccupations of the curriculum and the world outside. When a law student now mentions "the real world," she usually means the world of law practice; but in 1968, of course, "reality" was the incredible political chaos outside. The contrast with the orthodox agenda of legal education was probably one of many factors that broke up the authority of the old curriculum along with that of the teachers who expounded it, in a way from which they have never quite recovered.

Basically, the teachers taught us to do two things: doctrinal analysis and policy analysis. Doctrinal analysis was (as I now recognize) a kind of toned-down legal realism: we learned how to take apart the *formal* arguments for the outcome of a case and to find the underlying layer of justifications that would *really* explain the case, a layer of "principles" and "purposes" behind the rules. Policy analysis was a kind of quickie utilitarian method for use in close cases—it was supposed to enable us to argue for outcomes that could efficiently serve social policies somehow inhering in the legal system. The policies were derived either by appeal to an assumed general consensus of values (personal security, economic growth), or to an assumed (and assumed to be good) trend of historical development (such as from protecting producers to protecting consumers). Sometimes there would be competing policies, representing conflicting "interests"; here the function of policy analysis was to provide an on-the-spot rapid-fire "balancing" of interests.

A really "smart" lawyer who was adept at all these techniques would be able to discover—by the use of legal reasoning alone—socially optimal solutions for virtually all legal problems. The image of the ideal lawyer was that of the technocrat with mildly reformist-liberal sympathies—half hotshot, half benevolent country squire. Smart corporate lawyer-technicians on one side would be counterbalanced by smart government lawyer-technicians on the other. Moreover, the corporate types, trained to see deeper purposes, policies, and historical trends underlying the rules, would advise their corporate clients to play by the deep-level rules in their own long-term interests, and would engage in law-reform efforts in their spare time to keep the rules consistent with principles and up-to-date with changing conditions.

Outside politics must have made it easier for law students of the late 1960s and early 1970s than it had been for those who had graduated just before then to see what was wrong with this vision of law as neutrally benevolent technique. The appeal to a deep social consensus was hardly a winner in a society apparently splintering every day between blacks and whites, hawks and doves, men and women, hippies and straights, parents and children. The appeal to the underlying march of historical progress was in trouble for the same reason. The vision of law as a technocratic policy science administered by a disinterested elite was tarnished, to say the least, for anyone who watched the "best and the brightest" direct and justify the war in Vietnam. The fluent optimistic jargon of policy science in the middle of such unspeakable slaughter and suffering seemed not only absurdly remote from any real world of experience but literally insane.

Under these conditions young lawyers became desperate for a more plausible and less compromised view of the social uses of law; and many of us found it in the emerging vocation of the liberal but antiestablishment, activist reform lawyer, who would deploy the techniques of the system against the system, work for good, substantive rule change, more open and representative procedures, more responsive bureaucracies, and, in general, who would try to make effective and real the law's formal promises of equal justice.

The focus here is not on the concrete achievements of lawyers who adopted this vocation (though personally I think those achievements substantial), but on how actually doing this work may have contributed to their intellectual development. The greatest contribution was probably an education in all the myriad ways in which the system was not a set of neutral techniques available to anyone who could seize control of its levers and pulleys but a game heavily loaded in favor of the wealthy and powerful. Procedure was so expensive and slow that one's side could be exhausted in a single engagement with an enemy who could fight dozens. One was likely to obtain the most favorable rule outcomes just where enforcement of them seemed most hopeless. And even the doctrinal victories peaked all too early: just as a promising line of rules opened up, it would be qualified before it became truly threatening (e.g., antidiscrimination doctrine became quagmired at sanctioning intentional state action against individuals, not quite reaching systemic private action against groups; equal protection doctrine flirted briefly with remedies for wealth inequalities, then scurried into retreat[2]).

At this point, the felt need for a theory that would help explain what was going on became acute; and the kind of theory that seemed called for was one that connected what happened in the legal system to a wider political-economic context. Here orthodox legal thought had almost nothing to offer because even though liberal lawyers had learned from the legal realists that all law was social policy, their working methods kept technical (narrowly legal) issues at the forefront of legal analysis; the conventions of scholarship dictated that if social context were to be discussed at all, it had to be done casually and in passing. Liberal activist lawyers in the process of radical disillusionment had to reach back to the sources of social and political theory, which law school had pushed out of focus. When they did, it was like discovering that what had happened to them was something they had known all along but had partially suppressed.

The main kinds of common-sense explanations available to them were what are sometimes called instrumental theories of the relationship between law and society.[3] In the *liberal* version, law is a response to social "demands." These demands are frequently those of specific interest groups that want some advantage from the state; law represents the compromise bargains of multiple conflicting interest groups. Other times the demands are more generally expressed as those of the functional "needs" of "the society" or "the economy"; e.g., "the market" needs stable frameworks for rational calculation, which the legal system responds to with contract enforcement, security devices, recording of land titles, etc. In the *orthodox Marxist* version of instrumentalism, of course, bourgeois law is a product not of just any group's demands but specifically those of the capitalist ruling class. In both versions, a "hard" world of economic actions (or "material base") determines what happens in the "soft" world of legal rules and processes (as part of the ideological "superstructure"). Also common to both versions is a deep logic theory of historical change. In the liberal version, this is usually: feudalism→mercantilism→industrial capitalism→organized capitalism→modern welfare capitalism; in the Marxist version, much the same with slightly different terms. Both versions assume that legal systems go through different stages that are necessary functions of the prevailing economic organization. Liberals, for example, explained nineteenth-century tort rules that put all the risks of accidents or product defects on workers and consumers either as functional to that stage of industrial development (because infant industries needed to keep their costs down) or as the result of a temporary (and soon remedied) imbalance of political power in favor of capitalists; the instrumentalist Marxists said much more straightforwardly that capitalists just imposed these costs on workers.

If one had to choose between these theories—both purposely depicted here in their crudest form and *not at all* meant to represent the best that either liberals or Marxists have to offer—the Marxist version would have considerably more explanatory bite, since the liberal-pluralist notion that any interest group could capture the system and make it play the right tunes seems to contradict historical experience as well as the practical experience of the recently embittered lawyers. The liberal versions do not really explain why the masses have not just taken over the system, or why it seems to function so as to reinforce class, racial, and sexual inequalities: it seems to have a built-in tilt toward reproduction of existing class relations.

Nonetheless, anyone who thought about it would begin to see a great many problems with crude instrumentalist theory. The capitalists did not seem to win all the time through state policy and law: workers had been granted rights to organize and bargain collectively out of it, blacks had received the abolition of slavery and some affirmative government action promoting their rights, radicals had been granted some rights to teach and write, the poor had received some welfare entitlements, etc. Obviously, all this could be rerationalized as serving the long-term interests of the capitalist ruling class, but that would take considerable refinements of the theory. Some writers spoke of the strategy of "corporate liberalism"—the ruling class promotes government social-welfare programs and regulation of business in order to prevent political (through popular risings) and economic (through chaotic competition) destabilization of the social order. Other writers, borrowing from European neo-Marxist sources, began to speak of law as a means of "legitimating" class society: in order to be bearable to those who suffer most from it, law must be perceived to be approximately just, so the ruling class cannot win all the time. Still others, extending the point, saw the "legitimacy" of capitalist society as importantly inhering in (among a number of other factors, such as a certain degree of social mobility, social security for everyone, and apparently meritocratic criteria for determining people's shares of income and wealth) the legal system's promises to protect rights of freedom and security for everyone in the society equally—promises that must sometimes be made good.[4] So, since the legal system must at least appear universal, it must operate to some extent independently (or with "relative autonomy," as the saying goes) from concrete economic interests or social classes. And this need for legitimacy is what makes it possible for other classes to use the system against itself, to try to entrap it and force it to make good on its utopian promises. Such promises may therefore become rallying points for organization, so that the state and law become not merely instruments of class domination but "arenas of class struggle."[5]

Once leftist lawyers became accustomed to thinking this way, a whole new set of problems and questions opened up. One was that given this view of the matter, hard-won struggles to achieve new legal rights for the oppressed began to look like ambiguous victories. The official legal establishment had been compelled to recognize claims on its utopian promises. But these real gains may have deepened the legitimacy of the system as a whole; the labor movement secured the vitally important legal rights to organize and strike, at the cost of fitting into a framework of legal regulation that certified the legitimacy of management's making most of the important decisions about conditions of work.[6]

In any case, once one begins to focus closely on problems such as these, one begins to pay much more attention to what instrumentalists think of as the "soft" or "superstructural" aspects of the legal system. If what is important about law is that it functions to "legitimate" the existing order, one starts to ask how it does that. And for the purposes of this project, one does not look only at the undeniably numerous, specific ways in which the legal system functions to screw poor people —though it is always important to do that too, to point it out as often and as powerfully as possible—but rather at all the ways in which the system seems at first glance basically uncontroversial, neutral, acceptable. This is Antonio Gramsci's notion of "hegemony," i.e., that the most effective kind of domination takes place when both the dominant and dominated classes believe that the existing order, with perhaps some marginal changes, is satisfactory, or at least represents the most that anyone could expect, because things pretty much have to be the way they are.[7] So Gramsci says, and the "critical" American lawyers who have accepted his concept agree, that one must look closely at these belief-systems, these deeply held assumptions about politics, economics, hierarchy, work, leisure, and the nature of reality, which are profoundly paralysis-inducing because they make it so hard for people (including the ruling classes themselves) even to *imagine* that life could be different and better.

Law, like religion and television images, is one of these clusters of belief—and it ties in with a lot of other nonlegal but similar clusters—that convince people that all the many hierarchical relations in which they live and work are natural and necessary. A small business is staffed with people who carry around in their heads mixed clusters of this kind: "I can tell these people what to do and fire them if they're not *very* polite to me and quick to do it, because (a) I own the business; (b) they have no right to anything but the minimum wage; (c) I went to college and they didn't; (d) they would not work as hard or as efficiently if I didn't keep after them; a business can't run efficiently without a strong top-down command structure; (e) if they don't like it they can leave," etc.—and the employees, though with less smugness and enthusiasm, believe it as well. Take the ownership claim: the employees are not likely to think they can challenge that because to do so would jeopardize their sense of the rights of ownership, which they themselves exercise in other aspects of life ("I own this house, so I can tell my brother-in-law to get the hell out of it"); they are locked into a belief-cluster that abstracts and generalizes the ownership claim.

Now, the point of the work (usually called anti-positivist or interpretive) that some of the "critical" lawyers are doing[8] is to try to describe—to make maps of—some of these interlocking systems of belief. Drawing here on the work of such "structuralist" writers as Lévi-Strauss and Piaget, they claim that legal ideas can be seen to be organized into structures, *i.e.*, complex cultural codes. The way human beings experience the world is by collectively building and maintaining systems of shared meanings that make it possible for us to interpret one another's words and actions. Positivist social scientists (who would include both liberal and Marxist "instrumentalist" legal theorists) are always trying to find out how social reality objectively works, the secret laws that govern its action; they ask such questions as, "Under what economic conditions is one likely to obtain formal legal rules?" Anti-positivists assert that such questions are meaningless, since what we experience as "social reality" is something that we ourselves are constantly constructing; and that this is just as true for "economic conditions" as it is for "legal rules." If I say, "That's a bus taking people to work," I'm obviously doing much more than describing a physical object moving through space; my statement makes no sense at all except as part of a larger cultural complex of shared meanings: it would mean little or nothing to you if your culture were unfamiliar with bus technology, with "work" as an activity performed in a separate place outside the family compound, or indeed with "work" as distinct from "play" or "prayer."

"Law" is just one among many such systems of meaning that people construct in order to deal with one of the most threatening aspects of social existence: the danger posed by other people, whose cooperation is indispensable to us (we cannot even have an individual identity without them to help define it socially), but who may kill us or enslave us. It seems essential to have a system to sort out positive interactions (contracts, taxation to pay for public goods) from negative ones (crimes, torts, illegal searches, unconstitutional seizure of property). In the West, legal belief-structures, together with economic and political ones, have been constructed to accomplish this sorting out. The systems, of course, have been built by elites who have thought they had some stake in rationalizing their dominant power positions, so they have tended to define rights in such a way as to reinforce existing hierarchies of wealth and privilege.

Even more important, such system building has the effect of making the social world as it is come to seem natural and inevitable. Though the structures are built, piece by interlocking piece, with human intentions, people come to "externalize" them, to attribute to them existence and control over and above human choice; and, moreover, to believe that these structures must be the way they are. Recall the example given earlier of the person who works in a small business for the "owner" of the business. It is true that the owner's position is backed up by the ultimate threat of force—if she does not like the way people behave on her property, she can summon armed helpers from the state to eject them—but she also has on her side the powerful ideological magic of a structure that gives her the "rights" of an "employer" and "owner," and the worker the "duties" of an "employee" and "invitee" on the "owner's property." The worker feels he cannot challenge the owner's right to eject him from her property if she does not like the way he behaves, in part because he feels helpless against the force she can invoke, but also because in part he accepts her claim as legitimate: he respects "individual rights of ownership" because the powers such rights confer seem necessary to his own power and freedom; limitations on an "owner's" rights would threaten him as well. But the analogy he makes is possible only because of his acquiescence in a belief-structure—liberal legalism—that abstracts particular relationships between real people (this man and the woman he "works for"; this man and the brother-in-law he wants to eject from his house) into relations between entirely abstract categories of "individuals" playing the abstract social roles of "owner," "employee," etc.

This process of allowing the structures we ourselves have built to mediate relations among us so as to make us see ourselves as performing abstract roles in a play that is produced by no human agency is what is usually called (following Marx and such modern writers as Sartre and Lukács) reification.[9] It is a way people have of manufacturing necessity: they build structures, then act as if (and genuinely come to believe that) the structures they have built are determined by history, human nature, economic law.

Perhaps a promising tactic, therefore, of trying to struggle against being demobilized by our own conventional beliefs is to try to use the ordinary rational tools of intellectual inquiry to expose belief-structures that claim that things as they are must necessarily be the way they are. There are many varieties of this sort of critical exercise, whose point is to unfreeze the world as it appears to common sense as a bunch of more or less objectively determined social relations and to make it appear as (we believe) it really is: people acting, imagining, rationalizing, justifying.

One way of accomplishing this is to show that the belief-structures that rule our lives are not found in nature but are historically contingent; they have not always existed in their present form. (Elizabeth Mensch's essay in chapter 2 of this volume summarizes the history of various forms of American legal thought over the last two hundred years.) This discovery is extraordinarily liberating, not (at least not usually) because there is anything so wonderful about the belief-structures of the past, but because uncovering those structures makes us see how arbitrary our categories for dividing up experience are, how nonexhaustive of human potentiality. Another useful exercise is just simple empirical disproof of the claim of necessity. When it is asserted that strict, predictable rules of private property and free contract are necessary to protect the functioning of the market, maintain production incentives, etc., it can be shown that the actual rules are not at all what they are claimed to be, that they can be applied quite differently in quite different circumstances, sometimes "paternalistically," sometimes strictly, sometimes forcing parties to share gains and losses with each other, and sometimes not at all.[10] Or it may be asserted that certain hierarchical ways of organizing are necessary for efficient realization of economies of scale. One can use historical (nineteenth-century worker-organized steel production) or comparative (Japanese, for instance) examples to demonstrate that "efficient" production can occur under all sorts of conditions.[11] Or one can try to show that even at the level of theory, the claim of necessity is, on its own terms, incoherent or contradictory; this approach is currently being practiced on the various forms of "legal economics" that claim that certain regimes of legal rules are "efficient."[12] One can bring similar critiques to bear on claims that things must be the way they are because of some long-term logic of historical change ("modernization," "what is, after all, an inevitable consequence of social life in industrialized societies," "the price of living in a modern pluralistic society," "an inevitable consequence of the declining rate of profit under monopoly capitalism," etc.). It turns out that these theories of development cannot be applied to the concrete histories of particular societies without being so qualified, refined, or partially repudiated that they lose all their force as determining theories—at best, they are only helpful insights or ways of organizing thinking about the world.

If we start to look at the world this way—no longer as some determined set of "economic conditions" or "social forces" that are pushing us around but rather as in the process of continuous creation by human beings, who are constantly reproducing the world they know because they (falsely) believe they have no choice—we will obviously bring a very different approach to the debate over whether legal change can ever effect real ("social and economic") change, or whether law is wholly dependent on the real, "hard" world of production. For if social reality consists of reified structures, "law" and "the economy" are *both* belief-systems that people have externalized and allowed to rule their lives. Moreover, if the critiques of legal belief-structures are accurate—that even in their theoretically ideal forms they are contradictory and incoherent, and that in practical application they depart constantly from the ideal in wildly unpredictable fashion —it follows that no particular regime of legal principles *could* be functionally necessary to maintain any particular economic order. Similarly, no given economic order can be thought of as requiring for its maintenance any particular bunch of legal rules, except of course those that may be part of the *definition* of that economic order, as "private property" of some sort is to most people's definition of capitalism.

So—if one were to adopt this approach—one would no longer be inclined to look for "scientific" or "positivist" explanations of how the world works in large-scale theories of historical interrelations between states, societies, and economies (one would actually be trying to knock down such theories). It may be that the place to look is somewhere quite different—in the smallest, most routine, most ordinary interactions of daily life in which some human beings dominate others and they acquiesce in such domination. It may be, as Foucault's work suggests,[13] that the whole legitimating power of a legal system is built up out of such myriad tiny instances.

I do not want to give the impression that everyone in the critical legal-studies movement has adopted the approaches I have just described. On the contrary, these approaches are hotly debated. Some of those who most fiercely dispute the validity of these approaches do so in part on political grounds. I will mention a few of these criticisms and briefly respond to them.

One criticism is that the view that law and the economy as we know them are structures inside people's heads is a form of "idealism"; it assumes that the world can be changed merely by *thinking* about it differently. This charge is, I think, both true and not true. It is true in that the belief it criticizes is indeed that the main constraints upon making social life more bearable are these terrible, constricting limits on imagination; and that these structures are as obdurate as they are because they are collectively constructed and maintained—we *have* to use them to think about the world at all, because the world makes no sense apart from our systems of shared meanings. But the charge is not true if it means to imply that we believe that all constraints on human action are imaginary, alienated ideas of "false necessity." Obviously there are many constraints on human social activity—scarcities of desired things, finite resources of bodies and minds, production possibilities of existing and perhaps all future technologies, perhaps even ineradicable propensities for evil—that any society will have to face. What is false is to think that these constraints somehow necessarily dictate that we must have some specific set of social arrangements that we are already familiar with, in history or in our own time; that the human race can live only within its real constraints in a few specific ways (e.g., that it *must* choose between liberal capitalism and state socialist dictatorship).

The notion that there are no objective laws of social change is in one way profoundly depressing. Those who have come to believe it have had to abandon the most comforting hopes of socialism: that history was on its side, and that history could be accelerated through a scientific understanding of social laws. It no longer seems plausible to think that organization of the working class or capture of the state apparatus will *automatically* bring about the conditions within which people could begin to realize the utopian possibilities of social life. Such strategies have led to valuable if modest improvements in social life, as well as to stagnation, cooptation by the existing structures, and nightmare regimes of state terror. Of course, this does not mean that people should stop trying to organize the working class or to influence the exercise of state power; it means only that they have to do so pragmatically and experimentally, with full knowledge that there are no deeper logics of historical necessity that can guarantee that what we do now will be justified later. Yet, if the real enemy is us—*all* of us, the structures we carry around in our heads, the limits on our imagination —where can we even begin? Things seem to change in history when people break out of their accustomed ways of responding to domination, by acting as if the constraints on their improving their lives were not real and that they could change things; and sometimes they can, though not always in the way they had hoped or intended; but they never knew they could change them at all until they tried.

NOTES

1. Duncan Kennedy, "The Structure of Blackstone's *Commentaries*," 28 *Buffalo Law Review* 205 (1979); Peter Gabel, "Reification in Legal Reasoning," *Research in Law and Sociology*, vol. 3, ed. Stephen Spitzer (Greenwich, Conn.: JAI Press, 1980), pp. 25–51; Thomas C. Heller, "The Importance of Normative Decision-Making: The Limitations of Legal Economics as a Basis for Liberal Jurisprudence as Illustrated by the Regulation of Vacation Home Development," 1976 *Wisconsin Law Review* 385 (1976).
2. *See* Alan D. Freeman, "Legitimizing Racial Discrimination Through Anti-Discrimination Law: A Critical Review of Supreme Court Doctrine," 62 *Minnesota Law Review* 1049 (1978); Derrick A. Bell, "Bakke, Minority Admissions, and the Usual Price of Racial Remedies," 67 *California Law Review* 3 (1979).
3. Some classic instrumentalist texts are David B. Truman, *The Governmental Process: Political Interests and Public Opinion* (New York: Alfred A. Knopf, 1951); and Ralph Miliband, *The State in Capitalist Society* (New York: Basic Books, 1969).
4. *See* Edward P. Thompson, "The Rule of Law," *Whigs and Hunters* (New York: Pantheon Books, 1975); Douglas Hay, *et al.*, *Albion's Fatal Tree: Crime and Society in Eighteenth-Century England* (New York: Pantheon Books, 1975); and Mark V. Tushnet, "A Marxist Analysis of American Law," 1 *Marxist Perspectives* 96 (1978).
5. *See* Thompson, *supra*; David M. Trubek, "Complexity and Contradiction in the Legal Order: Balbus and the Challenge of Critical Social Thought About Law," 11 *Law & Society Review* 527 (1977).
6. *See* Karl Klare, chapter 4, *supra*.
7. *See* Antonio Gramsci, *Selections from the Prison Notebooks*, ed. and trans. Quinton Hoare and Geoffrey Nowell-Smith (New York: International Publishers, 1971), pp. 195–96, 246–47.
8. *See, e.g.*, Kennedy, *supra* note 1; Isaac D. Balbus, "Commodity Form and Legal Form: An Essay on the Relative Autonomy of the Law," 11 *Law & Society Review* 571 (1977); Thomas C. Heller, "Is the Charitable Exemption from Property Taxes an Easy Case? General Concerns About Legal Economics and Jurisprudence," *Essays on the Law and Economics of Local Governments*, ed. Daniel Rubinfeld (Washington, D.C.: Urban Institute, 1979), pp. 183–251; Al Katz, "Studies in Boundary Theory: Three Essays in Adjudication and Politics," 28 *Buffalo Law Review* 383 (1979); Roberto Mangabeira Unger, *Knowledge and Politics* (New York: The Free Press, 1975).
9. *See generally* Gabel, *supra* note 1.
10. *See, e.g.*, Duncan Kennedy, "Form and Substance in Private Law Adjudication," 89 *Harvard Law Review* 1685 (1976); Karl Klare, "Contracts, Jurisprudence and the First-Year Casebook," 54 *New York University Law Review* 876 (1979). *Cf.* James B. Atleson, "Work Group Behavior and Wildcat Strikes: The Causes and Functions of Industrial Civil Disobedience," 34 *Ohio State Law Journal* 750 (1973).
11. *See, e.g.*, Katherine W. Stone, "The Origin of Job Structures in the Steel Industry," 6 *Review of Radical Political Economy* 61 (1974).

12.   *See, e.g.*, Mark Kelman, "Choice and Utility," 1979 *Wisconsin Law Review* 769 (1979); Kelman, "Consumption Theory, Production Theory and Ideology in the Coase Theorem," 52 *Southern California Law Review* 669 (1979); Thomas C. Heller, *supra* notes 1 and 8; Morton J. Horwitz, "Law and Economics: Science or Politics?" 8 *Hofstra Law Review* 905 (1980); Duncan Kennedy and Frank I. Michelman, "Are Property and Contract Efficient?" 8 *Hofstra Law Review* 711 (1980).

13.   *See especially* Michel Foucault, *Discipline and Punish: The Birth of the Prison*, trans. Alan Sheridan (New York: Pantheon Books, 1977).

15 TOWARD A THEORY OF LAW AND PATRIARCHY
Diane Polan

The goal of this essay is to suggest ways to broaden critical legal theory beyond a Marxist analysis of the ways in which law and legal traditions have supported and/or perpetuated existing economic and social relations and class domination to include a feminist analysis of the role of the law in maintaining male domination, or patriarchy.[1] What is needed is a critical examination of the relationship between law and women's subordination that integrates feminist and Marxist theoretical perspectives.[2] This essay is an attempt to assess the applicability of critical legal theory to the relationship between law and patriarchy, and to suggest the beginnings of a Marxist-feminist approach to law.

To begin with, the essay agrees with the stance of all critical theory that law does not operate neutrally, ahistorically, or independently of the underlying power relationships in society.[3] For the purposes of a *feminist* critical theory, those "underlying power relationships" must be understood as having both a class and a gender dimension. Thus, if critical legal theory is grounded on a belief that the

In working on this essay, I have received support and encouragement from many people, especially from the women in Marxist-Feminist I, a group I have belonged to for more than six years; and, most recently, from several people who encouraged me and helped me with my thinking for this article: Nadine Taub, Susan Besse, David Kairys, and Ann Freedman.

294

legal system of a capitalist society ultimately supports the existing capitalist social order, a feminist critical theory likewise supposes that the legal system of a patriarchal society enforces and maintains a male supremacist social order as well. The questions asked by critical legal theory focus on how the legal system fulfills that role and how the role of the law has changed as capitalism itself has developed and changed. At the least, a feminist critical theory would ask those same questions about the relationship between law and patriarchy. While those areas of inquiry may not, by themselves, prove adequate to the task of understanding the complex relationship between law and sex oppression, they can serve as a useful starting point. In this effort, the analytic concepts developed by critical theorists will be used to examine the relationship between law and patriarchy. But before proceeding further, it is important to point out and briefly discuss some problems and limitations inherent in this approach.

PROBLEMS OF INTEGRATING MARXIST AND FEMINIST APPROACHES TO THE LAW

First, feminist theory is fundamentally different from Marxist theory. While Marxism locates the basis of class oppression in the control of the underlying productive resources of society, there is no analogous feminist explanation of the origin of female oppression. Moreover, capitalism developed at a particular historical moment and adapted the institutions of the law to its own purposes, while patriarchy has been a social institution for a far longer time and antedates modern legal systems. Thus, it probably is correct to say that any legal system that developed in a patriarchal culture, including the Anglo-American legal system, would be, by definition, a patriarchal institution.

Second, given that capitalism is a relatively recent historical development, whereas patriarchy seems always to have been with us, it is a far more difficult task to arrive at one satisfactory explanation of the genesis of patriarchy.[4] But, whatever the explanation of the origin of male supremacy, and regardless of whether patriarchy predated capitalism,[5] it seems clear that by now the capitalist system has so integrated and institutionalized the arguably preexisting subordination of women that modern women's inferior status and powerlessness must be seen as the product of the interaction of two separate systems of domination: capitalism and patriarchy.[6]

In the past decade, a variety of Marxist-feminist approaches and theories have been developed.[7] While they differ significantly, they all share a dissatisfaction with both the failure of classical Marxism to recognize male supremacy as a separate and distinct source of women's oppression, and the failure of liberal feminist analyses to examine the historical relationship between sex oppression and capitalist economic development. Rather than trying to discover the origin of male supremacy, Marxist-feminists have focused on the interactions of capitalism and patriarchy in maintaining women's oppression in modern society. In so doing, they have demonstrated that the oppression of women has not remained static over time but has changed historically in a dialectical relationship to changes in economic and social development and related changes in the role of the family.[8]

Third, capitalism and patriarchy do not always operate in analogous ways, which has implications for an understanding of the role of the law in relationship to each of these systems. For example, while it is possible to roughly describe and identify a capitalist "ruling class," whose interests are served by certain legal decisions, rules, and arrangements, it is much more problematic to identify an analogous patriarchal "ruling class," whose "interests" the law serves. The fact is that *all men* benefit from laws and legal decisions which disadvantage women or render them legally powerless—for example, laws that exclude husbands from prosecution under criminal rape laws. At the same time, because the law operates in support of *both* patriarchy and capitalism, people stand in different relationships to the legal system by virtue of their sex and class positions. To use a simplified example, a male worker may, at the same time, be oppressed by laws that punish union organization but benefit from laws that exclude women from certain occupations. Similarly, while it is certainly true that all women are subordinated by male supremacist laws, some women—by virtue of their class position—do benefit from the legal system.

Lastly, the law may, in fact, play a much different (and possibly less significant) role in the maintenance of patriarchy than it has in the perpetuation of capitalism. It can be quite persuasively argued that patriarchy has been primarily maintained not by legal means but by nonlegal forces and social institutions, in particular, the family.[9] Nevertheless, at least on the level of ideology, the law may be seen to play a similar role in maintaining exploitative relationships of domination and subordination between both class- and gender-based groups. Patriarchal ideology—ideas about women and their "place" in society —has probably played at least as important a role in the modern subordination of women as capitalist ideology has played in supporting advanced industrial capitalism. Particularly at those historical moments when significant material and technological changes, with the capacity to alter women's social and economic position, have occurred, ideology has been successfully used to maintain women's oppression.[10]

HOW DOES THE LAW PERPETUATE PATRIARCHY?

Applying a traditional Marxist concept, we might ask whether the legal system maintains patriarchy by operating directly against women, as an "instrument" of patriarchal power. Alternatively, using the neo-Marxist categories of critical legal theory, different questions might be appropriate: If the law has played a direct role in keeping women subordinate, to what extent has that role changed? And is it more accurate to view the law today as playing a more hegemonic role, whose ultimate purpose is to legitimate a status quo in which male supremacy is accepted as natural and unchangeable? A corollary question might be: To what extent has the legal system, as part of an overall hegemonic function, operated independently of, or even in apparent conflict with, the immediate interests of male supremacy?

Prior to the twentieth century, Anglo-American law, legal rules, and judicial decisions gave absolute and clear-cut support to male supremacy. Thus, it is indisputable that our legal system has operated directly to maintain women's subordination.[11] However, this is not a full or sufficient explanation of how the law operates to support patriarchy. Over the past century, the legal system has rejected some of its most blatant sexist notions and expressions without ceasing to reinforce male power and female subordination. For this reason, it is essential to examine and try to understand the less direct and instrumental ways in which the legal system operates to perpetuate male supremacy.

Like capitalism, patriarchy has never operated solely on the level of physical coercion, although it is striking to what extent the subordination of women *has* been maintained through the use or threat of physical force or violence by men.[12] Throughout history, ideas about women, the family, and the relationship between women and the outside world have been effectively used to rationalize inequality and the inferior status of women. Patriarchal ideology has been successful to the extent that it has convinced women that our social, political, and economic subordination and our psychological feelings of inferiority are the result of natural forces rather than exploitative social relations. Although patriarchal ideology has itself undergone changes over time, particularly in response to developments in the capitalist economic system and the labor force needs of particular periods, its overall function—the legitimation of male supremacy—has remained the same.

The ideas about women expressed in American legal decisions have generally tracked prevailing patriarchal ideologies. For example, Supreme Court opinions in the late-nineteenth and early-twentieth centuries reverberated with an ideology that has been described as the "public/private" split.[13] The essence of this ideology was that the world was naturally divided into two parts, or spheres: one, a public sphere, of work and politics, inhabited by men; and the second, a personal or domestic sphere, encompassing home and family life, which was deemed the realm of women. Not surprisingly, these ideas gained currency at a historical moment when the development of capitalism had resulted in the movement of production out of the home and into the factory.[14]

The public/private ideology served at least two distinct and identifiable purposes. One was to convince women, by use of assertions about their natural domesticity and their primary role as childbearers and child rearers, to stay at home and out of the workplace. Equally important was the function that this ideology played as a justification for *actually* barring women from participation in the world outside the home. The manipulation of this ideology within the legal system performed both of these functions.[15]

The legal system has also used the public/private dichotomy in another, more subtle fashion that has further reinforced patriarchy. By placing the operation of law squarely in the public realm and, at least rhetorically, removing itself from the "private realm"[16] of personal life and the family, the legal system created a distinction between a public realm of life, which is a proper arena for legal or social regulation, and another, fundamentally different, personal sphere, which is somehow outside the law's or society's authority to regulate. Thus, the legal system has functioned to legitimate that very distinction by asserting it as a natural, rather than socially imposed, ground for different treatment.

One practical result of the "hands-off" rhetorical stance of the law toward activities within the "private realm of the family" has been to license men's exploitation of women within the family unit.[17] In essence, by purportedly withdrawing itself from regulation of the private sphere, the legal system has lent its actual support to male supremacy by permitting men to completely dominate and control family life. Even today, it is difficult to get courts to intervene in domestic violence situations because of a supposed deference to the "privacy of the family."

Closely related to the law's role as an exponent of particular ideologies that support male supremacy, such as the public/private ideology, is its hegemonic function in support of patriarchy. While the concept of hegemony has thus far been articulated and applied in the context of understanding and explaining the *class* domination of advanced industrial society, it may also be useful to apply this concept in trying to understand how male supremacy is maintained. In respect to patriarchy, a set of ideas could be said to operate hegemonically to the extent it succeeds in convincing women that their inferior political, economic, and social status, as well as their subordination to husbands and fathers within the family unit, is a result of a *natural* division of the world into separate spheres and *natural* differences between male and female personalities that suit women and men for different roles, rather than the result of exploitation and domination.

Laws and court opinions that embody and express these kinds of ideas can play an important part in maintaining patriarchal hegemony. Interestingly, this hegemonic effect has sometimes occurred in the context of legal decisions that appear to actually *improve* women's lives. For example, beginning in the mid-twentieth century, a series of Supreme Court cases struck down restrictions on the use of contraceptives and then abortion as an unconstitutional state interference into people's private sexual lives. In all of these decisions, the Court emphasized the privacy of the family and asserted that sexual relations are part of a private sphere that is outside the state's authority to regulate. Thus, while the outcome of the birth control and abortion cases was beneficial to women by giving at least some women a greater degree of control over their reproduction, these decisions must also be understood as serving a hegemonic function, by legitimating the notion that there are naturally separate private and public spheres of human existence. Since it is the ideological construct of the public/private split that has been used both to exclude women from the public sphere and to devalue the social work women perform in the home, the law can be seen as operating in support of patriarchy when, by asserting that different legal rules govern public and private matters, it legitimizes that distinction as natural rather than as socially imposed.

Finally, the related notion of the "relative autonomy of the law" has been advanced by those arguing in favor of the law's hegemonic role. It is difficult to apply this concept to the historical experience of women (and nonwhites) within the American legal system because our legal system—at least until very recently—has not operated at all "autonomously" of the interests of white or male supremacy. Rather, our laws and judicial interpretations of them have directly enforced both sexism and racism. Although it may be true that the law has operated with the appearance of neutrality and even-handedness toward white men of both the upper and lower classes, there has not been even the *appearance* of fairness or equal treatment in the operation of the American legal system toward blacks and women. As a result, the legal system has in the past had very little legitimacy in the minds of many blacks and women, who have quite correctly viewed it as an instrument or tool of their domination and as an integral aspect of their subordinate status in society.

However, that situation has been changing in some limited ways over the past several decades. With the rise of the feminist and black liberation movements, the legal system has been forced to accommodate some of their demands in order to preserve the threatened legitimacy of the social order. To the extent that the legal system has taken some steps to repudiate its past racism and sexism, some sort of relatively autonomous role for the law in relation to both blacks and women may be developing. If the relative-autonomy concept is valid, one would expect to see greater legitimacy accorded to the legal system by those groups who have been previously excluded from the law's purported justice and equal treatment as well as greater enthusiasm on their part for pressing their demands within the legal arena. The response of the legal system to these demands in turn has a direct effect on social stability: when oppressed individuals and groups believe that they can rely on the legal system to redress their grievances and remedy their subordinate status in society, there is a decreasing likelihood that they will seek more radical solutions to their situation.

Thus, a subtle testimony to the law's success in achieving legitimacy is that women, and other groups who are oppressed and dominated within society, now largely accept the law's categories and its modes of discourse. To the extent that those groups choose to articulate their social criticism and their grievances in the law's limited categories—"equal rights" and "equal opportunities"—and confine their action to litigation and lawmaking rather than struggle in such alternative arenas as the workplace, the family, and in organized religion, they are giving up the battle, because in so doing, they are tacitly approving the underlying social order and thus undermining more radical challenges to the overarching male supremacist and white supremacist structure of society. This suggests that the law, in the very process of reducing its role as a direct instrument of patriarchal power, is effectively maintaining sex oppression in different, more subtle ways. Its success in establishing its own legitimacy among previously excluded and disenfranchised groups allows the law to operate hegemonically, thereby coopting the radical impulse behind the struggle against patriarchy and diverting the energy of the women's liberation movement into a narrow focus on legally articulable claims.

CONCLUDING THOUGHTS

This analysis does not necessarily mean that the law should be abandoned or ignored in the fight against sexism. Some victories may be won in the courts and legislatures. It is quite clear that the law's own rules and precedents can and have been used to expand women's rights, and sometimes they do deal effective blows to patriarchy. For example, while the Supreme Court's early birth-control decisions applied only to the right of married couples to use contraception, the rhetoric and logic of those cases has been successfully used to expand constitutional protection to single women's right to control their own reproduction.[18] As recent abortion decisions make clear, however, the logic of the prior decisions carries only so far: apparently, only women with adequate financial resources have constitutionally protected rights to control their reproduction.[19]

Second, it is important to recognize that legal gains for women depend on a variety of social, economic, and political circumstances, including the relative strength of women's movements and conflicts between patriarchy and the needs of the capitalist economic system. For example, the controversy concerning coverage of pregnancy-related disabilities by employers' insurance programs reflects underlying tension between the economy's need for women workers and patriarchy's interest in keeping women economically dependent by hindering their participation in the work force.[20] We must therefore try to identify and understand these potential contradictions, as well as the particular historical context of any given legal battle, in order to successfully exploit them for the benefit of women.

Finally, we cannot underestimate the practical limitations we face with any law-oriented strategy. The experience of going to court on a regular basis underscores the pervasive maleness of the legal system: it is a system infused with sexist values. Regardless of the language of a statute, it is individual judges who decide cases. The judiciary remains overwhelmingly male. Judges have grown up in a patriarchal culture; their attitudes are inevitably shaped by their life experiences and by their position as the beneficiaries of male supremacy. Similarly, the juries who weigh women's claims of sex discrimination and pass judgment on the guilt of rape defendants are made up of people who have lived their entire lives in a male supremacist culture. Thus, even while attempting to educate judges and jurors, this fundamental limitation on the usefulness of the legal system in the fight against male supremacy must be faced. Furthermore, even if sexism were formally eliminated from the legal system, and even if half the lawmakers and legal decision makers were women, the legal system would not become a nonsexist institution. The whole structure of law—its hierarchical organization; its combative, adversarial format; and its undeviating bias in favor of rationality over all other values—defines it as a fundamentally patriarchal institution.

Thus, it is not so much that laws must be changed; it is patriarchy that must be changed. Actions taken within the legal system cannot by themselves eliminate patriarchy, which is a pervasive social phenomenon. Because law is one, but only one, locus of male supremacy, legal efforts to end women's subordinate status cannot effectively challenge or cripple patriarchy unless they are undertaken in the context of broader economic, social, and cultural changes.

NOTES

1. For my purposes here, "patriarchy" may be defined as a system of social relations in which men as a group have power over women as a group; it is a system that is characterized by relationships of domination and submission, superiority and inferiority, power and powerlessness, based on sex.

2. Unfortunately, there has been no adequate integration of feminist and Marxist theories concerning the relationship between the law and women's oppression. The feminist legal scholarship that exists lacks an economic analysis, see, e.g., Kathryn Powers, "Sex Segregation and the Ambivalent Directions of Sex Discrimination Law," 1979 *Wisconsin Law Review* 55 (1979), while Marxist-oriented critical approaches have thus far confined their analyses to social relations within the public sphere, ignoring the private sphere that is so central to women's lives and women's subordination.

3. See David Kairys, "Book Review: M. Tigar and M. Levy, *Law and the Rise of Capitalism*," 126 *University of Pennsylvania Law Review* 930 (1978).

4. This problem has been the focus of much writing, debate, and disagreement among feminist theorists. See, e.g., Shulamith Firestone, *The Dialectic of Sex* (New York: William Morrow, 1970); Susan Brownmiller, *Against Our Will: Men, Women and Rape* (New York: Bantam Books, 1975); Simone deBeauvoir, *The Second Sex* (New York: Vintage Books, 1974); Gayle Rubin, "The Traffic in Women: Notes on the Political Economy of Sex," *Toward an Anthropology of Women*, ed. Rayna Reiter (New York: Monthly Review Press, 1975).

5. Engels and others have argued that women's subordination is historically related to the development of capitalism, private property, and the property-based family. See Frederick Engels, *The Origin of the Family, Private Property and the State* (New York: International Publishers, 1972); Evelyn Reed, *Women's Evolution* (New York: Pathfinder Press, 1975); Kathleen Gough, "The Origin of the Family," in Reiter, *supra* note 4. Many contemporary feminists disagree. See note 4 *supra*.

6. The term "capitalist patriarchy" has been used to describe and emphasize the "mutually reinforcing dialectical relationships between capitalist class structure and hierarchical sexual structuring" in the modern subordination of women. Zillah Eisenstein, *Capitalist Patriarchy and the Case for Socialist Feminism* (New York: Monthly Review Press, 1979), p. 5.

7. See, e.g., Juliet Mitchell, *Women's Estate* (Harmondsworth, England: Penguin Books, 1971); Ann Oakley, *Women's Work* (New York: Vintage Books, 1974); Eli Zaretsky, *Capitalism, the Family and Personal Life* (London: Harper Colophon Books, 1976).

8. See Mitchell, *supra* note 7; Zaretsky, *supra* note 7.

9. See, e.g., Dorothy Dinerstein, *The Mermaid and the Minotaur* (New York: Harper and Row, 1976); Nancy Chodorow, *The Reproduction of Mothering: Psychoanalysis and the Sociology of Gender* (Berkeley: University of California Press, 1978).

10. See Mitchell, *supra* note 7; Oakley, *supra* note 7; Zaretsky, *supra* note 7.

11. Examples abound: laws restricted married women's control of property and

eliminated their contractual rights; the marital "merger" of husband and wife meant that the wife lost all legal existence; the judiciary upheld state laws that barred women from entering professions; women were denied basic political rights; rape laws excluded husbands from prosecution, etc. *See, generally*, Barbara Babcock et al., *Sex Discrimination and the Law: Causes and Remedies* (Boston: Little, Brown, 1975); Kenneth Davidson et al., *Text, Cases and Materials on Sex-Based Discrimination* (St. Paul: West Publishing Company, 1974).

12. *See* Brownmiller, *supra* note 4.

13. *See* Nadine Taub and Elizabeth Schneider, chapter 6 *supra*; Powers, *supra* note 2; Diane Polan, "Patriarchal Ideology in the Supreme Court: A Critical Look at Nineteenth-Century Cases About Women, Marriage and the Family" (Unpublished manuscript, March 1980). On the role of ideology generally, *see* Douglas Kellner, "Ideology, Marxism and Advanced Capitalism," 1 *Marxist Perspectives* 43 (1978).

14. *See* Viola Klein, *The Feminine Character: History of an Ideology* (New York: International Universities Press, 1949), p. 10; Oakley, *supra* note 7, at 33; Zaretsky, *supra* note 7, at 49.

15. *See* discussion of Bradwell v. Illinois in Taub and Schneider, chap. 6, pp. 125–27.

16. In Prince v. Massachusetts, 421 U.S. 158, 64. S. Ct. 438, 442 (1944), the Supreme Court reified "the private realm of the family which the state cannot enter."

17. *See* Powers, *supra* note 2; Taub and Schneider, *supra* note 13.

18. Griswold v. Connecticut, 381 U.S. 381 (1961) (married couples); Eisenstadt v. Baird, 405 U.S. 438 (1972) (single women).

19. *Compare* Roe v. Wade, 410 U.S. 113 (1973) *with* Maher v. Roe, 432 U.S. 464 (1977) *and* Harris v. McRae 448 U.S. 297 (1980).

20. Soon after the Supreme Court upheld the exclusion of pregnancy-related disability benefits from state-funded and private employers' disability insurance programs, *see* Geduldig v. Aiello, 417 U.S. 484 (1974) and General Electric v. Gilbert, 429 U.S. 125 (1976), Congress passed amendments to Title VII of the Civil Rights Act, which specifically prohibited such insurance exclusions as illegal sex discrimination.

16 ANTONIO GRAMSCI AND "LEGAL HEGEMONY"
Edward Greer

Neither instrumentalism nor structuralism is satisfactory as a description of the American political reality or adequate as an explanation of the nature of the legal system.[1] This essay addresses an alternative approach, also in the Marxist tradition, that is based on the work of Italian theorist Antonio Gramsci (1891–1937).

Gramsci was a contemporary and enthusiast of the Bolshevik Revolution, and a leader of a similar working-class insurrection in Italy.[2] Almost immediately he realized that in the countries of Western capitalism the Leninist Party could not primarily orient itself around the preparation for armed struggle. The failure of the Bolshevik Revolution to be replicated elsewhere led Gramsci to focus—even as he was helping to create the Italian Communist Party—on the decisive social differences between the Soviet Union and Western Europe, and the strategic implications of these differences for the Left.

The central difference in his opinion was the far more elaborated "civil society" of Western capitalism:

When the state trembled, a sturdy structure of civil society was at once revealed. The State was only the outer ditch, behind which there stood a powerful system of fortresses and earthworks.[3]

By 1926 Gramsci had developed, at least embryonically, the concept of "hegemony" in response to the failure in the West of the Bolshevik model of insurrection.[4]

Gramsci's approach commenced with an evaluation of the practical question of how the capitalist class rules in advanced capitalist society. His original formulation was that such rule is based on a combination of force and consent. The role of coercion in the exercise of state power is well known and does not need discussion here. The more interesting question is how the capitalist class obtains the consent of the ruled to their ongoing exploitation and oppression. Fundamentally, this consent flows from the capitalists' hegemony over both the state and civil society. Carl Boggs has described Gramsci's concept of hegemony:

By hegemony Gramsci meant the permeation throughout civil society—including a whole range of structures and activities like trade unions, schools, the churches, and the family—of an entire system of values, attitudes, beliefs, morality, etc. that is in one way or another supportive of the established order and the class interests that dominate it. . . . To the extent that this prevailing consciousness is internalized by the broad masses, it becomes part of "common sense"; . . . For hegemony to assert itself successfully in any society, therefore, it must operate in a dualistic manner: as a "general conception of life" for the masses, and as a "scholastic programme" or set of principles which is advanced by a sector of the intellectuals. . . . [Gramsci observed that where] hegemony appeared as a strong force, it fulfilled a role that guns and tanks could never perform. . . . [I]t encouraged a sense of fatalism and passivity towards political action; and it justified every type of system-serving sacrifice and deprivation. In short, hegemony worked in many ways to induce the oppressed to accept or "consent" to their own exploitation and daily misery.[5]

Thus, rejecting mechanistic and "scientific" Marxism, Gramsci's Marxism conceived of the world of the ruling class as "implicitly manifest in art, in law, in economic activity and in all manifestations of individual and collective life," encompassing virtually everything that organizes the life activities of the masses.[6]

To give one illustration: the view that "human nature is acquisitive" is not a trick of the capitalists on the masses. Rather, it is an idea about human nature that is consented to and agreed with generally by persons observing the nature of those living *in capitalist society*. It therefore justifies and legitimates institutions based on private ownership and competition. Bourgeois hegemony of this sort thus stands as a principal barrier to socialist politics. The most common obstacle to convincing someone to become a socialist is not disagreement with the ideal of the "socialist commonwealth" but the profoundly held notion that true socialism is impossible because the *inherently* acquisitive nature of humans will quickly turn such a society into a tyranny.

From this insight Gramsci did not draw the conclusion that politics is primarily a conflict of contending ideas. Rather, as a Marxist, he identified a material basis for this hegemony of capitalist ideas among the population; to wit, that the capitalists organize and play the decisive role in the organization of production.

Undoubtedly the fact of hegemony presupposes that account be taken of the interests and tendencies of the groups over which hegemony is to be exercised, and that a certain compromise equilibrium should be formed—in other words, that the leading group should make sacrifices of an economic-corporate kind. But there is also no doubt that such sacrifices and such a compromise cannot touch the essential; for though hegemony is ethical-political, it must also be economic, must necessarily be based on the decisive function exercised by the leading group in the decisive nucleus of economic activity.[7]

But there is considerably more to Gramsci's notion of hegemony that is relevant to us here: he believed that the capitalist class actually performs vital social functions that serve the society in general. At the trivial level, the maintenance of traffic lights and control of violators of traffic signals protects the well-being of the workers. (This enables bourgeois liberal law professors to "win" many arguments with radical law students, as the professors can demonstrate that a plurality of legal rules and processes are assimilable by such a model of service to the population as a whole.) At a more complex level, the population is constrained to limit public-policy choices to those that do not result in massive capital flight; governments must remain within the restraints imposed by investor confidence;[8] and the judiciary must tailor its holdings to the fundamental social limits imposed by a capitalist order regardless of personal values.

In contrast to the structuralists, however, Gramsci emphasized that there is no inevitable requirement that such occur. The ruling class, if it is not to find its power usurped, must be willing and able to act affirmatively on behalf of society as a whole. If it lacks this capacity or will, its power will rapidly shrink to that of its military capacity for terror, and soon even the mightiest Shah will be gone.

To be the head of a historic bloc that holds state power, a class must have its interest "conceived of and presented, as being the motor force of a universal expression, of a development of all 'national' energies."[9] Under that circumstance, a class imposes its fundamental economic and political aims together with its intellectual and moral unity upon the society; and it does so in the political sphere as well as in the various institutions of civil society, such as families, churches, and trade unions.

The contest for hegemony in an advanced capitalist country such as the United States therefore requires going far beyond the activities and programs traditionally associated with community organizations, trade unions, and reformist socialist political parties striving for electoral power. Juridically, that traditional reformist approach does pose the problem of control over the state, but

only in terms of winning politico-juridical equality with the ruling groups: the right is claimed to participate in legislation and administration, even to reform these—but within the existing fundamental structure.[10]

In short, Gramsci would hardly take seriously the idea of creating a socialist commonwealth by mere constitutional amendment.

In the history of Marxism, Gramsci is a very disputed figure. On the one hand, there are those (like myself) who perceive him as fundamentally a Leninist. On the other, there are those who see the notion of hegemony as a qualitative break with Leninist ideology, or at least view Gramsci as a transitional figure foreshadowing that break. The crux of this dispute inheres in the way in which Gramsci called into question what had been the traditional Marxist stance on the relationship between the state and civil society, for Gramsci's articulation of the concept of hegemony expanded the state to include civil society.[11]

At the one end of the ideological development of the Left in the wake of Gramsci's conceptual revolution there are those who assert that traditional Marxism is essentially superceded. Notions of "legitimation theory" are seen as a more accurate way of understanding advanced capitalism. While legitimation theorists regard Gramsci's ideas on hegemony as useful (especially as a way of attacking vulgar Marxist approaches), their political orientation is quite far from Lenin's. Some of these thinkers tend to entirely eliminate coercion as part of the advanced capitalist state and to make "consciousness" the focal point of their politics. They similarly reject the dispute between instrumentalists and structuralists as not so much wrong as irrelevant. At the other end are those who feel that the classical Marxist formulations on the state are basically sound and adequate. Thus, many exponents of instrumentalism and structuralism are largely indifferent to Gramsci's perspectives.

My own notion is that the core of Lenin's view of the state—namely, the need to destroy it in order to replace it with something quite different in kind[12]—can only be appreciated theoretically and worked out practically in the light of Gramsci's observations about hegemony. The expanded Gramscian state (one encompassing both the governmental apparatus and civil society) surpasses both instrumentalism and structuralism as explanatory frameworks.

The immediate consequence of a Gramscian approach is that it
no longer makes sense to view the law as merely reflective of the
power of the ruling class in the state (instrumentalism) or of the
inevitable logic of capitalism (structuralism). Neither, as some radicals
and liberals argue,[13] is the law an antonomous system of rules and
concepts. It would not even be correct to see the law as a reflection of
the class compromise between the capitalists and other social classes—
although this position points in the direction of a Gramscian posture.
Rather, the law should be conceptualized as being in major part constitutive of the capitalist state power. Absent the legal apparatus,
bourgeois society could not exist.

The rich density of Gramsci's contribution bars any mere evocation of the law as a tool of the ruling class. It is instead a mosaic of
ideas, rules, traditions, allocations of power—and a creator and destroyer of institutions (and even social strata)—that must be criticized
in the context of our ongoing political battle[14] to wrest power from
those few who now control it and to share it among the many.

NOTES

1.   Structuralism is an approach that contends that a capitalist economy necessarily yields a capitalist government; instrumentalism is defined in Robert
      Gordon's essay in this part. For a detailed critique of these approaches to
      government and law, *see* Edward Greer, *Big Steel: Black Politics and Corporate Power in Gary, Indiana* (New York: Monthly Review Press, 1979);
      Karl Klare, "Law-Making as Praxis," 40 *Telos* 123 (Summer 1979).
2.   John M. Cammett, *Antonio Gramsci and the Origins of Italian Communism*
      (Stanford: Stanford University Press, 1960); Paolo Spriano, *The Occupation of the Factories: Italy 1920* (London: Pluto Press, 1975).
3.   Antonio Gramsci, *Selections from the Prison Notebooks*, ed. Quinton
      Hoare and Geoffrey Nowell-Smith (New York: International Publishers,
      1971), p. 171.
4.   This point is elaborated in Maria-Antonietta Macciocchi, *Pour Gramsci*
      (Paris: Editions du Seuil, 1974).
5.   Carl Boggs, *Gramsci's Marxism* (London: Pluto Press, 1976), pp. 39–40.
6.   Christine Buci-Glucksmann, *Gramsci and the State* (London: Lawrence &
      Wishart, 1980), pp. 47–63.
7.   Gramsci, *supra* note 3, at 181.
8.   *See* Greer, *supra* note 1; Paul Peterson, *City Limits* (Chicago: University of
      Chicago Press, 1981).
9.   Gramsci, *supra* note 3, at 182.
10.   *Id*. at 181.
11.   *See* Buci-Glucksmann, *supra* note 6.
12.   This idea is elaborated by Lucio Colletti, "Lenin's State and Revolution,"

in Lucio Colletti, *From Rousseau to Lenin: Studies in Ideology and Society* (London: New Left Books, 1972).

13.   *See, e.g.,* H.L.A. Hart, *The Concept of Law* (London: Oxford University Press, 1961).

14.   For some applications of these concepts to the world of legal practice, *see* Edward Greer, "Class Targets," *Guild Notes* (July/August 1981); and Edward Greer, "On Reforming Court Rulemaking," 38 *NLADA Briefcase* 53–55 (Fall 1981).

17

THE RADICAL TRADITION IN THE LAW

Victor Rabinowitz

On June 27, 1905, the founding convention of the Industrial Workers of the World (IWW) met in Chicago, pursuant to a call urging the creation of "one big industrial union" to be "founded on the class struggle." The Credentials Committee reported the attendance of nearly two hundred delegates—socialists, anarchists, members of industrial trade unions, and a handful of representatives from craft unions. The Committee recommended the seating of the delegates and also recommended the seating, as a fraternal delegate, of a lawyer from New York. A long and bitter debate followed. Lillian Forberg, speaking against the recommendation to seat the lawyer, said:

This is the first convention, to my knowledge, that has ever been called to organize the working class into an organization by which they can fight the capitalist class. The only thing that an attorney ever did in this world was to support the capitalist class. The only way in which attorneys at law ever express their friendship to the working class is by fighting for injunctions before the courts of law against the working class. I think it is a well-known fact that no attorney of law could be anything else but a parasite. We are here to fight the whole parasitical class and to organize the working class.

Daniel De Leon, also a delegate, said:

. . . Not only must we exclude people who are themselves living on interest that they draw directly, but we must exclude those who live as parasites upon those who draw interest. If you admit a lawyer because he nominally works and does not derive interest—though every dollar that goes into his pocket is tainted with the blood of workingmen in some way or other, because he lives upon interest indirectly—if you allow such a man in here, by what process of reasoning can you exclude the policeman? . . . I would say that I know of no lawyer who deserves any place in the labor movement. . . . What does the class struggle mean but that the material necessities of a man control his action? And will you deny that the material necessities of the lawyer will compel him to commit the crimes against the working class that every lawyer in the country commits today?[1]

The convention resolved not to seat the lawyer, after refusing to permit him to address the convention.

The New York lawyer was Louis B. Boudin. His exclusion by the IWW convention did not put an end to either his political or his legal career. He became a part of the leadership of the Socialist Party and, during World War I, was prominent in the left-wing of the party, which opposed U.S. participation in the war effort. He was the author of *The Theoretical System of Karl Marx*, a book highly regarded in Marxist circles. In the thirties he was one of the most active, and perhaps the most learned, of the radical lawyers in this country. He represented Communist Party leaders in the AFL unions who were struggling against a bankrupt and corrupt national leadership. He participated in the litigation that culminated in the establishment of radical leadership in the food workers union, the furriers union, the hotel workers union, and many others. After the formation of the CIO, he represented many of the new unions in their early and most militant struggles. He similarly acted for scores of radicals brought up on criminal charges or faced with deportation. He participated in the formation of the National Lawyers Guild. One could hardly argue that his contributions to the radical movement of his day were not considerable.

The debate over the role of the law (and the lawyer) in the class struggle has not abated since 1905, and the nature and significance of the legal system in Marxist theory continue to be the subject of extensive discussion. In 1971 a collection of essays by radical lawyers in the United States, edited by Robert Lefcourt, was published under the title *Law Against The People*.[2] The editor, in his preface, quoted Herbert Marcuse:

... there is no (enforceable) law other than that which serves the status quo, and ... those who refuse such services are *eo ipso* outside the realm of law even before they come into actual conflict with the law.[3]

Over half of the essays in the volume argued what the title of the collection implied: that the law as an institution is an instrument of the bourgeoisie designed to deceive and oppress the mass of the people, and the lawyer is necessarily a part of this machinery. Florynce Kennedy, a prominent militant lawyer, wrote, in characteristically blunt language:

Ours is a prostitute society. The system of justice, and most especially the legal profession, is a whorehouse serving those best able to afford the luxuries of justice offered to preferred customers. The lawyer, in these terms, is analogous to a prostitute. The difference between the two is simple. The prostitute is honest—the buck is her aim. The lawyer is dishonest—he claims that justice, service to mankind, is his primary purpose.[4]

This is, perhaps, a fair approximation of a view held by many Marxists who consider themselves as representing an "orthodox" view. An abstraction called The Law is seen as an instrument through which another abstraction called The State exercises power on behalf of the bourgeoisie. The Law, while pretending to be a benign, neutral force dispensing justice, equality, and due process, actually is but a fraudulent cover-up for the force through which The State rules.

I suggest that the IWW-Marcuse-Lefcourt position is in error. It proceeds in disregard of centuries of history and is the result of an intellectual view based on a priori reasoning, bearing little relation to reality. Moreover, it is a self-fulfilling error. It encourages cynicism about our legal structure and gives up the battle that both the mass of the people and a handful of lawyers have carried on for centuries—a battle for progressive, socially desirable laws and against retrogressive laws—by failing to distinguish between them or even to admit that such differentiation can exist.

This paper is written with a few assumptions in mind, which should be set down. No society of even moderate complexity, whether it be feudal, capitalist, or socialist, can exist without law. All systems of law are constructed to protect the state and its economic base. Conduct that seriously threatens the survival of the state or that would effectuate a basic change in the economic system is, *ipso facto*, "illegal." Those in whose interests the state exists will necessarily make laws to protect that state, and a government that will tolerate effective seditious conduct is almost beyond our imagination.

Having said this, there are several points to be made.

The law sets up standards and rules by which the state agrees to exercise its power and which, by definition, set limits on that exercise. These standards and limits are, of course, self-imposed, but in the long run every state finds it necessary to impose some restrictions upon itself because no structured society can exist for long if state power is lawless and completely arbitrary. Most capitalist states find it desirable to act by these standards. Thus, in England, France, the United States, and other developed capitalist countries, there has grown up a mass of laws and regulations that curb the state's conduct. The state relinquishes its power to act except in conformity with certain rules. Whether those rules give adequate protection to the people will vary greatly in different situations, but the existence of rules provides some protection against totally arbitrary state action. To the degree that state power is exercised in an arbitrary manner, the state itself becomes unstable and subject to the constant threat of revolutionary violence. When that happens, one of the necessary demands of the people is for a return to the proper law, which is seen as a vehicle through which justice can be provided.

In fact, revolutionary movements have been carried on in the name of "the law." Fidel Castro, in his address to the court when on trial for the Moncarda Barracks raid, did not attack the law as a sham and an illusion but rather urged that the law, as set forth in the Cuban Constitution and the Code of Social Defense, be enforced. He argued that it was the Batista regime that was destroying the institutions of Cuban law and justice.[5] It was Castro's position, as it should be ours, that the laws that generally promise justice and equality ought to be enforced and not denigrated as foolish illusions.

In a bourgeois state, the law does more than establish standards by which the state promises to conduct its business. In such a state there is a working class sufficiently well educated and sufficiently articulate not only to carry on the role required of it in a capitalist society but also, in the long run, to demand certain action by the state. Capitalist law (and even precapitalist law in the English common-law tradition), under great pressure from the mass of the people has, from the earliest days, promised to those masses equality of treatment, justice, fair play, due process, and other abstract idealizations. In this country, the law even promises freedom of speech, press, religion, and assembly, freedom from unreasonable search and seizure, and all of those other good things set forth in the Constitution.

It is true that these promises are often broken, perhaps more often than not. It is also true that many of those who made the promises in the first place never intended that they should be kept. Capitalism seldom delivers on such promises of equality, justice, and freedom. But the promises are made; and the fact is that very large numbers of the people accept, believe in, and rely on these abstract principles. Often they demand that the promises be kept; they may even be willing to march and riot in the streets, and sit down in factories and churches. Belief in and devotion to these principles are not confined to the working class; many members of the middle class, including even some members of Congress and some judges, believe in these promises or are unwilling to repudiate them.

For example, the trade-union movement of the 1930s and 1940s, the civil rights movement of the 1950s and 1960s, and the antiwar movement of the 1960s and 1970s would not have been possible had we not had a deep tradition of respect for freedom of speech and assembly. It is a mistake to minimize the significance of that tradition in our history. This and related traditions are deeply embedded in the consciousness of most of the American people even though these traditions are frequently frustrated in practice; and much progress has been made because these rights have been assumed by most of us.

For who can deny that progress has been made? Certainly not one who has read Mayhew or Dickens or even Stephen's *History of the Criminal Law*.

A century and a half ago, poor people spent years in custody because they could not pay their debts; in England, many were transported to the other side of the world for such "offenses." Today there are no debtors' prisons in the United States or England, and transportation is no longer accepted. Less than two centuries ago, trade unions were deemed unlawful conspiracies in the United States; in the past half-century, unions have been given recognition, approval, and encouragement by the state. The factory and housing conditions that characterized the growth of the industrial revolution in England and the United States have largely been ameliorated by the passage of housing, factory, and child labor laws; the conditions under which men, women, and children customarily worked in Birmingham, England, and Lowell, Massachusetts, would not be tolerated today in any advanced capitalist state.

The right of privacy prohibiting unlawful search and seizure has been strengthened. Censorship of written material has been relaxed; only a few decades ago, Joyce's *Ulysses* could not be imported into the United States or transported through the mails. The situation today is quite different. Less than two centuries ago, there were five hundred crimes punishable by death in England, and public executions were commonplace; today, there is no capital punishment in England. In this country, executions averaged almost one every other day in the 1930s; the number of executions in the United States since 1967 is less than a score. And, of course, the greatest progress of all has been made with respect to the rights of minorities and women in our society.

The catalogue could be extended at length. It would show that, overall, changes in the law have been in the direction of those very qualities of justice, equality, and fair play which the orthodox Marxist view holds to be irrelevant to the legal system. That view simply denies the reality and importance of these changes.

It is true, of course, that changes in the law have not transformed a capitalist system into a socialist system; they have not abolished poverty, nor have they eliminated economic classes in our society. But the law was never intended to perform those tasks and, if our earlier assumptions are true, cannot be understood as having so promised. Those changes can be brought about only by extra-legal means.

Nor should any of this be understood as suggesting that the law gives adequate protection to the working man and woman. This can never be so long as there are inequalities in wealth and power, and such inequalities will always exist under capitalism. In some respects the law has not significantly improved much in two or three centuries. The election laws are, generally speaking, still rigged to frustrate the democratic process and are helpful principally to the wealthy; the tax laws still impose the heaviest burden on the working class; and the laws relating to real property still leave a tenant with little power. It is also true that now, as in Jefferson's day, eternal vigilance is the price of liberty, and many of the gains that have been made are constantly threatened and will continue to be threatened under a capitalist, socialist, or any other kind of economic system. Failure to exercise that vigilance exacts a heavy price, a price we are called upon to pay.

It is often argued that these legal reforms have the effect of preserving the capitalist system and serve to postpone basic change as well. To some extent this is true. Certainly the unemployment insurance and Social Security laws, the extension of suffrage to blacks in the South, and even child labor laws were required to bring the industrial revolution to fruition; and objectively they stregnthen, not weaken, capitalism. Had these reforms not occurred, economic and social conditions would be much worse than they are; but who would advocate their repeal to bring the revolution closer? This argument puts progressives in the untenable position of advocating misery and assumes that misery will lead to progressive change.

Moreover, while capitalism was strengthened, it does not follow that the "ruling class" permitted such reforms in order to preserve the economic system. The contrary is true. The New Deal measures were adopted during the thirties in the context of powerful working-class movements demanding substantial progressive changes. These demands and movements were fought tooth and nail by the capitalist class, to whom President Franklin Roosevelt was the devil incarnate; Roosevelt reciprocated with his attacks on the "economic royalists." Who was responsible for those laws is a complex question and beyond the scope of this paper, but there is no evidence that those laws were merely bones thrown by the leaders of capitalism to the working class to pacify it, or that they were the result of prescient and sagacious planning by United States Steel, General Motors, Chase National Bank, Metropolitan Life Insurance Company, *et al.*

Let us take but a quick look at some of the major developments in our constitutional law in the recent past.

In *Gideon* v. *Wainwright*,[6] the Supreme Court held that all persons charged with serious crimes are entitled to a lawyer and that the court must appoint one where the defendant is indigent. In *Miranda* v. *State of Arizona*,[7] the Court held that persons in police custody must be warned of their constitutional rights and advised of their right to get legal counsel. In *Mapp* v. *Ohio*,[8] the Court held that evidence illegally seized by the police from the defendant may not be used in criminal proceedings against him. In *Furman* v. *Georgia*,[9] the Supreme Court in effect held unconstitutional the capital punishment laws in forty-one of the states. These and many other decisions provided a much greater measure of protection to individuals charged with crimes, but they have no measurable effect one way or another on the continued survival of capitalism.

In *Griswold* v. *Connecticut*,[10] the Court held that a statute prohibiting the use of contraceptives was unconstitutional, with the result that the sale and use of contraceptives are now both legal and commonplace. And in *Roe* v. *Wade*,[11] the Court struck down statutes, effective in most states, prohibiting abortions. These holdings as well as statutes, regulations, and court decisions over the past decades have markedly alleviated harsh conditions of life for many members of the working class. Can it be argued that they have, in one way or the other, substantially affected the economic system of the United States, or that the judiciary and legislatures were acting merely as instruments of capitalism? Or can it be said that the changes are not real or that they are merely transient, to be abandoned by later generations? The representation of defendants in criminal cases by legal aid societies or public defenders is, in most jurisdictions, a great deal more effective than the representation provided by the lawyer a working class defendant is usually able to retain. Likewise, the efforts on the part of federal and state governments to limit the right to an abortion or to restore some degree of capital punishment have little bearing on the argument. All progress is uneven, and occasionally battles for important principles can be lost.

A long-term view cannot support the conclusion that progress has not been made in many areas where the economic system seems an irrelevant or marginal factor. It is by no means clear—and I believe it is simply untrue—that state action in relating to, for example, the protection of the environment has either the purpose or the effect of safeguarding the capitalist system; there is no doubt that the enactment of environmental protection laws was due to overwhelming pressure by people who wanted nothing more than a good life.

I suggest that the law develops a dynamic and a life of its own which is independent of capitalism or any other system of economic relationships. It grows out of the pressure of the people for a better, more rational, and more bearable existence, and out of changes in the moral and ethical systems of a society that require changes in the law even when there is no economic reason or popular demand therefor. Even the most conservative judges can be moved, on some occasions, by the horrors of capital punishment, by the fearful consequences of laws against abortion, and by the terrors of police abuse; even conservative state legislators suffer physical discomfort at having to breathe the air of Los Angeles and New York.

Any capitalist legal system undoubtedly crystalizes class relations and masks injustice created by those relations. But what is the alternative? The exercise of naked, arbitrary power without even the forms of law can hardly constitute an improvement. The fact is, as Edward P. Thompson has said so eloquently,[12] that any legal system, including a legal system in a capitalist society, carries with it large components of equity and justice that can provide some degree of protection to the masses of the people, that provide a platform from which further progress can be made, and that also provide a vision of social justice that inspires action.

What, then, should be the reaction of the progressive citizen and the radical lawyer to the law? Shall we proclaim that the law is a fraud and that, to use Kennedy's epithet, lawyers are prostitutes who sell themselves to the highest bidder; or should we as progressives interested in creating a better world use the law as a vehicle through which we seek to compel the state to keep the promises it makes—the promises contained in the Constitution and in the Fourth of July orations? When the law fails to keep these promises, is it not our duty to promote a confrontation between the people and the state to compel the latter to move toward the dream of a better world we share with all others?

There is certainly enough to be done. We can do our best to keep radical activists out of jail and on the streets. We can seek to extend to their ultimate limit the rights of free speech, due process, freedom from unreasonable searches, and similar rights; to make more possible major changes in our economic system. We can expose police abuse and protect the right of privacy, both in political and personal affairs. We can, as lawyers and legal workers, join with rank and file trade-union groups in the struggle for the establishment of democracy in the trade unions. Many of us have legislative skills that can be put to good service. The tradition of Louis Boudin and Clarence Darrow is, I urge, a more productive tradition than the negative and self-defeating role accepted by those who see the law and the state simply as the instruments of the capitalist elite.

And most important of all, we can join with other radical lawyers in developing a modern Marxist theory of the role of the law and the radical lawyer in our society. The office of such a theory will be to point a direction for such lawyers. It will help us to distinguish between reforms that carry the seeds of oppression and developments that truly represent an improvement in the lot of humankind. Such, we understand, are the tasks undertaken by this volume of essays.

NOTES

1.   Proceedings of the First Convention of the Industrial Workers of the World (New York: New York Labor News Co., 1905), pp. 26, 67–70.
2.   Lefcourt, ed., *Law Against the People* (New York: Random House, 1971).
3.   *Id.* at 11.
4.   *Id.* at 81.
5.   There are many translations of the Castro speech, usually entitled "History Will Absolve Me," in general circulation. The reference in the text can be found at pp. 10, 50, 56–60 of the pamphlet published under that title by the Center for Cuban Studies, 220 East 23rd Street, New York, New York 10010.
6.   372 U.S. 335 (1963).
7.   384 U.S. 436 (1966).
8.   367 U.S. 643 (1961).
9.   408 U.S. 238 (1972).
10.   381 U.S. 479 (1965).
11.   410 U.S. 113 (1973).
12.   Edward P. Thompson, *Whigs and Hunters* (New York: Pantheon Books, 1975).

CONTRIBUTORS

Richard L. Abel is professor of law at UCLA. He has been the editor of *Law and Society Review* and recently co-authored and edited two volumes of essays, *The Politics of Informal Justice*.

W. Haywood Burns is Director of the Center for Legal Education at the City College of New York. He is a former executive director of the National Conference of Black Lawyers.

William J. Chambliss is professor of sociology at the University of Delaware. The author of several books on criminology and law, he recently co-authored, with Robert Seidman, the second edition of *Law, Order and Power*, and, with Alan Block, *Organizing Crime*.

Jay M. Feinman is associate professor of law at Rutgers University, Camden.

Alan D. Freeman is professor of law at the State University of New York, Buffalo. He is co-author of *The Rights of Older Persons*.

Peter Gabel is professor of law and co-president of the New College of California.

Robert W. Gordon is professor of law at the University of Wisconsin.

Edward Greer practices law in Brookline, Mass. He is the author of *Big Steel: Black Politics and Corporate Power in Gary, Indiana.*

Morton J. Horwitz is Charles Warren Professor of American Legal History at the Harvard Law School. He is the author of *The Transformation of American Law, 1780–1860.*

David Kairys is a constitutional lawyer in Philadelphia with the firm Kairys, Rudovsky & Maguinan and local counsel to the National Emergency Civil Liberties Committee. He has represented a variety of progressive groups and activists in leading national and local cases. He also teaches part-time in sociology at the University of Pennsylvania. He is Chair of the Theoretical Studies Committee of the National Lawyers Guild and a member of the Organizing Committee of the Conference on Critical Legal Studies.

Mark Kelman is associate professor of law at Stanford University.

Duncan Kennedy is professor of law at the Harvard Law School.

Karl E. Klare is professor of law at Northeastern University and visiting teaching fellow at the Legal Services Institute. He formerly practiced labor law with the National Labor Relations Board and then with a private firm.

Elizabeth Mensch is assistant professor of law at the State University of New York, Buffalo.

Diane Polan practices law in New Haven, Conn. She is co-author of *The Pro Se Dissolution Kit: Getting Your Own Divorce.*

Victor Rabinowitz is a constitutional and labor lawyer in New York and Assistant General Counsel to the National Emergency Civil Liberties Committee. He is a former president and founding member of the National Lawyers Guild.

Rand E. Rosenblatt is professor of law at Rutgers University, Camden. He was formerly a staff attorney at the Health Law Project of the University of Pennsylvania and counsel to legal services programs and welfare, health and consumer organizations.

David Rudovsky is a constitutional lawyer in Philadelphia and local counsel to the National Emergency Civil Liberties Committee. He is co-author, with Michael Avery, of *Police Misconduct: Law and Litigation.*

Elizabeth M. Schneider is a constitutional lawyer with the Constitutional Litigation Clinic of Rutgers Law School, Newark. She was formerly an attorney with the Center for Constitutional Rights and has pioneered in the development of the law concerning women's self-defense claims.